D0097921

RED NILE

RED NILE

A Biography of the World's Greatest River

ROBERT TWIGGER

Thomas Dunne Books
St. Martin's Press
New York

THOMAS DUNNE BOOKS.
An imprint of St. Martin's Press.

RED NILE. Copyright © 2013 by Robert Twigger. All rights reserved.
Printed in the United States of America. For information, address St.
Martin's Press, 175 Fifth Avenue, New York, N.Y. 10010.

www.thomasdunnebooks.com
www.stmartins.com

Library of Congress Cataloging-in-Publication Data

Twigger, Robert, 1964–
  Red Nile : a biography of the world's greatest river / Robert
Twigger. — First U.S. edition.
    p. cm.
  Includes bibliographical references and index.
  ISBN 978-1-250-05233-9 (hardcover)
  ISBN 978-1-4668-5390-4 (e-book)
  1. Nile River—History. 2. Nile River Valley—History. I. Title.
  DT115.T94 2014
  962—dc23

                                                    2014022126

St. Martin's Press books may be purchased for educational,
business, or promotional use. For information on bulk
purchases, please contact Macmillan Corporate and Premium
Sales Department at 1-800-221-7945, extension 5442,
or write specialmarkets@macmillan.com.

First published in Great Britain by Weidenfeld & Nicolson, an
imprint of Orion Books Ltd, an Hachette UK Company

First U.S. Edition: October 2014

10   9   8   7   6   5   4   3   2   1

CONTENTS

ILLUSTRATIONS

Papyrus from the Book of the Dead of Nakht, showing Spell 110. Thebes, late Eighteenth Dynasty, 1350–1300 BC (*The Trustees of the British Museum*)

Back view of a crocodile-skin suit of armour from the third century AD, discovered near Manfalut (*The Trustees of the British Museum*)

Map showing Egypt to Ethiopia from the Ptolemy manuscript, illustration from *Memoires de la Societe Royale de Geographie d'Egypte*, c.1470 (*Private Collection/Bridgeman*)

Photograph of the Great Pyramid of Cheops reflected in the Nile overflow, c.1950 (*G. Eric and Edith Matson Photograph Collection/Library of Congress*)

Aerial photograph of the Aswan Dam, looking north, c.1936 (*G. Eric and Edith Matson Photograph Collection/Library of Congress*)

Fifteenth-century illumination from *Les Grandes Chroniques de France*, showing Louis IX's battle against the Saracens on the Nile (*AKG/ Erich Lessing*)

The Nilometer, Rhoda Island (*Radius Images/Corbis*)

The Battle of the Nile, 1 August 1798 at 10 p.m. by Thomas Luny, 1834 (*Bonham's, London/Bridgeman*)

Map of Speke and Grant's route from Zanzibar to the Nile, drawn and coloured by Grant with explanatory note by Speke dated 26 February 1863 (*Royal Geographical Society*)

Tissisat Falls (*Christophe Bolsvieux/Hemis/Corbis*)

Albumen print of a house and garden in the French Quarter, Cairo, with Gustave Flaubert, 1850 (*Private collection/Christie's/Bridgeman*)

Photograph of a *dahabiya* in Cairo, c.1860–90 (*Library of Congress*)

Photographic print of boys shooting the rapids of the Nile on logs, c.1901 (*H.C. White Co./Library of Congress*)

MAPS

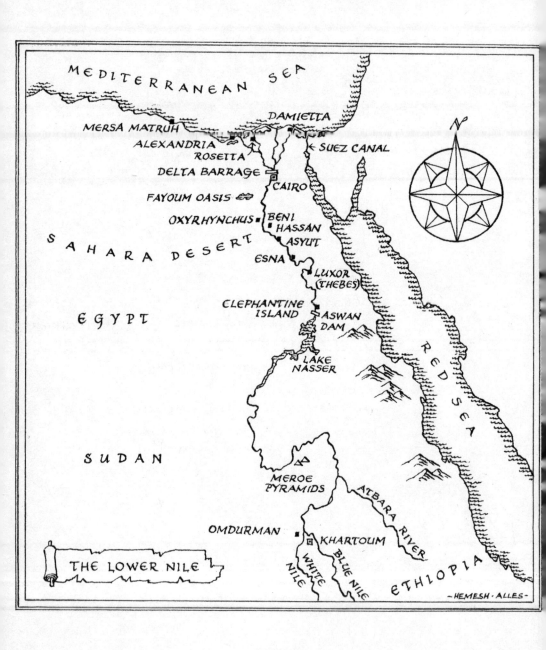

MEDITERRANEAN SEA

DAMIETTA
MERSA MATRUH
ALEXANDRIA ← SUEZ CANAL
ROSETTA
DELTA BARRAGE
CAIRO
FAYOUM OASIS

S A H A R A   D E S E R T

OXYRHYNCHUS BENI
HASSAN
ASYUT
ESNA
LUXOR
(THEBES)
ELEPHANTINE
ISLAND
ASWAN
DAM

E G Y P T

LAKE
NASSER

RED SEA

S U D A N

MEROE
PYRAMIDS
ATBARA RIVER

OMDURMAN
KHARTOUM

WHITE NILE
BLUE NILE
ETHIOPIA

THE LOWER NILE

−HEMESH·ALLES−

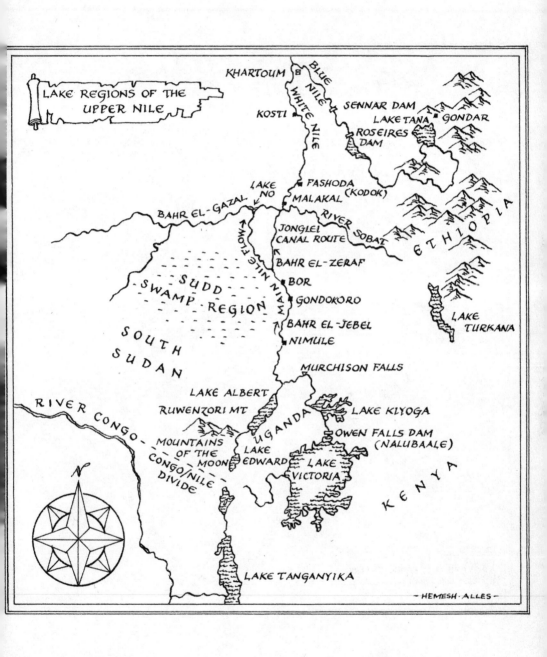

LAKE REGIONS OF THE UPPER NILE

KHARTOUM
BLUE NILE
WHITE NILE
SENNAR DAM
KOSTI
LAKE TANA
GONDAR
ROSEIRES DAM
LAKE NO
FASHODA (KODOK)
MALAKAL
BAHR EL-GAZAL
RIVER SOBAT
JONGLEI CANAL ROUTE
ETHIOPIA
MAIN NILE FLOW
BAHR EL-ZERAF
SUDD SWAMP REGION
BOR
GONDOKORO
LAKE TURKANA
BAHR EL-JEBEL
SOUTH SUDAN
NIMULE
MURCHISON FALLS
LAKE ALBERT
LAKE KIYOGA
RIVER CONGO
RUWENZORI MT
UGANDA
OWEN FALLS DAM (NALUBAALE)
MOUNTAINS OF THE MOON
CONGO/NILE DIVIDE
LAKE EDWARD
LAKE VICTORIA
KENYA
N
LAKE TANGANYIKA
~ HEMESH · ALLES ~

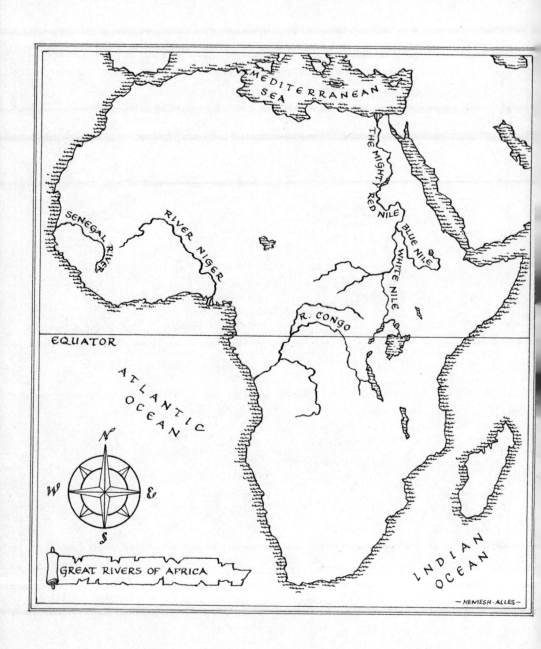

GREAT RIVERS OF AFRICA

— HEMESH·ALLES —

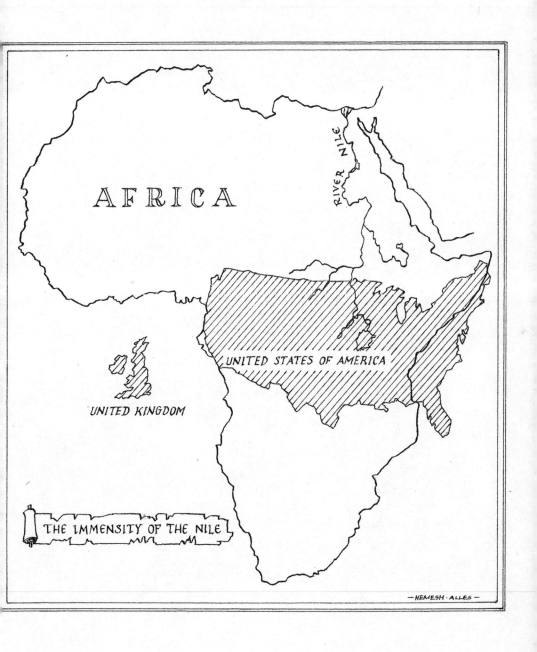

AFRICA

RIVER NILE

UNITED STATES OF AMERICA

UNITED KINGDOM

THE IMMENSITY OF THE NILE

—HEMESH·ALLES—

Two dams that changed the Nile forever

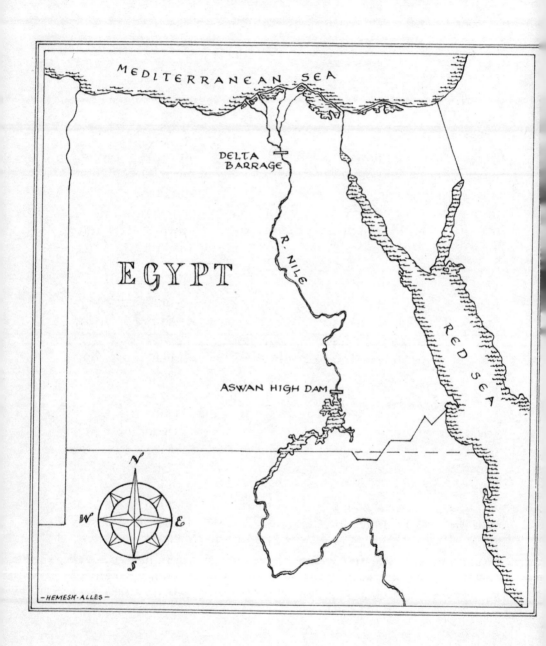

INTRODUCTION

Red river

Picture a river that flows through a quarter of all Africa, a river fed by smaller streams and other rivers, yet retaining in our mind a unity, a single identity, despite the diversity of the nations and tribes it passes through. One molecule of the water that rises in the forests of Burundi or in Lake Tana in Ethiopia can make its journey all the way to the Nile delta in Egypt and flow into the Mediterranean, and so justify our referring to the mighty system of the Nile as one river.

The Nile is mighty. If the Thames were on the same scale it would not end at Gravesend – it would swim the Channel, continue through Europe, cross all of Turkey and enter Iraq to issue like the Euphrates into the Arabian Gulf. Imagine travelling such a river, wanting to own it and control it. This has been the dream of men and nations since nations began with the world's first – the country known as Misr, Egypt.

These attempts at control have faded, the influence and consequences all forgotten. Only the stories remain. And the ruins of great buildings, old dams, temples and statues? Don't these exist too as the stories we tell of such buildings and their makers? Only the stories remain.

And what is the colour of such stories? A trick question. The stories that remain are always the most highly coloured, the most passion filled or the most blood curdling. Naturally, their colour is red.

Red. The real Nile isn't White or Blue or even Green. It's Red. For a moment when the Blue Nile in full flood enters the White Nile it backs up the river, reversing its flow for five miles, mixing its load of sediment with the clearer waters of the White Nile to make, for a few days, a blood-red river. This moment, in time and place, where Blue and White meet in the Sudan in early summer near Khartoum, is a magical metaphor for the world's greatest river: a river of blood, of life, of death. When Moses demanded that the Pharaoh allow the Israelites to leave, ten plagues were visited upon the Egyptians – the first being that the Nile turned into blood and all the fish died. Some commentators suggest this was a 'red tide', a rare algal bloom on the river's surface, but we will, in a short while, discover better explanations for this seeming miracle. Later, in 1249, 'Bloody' Baiburs, the Mamluk defender of Egypt, put 3,000 French crusaders to the sword in the delta and turned 'the mighty Nile red with blood'. This is a river that naturally runs red throughout history, the colour of wars, of creation, of struggle, of pilgrimage, of sickness, of triumph.

The White Nile and the Blue Nile are rivers, amazing rivers, but riverine in scope and history, like rivers, admittedly big rivers, the world over. The lower Nile, the only river to cross the Sahara Desert, is extraordinary in its own right too. But take them together – the Blue, White and lower Nile – and you have something truly remarkable. This is what I choose to call the Red Nile. It is the entire system of Niles, and it is without doubt the greatest and most influential river system in the world.

The Nile inspired Alexander the Great in the fourth century BC to seek its source to discover the explanation for its miraculous flood – which happens in summer. All other rivers in the ancient world flooded in winter. One reason for the incredible plenty of Egypt, which allowed it to amass grain and establish an urban culture (and the world's first nation state), is the fact that just when you need water, when it's hot and dry, you get a ton of it. A veritable flood, an inundation that bursts banks and brings life-giving silt into every field. And the sheer quantity of silt, which comes from the Ethiopian highlands, was unsurpassed in growing power until the advent of chemical fertilisers. With flood and flood-borne silt you have the makings of a country that the Romans would call the 'breadbasket of the Empire'.

Alexander's emissaries never did get to the source. Instead he turned to the Oracle in Siwa. The Boy King asked it to explain the summer inundation. There is no record of the oracular answer. But we now know the flood arises in the summer monsoon rains that deluge the Ethiopian highlands.

Creation's river

The banks of the Nile are smoking with the fires of the river dwellers. There are crocodiles and hippos, gazelle and ibis. Hyacinth floats midstream. A sacred river, old and contorted as a creation myth, the Red Nile absorbs all life and death and moves on. It swirls its way deep into Africa, its scale beyond comprehension.

So much begins on the banks of the Red Nile, on the palm-tree bank, the papyrus bank. All religion, all life, all stories. The script we write in, the language we speak. The gods and the legends and the names of stars. This great river, somehow unhurried, yet always swiftly moving on, has been history's greatest and most sustained creator.

The first people of the Red Nile were very probably the first people anywhere. They came up the Nile valley, an extension of the Great Rift Valley of east Africa. The rift was where all the little competing groups of humanoids first emerged. Eventually *Homo sapiens sapiens* made it up the rift and up the river, into Europe and the rest of the world.

These first humans were far from unimaginative. We encounter them through their art, drawn exquisitely on scooped-out cave walls, and through their tools: hand axes, heavy and scalloped, and flint arrowheads chipped from silica, a rare natural glass found only in the Egyptian Sahara, thought to have been formed by a meteor of massive proportions smashing into the sand and fusing with the Great Sand Sea into a wondrous aquarium green. (Millennia later, a large piece of this glass was transported by donkey and then up the Nile, so that the Pharaoh Tutankhamen could have it carved into a scarab and set in gold around his neck.)

Stories remain

Older than Egypt, older than the current course of the Nile, is the *Crocodylus niloticus*, the Nile crocodile. There is one outside my window in Cairo, where the Nile moves with effortless ease, always wind lapped, always flowing north. The crocodile's appearance, usually among the reeds of some Nileside suburb of Cairo, gets reported every two or three years. This time it surfaces in Maadi, where I live, a few miles from the centre of the city. Instead of being a wild creature it is a pet released by a bored owner. In ancient Egypt, the crocodile was a symbol of protection. It's comforting to have him near.

My home is one road back from the Corniche, the once grand, now faded and tatty avenue that runs alongside the Nile in Cairo. I can see the water between two new buildings: an oblong of river, a single palm and a patch of blue sky. In the late afternoon I can see, in this oblong, the sun setting directly behind the Pyramids, ten miles away – when the smog isn't too bad, that is. The Pyramids were built with giant limestone blocks carried to the Giza plateau by the floodwaters of the Nile. If you tried to build them today using the methods of the Pharaohs you couldn't, because the Aswan high dam has reduced the summer flood to no more than a quickening of the flow and a rise of a foot or so; this is all that remains of the great flood of the past. There is almost always a breeze blowing up or down the river and, remarkably, it is never crowded. On it sail pleasure boats, small dhows called feluccas named by the British after the Portuguese boats, also of Arab origin, that look similar. Far older are the rowing boats plied by the fishermen. The design, with an upturned bow and stern and square-shaped oars, is the same as those found in ancient tombs in Saqqara.

Families of fisherfolk live year round on the water. While the men usually have an outboard motor, the women and young men still have to row using big ungainly oars. They cast their nets and beat the water to drive the fish into them; as with the boats, there are 3,000-year-old friezes, in the tombs of Beni Hassan, depicting fishermen beating the waters, doing exactly the same as they do today. There is another type of fisherfolk I can only see when I get closer to the river, usually from the outdoor terrace of TGI Friday's, which serves ice-cold beer and overlooks the water. It is the Nile kingfisher, black and white to our kingfisher's blue, and it plunges from on high to splash into the water, a sudden flicker like a flash photo, surfacing with a blood-stained silvery fish in its beak. Not long ago, in a small rubber boat more suited to a beach than the Nile, I floated downstream for six miles, from my suburb to the city centre. I passed an island where, according to legend, Moses was left in his basket; a few miles further downstream was the spot where Joseph and Mary landed after their flight to Egypt. The present population were busy killing a lamb for the *eid* festival, there on the beach – they waved at me to join them and the kids jumped into the bloodied river to grab hold of my boat. The Red Nile won't let you get away from history – it's the source and the sauce in more ways than one.

People set eyes on the Nile and they are beset by a curious urge to travel up it, discover its secrets, own it, control its bounty. Most of the stories, the human stories, concern attempts successful or not to control this river. For millennia the Nile's flood was controlled by building up high banks or levees along the river. These would contain the flood. Then at right angles other embankments directed the flood's might right and left into large square basins, a patchwork of small lakes over which the populace would sail on papyrus rafts, wooden boats or even floating logs. The basins would dry up and be planted with grain which grew abundantly on such well-silted and well-watered soil. What follows is not the mainstream of history, chuntering on, year in, year out. Instead I have followed the metaphor a step further, written stories borne on the back of the Red Nile's flood, stories of excess, love, passion, splendour and death. Plenty of death.

But, while necessarily limiting myself to the bloodiest and best narratives, I found something odd happening. This patchwork of stories began to join up in most unexpected ways. Just as floodwaters link up overlooked canals and waterways I started to expect rather than be surprised by the often extraordinary connections between stories I uncovered. Who would have thought that the place where the crusaders' blood filled the Nile – Mansoura – would also be the place where, only a few years later, the first accurate description of the blood's circulation would be made? That Cleopatra would not only be the mistress of Caesar and travel up the Nile on a state boat with him, but also have an affair with the same King Herod who would later drive Mary and Joseph to embark on a less exclusive Nile cruise with their infant son Jesus? Or that an island in the Nile with the oldest flood-measuring device should also be the headquarters of the slave warrior Mamluks later to be exterminated by Muhammad Ali, the first man to interfere with the flood by building a barrage across the Nile? Or that Napoleon would inadvertently be the cause of both the Suez Canal and the translation of hieroglyphics? Or that Flaubert would almost literally walk in Florence Nightingale's footprints in the sand as he was only a few days behind her on a Nile cruise? Or that the Stanley who discovered Livingstone was the first man to visit the Blue Nile source before the White Nile source when he covered the little-known elephant war of 1868 in Ethiopia (accompanied coincidentally by James Grant, who had already been to the source of the White Nile and was now visiting the Blue Nile)? Or that the man whose brainchild was the Aswan high dam was a lone Greek inventor, who was inspired by the first Arab to try and dam the Nile, Ibn al-Haytham, who incidentally also invented the camera? Or that the first man to photograph the Nile, Maxime du Camp, would also be the man inadvertently to cause Flaubert to write *Madame Bovary*, the world's first modern novel? And these are only a few of the canals, irrigation ditches, patches of shining water that accompany any historical journey down the Nile.

I made the easy decision not to travel from the source to the sea in the rubber boat I travelled through Cairo in (or even one a little more seaworthy). I left my hang glider at home, so to speak, and forwent, rather easily, the temptation to jet ski like James Bond from Uganda to the Med. I'd need to read as much as make miles. Rather, I would travel at my own pace, and try to uncover the best stories, in all their light and darkness, the stories red in tooth and claw, the more bizarre the better, the blood and the guts of this river which spills into history. Only the stories remain.

Part One

NATURAL NILE

Beasts and beginnings

1 · The source

The strength of the crocodile is the water. Ugandan proverb

One should always begin at the beginning, and with a river that means the source. But where exactly is it? Despite, and maybe because of, a universal longing to 'find the source of the Nile', even now the exact location of the source is still disputed.

Searching for the real source of the Nile, in fact, is rather like visiting Stratford and discovering that the commercial attraction known as 'Shakespeare's Birthplace' is simply a nineteenth-century invention, and that, in reality, Shakespeare has several competing birthplaces. (According to the most informed, the real site of the bard's birthplace is now currently a car park.)

In antiquity the twin sources of the Nile – the Blue Nile and the White Nile – were often confused when it came to naming the true source. The Blue rises in Ethiopia, the White in central Africa. The Blue Nile, in the wet summer season, provides 85 per cent of the water that crosses the Sahara Desert and enters Egypt. But in the dry winter season the Blue Nile's contribution is negligible, less than 5 per cent, and the White Nile is the main provider. So in summer you could argue the Blue Nile is the source and in winter the White Nile.

Another definition, more acceptable, is that the source is simply the furthest point on the river from its end, from the delta on the Mediterranean where it enters the sea. The White Nile is by far the longest contributory branch and its official start is where it leaves Lake Victoria at the town of Jinja.

But rivers feed Lake Victoria too and the longest of these is the Kagera. A river of considerably greater girth and power than many European rivers, it makes the Thames look rather small and unimportant. Though it doesn't bear the Nile's name the Kagera is, in a sense, the mother to the Nile; 450 miles long, it is a mighty river in its own right. It is navigable in its lower stretches, but higher up it weaves through deep clefts and swampy patches occluded with papyrus. Higher still it takes on the vivacity of a mountain stream as it drains the western lake mountains that extend from the Ruwenzori range, known in antiquity as the Mountains of the Moon.

So the true source of the great River Nile, arguably, and most do argue this, is the source of the Kagera river. It was this that I had come in search of. It wasn't the first of my Nile explorations – I had been travelling up and down the river for some years, ever since moving to Cairo in 2004 – but it felt like the start of the current phase, 'the Nile-book phase' as I had come to think of it.

But the complications multiplied. The Kagera has several sources of its own, mostly in damp and hard-to-get-to forests. And river measuring – from maps and satellite pictures – is never an exact science. Do you, for example, measure along the inside curve, the middle or the outside? Presumably the middle. But what about when it went around islands – islands, which, in the case of the vast Sudd swamp in Sudan that the Nile traverses, actually moved?

On a previous expedition I had been involved in the tricky task of measuring long snakes, pythons that refused to straighten out. Pythons are strong – the best you can expect in terms of straightness is a wavy line, like a river; finding their length as they squirm is more art than science despite the technology of exact measurement.

A 2006 expedition that had gone up the Nile in powered rubber boats equipped with hang-glider wings for flying over rapids had measured their route as they went. From this practical rather than theoretical measuring we get the official length of 4,175 miles – 6,719 kilometres. This expedition had also made a diligent search for the furthest source they could find. It was this source I had decided to seek out.

It should have been rather momentous, plodding towards this most sought-after of places. Think of the history, I kept telling myself, but here, in the Rwandan Nyungwe Forest, the dripping Nyungwe Forest, I sensed nothing significant at all. At first. Not even the troop of olive baboons that sidled away could interest me. 'Them scared of bushmeat hunters,' I was told.

I thought I knew about rivers. I had followed one of Canada's longest, the Peace, from its finish in Lake Athabasca to its start in the pine-clad Rockies. I'd written about my three-season journey against its vicious current in my book *Voyageur*. I say vicious because the Peace river was plain mean compared to the strong but benign Fraser. Every river has a moral character, strange but true, and you find it at your peril usually by going against it, drinking it, pissing in it, watching it in its moods of repose and anger. If you ride with a river it's harder to get to know it. It's the same with people – you only find out the real person when you come up against them, anger them or they anger you, or you strive together against some joint adversity. If you submit to another and just get carried along you're more likely to go to sleep than learn anything. Not that I was going to do anything as crass as follow it geographically from start to finish, or finish to start as that group of adventurous folk did using powered hang gliders to jump over the rapids. I suspected that this would be about the dullest way to approach a river as rich historically as it was geographically. My own experience as a latterday explorer making long and difficult journeys where others hadn't been (in recent memory at least) was that the very difficulty in remaining authentic – ignoring handy lifts from pick-ups, stops in towns, going on local tours – actually kept you from interacting with, and keenly observing, the country you travelled through. It was like the whitewater rafting I was later to do during my Nile journey. Every raft experience was more like the previous one than different. The guides sought to turn every evening into a beach party with beer, boombox and barbie tickling your senses with the scent of meat fat crackling over the glowing embers. The more a trip becomes a physical test the more you have to ignore the non-physical – everything else, really. But the Nile wasn't just a series of Class 5 rapids separated by a lot of boring flat water, it was a river of immense human significance.

At first. But just as I glimpsed the puddle that I knew immediately was the source a strange sense of contentment came over me. It wasn't the exultation I had anticipated long ago when making plans, buying tickets, telling people. Rather it was a sense of wondrous contentment, and, at the risk of ridicule, it was not unlike the sentiment I first felt visiting Legoland. The sheer size of the tiny Legoland world (all built out of Lego – mountains, towns, cities, harbours, jungles) on my first visit made me feel awe mixed with cosiness, a kind of pet-owners' generosity of spirit – a world in your palm, but still a world.

And the source of all this was a small puddle in the middle of the jungle in Rwanda. I had forced our guide, called Pius, using my cheap yellow eTrex GPS, which I already thought of as a dear friend, to follow a route he thought both improbable and pointless, through strange bushes equipped with a thousand thorns and up and down ditches and over rotten logs soft as pie crust to get to the spot explorers earlier that year had decided was the real true source of the Nile – in their eyes

– as it was the longest distance from its end in the Egyptian delta that flows into the Mediterranean. I sat by the puddle and produced to great interest and some hilarity my secret weapon, my piece of business, my magic. Si-105 was a mini-pump filter that was guaranteed to clean fifty-five litres (twelve gallons) before it was used up. It was about the size of a big tube of toothpaste with rubber pipes that allowed one to suck up water from a tree bole, for example, or a handy crevice. The great thing about Si-105 was the built-in filter over the sucking end – it sort of flared out and had a micromesh net over it. This stopped the thing getting clogged, something that had happened with previous pump water filters I had used. The idea was simple, diabolically simple – I would drink my way down the Nile, imbibing it at every point of interest, historical, psychological, mystical and any other significance I could think of. I'd be able to make fifty-five samples, more than enough. I hoped I wouldn't get ill – but hell, no pain, no gain, and I knew of no other way to discover the river in all its pride and glory. Except one – swim it. I already had my sweaty Gore-Tex boots off and was dangling my toes in the slime. I removed them before I started pumping, recalling a story told about Orde Wingate, the enigmatic Abyssinian campaigner who insisted on rushing to the head of his military column when they arrived at a water hole – and stripping off and dunking his behind in the water ... before any of his men could take a drink. But that was at the other source – the Blue Nile.

The water came out clear and enticing. I thought Pius and his friend Peter would be vaguely insulted. Instead they gave broad grins and were keen to share the half-litre or so of liquid I managed to pump into my Sigg water bottle, another friend (you cling to travel kit, turn the everyday into the iconic as a way of normalising the new and unexpected).

It had been my ambition like the venerable Roger Deakin, who swam his way across England, to swim and drink my way down the Nile. I stuck to it, for a while, and then it began to seem a bit silly. Why risk getting ill or eaten just for a book? It served its purpose I suppose, it got me moving, really looking at the river and seeing it as the main source of water and movement for the entire region – since earliest times until this century, when air travel and mineral water served up from wells drilled deep into the Nubian aquifer began to take over. And even now it is really only the rich who can afford to ignore the Nile's bounty.

I intended to meander. That was important. I eschewed, out of epistemic necessity, the purely linear way of approaching the river; that left the vaguely historical, the psychogeographical and the purely personal and meandering. History was definitely my major resource. Psychogeography was less promising; while I applauded the works and methods of the psychogeographers, I knew such occidental urbanity would be chewed up and utterly masticated by the immensity of Africa. As for the neat interpretations of psychology, they tend to become dwarfed and tortured into mythology when they leave the comfortable confines of the Western city, the cosy suburbanalities of the campus. What sort of psychological analysis can one apply to Lord's Resistance Army leader Joseph Kony, who had his men remove the lips of children who displeased him? Or to Napoleon invading Egypt in 1798 with his sights set on Persia, India and the world? Or to the first Sultana of Egypt, Shajarat al-Durr – who murdered one husband in his bath and pretended another was still alive when he wasn't? The personal and meandering had always served me surprisingly well in the face of other such enormities. I hoped, with such a long meandering river in my sights, it would serve me well again.

2 · A high-speed journey down the Nile

Where there is the Nile they do not wash by using water drip by drip.
Egyptian proverb

The problem with any book attempting to tell both a geographical and a historical tale, or a linked series of tales, is that geography starts at the source (if we are talking about rivers) and ends at the sea, while history can zip up and down the river a couple of times each generation. Certain spots attract more history than others – Cairo, obviously, and also the dark jungles of the upper Nile – but, whatever way you cut it, any history of the Nile involves knowing a lot of geography before you can even start. Otherwise, as one zips up and down the river, following, say, General Horatio Kitchener on his mission to avenge Gordon and at the same time steal the Nile from the French pushing in from the Congo, one needs to know where one is. The names of places. The rapids, waterfalls and tributaries. Maps help a lot, and we have included a few in this book, but you still need a solid mental picture of the river before we start. Hence the instant jetboat and Cessna plane descent,

taking, I hope, no more than ten pages and keeping you fully engaged
in what is actually a very, very long river with its fair share of longueurs
between all the very exciting bits.

First, for those who have never seen the Nile, what is it like? I'll
never forget the disappointment I felt on seeing the mighty Mississippi
in New Orleans. Muddy, dull, forgettable. It didn't help that I had just
been mugged on the viewing platform. My main thought was: it ain't
that wide. I was expecting something like the Brahmaputra – so wide
you can't see the other side, something more reminiscent of a great
lake or the sea than a river. Nope, the Mississippi is ordinary, like the
Thames at Deptford, the eminently missable Mississippi. (I'm talking
about New Orleans here – it widens out elsewhere.) In Cairo, when
the Nile filters around mid-river islands, it too can look rather narrow.
But get down to the riverside and the grandeur, the stately calm of the
river, is all too apparent. This is a river that has been places – and with
its unhurried air it seems not a jot tired of its journey, not yet at least. It
is a fast river, a continent-crossing river – fast compared to a big English
river. There are parts where the river widens out – Lake Kiyoga north
of Lake Victoria, in stretches in Sudan and Upper Egypt – but this is
never a river like the Congo and the Amazon, rivers watered along their
entire length by tropical downpours. The Nile spends most of its time
crossing desert or dry savannah – it is less of a drain than a life-bringing
irrigation stream. There are no big cities south of Egypt on the Nile,
apart from Khartoum. It is a clean river and looks clean. Oh you get
rubbish in the canals, and a few beaches and washing places in Cairo,
places where, even today, women take pots and pans down to the river
to wash them; there may be Coke bottles and plastic bags. But there is
nothing like the garbage you see on the streets around the overflowing
skips (which replaced the highly efficient donkey-cart-driving rubbish
collectors who were deemed too 'old fashioned').

But what of its character? I have written that all rivers have a
moral character. This is indefinable, but appears to those who spend a
long time in their company. The Nile's character is *sui generis*, one of
dependability. For all its floods and famines and small tantrums, this
is a river you can rely on. It won't rush you to your death if you fall in.
It will carry you along, perhaps to the shore. I should say I am talking
about the lower Nile here – the mixture of the White and the Blue.
And, despite its cataracts and waterfalls, the upper White Nile too has a
similarly dependable feel. The Blue Nile is altogether wilder and more

unpredictable. The character of the Blue Nile is unlettered wildness, the wildness of a falcon or bird of prey that can be yoked into work but never entirely trusted. Turn your back on the Blue Nile, one feels, and it will drown you.

Now we have the several sources to skim over and observe: the Blue Nile rising in Ethiopia – at Lake Tana, or, rather, thirty miles from Lake Tana; the White Nile in that part of Africa where a great many countries seem to get drawn together: Uganda, Kenya, Sudan, Congo, Rwanda. The sources dominate men's imaginations, but they are only a small part of the river's identity, an identity largely forged by the terrain the river travels through. With its huge summer flood, literally pregnant with water, the Mother of the Nile would have to be the Blue Nile. But we'll start our quick journey with the broadly agreed beginning of the White Nile, the father of all the Niles. The Kagera river, the ultimate source of the White Nile, snakes its way from the montane jungles of Rwanda to the west coast of Lake Victoria. But where does the water actually come from? Just as the Blue Nile is charged by the monsoons that pound the Ethiopian highlands, the White Nile receives its rainfall from the south Atlantic gales that arrive burdened with moisture on the African coast. Meeting no real resistance until they strike the mountains of the central rift, the rain falls and is channelled north. The precipitation that hits the mountains lower in the chain around Lake Tanganyika drains into the Congo basin and back into the Atlantic. Interestingly Lake Victoria, being only 300 feet deep and over 25,000 square miles in area, is actually a net loser of water – more flows into it than flows out – the rest being lost to the wind as evaporation.

For the first part of its life after the Owen Falls at Lake Victoria the Nile follows a chain of rapids through forest traditionally unoccupied, due to the prevalence of sleeping sickness. The river is wild and only with the coming of whitewater rafting has it been possible to descend safely. The thick, subtropical forest on either side was traditionally penetrated only by elephants, whose huge trails became the paths for inquisitive explorers who, in the late nineteenth century, ignored the local avoidance of the disease-ridden area – and suffered for it. Dealing with strange fevers, boils, mysterious sheddings of skin, bone ache and ague became the stock in trade of all who dared penetrate to the heart of Africa.

Around 50,000 people a year in Africa are still supposed to die from sleeping sickness. Spread by the tsetse fly, the disease is a parasitic amoeba that eventually invades the nervous system, causing, if it is not treated, disability and death. There are now several lines of defence, various drugs and treatments. This has led to eradication from some areas. Spread further by Arab slavers, colonisers and modernisers from its original location in the upper Nile regions, sleeping sickness is now more of a problem elsewhere than in the lands above Lake Victoria.

So, with less disease and tamer rapids, thanks to the Owen Falls dam (now renamed the Nalubaale), the first forty miles of the White Nile are not so wild as they once were. As it drops 600 feet in those forty miles it is easy to see why, in the 1860s, the explorer John Hanning Speke chose to avoid a direct descent of the river – though, if he had braved disease and cataract, he would have found the next 120 miles perfectly navigable. The Nile widens to a third of a mile and the forest begins to recede. It is as if someone has employed a forestry company to thin the trees in a charming manner in keeping with the landscape; only it is nature that has performed this task.

The river gets to a mile wide and the river's floor gets nearer and nearer – less than ten feet deep. You can see the fish rising for air – Nile perch and catfish, tilapia, elephant fish. The river becomes wider still and transforms into Lake Kiyoga, a broad muddy sheet of water choked in parts with weed; it is a presentiment of the swamps to come. As the river flows through this lake for sixty miles it carries a pale-blue water lily that lies like a Chinese carpet on the moving surface.

The lake receives another wild tributary, the Kafu, at its northern end. This is just as well – if the tributary entered earlier on in the swampy lake its force would be absorbed and negated. Just as it was thousands of years ago, the Nile would be finished, spent of all motive force before it had half started.

After the join, the river begins to loop, and following its hypnotic swirls I am reminded of the philosopher's conundrum about the identity of a broom which has had its brush and handle changed many times. Is it still the same broom? Similarly the Nile is rejuvenated all along its path and loses much of its source water long before it reaches the sea; yet it maintains its identity by some mysterious process.

The first of the swamps abruptly changes and the scoured rocky river floor is gained again as the Nile sweeps west and becomes again a mountain stream – an epithet uttered by Speke and the cause of much mockery from the bewhiskered stalwarts of the Royal Geographical Society. The mighty Nile – a stream! The insult! Yet only those who have seen both the mile-wideness of the Nile and its ferocity squeezed into a gorge twenty feet wide can understand that it can be both of these things. It is here, at the Murchison Falls, first seen by the explorer Samuel Baker, that the Nile is squeezed and then dashed from ledge to ledge surmounted by a constant rainbow, which Baker took to be a symbol of good fortune.

The foam stays on the river long after the bruising 141-foot Murchison Falls, but the river again quickly broadens as the rocky outcrops become less pronounced. It is here that hippos proliferate; and crocs – hundreds of them basking on rocks; both animals waiting, it seems, for rafters and kayakers who are too cocky or too unlucky to ply these waters carefully. Now the Nile enters, again at its head, another lake – the Albert. On its banks grassland alternates with forest and all manner of wildlife proliferates; and again the Nile is recharged, this time by the waters gathered in Lake Albert from the Ruwenzori – the Mountains of the Moon.

The Mountains of the Moon are fascinating in their own right, and we will return for a closer look. For the time being we will just glimpse them from the plane window, shrouded for 300 days a year in cloud, with the snowy peak of Mount Stanley poking through like a bewitched island rising from an enchanted lake.

Very quickly the river loses its pace and begins to resemble the intestines of some giant beast. The banks of the river are scrubby savannah – thick patches of low trees. As it widens and loops the river's speed of flow drops so low it would be very hard to say which direction it is flowing in. As with a patient in a coma only the most advanced equipment can detect if it is alive or not. We are entering the world's largest swamp – the Sudd.

Solitude of a stifling kind settles over the Sudd country. Here the Nile is almost lost in its wanderings and in the absorbent mulch of the world's biggest marsh. In previous versions of the Nile, a million years ago, the Sudd would have been the true end of this part of the river, yet now it is only a hindrance, a massive hindrance, but one that the river finally overcomes.

The river widens but keeps to its banks, even in flood times, the excess simply absorbed by the land. The floating islands are a sign of further swamps ahead. From Bor to Lake No, 300 miles north, swampland predominates. Flying low over it in a six-seater Cessna the red-brown Nile seems vaguely undulating, held together by white slime.

Backwaters, pools and marshes unravel the river into shoals of heaving papyrus and elephant grass. Nourished by boggy soil, grasses predominate in the swamps.

That the Sudd was not really conquered until 1900 is easily understood when the process of travel within the swamp is revealed. Though the first water crossing of the barriers of island, mud and marsh was made in the 1880s, it was the British in 1900 who decided to make it properly navigable. The process was laborious in the extreme. The first problem was to identify which part of the vegetation blocking the river was part of the bank and which part of a moveable island. If island, stakes would be driven in and attached by cables to the steamer, which would then reverse downstream ripping away the barrier of foliage. Like a dentist pulling teeth the blockages were torn away piece by piece. Sometimes islands could be burned first, then the roots would be hacked away by a hundred natives waist deep in water heaving with mattocks and spades. Five miles of swamp took three months to clear. It took five steamers and 800 Nubian prisoners – all surrounded by warlike tribes, mosquitoes and fever. This gigantic task of clearage has ever since always been under threat. The true path of the river always changes and still becomes blocked. In the 1990s, during the second civil war in Sudan the swamp again became impassable for months at a time.

We fly over the white and grey, somehow dilapidated-looking towns and villages, but they are as nothing compared to the relentless pull north of the winding river. This is the defining feature of the region. Around each village and town there is nothing like the amount of vegetation we see along the river.

From Bor northwards for 300 miles papyrus and elephant grass dominate the swamps. Papyrus is the Nile plant par excellence – it provided the first boats and the first paper. On the walls of tombs papyrus boats are depicted, similar to those still used on the Nile. The virtues of papyrus are recorded also on ancient pieces of papyrus mummified by the desert air at Oxyrhynchus and Fayoum. Papyrus in the Sudd grows over eighteen feet tall in places, forming dark-green forests, the younger lower plants a paler shade from lack of light. The papyrus rustles and creaks, forcing itself right into the Nile at the water's edge.

Elephant grass, with its stems like bamboo, looks much stiffer and less graceful than papyrus. It has a brown feathery crown and pointed upright leaves. Another grass is the 'um-soof' with its green hairy fur;

its name means 'mother of wool'. Towering above all of them is the ambatch, a fibrous pithy plant twenty feet high and six inches thick. Often it is festooned with huge blue-flowering convolvulus. With its tiny thorns it isn't so easy to work as papyrus, but like papyrus this is a great material for making rafts.

We swoop on over the flames of oil platforms – the Sudd was drilled for oil by Chevron in the 1970s, but ongoing troubles in the region have always made it a hard place to maintain production.

After the swamps, after the oil-bearing swamps of the Sudd, the Nile begins again with a no, a giant no, Lake No in fact. This is the first lagoon after the great marsh. It is really the beginning of a new epoch in the Nile's existence. From now on it is downhill all the way. Almost.

Here, in the south of Sudan, around latitude 10 degrees North, the Nile regains a firm bed, which it keeps until it reaches the delta in Egypt. There are no more swamps. This is the region where the Bahr el-Ghazal – 'the island sea' – meets the Bahr el-Jebel – 'the mountain sea' – at the western end of Lake No. Though the Ghazal is the tributary and the Jebel the original continuation of the Nile, the Ghazal is a mighty river in its own right, dumping, on its earlier path through the swamps, as much water as the Nile itself. Another tributary is the Bahr el-Zeraf – 'the giraffe sea' – which, seen from a plane as it enters the Nile, looks like some malignant disease eating away at the land. This is the furthest point that anyone from antiquity reached on the Nile. The Emperor Nero's men knew this point, as did, most probably, Greeks of an earlier age. Seneca wrote about Nero and the two centurions he sent up the Nile in the first century AD. He reports that they said on their return, 'we came to immense marshes, the outcome of which neither the inhabitants knew nor can anyone hope to know, in such a way are the plants entangled with the waters, not to be struggled through on foot or in a boat, because the marsh, muddy and blocked up, does not admit any craft unless it is small and containing one person'. That this is a precise description of the Sudd swamp and its rafts of papyrus can hardly be disputed. It is remarkable that this feat of exploration was not to be replicated for nearly 2,000 years.

The Nile now enters the dry lands, and it will never leave them. The earth is red laterite, and when it is damaged by vehicles you can see the scars scorching through the land and along the river banks. At the point where the Nile at last turns north again, the Sobat enters into it. The first of the Ethiopian rivers, it carries silt down from the south-western highlands. It is a powerful river supplying 14 per cent of the water carried by the White Nile to Khartoum. In this stretch the river is not deep – perhaps fifteen feet, though in places as little as six. On either side the land flattens out and acacia replaces papyrus. There are no rapids in this section of 750 miles – from Lake No to Khartoum – and low undulations on either side protect the land from floods and swamps, holding the stream within firm banks. There are eleven varieties of acacia growing on the plain along this stretch of the river and traditionally the Shilluk made everything from boats to waterwheels, firewood, tanning materials and gum from these trees that stand like black skeletons stark against the midday sun of the plains.

This is the point where invading Asia meets escaping Africa along the Nile. The conical huts of the Dinka and Shilluk give way to the square houses of the Arabised northerners. Donkeys and camels walk by the Nile now and people cover their heads and bodies almost completely. The hippo becomes rarer and rarer. At Kosti there is the third bridge over the Nile since its beginning 2,000 miles away.

It is here that the migrating birds of the north spend their winter: the swallow, the increasingly rare corncrake, storks, orioles, terns, snipe and lapwing. What is most strange is that the Egyptian swallow flies only a short length down the Nile. The ones furthest south are those who have come from the furthest north, and this is true of the cranes and storks who migrate further than the native species, as if this travel were necessary for some reason other than mere survival, as they too, like our ancestors, sought to penetrate as far along the Nile as possible.

We arrive at Khartoum and observe the relentless spread of the city. If we are lucky and are hovering overhead sometime in summer we will catch a glimpse of the birth of the Red Nile, the powerful miscegenation of White and Blue, the Blue Nile so overwhelmingly powerful at this time that it punches the old White Nile back upstream. The silt – orange, red, pink depending on the exact conditions – pours into the widened river as it flows on towards the cataracts of northern Sudan.

From above, rapids look like drippings of toothpaste on a grey floor. By some curious optical illusion the river is stopped, freeze-framed, as you watch from a small plane window. Down on the ground the noise is deafening.

We pass the 200 or more mysterious steep-sided Pyramids of Meroe, home to the 'Black' Pharaohs, who lived here from 800 BC to around AD 230. From on high these Pyramids look like a series of diagonal crosses; when the plane banks you get a side-view and they resemble somehow the tiny wooden houses left over from an old-fashioned Monopoly game.

The Nile reaches Lake Nasser. One of the world's largest man-made lakes – over 250 miles long – it takes an hour to fly over in a twin-prop Beechcraft. All that water! And so hypnotically blue, patterned with algal green around the shores. The lake makes mini-fjords along its banks, the dry valleys or wadis it has filled up. Surprisingly, for a lake less than fifty years old, there are already some sandy beaches developing along its edges.

We swoop over the two dams, missing the ruins of Philae, camouflaged in their rocky brown from above. The agricultural benefits of the Nile are now apparent: bright-green fields about the darker-green belts of densely planted palm trees. Everything looks tilled, cared for, and then, without warning, it is yellow, pure sand – the desert. The life-giving river is never more apparent than when seen from above with its fragile fertile margins clinging to each side.

We fly over the great temple at Luxor and cross the small dam, or barrage, at Asyut. The river widens and narrows for no apparent reason, waxing and waning. At Cairo there is a kind of explosion. The city is everywhere, the river dwarfed but still vital, still pumping away like the main artery it is. We cross the first dam ever built on the Nile – the barrage at the delta, which sits at the fork of the two main branches. The delta spreads out around us. It is the original of all deltas, shaped as it is like a Greek letter 'D'.

Finally the sea. The white line of surf appears stationary, like the rapids we saw earlier. Dots, or rather people, on the beach. The sea greenish – lighter now that it is denied the silt that used to flood into it, feeding the great schools of sardines that are now all but gone. The river spreads into the sea, its home, and is lost.

3 · A river of change

The person whom God has cursed trades butter in the hot season and salt in the rainy season. Sudanese proverb

So, been there, done that. Having flown the Nile, skimmed its surface, it's time to dig deeper, unearth what we can. For a start, the most interesting thing, I think, about the Nile is how young it is, how much it has changed, and continues to change. In a sense, all rivers are old, and the Nile is, in parts, an old river; but it is also, geologically, a young river. The Nile's earliest valleys are millions of years old. Yet, in its current path, the Nile is shockingly new (in geological terms): only 12,500 years old. It is, above all else, a river that has been through many transformations and incarnations.

If there is one idea I want to keep in mind when thinking about the Nile it is the utterly simple and all too slippery notion of change. The Nile has changed; it changes things. When people come into contact with it they change – by moving along it, settling by its side, inventing irrigation, writing, forming an embryonic civic society, or using it as an excuse to invade, convert, plunder, rule. The Nile changes; it is a catalyst for change. Is it too general a concept to be of any use? We'll see.

What remains? After the red river has flooded, what remains? The land, the black land. The land, black with silt, the nutrient-heavy silt that allowed ancient Egypt to flourish. In the water, suspended and moving, it appears red, like blood; again like blood, when it dries and congeals and ages it becomes black. There is always a risk with running such metaphors too far and for too long; but they seem to hold, and in the Nile's case, with a river so vast in scope and length, it was the only way, with such flimsy strategies, that I could sort my own version of the nutrient silt, the mountains of research, story, history, science, myth and fiction that were piling up around me in my Nileside study. As I sat in my little brightly lit room at number 32, Road 100, just up from the gas station at Maadi I made sure, when I looked up from the computer, that I had a view of the Nile, an uninterrupted view. I took down the curtains, as they were of heavy material that intruded into my vision. The blank square was better, even better when I opened the metal-framed window. The river looked like a small swatch of greenish brown trapped in the gap between two buildings. One building was very high, over twenty storeys; it had been built only a few years previously. The other, suggestively I felt in the current mad phase of urban development in Egypt, was a home for the mentally ill. Often I heard them screaming and yelling. Well, once a week or so. I asked my wife about that and she said placidly, 'It means one of them has escaped.' 'You mean it's not the mad people who are screaming?' 'No, it's the nurses.'

The first building that blocks or curtails my view is, as I mentioned, a new block – for the newly rich, those richer than myself presumably. The proof being: they live nearer to the Nile than I. (Proximity to the river has always been a priority in Egypt, but the injection of high finance and the profits of real estate have elevated this concern to the same levels of hysteria you find in London and Paris with the Thames and the Seine. Strangely, New Yorkers seem still to prefer Central Park to the Hudson; tainted by commerce still perhaps.)

How to get enough of an angle on change, metamorphosis, transformation, evolution, revolution, mutation, transfiguration, translation, transmutation, alteration, rebirth? One angle: the river's course as palimpsest – dig down deep enough and you will reveal successive layers of inhabitation, geology, agriculture. Simple enough. Or, ignore those layers. Be an anti-archaeologist, an anti-palaeontologist. While the academics deal with what is there, the evidence, another more radical form of research might be to focus on what isn't there, the gaps in the fossil record, the glaring absences, the ignorance, the lost tribes and missing persons.

Perhaps the way forward is to look at the *other*. The river's opposite – stagnation. A river flows, provides life. When it stagnates it becomes a lake or a canal – something that is held by some shape, some depression, some ditch in the landscape. It is as if the land has killed it, made it dependent instead of alive. And it is true – canals leak and have to be puddled with clay or else all the water will escape.

The stagnant may be useful, but it has a short shelf-life. Without attention, without gardening, without human intervention it gathers the surface decay of stagnancy, it harbours disease, it actually becomes a danger to man; it can, in the breeding of mosquitoes and the harbouring of parasites, become the death of us.

Yet, even knowing this, our first instinct is always to make the river stagnant – to turn it into a 'useful' lake. We want more, we want every golden egg and we'll kill the goose for it.

It reminds me of Paul Celan's poem 'Death Fugue' – 'Black milk of daybreak we drink it at nightfall': we constantly want to exchange the living red river for black milk. Life seems to bore us. We need to know how much death we can imbibe, sip, tipple away on, unnoticed in the corner.

The word 'alcohol' comes from the Arabic *al-kohl* – the black powdered eyeliner so favoured by ancient Egyptians and later adopted by the Arabs. Making *al-kohl* involved distillation of antimony, so 'alcohol' came to mean any process involving distillation (a curious irony that those who oppose distilled spirits invented the process).

For all its blessings our favourite drink can also be a poison. In the form of methanol, alcohol can blind and kill. In the form of ethanol it simply makes us drunk. But pure ethanol is not very palatable, so all the preferred forms of alcohol contain varying amounts of methanol, pure poison. Death provides the taste.

Back to black. The kohl-lined eye is one of the most characteristic images of ancient Egypt – depicted in hieroglyphs as the eye of Horus. As befitting a falcon-headed god, Horus' eye resembles that of a bird of prey. The eye watched over and protected the Pharaoh in the afterlife, and was painted, for similarly superstitious reasons, on the bows of ships, a practice that spread to the whole Near East. Even today you'll see the eye of Horus on the bow of a dhow or felucca plying the Nile. The eye in ancient Egypt was thought of not as a passive organ of mere recording, but as an instrument of action, intention, wrath. The eye that guards against the evil eye. Perhaps from merely recording what I see I should take the hint and go out on a limb. Ride the river.

Black milk, evil eyes. At what point does change kill, become a form of death? At what point does tradition stifle and choke and become a cause of death? This is all too apparent in Egypt, where the ultra-modern butts up time and again against the immemorial. People living in the tombs in the city of the dead logging on with a Mobinil smartphone.

The black land, as the ancients called Egypt. The land remains the same – in the delta they farmed until the mid-twentieth century in the same way as they had 3,000 years ago. Even now there are many similarities in the poorer communities along the Nile. The land remains the same, the river changes.

Tradition is bad. That's one dogma. But tradition could be called a preservative, preserving ways of living, life. Change could involve killing what we need but temporarily no longer want. Because it has slipped out of sight.

One thing I am sure about, though: the piloting of the material, the navigation down the river from my little cabin-like study, lined with books, no curtains, view of the Nile night and day (the sunsets are amazing), the documenting of that journey, the pilot's log so to speak – that will be as vital a journey as the log of any real journey I might make. There had been any number of Nile trips recently, from the very adventurous to the strictly televisual; some had recorded changes in the river, some had not. Some had sought to emphasise that nothing had really changed. Others that everything had. It was all about what you looked at, where the black, kohl-rimmed eye looked.

Certainly, looking at the life of the Nile, over the longest period of time, will help us delineate better the roles of rebirth, death, change and tradition. These are the real questions, aren't they? I am hoping for it, sipping my Sakkara beer, alcohol of a refined kind, courtesy of the Al-Ahram brewery, sitting at my little window watching the sun set in my own little square of eternity.

4 · A child of the Rift

Only two things in this world are innately good: water and one's mother.
Sudanese proverb

Alfred Wegener, a German explorer and scientist, was disbelieved and ridiculed for his continental-drift theory – the theory, put forward in 1912, that the world was fissured, like an infant's skull, and yet that these fissures were actually fruitful, fructifying with molten magma deep under the sea, expanding, sliding over each other. Wegener was ignored from his untimely death in Greenland in 1930 until the 1950s, a warning shot to those who would propose a theory that looks right but can't be easily explained.

Wegener, from an early age, noticed what every schoolchild notices: South America fits into the right angle of west Africa; in fact the land mass of the earth all looks as if it was once joined. Wegener searched for evidence of his theory – finding rocks and fossils that matched on either side of the Atlantic Ocean. He provided the evidence but no mechanism and was opposed heatedly by such august organisations as the American Petroleum Society. He sought solace in making expeditions to the frozen north. On his last trip to Greenland conditions were so harsh he had to amputate a team member's frozen toes with his penknife. Temperatures dropped to 60 degrees below freezing; then Wegener, aged fifty, a heavy smoker who had spent too long in his study, died.

The discovery in the 1960s that the sea floor really did spread as Wegener had speculated, with magma bubbling up along tectonic plate lines, finally brought respectability to a theory that had been derided and lampooned. Scientists agreed that the circulating hot liquid centre of the earth was how the plates, with the continents sitting on top of them, moved. Just as rice in a pan of boiling water will circulate, so the surface of the earth was in constant movement, shoved by the circulating movement of the magma below.

I think it is salutary to note that the current theory about the birth of the Nile – in a valley made by tectonic plates shifting – was, until the 1960s, considered pure poppycock. I think we are all apt, especially non-scientists, to underestimate the transitory nature of scientific 'truth'. By definition such truth can only be a groping towards better and better explanations. I think we need to maintain a sense of lightness, of the faintly absurd, whenever a theory becomes too heavy, too fundamentally essential. In a few years, it too could be poppycock.

But for the time being we have Wegener and his moving plates. The Red Nile and the Red Sea are two children of the Rift Valley, the tectonic twins. The Rift Valley starts in east Africa and shatters its way north to that other fracture zone – Palestine and the Levant. The Red Sea is one result. The Nile valley is the other.

This combination river, the Red Nile, was born in the extreme violence of tectonic shifts and climate change so huge it makes our present concerns look like a quibble over the thermostat setting. We're talking aeons of time when whole seas disappeared alternating with floods in a manner that is starkly reminiscent not of hard science but of the chronicles of Ur and the Bible.

But long before the Bible was written, seven million years ago, the Mediterranean evaporated and became just another puddle. In those days Gibraltar was joined to Morocco and the global temperature was so frizzlingly high that most of the water just boiled away leaving behind a giant saltpan and the aforementioned puddle. Because of the current worries over global warming it's easy to think that the earth has never been very hot before, but, in between ice ages, temperatures have soared to 15 or 20 degrees above current averages. Fancy a day out when it's 60 degrees? Naturally such high temperatures resulted in some serious evaporation. Add to this tectonic shifts resulting in new land bridges and you have the reason for the Mediterranean's fickle nature.

With a tiny amount of water in the Mediterranean the sea level was much, much lower. This meant that any river flowing into the Mediterranean had a lot further to fall. This increase in drop speeded rivers up and meant they cut deep canyons as they approached the coast. The Nile in Egypt – it was wholly contained within Egypt then, fed by the rains of the lush plains (it was not yet a desert) – cut a canyon miles deep. Cairo sits on that canyon, now silted up by subsequent Niles. If we could go back seven million years or so we'd see something like the Grand Canyon, spewing into a dried-up sea. At Cairo the canyon would be more than a mile deep, at the delta it would have been an incredible two and a half miles deep. You could comfortably BASE-jump off the top and have a cigarette on the way down. Or two, even.

Life on the banks of the Nile seven million years ago would include giant crocodiles sixty feet in length, long-extinct ancestors of the lion replete with huge teeth and bigger appetites, giant turtles and perhaps a few primates.

The Mediterranean eventually recovered – much to the pleasure of all future holidaymakers. The land bridge between Gibraltar and Morocco that had corked up the Med and allowed the evaporation was overwhelmed by rising Atlantic sea levels. This was about five million years ago. Sea levels continued to rise in a dramatic way. The canyon river was flooded hundreds of miles upstream. The entire River Nile became a huge bay, a gulf, over seven miles wide at Aswan, 525 miles upstream.

Then it became dry again, very, very dry. I know this is all getting a rather Old Testament feel, but this is really what happened according to the best science we have available. Two million years ago the entire Nile river dried up and became a dusty valley, a wadi; all was desert, all was sand.

Then 800,000 years ago the earth began to move, or rather its surface began to shift in a different way; slowly the Ethiopian plate lifted up and tilted towards the Nile and away from the Red Sea. So instead of water running into the Red Sea it started to drain into the Nile. Remember, up to this point the Nile had been confined to Egypt, but now, with the favourable tilt of Ethiopia, and its new rivers feeding the Nile, the great river stopped being a dry valley and was extended backwards into Africa as a living waterway.

Meanwhile, in central Africa, water flooded from what would become the Congo basin and the future Nile basin in Sudan to create the Sudd – the world's biggest dead end. The rivers all turned inward and had nowhere to exit, no route to the sea. So they simply waterlogged an area bigger than France, creating the world's largest marsh. Imagine putting on your wellies in Boulogne and squelching all the way to Marseilles, with a few muddy swims in between. That was the Sudd.

The name Sudd comes from the Arabic for 'barrier' – and it would remain a barrier until the ice, during the maximum period of glaciation, some 15,000 years ago, began to recede. In this last ice age the mountains of central Africa such as the Ruwenzori would have been snow white all year round. They would have looked to ancient man like something alien and glowing in the morning sun. Perhaps their mythical name, Mountains of the Moon, dates from some ancient story preserved from this time.

New rivers formed to take the melting snows away. The new mountain rivers, enhanced by glacial water, were like a giant dam burst, pumping through the Sudd swamp and connecting it up with the Ethiopian rivers of the Nile.

At this point the Nile started at Lake Tanganyika, flowed through Lake Albert and finished up at the sea in what would become Egypt. Further tectonic activity shut off Tanganyika, leaving the start of the Nile in the area of Lake Edward and Lake Albert.

This was the Nile, almost as we now know it. Finally Lake Victoria – some 12,500 years ago – rose sufficiently high to overwhelm the rocky slabs at its northern end. The lake overflowed and broke through to the Albert Nile drainage, to create the modern Nile. This period was extremely wet – vast torrents unblocked the Nile of sand dunes and reeds making a huge, wide, dangerous river, a river to be feared and avoided.

This wet phase – from 12,500 BC until 4000 BC – meant people lived in the desert in preference to living beside the river (the desert was still much more hospitable, much more like savannah as late as 2450 BC during the Fifth Dynasty of ancient Egypt). Desert remains, hundreds of miles from the Nile, indicate wells and rain-fed lakes in country that is now completely desiccated, pure sand and rock.

These desert dwellers fled the rolling plains as they dried up, and found that the raging river had become quieter, more manageable. They brought with them their desert iconography: pyramids that mimicked star dunes, sphinxes that looked like wind-formed yardangs or 'mud lions'. They found they could manage the river's yearly flood, and invented irrigation methods still in use today. Civilisation grew and the world's first nation state formed along the banks of this river. The taming of the Red Nile had begun.

Along with the settlement of the Nile came the stories – myths about its origin, stories about its source which have a semblance of truth about them even now. The stories fed into the traditional tales of Africa, Egypt and even Greece. As they were passed down orally and then set down in texts, the Nile became the first river of ancient literature.

5 · Out of Eden bearing gifts

Laughing she got pregnant; crying she delivered. Ethiopian proverb

So we have a river, but what of the people that inhabited it? Sixty miles from the Nile valley, walking over dunes in the Egyptian desert, I accompanied executives from Oracle, the computer company, there on a company team-building exercise. My role was to reveal the secrets of the desert, but it was the company head of sales who found a hand axe. She didn't realise its significance. It had been left there maybe 200,000 years ago by one of the earliest dwellers along the Nile valley.

It was an Acheulean hand axe, as much leading technology in 200,000 BC as an Oracle database was in the twenty-first century. The early Nile dwellers have left behind no bones, no hearths – the desert has destroyed all that. All we have are their tools. And they are scattered everywhere in the desert, proving that the bounty of the Nile extended deep into what are now dry deserted lands. As I explained this, the executive saw my excitement and gave me the hand axe. It was too good a gift to pass up. 'Besides,' she said, 'it's too heavy for hand luggage.'

In the Book of Genesis we read: 'And a river went out of Eden to water the garden; and from thence it was parted, and became into four heads.' Was that river the Nile, the main artery of the human race? Down (and up) this artery humankind has spread and developed since the very formation of the River Nile.

As we have seen, the Nile in its current formation is, as rivers go, relatively recent. A proto-Nile that ran into the Tethys Sea – what is now the Mediterranean – existed several million years ago. But it was not until the Ethiopian highlands tilted away from the Red Sea that the Nile could extend backwards out of Egypt. This was around 800,000 years ago.

This new riverine link provided a certain band of hominids with the chance to break free of their isolation. They went on to dominate the world and outlast any other group, outliving *Homo erectus* in the Far East around 50,000 years ago and dominating *Homo neanderthalensis* through interbreeding. Yet *Homo sapiens sapiens* could easily have remained marooned in the Ethiopian highlands. Without the river they might have stayed in their own Eden – perhaps to have perished and become extinct as many earlier hominid groups had done.

The Nile valley was their exit route.

Early *Homo sapiens sapiens* had one advantage over his predecessors *Homo ergaster, erectus* and *neanderthalensis*. He was what he still is: a gift giver. Early hominids worked out how to use fire for their own purposes nearly a million years ago – there are fire-baked clays, evidence of controlled fire use dating from this long ago. Even earlier we see tool use that develops into the Acheulean hand axe, a ubiquitous tool that hardly changed its form in 500,000 years. A massive teardrop-shaped piece of stone, the hand axe was ideal for bashing out marrow from the scavenged and hunted long bones of large prey – deer, buffalo, eland, rhinos and giraffe. Marrow was crucial as a foodstuff as it is high in fat. This allows one to digest the protein of the kill. Without fat one can die of malnutrition, however much protein abounds – as survivalist Chris McCandless showed when he died in the Alaskan wilderness despite shooting plenty of lean game. He had no hand axe to bash out the marrow and died only twenty miles from the highway.

So even 500,000 years ago ancient man had worked that one out. He had started funeral rituals – arranging the way the body was laid out after death – and there is even rudimentary art among Neanderthals. But only *Homo sapiens sapiens* is buried with trade goods from far away, way outside his own living area. Burials in the Pyrenees turn up with obsidian carvings from central Europe. Northern Europeans have Mediterranean beads. These are the descendants of the first *Homo sapiens* who swarmed up the Nile and out of Africa, swapping their goods as they went.

We assume they were trading, but looking at the nearest living equivalent that is still around today – hunter-gatherer groups – it is much more probable that they simply gave these things away. The !Kung tribesmen, a remote group of the so-called San Bushmen of the Kalahari, are gift givers not traders. They also have no leaders. As one put it, 'We have headmen, every man is a headman over himself!' This was said as a joke to anthropologist Richard Lee as he studied their highly efficient way of life.

Trade is so central to our own ideas of what is essentially human that we may assume gift giving as an aberrant or naive proto-behaviour. Yet hunter-gatherers – such as the !Kung – as well as those early *Homo sapiens* had no need of trade nor any incentive to practise it, living as they did in groups of around thirty members, which is the ideal size for a hunting unit. Though the so-called Dunbar number is often repeated as marking the ideal size of a human community (150 members), this is a theoretical construct derived from extrapolations from primate studies. The lower figure of thirty better reflects the requirements of feeding a group who have no recourse to farming. Early hunter-gatherer man carried only twenty-five pounds of worldly goods when he moved, which he did periodically to find new game. We can assume that a great river, replete with game living off its bounty, would have worked as a natural magnet, pulling these hunter-gatherers ever further north. They had no need to trade – their twenty-five-pound bundle contained all they needed – but they would certainly have given goods away as gifts. When you are on the move you want as light a bundle as possible; there is no benefit in excess baggage.

!Kung women give birth roughly every four years. They suckle their young for that long, which acts as a natural prophylactic, a necessary one since it is hard to move and carry two infants at a time. But it is also an ecological solution. Only with the coming of agriculture can man turn his womenfolk into the breeding machine that for so long was seen as the natural state. Hunter-gatherer women, as opposed to the women of pastoral nomads and nomadic agriculturists, have a great deal of equality with men. This is not mere romance – it stems from the importance of their role in both gathering food and shouldering the burden of moving around.

The !Kung do not trade because all they carry are a few tools and perhaps a musical instrument. The necessity of movement means they cannot develop the greed that is an everyday part of the settler's life. Is it possible, then, that in that first breakout from Eden early man really did fall from grace? The !Kung settle their differences through talk, not through war – just as the Penan hunter-gatherers of Borneo are reported to do, as do the other endangered and scattered survivors of *Homo sapiens* who stuck to the original plan and weren't tempted by the lure of grain and grazing animals. It seems to me that to have no leaders is better expressed as having no followers. It is the followers who cause all the problems, and early man had solved this before he took that river out of Eden.

The details are also correct. The Nile now splits into two main branches in the Egyptian delta. A thousand years ago there were three branches. In prehistory there were four, just as it states in Genesis.

It is tempting to want to turn the clock back. But the whole gist of the story of the Fall, the first Nile story if you like, is about the impossibility of doing just that. Adam and Eve are kicked out and can never return. Early man left Eden and found a river that drew him north to the rest of the world. But this river would later encourage agriculture and the plenty required to start trade. Change happens. But *Homo sapiens* vanquished *Homo erectus*, *neanderthalensis* and *heidelbergensis* before he ever began to trade.

Naturally there is great controversy over what traits made *Homo sapiens* the hominid winner. Gift giving is actually more advanced than trade. Chimpanzees and bonobos trade in as much as they gain advantages through exchanging goods and services. Gift giving requires the ability to empathise and imagine what another might want. It is also the start of selflessness. Surely the first stage in being human is when we realise that being connected to others means more than the selfish survival of a lone individual, which is the condition of any animal.

We no longer live in groups of thirty, nor do we hunt and gather for a living, have babies every four years and walk great distances to find new sources of berry and nut. We are civilised now, thanks to the Nile, yet one of our highest qualities is the one that remains: generosity, gift giving. The ancient Greek historian Herodotus famously wrote that 'Egypt is the gift of the Nile.' Perhaps, despite the temptations provided by the Nile, the escape route from Eden, we retain the ability to give.

6 · River gods

The baboon, because he cannot see his bald behind, laughs greatly at the defects of others. Sudanese saying

I was at the 'other' source of the White Nile: in Jinja, at the Nile's exit from Lake Victoria. It was here that Mahatma Gandhi had some of his ashes scattered (as well as in several Indian rivers and a shrine in Los Angeles). That is the magic of the source – Jinja being the generally accepted start of the Nile in travel guides and the like (the whole Kagera thing being too complicated for a fleeting Fodor reference). By some peculiar circularity Gandhi has helped publicise Jinja as a source of the Nile – fame helping fame. In Jinja there is also a Buddhist temple, a mosque and several churches. Religion provides its own narrative about ultimate beginnings, and like calling like perhaps feels at home with other sources that have, over time, achieved mystical qualities. Or at least the power to bewitch.

But I was here to worship nature rather than investigate religion. I had just been river rafting, a fun thing to do on any river, and here, at the Bujagali Falls, is some of the best rafting around (as well as bungee jumping, quad biking etc).

Now it gets complicated – all these waterfalls and dams, some of which got renamed when a new regime took over. The gist of it is: originally the Nile flopped out of Lake Victoria over some rock slabs. This was named the Ripon Falls after Lord Ripon, a patron of John Hanning Speke, the first European to see the spectacle. Just below the Ripon Falls were some more – the Owen Falls – and about four miles further on some more: the Bujagali Falls. Actually they are more like wild bouldery river rapids than falls in the Niagara sense of the word. At the Owen Falls they built a dam in the 1950s that flooded the Ripon Falls. There used to be a plaque there commemorating their discovery by Speke. Now it's under water.

For many years they have been planning to build another dam which will flood the Bujagali Falls – over which I had just slithered and shot in a sixteen-foot Avon rubber raft. As you read this it will already be too late to do the same thing. Amazingly, the planning has stopped and the building has started. Work on the dam started in late 2011.

In a way, what with all the religious possibilities in town, it seemed right that I was here to mourn the passing of the Bujagali Falls, which will be submerged by the new dam, some two miles from the Owen Falls dam. Yep, the river hasn't really started and we've already stopped it. Twice.

So. More submergence. Dams drown things. The Aswan high dam drowned Nubia, making a hundred thousand people homeless. Fewer will be affected by the Bujagali dam, and of course Uganda does need the electricity. Why, one asks, in a place with immense amounts of sunshine do they need to dicker with the river? Dams, like nuclear power stations, are big business. You can get a mighty big kickback on a dam contract. Solar power doesn't have quite the same remunerative effect on a government minister.

The Bujagali Falls are of religious significance quite apart from the interest shown by Hindus and Buddhists and New Agers. Ja Ja Nabamba Budhagali (irreverently one is reminded of the water people of whom Jar Jar Binks in *Star Wars* is a member) is a ninety-five-year-old man, and their thirty-ninth guardian. He has announced that he is royally pissed off by the dam as it will flood the graves of his thirty-eight ancestors and all the islands where he gets his healing herbs.

I had wanted to meet Ja Ja Budhagali but it wasn't possible. He was busy, or out looking for a new place to get herbs. Some people told me he was ninety-seven, others ninety-five and one 'over eighty'. At first I had thought that I should find instances of river worship as a key part of this book, that worship was the natural relationship of humans to a river: be it for the life-giving flood or a life-enhancing thrill sport. But I was beginning to see that, though we do worship rivers, the river itself is about change. The water is always changing, the course sometimes changes and man throws in his own changes just for good measure. And in the lifetime of the human race (which all agree is piffling compared to the lifetime of say cockroaches or crocs) the Nile has emerged, has *become*, so to speak. Changed, certainly, out of all recognition. The skill was in knowing when to let go and when to hang on. Kind of like in rafting. For a long time Ja Ja Budhagali wouldn't say if the river spirits would stay after the dam was built, but now he says they will, even if their traditional home is under water with everything else. In 1994, it was Ja Ja Budhagali who cleared the falls of bodies washed down from the Rwandan genocide.

Right now the Bujagali Falls look wonderful. They sound good too, a constant motorway roar, not white noise but whitewater noise. The falls are a series of massive steps over which the muscular river bounds, the lucent bulge of blue water waiting to be broken, shattered into whitewater. You can raft the lot, though it's tricky. You can even swim the lot – if you're brave and have a twenty-five-litre jerry can. For $3 a young Ugandan will ride all the main rapids clinging to a yellow plastic jerry can, though one boy was drowned in 2011. If you want to see it done, go on to YouTube and check it out.

Work started on the new Bujagali dam in October 2011 and the official last day of rafting was 27 February 2012, so what I saw will now be gone. Well, the first three miles will be gone, but the rafting company were keen to persuade me that they will simply move operations downstream and that the rapids there are almost as good.

I'm no fan of dams, but I can still admire the incredible nineteenth- and early twentieth-century confidence that goes into building them. In fact the Owen Falls dam, built in the 1950s, was conceived by British hydrologists as part of an ambitious plan to control the entire Nile from source to sea. In 2006 it was discovered that fifty years before there had been another, top-secret plan by the British to use the Owen Falls dam to turn off the tap of the Nile to force Egyptian President Gamel Nasser to hand back the Suez Canal – which he had just seized. They didn't do it, though they persisted with their ambitious meddling for a few more years. It included constructing a 200-mile canal through the giant Sudd swamp, damming the Blue Nile and other grandiosities. Not much of this was completed at the time and the Nile is yet to be controlled. British plans to tame the river took no account of the independence of Sudan and Uganda and Egypt. To further complicate matters, this was the schizophrenic independence obtained within borders decided by previously hated colonial powers; wars and pestilence must needs follow.

The old Ripon Falls in Uganda, the exit point of the Nile from Lake Victoria discovered by John Hanning Speke in 1862 and confirmed by Henry Morton Stanley in 1875, would have been a charming place. But I was too late to see it. I made do with seeing a dam.

The Owen Falls dam has that diarrhoea-coloured concrete that all dams in Africa seem to acquire. The idea of the dam had been mooted as long ago as 1904 and was encouraged by Winston Churchill in his 1908 book *My African Journey*. 'What fun', he scribbled, 'to make the immemorial Nile begin its journey by diving through a turbine.' What hateful, careless words, I thought, as I gazed at the sorry-looking structure that submerged not only the touching plaque to Speke but also the twelve-foot Ripon Falls as the water now backed up into Lake Victoria. I'm suspicious of big dams, though small dams seem acceptable. Fish can get around small dams without a problem. Speke wrote about the teeming quantities of fish leaping up the falls to ascend into Lake Victoria. Alas, no more; at the Owen Falls dam it was deemed an unnecessary expense to make a fish weir. Passenger fish used to make their way up the falls into Lake Victoria. And the resulting explosion in Lake Victoria's Nile perch population is almost certainly due to the damming of the river. To want to limit a great river – what folly and arrogance, and yet it shows an admirable freedom from fear: fear of nature's revenge, fear of God's revenge for meddling with His world. I must admit to being partisan. I had long been poisoned against Churchill by a great-uncle who had fought with the White Russians and spent a year in Moscow's Lubyanka prison (he despised Churchill for sending the Cossacks back in 1945 to be murdered under Stalin's orders).

We'll run into Churchill again – when he fought in the 'river war' of Omdurman – but for the time being I stare at the dam spewing out water like a beast that has been ignobly caged and is now allowed freedom but is damaged and scared to the core. The dam, completed in 1954, was partly paid for by Egypt as a portion of the water held back could be released to ease the low winter water levels (obviated later by the building of the Aswan high dam). The Queen of England attended the Owen Falls dam opening. That makes you think – no modern dam would get the Queen, and Prince Charles, I am sure, would oppose its construction rather than celebrate it. Reports tell us a rogue hippo charged the royal enclosure but no one was hurt. The dam is half a mile wide, a hundred feet high and raised Lake Victoria by three feet, it is estimated. I can't ignore its colour. Not rust, not dirt, but some sort of continental concrete rot, very unhealthy. How long can a dam last if it isn't looked after? I'd been on a dam in Canada and it had developed holes in its earth barrage, holes big enough to swallow the wheel of a hippy camper crossing the top at the wrong time. They filled the holes, rescued the hippies; but how long can you keep playing catch-up with water, with holes, with rust, with time? The Nile is getting more dammed by the year. The word is appropriate, the echo no accident. The river is damned in many ways, not just by being hostage to rust and holes. Things fall apart in Africa faster than elsewhere. The desire to maintain and rebuild, as exemplified by the people of Coventry and Dresden, is largely absent. It is not an unusual sight in east Africa to see a tractor abandoned because it has run out of fuel. I can sympathise; part of me wants to discard my bicycle when it gets a puncture. You can get too owned by things, too owned. And dams own you – and one day, when the easy money runs out, they will stop rebuilding them.

So I am between dams, so to speak, having just spent six hours going downstream and forty-five minutes coming back, via a cleverly welded lorry with seats way up high on its back, like a tortoise with a seat on its shell. I am eating a chapatti rolled around an omelette, one of the best things to eat in Uganda if you are in backpacker land as I was at the Explorers' Lodge in Jinja.

I did my swim, well, my wade, with extreme caution at lunchtime. I am not a brave swimmer. I am a functional splasher. I once swam a mile – when I was thirteen – and haven't since taken it very seriously. I like swimming in clear water because of the optical illusion. I don't mind the cold as long as I have a hat on: it's the secret of rushing into icy sea and being tougher than anyone else – keep your hat on. But the Nile here is as warm as ... well, it isn't warm, it's rather chilly (though the air temperature was around 28 degrees), like a bath that has been allowed to cool, colder than you thought it would be.

The place where we stopped was a little inlet which Henry our river guide assured me was safe. He told me that there were no more hippos or crocs in this part of the river, though there were plenty lower down. No one joined me wading out like John the Baptist, though earlier the six young(ish) adventurers I was rafting with were all keen enough to jump off a high rock. I chickened out on account of wearing glasses, which I suppose I could have taken off but it didn't occur to me. I was also the only one in trousers; everyone else was in shorts. Somehow tombstoning in long trousers seems a bit silly, and I had vague worries too about such things as trapped air. Anyway now I made up for it by striking out in natty bermudas that I hoped would not attract a croc or a hippo or a baboon. Despite Henry's assurances, the Jinja golf club still allows a free hit if your ball has the misfortune to land in a hippo's hoofprint.

But hippos were not what worried Henry. He told me, 'I'm more careful about baboons than any other creature we come across along the river. More than crocs for sure, and actually more than hippos. A baboon can tear your jaw off.'

'But surely you have to provoke them first?'

He laughed, 'The crocodile likes to take people who are injured. Hippos – well, you just need to watch their territory. But baboons – they're smart *and* nasty, when they want to be.'

I had heard something about baboons in Jinja. A troop of them had staged a sit-down protest in the road after a big female had been hit by a driver. Eyewitnesses had stated that the driver had swerved mal-iciously to kill the female, and the troop would not leave the road – even when offered sugar cane. They were mourning the alpha female of the group. Since males transfer out of groups and females remain, the alpha female is the repository of the troop's knowledge of the area. They were mourning her because it was a real loss.

Baboons are brainy, they mourn their dead, and they are Nile crea-tures par excellence along with the hippo and the croc. The ancient Egyptians recognised the baboon in the figure of Thoth – god of wisdom, of writing, of bringing the gods together. He is depicted with a baboon's head.

I had seen in a rock cave deep in the Egyptian Sahara other evid-ence of baboon worship. There, painted perhaps two millennia before the desert dried out some 4,500 years ago, were baboon bodies with-out heads. It was like the mirror image of Thoth. And we know that the people who formed the nucleus of settlers who originated from what we know as ancient Egypt came from this same drying-out Sahara around 5,000 years ago. Even more mysteriously I'd discovered that the same headless baboon paintings could be found in caves in Botswana.

Some form of explanation was required. It might be this: a species of hominid, *Homo rudolfensis*, was driven into extinction by baboons, by competition with this Nile-dwelling primate, over a million years ago. Perhaps it was a near-run thing between baboons and early *Homo sapiens* too.

There is a compelling reason to believe that all our unfounded fears are the vestigial fears suffered by previous incarnations, evolutionary forms. We deprive fears of their power by noting and observing them. Drawing pictures of them. In the end we may grow quite fond of them, give their form to something we venerate. Perhaps the baboon-bodied creatures painted on rock were tribute paid to an ancient enemy.

This was an intriguing river meander, a sort of baboon version of Bruce Chatwin's thesis that a giant cat, *Dinofelis*, had threatened early man with extinction. Baboon paintings link directly with Thoth, though any connection with the Nile is indirect. The ancient Egyptians had a god of the flood, Hapi, but the Nile itself was simply known as Iterw – the river. Osiris, the Egyptian god most associated with the afterlife (and interestingly depicted as a greenman, thus linking up with greenman myths in Europe), is sometimes associated with the Nile, but the river's sheer ubiquity seems to have caused the ancient Egyptians to overlook it.

All scribes worshipped Thoth, as he invented writing. So, in a book containing the written stories of the Nile, Thoth is the god to invoke here. The god who brought us, just as the Egyptians did, writing – as well as the hermetic tradition (Hermes was the Greek version of Thoth) of hidden knowledge, wisdom, mysticism, alchemy. It was Thoth who made sure that neither good nor evil had a decisive victory over the other.

There is an ancient Egyptian story which refers to a text known as the Book of Thoth. This book contains a spell allowing one to understand the speech of animals. The book was originally hidden at the bottom of the Nile, so the story goes, guarded by seven serpents. An Egyptian prince tried to steal the box containing the Book of Thoth, but when he did, calamity rained down upon him, his children and his children's children. The message was simple: the knowledge of the gods is not for humans to obtain except at their own peril.

The baboons were skulking by as we drifted off that afternoon. No need to purify this water: I tasted its riverine stinkiness when Henry purposely flipped the raft on 'Easy Rider', a big friendly wave of a Class 4 rapid, a glossy green tongue of powerful water ending in a confusion of white foam and laughing people in helmets and orange lifejackets. Before this burst of excitement we'd watched a baboon troop, perhaps about thirty, loping along the bank like young thugs in an urban graffiti zone, looking for action, unworried, bigger than you'd think.

7 · Red sweat

The hippo coming out of the great lake licks the dew on the grass.
Ethiopian proverb

Baboons may be the most feared by river guides, but the lumbering hippopotamus is supposed to kill more people. Yet, when I delved into the statistics to find the Nile dweller that was the most deadly, crocs also came up. And then I began to think – how exactly are these stats compiled? Some places, such as southern Sudan, don't even know how many people are resident, let alone how many are bashed by hippos or gnawed on by giant crocs. Leave the dubious numbers behind and wade on, paying due attention of course to both hippos and crocs.

Though there are plenty of Nile crocodiles on the Nile even in Egypt – most of them being stopped by Lake Nasser – there are no longer any hippos. They were once so widespread as to be worshipped by the ancient Egyptians, along with the baboon-headed Thoth, and feared – Menes, the first ruler of the First Dynasty, the first Pharaoh in effect, was snatched and killed by a hippopotamus. The last one disappeared on the lower Nile in the early twentieth century after the construction of the first, British-designed dam at Aswan in 1900. Flaubert saw hippos when he travelled up the Nile in 1849, though the last hippo in Cairo probably died in the very early nineteenth century.

The hippo, or *Hippopotamus amphibius*, still lives on in the upper regions of both the Blue and the White Nile. It may not be as endangered as we think. The drug lord Pablo Escobar bought four Nile hippos in New Orleans and kept them at his Hacienda Nápoles estate about sixty miles from Medellín in Colombia. When he was captured in 1987 the hippos were left to run wild over the estate. By 2007 there were sixteen inhabiting the Magdalena river and causing trouble to both humans and cattle – attacking both and inflicting deep wounds with their two-foot-long tusks. Though hippos are vegetarian, mainly eating bankside grass, under stress they can become carnivorous despite being incapable of digesting meat properly. By 2009 the hunt was on for the leader of this renegade group of hippos, a highly aggressive male called Pepe by local law-enforcement agents. It was almost as if Escobar's life was being replicated by his outsize pets. Finally Pepe was cornered and shot by police authorised by the local government.

That hippos are dangerous is attested to by every raft guide you'll find on African rivers. A cursory check of YouTube reveals startling footage of a hippo taking on and beating a large Nile crocodile. A croc would only try and eat a dead hippo; a live one would be too danger-ous. In general hippos are feared more than crocodiles by man because of their greater aggression, a product of extreme territoriality. A bull hippo requires about 250 yards of bank, which he will defend to the last. Large flattened runs through the undergrowth at the river's edge are the places not to stop for a picnic – you may meet a hippo in a headlong rush aiming for the water he must defend. Females can also be aggressive, but less so, though it is hard to tell the sexes apart as they are of similar size.

When a hippo turns red you really need to take care.

That the ancient Egyptians depicted Set, the god of storms, the desert and chaos, as a red hippo suggests they knew about the so called 'red sweat' of the hippopotamus. As humans do, the hippo sweats during the heat of the day, but, unlike us, also when he – or she – is angry. And unlike any other animal studied the hippo even sweats under water. The red sweat has been shown to be both antimicrobial and UV pro-tecting – a combination suncream and antiseptic, Savlon meets Soltan – and it is effective. Hippos do not have the scales of many water dwell-ers (in fact they share a common ancestor with whales and porpoises), and the many cuts and abrasions they endure heal remarkably quickly despite constant immersion in mud and water. According to Kimiko Hashimoto and Yoko Saikawa, who devoted an admirable seven years to studying the red sweat of the hippopotamus, the active ingredients in the sweat have been named as a combination of hipposudoric and norhipposudoric acids. These acids suffuse the red secretion which turns brown as it gradually dries.

The other ancient Egyptian god represented by the hippo is Taweret, 'the great goddess', who appears as a pregnant female – often, interest-ingly, with a crocodile on her back.

It is easy to mistake a pod of hippos for something else. I once saw what I was sure was a grey rock. In fact it was a pod of hippos in a circle with their heads on the inside of the wheel. Even at a hundred yards their line of backsides looked just like the rounded limestone boulders of the upper Nile – until they heard the splashing of our oars and came swimming over to investigate. Hippos swim at 5mph so a kayaker can outpace them, but it'll be a close-run thing. If you are in a raft it is best to travel close to the bank even though that could be seen as an incursion into a bull's territory. The reasoning is that even if the boat is battered on the river side you can jump off on to the land and beat a hasty retreat while the hippo eats your rubber raft. But if the craft is upset midstream the hippo is quite capable of taking enraged chunks out of your splashing body. And unlike the crocodile the hippo *can* chew.

In a strange couple of incidents, Diana Tilden-Davis, a South African former beauty queen, was attacked by a hippo in the Okuvango swamp in 2007 only two weeks after another woman (on her honeymoon) had been killed. Ms Tilden-Davis survived but was still on crutches two years later. Both these attacks took place at the end of the dry season when water levels were low and food scarce. This is when males traditionally are most aggressive. If one sticks to deeper water and wetter conditions an attack is less likely.

Hippos often skulk in thickets during the day, and get aggressive if surprised, so it's best to avoid such places. The oxpecker bird has a distinctive alarm call – if you hear it there may well be hippos about.

If a hippo does attack, making a noise or clapping your hands is of no use at all. This is a creature that can break a crocodile's back in one bite. It has no fear. Your best bet is to climb a tree or hide behind a termite mound. A big termite mound.

8 · The biggest killer

Fighting a leopard is learned by watching the person who deals with them most: an owner of goats. Sudanese proverb

So you avoid the baboons and the hippos, which, despite everyone saying are so dangerous, you always thought were just a trifle *overrated*. Now, at last, you're facing the real killer. The land-going equivalent of the great white shark: *Nilus crocodilus*. Dolphins may be more efficient killers than sharks (and certainly sharks fear dolphin attacks), but there is something deadly and primeval about a shark that hits the fear button in a way a dolphin never could. It's the same with crocs.

The first croc I saw I thought was a stick, a six-inch stick with two bumps, the bumps being where further sticks may have sprouted from.

I didn't know, I wasn't watching, I didn't really care – I was admiring the shimmering width of the river as I passed the Sobat tributary in Sudan. But I knew enough not to be trailing my fingers in the water. The stick was drawn to my attention – it was going upstream, against the current, raising the tiniest of ripples in front of it. And it was drifting broadside on – unusual, to say the least. Then the head appeared, not slowly, but all at once, as shocking as something being born, some memory long buried in the oldest parts of the human brain. I've seen a lot of crocs since then, even eaten them at a restaurant (fishy tasting), but I still remain cautious. Something to do with their eyes.

Hendri Coetzee, killed by a crocodile at thirty-five, had already achieved what no other explorer had: a complete descent of the Nile river from its furthest source, the Kagera river, to the Mediterranean Sea. He had traversed the famed Murchison Falls area which has the highest concentration of massive Nile crocodiles anywhere on the planet. He had had years of experience paddling African waters. I first heard about him when I was rafting the Zambezi for a travel magazine. A kayaker making a video of the descent was a friend of Coetzee and spoke of his efficiency, helpfulness and coolness under pressure in awed terms. It was something that rang a strange bell down through the ages, reminding me of what people said about another explorer dead before his time – Arctic explorer Gino Watkins, who also died in a kayak but in the frozen north, not in the steaming jungles of central Africa.

Hendri Coetzee said that 'If I wanted surf I would never leave home. The nature of the beast is risk.' The beast was exploring uncharted rivers in the Nile/Congo headwaters in tiny creekboats – eight-foot-long kayaks with more space than a playboat for food and gear, balancing the risk of greater weight against the need for supplies in such a remote spot. Like Watkins, who died at twenty-seven when his kayak was sunk by a freak calving ice floe in Greenland, Hendri had no warning when he was snatched from behind by a giant Nile crocodile on the uncharted Lukuga waters, once considered a possible source of the Nile (they actually drain into a source of the Congo).

I had wanted to meet Coetzee as he had more knowledge of the real conditions on the White Nile than anyone alive, and yet it seemed in some weird and atavistic way that his very challenge of the river, his domination of it by making the first complete descent (purists aside, who cavilled that by doing it in two stints it didn't really count), an achievement which could be seen as yet another act of arrogance by man towards the natural world, had angered the river gods in some way. And the greatest of the Nile river gods has always been the crocodile.

I could not escape the oppressive feeling that Gino Watkins had also courted his own death in some way. Watkins was the man who brought the Eskimo roll to the developed world. Before his year-long stay in Greenland it had been considered 'impossible for a white man to perform such an acrobatic manoeuvre in a craft of mere skin and bone'. But Watkins became so good at rolling his kayak – essential in the frozen Arctic seas – that he was often mistaken for a native hunter. However, he did one thing no native would ever do: he hunted alone, and when he was tipped by a plunging ice floe from his frail craft of sealskin-covered sticks and bones he had no one to help rescue him from the freezing waters.

I mention Watkins because that technique that he showed could be perfected (I, too, had benefited, learning years ago how to roll in a tiny canoe in a swimming pool in Oxford) was what enabled Hendri Coetzee to make his incredible journeys in such a tiny boat.

Coetzee knew the risks and he knew crocodiles, though it is possible that he subscribed to a myth about their stupidity that is undeserved. The Nile crocodile has the most complex brain of any reptile on the planet, but it is not the most recently evolved; the crocodile has remained more or less unchanged in sixty million years, and close variants of the crocodile have been around as long as the dinosaurs – from 200 or more million years ago. Walking thirty miles from the current Nile valley I have found the polished teeth of *Laganosuchus*, one prehistoric ancestor of the crocodile. At first you think they might be belemnites, a good size at an inch or an inch and a half long, but then you see the unmistakable shiny patina of fossilised enamel, and the cutting edge, like a slanting chisel on even the most pointed teeth, and you realise that this long-dead creature was designed like a living cudgel or nailed club, that one strike from this density of sharpened nail-like teeth would result in being mercilessly taken. And a Nile crocodile has sixty-six teeth. Strangely, in the upper White Nile, when the river is low, crocodiles of immense proportions will hide themselves away in comparatively tiny potholes and puddles in the river bed. Their self-imposed incarceration, mired in clay and quite immobile, makes our smallest zoo cages look quite commodious.

Hendri Coetzee warned his team to stick together – as one of them

put it, 'You appear not as one eight-foot-long kayak, but as a group-
ing that is larger; you appear as a larger organism.' Crocs, it seems,
don't think quite like this. Though this tactic had served Coetzee well
through such croc-infested areas as the Murchison Falls, these were
areas where people and river craft were not unknown. It is possible that
the 'picking off' strategy of the Nile crocodile had been blunted by the
experience that a group of people may react differently to a group of
deer, or pigs or Nile perch.

It is one of the other great survival mechanisms of the Nile crocodile that it can live off a frog or consume a zebra. By basking on warm
riverside rocks it conserves energy and can go long periods without
feeding.

The 'picking off' strategy works for the croc in conjunction with
noise and splashing. Noise doesn't scare them away, it attracts them,
and here Coetzee was undoubtedly right in his constant injunction not
to panic when confronted by this sort of danger. With noise comes the
promise of a herd of wildebeest or a class of schoolchildren crossing a
river. The lamest, the slowest, *the one at the back*, that is the one the Nile
crocodile aims for. Coetzee and his two fellow paddlers were so close
they had to be careful their paddle blades didn't clash. They were doing
everything right if the theory of 'appearing big' worked. But Coetzee
was slightly to the rear and that was where the attack came from. He
was picked off by a crocodile which perceived this as a splashing group
of potential victims.

People constantly underestimate the intelligence of wild animals.
Often it is only the hunter (and the biologist who hunts with his dart
gun) who realises just how canny a creature that has survived sixty
million years can be. Not that the attack on Coetzee should mean that
kayakers should adopt a different strategy. Nile crocs are the biggest
animal killers in Africa, taking over a thousand people a year; no one
knows for sure, but these are the estimated figures. They seem to only
coexist happily with people who worship them – ancient Egyptians
and the Ghanaians living in the small town of Paga, who feed them
catfish and are so at ease with their crocs that they dry their clothes on
the crocodiles' backs as they bask in the sun. Could it be that the seeming stupidity of worshipping a killer predator is actually a very smart
strategy for coexistence with something that we can neither outrun nor
outthink in the game of survival?

The Nile crocodile, it must never be forgotten, has the highest bite

pressure per square inch of any animal recorded. Over 6,000 pounds.
That compares to about 300 pounds for a German shepherd dog, 600
pounds for a lion, 1,820 pounds for a hippo, 600 measly pounds for a
great white shark and 1,000 pounds for a snapping turtle. A human bite
is about 100 pounds per square inch.

It is interesting to discover that the ancient Egyptian crocodile cult
of Sobek built temples and sanctuaries at places – rapids and widening
bends – where crocodiles would be most dangerous and most numerous. In fact this is the only Egyptian deity whose dedicated temple
location is the result of an observable and pragmatic reason. For the
other Egyptian gods we are still more or less ignorant about why one
site rather than another was chosen. That the worship of the crocodile
was sincere and thorough is attested to by the huge crocodile cemetery found in Tebtunis in the Fayoum oasis. The greatest development
of Sobek's worship was in Ptolemaic times with the establishment of
Crocodilopolis in Fayoum. Given that this was the largest lake in Egypt
(until Lake Nasser was created by the high dam), one can guess that it
might have been a practical response to the quantity of crocs in Lake
Qarun.

Crocodylus niloticus is the animal par excellence of a bloody river. Yet
the crocodile does not choose to bite arteries and veins, though one
might try and club you with its tail. In fact the croc's preferred method
of killing is to grab the victim swiftly, without fuss, and drown him,
and it's usually a him – male deaths due to crocodile attacks outnumber
female four to one. Though it's tempting to use this as *prima facie* evidence of male stupidity, the more likely reason is that women, though
they may visit the river banks, don't in traditional societies tend to go
swimming and fishing in spots far from human habitation. Saltwater
and Nile crocodiles cause more human deaths than any other creature
that swims, crawls or runs upon the earth. It has always been so. The
nineteenth-century traveller John MacGregor, who was brave enough
to canoe the Nile in 1849, reported seeing two men killed by a twenty-
six-foot crocodile swinging its tail like a giant cudgel. A decade earlier
Irish traveller Eliot Warburton wrote that he found a lad crying beside
a dead crocodile, which had eaten his grandmother. He sold the crocodile for 7s 6d, with the old lady inside.

It is little wonder that the croc was worshipped, and is still worshipped. Sobek was the ancient crocodile god who achieved his greatest
popularity during the Ptolemaic era, around the third century BC. The

oasis of Fayoum, which was fed by the Nile, was called Crocodilopolis, the Greek word from which the modern name for the beast derives. Oddly enough, giant crocodilian fossils have also been found in the same oasis, extinct remnants of a proto-Nile. In apothecary shops in the spice bazaar of Cairo you will still see a stuffed croc hanging from the roof beams – for protection. Indeed you can buy one, for luck, in Khan al-Khalili souk. Mostly they come from Lake Nasser, the dammed Nile. It is damned in another sense: with a glut of over 70,000 crocs, it's not a place you want to explore in the dark. Still, the dam does keep them from floating down to Cairo. Most of them. Indeed, when there is a croc scare in town, it is usually the result of an unwanted pet being liberated into its natural environment.

A stuffed croc gracing a magician's den is a familiar sight in many supernatural films or TV programmes. This derives from the magical and alchemical traditions of Egypt, themselves inheritors of the cult of Sobek. Most 'magical' practices are debased forms of some practical endeavour. There are convincing arguments that prayer forms were originally sophisticated bodily movements designed to achieve optimal mental and physical health, rather in the manner of tai chi. The cult of Sobek, as we have seen, most probably derives from a desire to placate the biggest predator on the block, and from a sensible strategy of observation and appeasement that is maintained by elevating its status to the supernatural and ritualistic.

That the Nile is supremely important can be judged by the fact that it has no god; Khnum is the local deity of the Nile at the first cataract, near Aswan in modern Egypt, a place favoured by François Mitterrand and the Aga Khan, not to mention Agatha Christie and Winston Churchill, as a place of perfect climate in winter. It was also traditionally the source of all ivory – hence Elephantine Island, where the great mounds of tusks coming out of Africa were stored before being despatched in barges down the Nile. In a sense the first cataract is the gateway to Egypt, the first place where the flood will be noticed – and on the flood rested the prosperity and health of the nation. Sobek was seen at certain times as a primeval creator god, the one pulling the strings. This almost certainly pre-dates the cult of Ra and the sun gods and the association of light with the monotheisms, because earth religions are almost always displaced by light religions as civilisation develops. I have seen a clear example of this in northern Borneo where I was shown, by a now converted (to Christianity) Lundaiya tribesman, a crocodile-shaped mound where they used to worship (and hang the heads of their enemies). There were no crocodiles left in that region, if there had ever been; nevertheless the primal representative of the earth religion had held firm until the light religion of Christianity had replaced him.

A Nile crocodile can weigh up to a ton – the weight of a small car like a Honda Civic or a Ford Fiesta, but a Ford Fiesta can't rise up nine feet on its back legs and tail, using the swinging tail to maintain buoyancy as it lunges upwards from the water, jaws snapping, jaws that have the crushing power of a machine press. People who jumped from boats into the lower branches of trees have been pulled from those trees even though they were more than their own height above the water. On land, say strolling along a riverine beach, one needs to be a fair distance from the shallows. A stick with eyes can lunge thirty feet up on to a beach from its submerged position. And they've been doing this a long time. Remains of *Homo habilis* have been found at the Olduvai Gorge in the Great Rift Valley with tooth punctures from the Nile crocodile in their fossilised, million-year-old skulls.

The crocodiles – mother and father – will guard the nest until the piping of their young warns them to dig up the eggs to hatch. The mother will then scoop up the wriggling babies and carry them in a pouch in the bottom of her massive mouth. The babies are released in safe water and watched over for six to eight weeks. This is not a usual reptile strategy – where it is mostly a case of quantity over quality. If, over millennia, crocodiles which care for their young have outlasted those that simply have lots of eggs, then we must assume they are pretty good at it.

Crocs have huge mouths and are capable of over a ton of crushing power. However, the jaw-*opening* muscles are comparatively weak, allowing hunters (with more than a trace of Tarzan) the chance to hold the mouth shut until it is bound with rope. Crocs can't chew – the side-to-side motion needed means that the straight crushing power would be weakened; instead they settle for tearing off chunks, violently shaking a victim to rip off a piece, or, with a large animal, spinning round and round to tear off a morsel. There are cases of a snatched human spinning with the crocodile and being disgustedly dumped, alive, by the croc who cannot remove anything to eat. Once a chunk has been ripped they adopt the characteristic posture of neck back, throw the bit up and gulp it down.

That the eyesight of a crocodile is paramount in its attacks is shown by the way they are caught. Herodotus wrote that mud applied to the eyes of a Nile croc would render it passive; this echoes modern hunting techniques where a sack is thrown, at night, over the eyes of a crocodile. This is its Achilles heel, so to speak, or seems to be, the beast remaining passive until it is bound up and captured. Why doesn't it simply shake off the obstruction over its eyes? Like that other natural hunter – the falcon – it seems to switch off in darkness, accepting this as a signal to rest. Crocs have a third transparent eyelid, the nictitating membrane, that allows them to see clearly under water. Perhaps it is the presence of this third eyelid that has something to do with their passivity when deprived of any light. What is a fact is that this ability to see under water allows the croc to drown its victim and lodge it under a convenient rock and then return and feast on it when the meat has rotted down and become more pliable. A croc can routinely stay under for fifteen minutes during a struggle with a victim, and, if unstressed, for much longer – for hours in fact. There is one case of a crocodile remaining for eight hours in very cold water, which slowed its metabolism right down, allowing it to conserve oxygen.

Crocs love deep water since drowning is a preferred method of despatching a victim. That Hendri Coetzee was drowned is certain; his remains have sadly never been found.

9 • Croc yarns

Running water, over time, will make even a stone talk. Ethiopian saying

Herodotus mentions a bird, the trochilus, which he relates is the only bird allowed near a basking croc. It enters the mouth of the giant beast and devours the leeches there. The bird has been identified with the Egyptian plover – *Pluvianus aegyptius* – the only member of that genus. Uniquely this plover has a spur on each shoulder, something like a vestigial claw and reminiscent of the pterodactyl; this, according to myth, was used to scratch the inside of the croc's mouth should it forgetfully close its jaws on its helpful friend. Modern ornithologists are rather sniffy about the crocodile bird, or siksak as it is known along the Nile, though the reliable James Augustus St John, writing in 1840, relates, 'it is very certain that the crocodile is rarely seen unattended by one or more of these birds'. Dr Livingstone, further south, reported that its name south of the Sahara was setula-tsipi, the 'hammering iron', on account of its tinc-tinc-tinc alarm call. He mentioned its affinity to the crocodile but never saw it enter a crocodilian mouth. Some accounts suggest it lives on the parasites on a crocodile's back rather than in its mouth and that it is the alarm call that benefits the croc. Herodotus says that the Nile dwellers at Aswan, far from worshipping crocodiles as those lower down the Nile do, actually eat them. A piece of swine flesh is affixed to a hook and thrown into the middle of the river. Meanwhile, on the bank, a tethered hog is beaten with a bamboo rod until it squeals. The croc, confusing the two events, swallows the baited hook and is then drawn easily to the squealing hog. When it is near to the bank wet clay is slapped on both its eyes – rendering it quite docile, certainly passive enough to be killed without a fight. The famous Australian croc hunter Steve Irwin was fond of demonstrating just how easy it was to catch a croc by first dropping a jacket or cloth over the croc's eyes before roping it. Without this precaution a croc will fight for its life.

10 · Death kiss of the Nile

The river flows all day, never waiting, but it still gives a share to each person. Sudanese proverb

It's been fun running through all the dramatic ways the natural world can do you in on the Nile, but we've been skirting the real killer, the banal killer: disease.

It has always been disease. Illness spread less by the water than by what lives in and around water made the Nile of 10,000 years ago an inhospitable place. Ancient man preferred the drier savannah that later became the Sahara Desert. The desert is preternaturally disease free. The sodden, marshy river: the opposite. As the weather changed the Nile became more hospitable. Yet it was still a major vector in spreading disease. Bugs, flies, spiders, mosquitoes, amoebas, parasites, worms, mites. Welcome to the dangerous micro-world of the natural Nile.

Think of the noise of two camp actors greeting, kissing air in the vague vicinity of each other's face – mbwa, mbwa. Now try and tinge it with horror and foreboding. Hard, eh? Yet never again would I hear that (until now) empty ritual with anything other than distinct apprehension. Father Oswald told me, 'Beware the mbwa, mbwa.' Father Oswald was a Spanish missionary working the Sudd swamp with the kind of infinite patience that is needed in Africa if you want to avoid drink or high blood pressure. He did not smile when I explained the joke, the kissing allusion. Mbwa, mbwa was serious business. It is a fly: *Simulium damnosum*, a fly that hovers over the river in clouds easily mistaken for the smoke of a burning tyre. In the Sudd and the upper reaches of the river towards Lake Victoria, *damnosum* damns all. Known locally as mbwa, the sound of kissing air, these gnats are really blackfly – with a mean bite that harbours an embryonic parasitic worm. The worm causes tumorous growths that can cause great pain, disfigurement and, in extreme cases, blindness. Father Oswald told me all river rafters should beware as the fly lays its eggs in water and the larvae attach themselves to the kind of rocks it's handy to grab hold of in rapids and cataracts.

A benign cousin to *damnosum* inhabits the river beyond the Sudd, between the third and fourth cataracts in Sudan (a cataract is a rocky obfuscation, a short series of micro-ledgelike waterfalls across the river). This biting fly, onomatopoeically called nimiti, is designed to bite birds and donkeys – but men do just as well. It can, in its cloud-like swarms, invade the nose and eyes and ears, 'like putting your head in stinging water'. To keep this pest at bay, the people of the river can be seen carrying the end of a smoking rope like a priest with his swinging censer, said Father Oswald.

When I became ill I was in Cairo. No flies or parasites were involved; I simply aged overnight about fifty years. Was it the swim, an incautious jump, slightly fortified by drink, from Zamalek Island in Cairo to a moored houseboat on the western shore of the river? I couldn't be sure but I felt ... very strange. Fragile, ninetyish. I felt my back might break if I bent too quickly or too far; even tying my shoelaces was an operation fraught with danger. My insides turned everything to water, river water perhaps. Had I swallowed anything in that innocuous splashing about that evening? You always do. I had friends who regularly swam in the Nile and never got sick. Fishermen and their kids do it all the time. And a sewage expert told me that apart from the heavy metals in the river it's probably clean enough to drink, now that Cairo pumps its raw sewage out into the desert down five-foot-diameter pipes. Probably? I wouldn't drink Thames water either.

Maybe it was just a rare case of food poisoning (if you steer clear of Nile cruise boats in Aswan, it's rarer in Egypt than in England, I've found). But maybe it was the river. The canals in Cairo look horrible – rimed with garbage, and used for washing knackered dray horses and donkeys – but the river always looks clean. You hardly ever see floating rubbish on it and the banks have less plastic flotsam than the sea. It looks like a clean river, and, because it is a fairly fast river – maybe 3mph midstream in Cairo – it remains a clean river.

The Nile floods and lies stagnant in pools, yet malaria does not and never has proliferated along its length. The reason is that silt-laden water is immune to the breeding of mosquitoes. In Bengal, when silt-laden irrigation was abandoned and irrigation by rainwater introduced, malaria proliferated. In areas where building proceeds apace – so-called New Cairo out in the Eastern Desert – there are many more mosquitoes than you find by the Nile. The stagnant pools on building sites and in newly built gardens are to blame.

The ancient Egyptians planted along the banks of the Nile *bersim*, or clover. Every cart you see trundling around Cairo picking up garbage or selling fruit has a sheaf of the stuff on the back – it's the rocket fuel of a donkey-powered economy. It is also, like citronella, a mild mosquito repellent. And, just as importantly, it blooms repeatedly and can be cut repeatedly, and this action further keeps away mosquitoes from the ditches along the river that would otherwise be fertile breeding grounds. Some pharaonic cures – those involving goose excrement and turtles' testicles, for example – run counter to modern notions of medicine. But other diktats from the palace still make sense: it was forbidden for people in public service to eat uncooked vegetables, another guard against the spread of disease through eating plants nurtured with nightsoil and watered with stagnant water.

We might mention here William Willcocks, the mastermind behind the great British dam, the forerunner of the high dam at Aswan. Willcocks was straight as a die and wholly honourable, a worker, a builder. He irrigated vast parts of India, Iraq and Egypt. He developed the grand plan for controlling the Nile in its entirety. And he spent the latter part of his life occupied not with what he had achieved but with the Pandora's box he had opened in the form of spreading bilharzia and hookworm.

These diseases inhabited the canals he had made possible with per-ennial irrigation. With year-round water in the canals, the level of groundwater, and of cesspools, rose; this enabled the debilitating hook-worm to prosper. And as a kind of insult-to-injury coda, when the high dam was built the reduction in silt travelling downstream meant that mosquitoes could proliferate again.

Bilharzia is another nasty parasite, this one spread by a snail. The snail cannot live in flowing water, it needs a sultry ditch, a lake, a dull pond to make its mark, to increase unto the next generation. It is recorded even in the time of the Pharaohs that swift water was needed to avoid the disease.

The primary effect of bilharzia is tiredness and pain. The disease eats away at the body for years. Your health is broken, your strength gone. I was told in Nubia that the spread in the habitual use of bango (grass) and hashish coincided with the spread of bilharzia in the upper Nile – it dulls the pain wonderfully.

Previously there had been only tiny pockets of bilharzia in the delta, which increased as a result of the first perennial irrigation introduced after the building of the first dam on the delta, the barrage of the 1880s. But with the high dam at Aswan, the barrage at Asyut and all the other clever stoppages and diversions the snail spread throughout the much increased network of canals and ditches.

Since time immemorial the Egyptians had irrigated their land with the one-off rush of the Nile flood in the summer. Now the dams held back some of the water all year, allowing the canals to be fed year round. There was no longer one great surging, cleansing flood, ripping away the nooks and crannies beloved by the bilharzia snail, carrier of the disease bilharzia, also known as schistosomiasis.

This snail-carried parasitic trematode emerges (usually only during the day) and penetrates any human skin in its vicinity. Once inside the human being the creature visits the lungs and then makes a home in the liver and begins feeding on red blood cells. The parasite matures into a worm less than half an inch long which starts laying hundreds of eggs. Such worms may persist in the body for up to twenty years, resulting in chronic lethargy, liver ailments, fever and malnutrition.

Throughout the ditches and canals of Upper Egypt the snail spread and the disease spread. It reduced the strength of the Upper Egyptian workers in a measurable way. The P&O coaling station at Port Said had the highest recoaling rate anywhere in the world in the 1900s, when it was manned by hardy Upper Egyptians used to hours of back-breaking work. By the 1930s the Upper Egyptian population was raddled with bilharzia and the recoaling rates had fallen to a miserable level.

A cure was developed in Britain in 1918; the medieval compound of antimony known as tartar emetic was found to be effective. There were side-effects – odd seizures and vomiting – but in Nasser's new Egypt these were considered trifling. A huge programme of injection ran from the 1950s to the 1980s. There was another coda: unwashed needles were used again and again on the entire rural population of affected areas. This spread hepatitis C in Egypt, which today has the highest levels of infection in the world at around 10 per cent of the population. Bilharzia is now cured orally with an annual treatment of praziquantel.

Bilharzia had been present even in pharaonic times, though it peaked in the later periods, perhaps when knowledge of the need for fast-moving water to keep it at bay was lost. In ancient times myrrh was considered a cure. A modern drug containing myrrh, called Mirazid, was finally dropped in 2005 – because, though it worked, the current cure praziquantel was eight times more effective.

The bilharzia/injection/hepatitis C fiasco is another case of the iron law of unintended consequences. Yet, despite his lack of foresight, Willcocks was a fascinating man. Apart from his monumental work in two volumes, *The Nile*, he produced one of the most interesting books ever to be written on the adventures of Moses. Willcocks decided to look at the Bible from the viewpoint of hydrology and irrigation. Since the earliest civilisations were based on irrigation, it was an eminently sensible departure point. Look at the world from Moses' point of view, not our own. Despite his or her earnest training in flint knapping and ancient fire making, how is it possible for an archaeologist to look at the world – after the BA, the MA, the PhD and all the digs and volunteer jobs copying potsherds – with anything other than the eyes of an archaeologist? It seems peculiar to me that specialisation should involve developing a point of view that obscures the very subject you wish to study.

I knew from my time in the desert collecting stone tools that any place that looks interesting to us will have been interesting to ancient man. Caves, strange rock formations, interesting overhangs – in all of these places you will find the best artefacts – and these are all places a child, or someone still with the instincts of childhood, will gravitate towards. One of my best finds – three intact amphorae found in the Great Sand Sea – was the result of asking someone to climb on to an interesting rock for a photograph. The pots were buried at its foot.

Willcocks was an expert in irrigation, not in biblical studies, but his conclusions in *From the Garden of Eden to the Crossing of the Jordan* are never uninformed, never the flat-footed stuff engineers who chose to write about the mystery of the Pyramids tend to write. It is a fascinating, wonderful glimpse into the mind of a late nineteenth-century polymath.

He was of English descent though born in Mussoorie, a hill station in India. When I visited the place I recognised at once the steep hillsides and fragrant deodars that had been Willcocks' playground in his youth. He attended Indian schools and an Indian college of engineering. His ambition was to be like his father, a Devon man who had raised himself up from simple soldier to irrigation engineer by sheer determination and hard work. His father believed that the success of the British abroad was down to the quality of their gentry. Though of humble yeoman by birth himself he claimed, with the experience of a well-travelled soldier who had fought for the Carlists in Spain and with the British in Afghanistan and India, that there was no more generous landlord than the British gentry. Therein, he told his son William, lay the secret weapon of the British.

Willcocks lived an austere and disciplined life. 'Hardships and alertness, in my opinion, go together,' he wrote. He was fond, when out on a survey, of living in a tent as humble as those of his workers, if not more so. When local landowners came by to pay visits they assumed that no European boss was in charge and turned away, leaving Willcocks to get on with his precious work. Even late in life he would often be mistaken for a clerk rather than the chief of a large hydrological project. Described by his superior and eventual father-in-law Colonel Colin Scott-Moncrieff (brother of the Proust translator) as a human dynamo, without whom the indentured slavery known as the corvée would not have been ended nor the Aswan dam built.

A typical day for Willcocks started at 5.00 a.m. with him rising in his shared lodgings in Helwan, a health resort built about fifteen miles south of Cairo. His neighbours included the venerable German explorer Georg August Schweinfurth, whose path will crisscross with ours throughout the book. After a hasty breakfast of porridge Willcocks would spend twenty minutes doing his Sandow exercises. Willcocks was an early follower of Eugen Sandow along with another early body-builder, Arthur Conan Doyle. Indeed Sandow staged the world's first bodybuilding exhibition in the Royal Albert Hall in 1901 with Sherlock Holmes' creator as the head judge.

The half-Russian, half-Prussian 'father of modern bodybuilding', Sandow wrote books with the titles *Strength and Health* and *Movement is Life*. He was filmed in 1894 by the Edison film company (we will later encounter Edison making the first elephant snuff movie: he filmed the death of a rogue elephant). The Sandow film was a huge success and people marvelled less at his strength than at the bulge of his muscles. Sandow's fame was so great that a statuette of his resplendent phy-sique is the first prize for Mr Olympia, the world-famous bodybuilding contest that Arnold Schwarzenegger won six times in a row. It seems appropriate that the man who did more than any other to wrestle the Nile into submission should be a fan of bodybuilding.

Anyway, with his exercises finished by 6.20 a.m., Willcocks would spend the next hour walking very fast 'in a bee line up hill and down dale' in the nearby desert. At 7.30 a.m. he would leave for Cairo and return home at 5. From 5.30 to 7.30 he again hurried through the desert. Walking was his favourite pastime and when surveying a new canal or irrigation he walked tirelessly. He boasted of once walking twenty-five miles a day every day for 107 days in temperatures of over 80 degrees. Truly a man of steel. Back home he would dine at 8.00 p.m. and be asleep in bed by 10, readying himself for another day at the office changing the course of nature and history.

But Willcocks, despite his zeal, or perhaps because of it, managed to get on the wrong side of Lord Cromer, the dictatorial *de facto* ruler of Egypt. For the first time in his life Willcocks was passed over for promotion. It was enough, he wrote, to shake his conviction in a Creator God and persuade him to give up his wishful plans for the great dam. Indeed he was thinking these blasphemous thoughts while out speed-walking in the desert one morning. Suddenly he felt an arm on his shoulder and the ghost of his dead father appeared and walked with him for half an hour and argued with him, at length per-suading him never to give up his dream. Willcocks wrote, 'From then on I never looked back but went on straight with my project with redoubled zeal.'

The plans were accepted as first rate. The survey work in Aswan was pronounced faultless. He had thought of everything – designing the dam very high to accommodate archways through which the entire flood might run. This was Willcocks' intention, so that the river would carry the silt-reddened Nile down to the delta and not back it up behind the dam. The dam could be raised further at a later date. Again Willcocks had foreseen that opposition to the yearly flooding of the temple of Philae would lessen once the multiple benefits of the dam were felt. His design was so complete it required only the Forth bridge engineer Sir Benjamin Baker to turn it into a reality.

But nothing happened. A year or two went by. He worked even harder; during one survey he never took a Sunday off in eighteen months and insisted that he and his men sleep in tents, the rougher sort of tent too, for that entire period. Finally in 1897 he asked Lord Cromer if his plans for the Aswan dam would ever be realised. Cromer rid himself of this troublesome employee by replying that all Egypt's money was needed to reconquer the Sudan, and he doubted if the dam would ever be built in Willcocks' time. So Willcocks resigned and took a job with the Cairo water board. A year later work on the world-changing dam began. Finance from the private investor Ernest Cassel had been found, but Willcocks was no longer there to be the midwife to his baby: 'I well remember the feeling of humiliation which came over me when I stood on the four-foot diameter pipe which carried the whole of the water supply of Cairo and compared the dignity of looking after this water with that of designing structures for controlling the flood discharge of the Nile.'

Willcocks turned his back on building and started writing with a vengeance: his two-volume work *The Nile* is a masterpiece of detail and wonderfully drawn plans. He took up property speculation at the behest of the same Ernest Cassel who had funded the dam – and lost a lot of money.

But his zeal continued and he later worked in Iraq dealing with the irrigation problems of the Euphrates.

In later life Willcocks got into a dispute with Murdoch Macdonald, a man whom one immediately spots as a yes-man for the powers that be. The dispute ended as a libel suit, the traditional battleground of the English when all else has failed. Willcocks lost. The battle was about the flow rate of yet another dam to be built – this time on a major tributary of the Nile, the Atbara. Willcocks maintained that the figures were a lie. Whatever the truth of the matter, he lost. But the sheer venom of his attack seems unusual for this mild and industrious man. The reason, I believe, can be found in his realisation that dams can bring misery too. He simply didn't want another built.

All through those last years, the realisation slowly dawned that all that work, mountains of work, would not bring unalloyed benefits to mankind. The mountains of work. The dams, the canals, the pumps, the barrages – if anyone transforms the world it is the water engineer. He can raise fertile land from barren sea with polders and dykes, he can rewire the oceans with a giant canal, he can feed a nation that is starving. Instead of building useless stone monuments he builds useful ones (later we'll find just how close the Pyramids came to being demolished to make the first dam across the Nile). Instead of wailing about floods and famines he stops them dead in their tracks. Is there anything wrong with that? Is there a point beyond which one leaves behind honest agriculture and enters the vicious swerve ball of unintended consequences? Of building a dam that brings disease and misery as well as population growth?

We know that agriculture resulted in a drop in general health compared to hunter-gatherer lifestyles. Hunter-gatherers, for example, routinely keep all their teeth until old age. Once flour was milled, dental decay became usual among agricultural populations. So every step up the technological ladder results in a drop in individual health but an increase in population. Egypt's dams have coincided with vast population growth – from five million in 1890 to eighty-five million today. All living on the same strip of land – just better watered and more chemically altered than almost any black earth on the planet.

The connection, the symbiosis between exponential population growth and stopping the river, stopping the flow, seems important. There is no useful link, nothing a dedicated development official could get their teeth into, nothing solid like that. But if it was obvious we'd be fixing it already. If it was obvious the problem would be addressed. I wonder if all we are ever allowed is hints, vague associations, informal evidence, useful rumour. The world wants us to exercise judgement and we want to shirk it, we want it to be easy. Willcocks tried to make amends, but the damage was done, the path set, the die cast. Any way you turn you can't undo a dam. Only time can do that.

I recovered from my strange illness. You usually do. Willcocks retired to Egypt. He quite clearly loved the country. I'm not sure how he died.

11 · The Nile evaporates

No matter how thirsty you are you can't drink the whole river.
Bugandan saying

Willcocks, like many, if not most, techno-idealists saw every advance as almost uniformly devoid of serious problems. So he missed disease, and his successors missed evaporation. The recent attempt to divert the Nile at Toshka, 'to make the desert bloom' around the western edge of Lake Nasser, has met with resounding failure. A mega-project, a long-held fantasy, of Egyptian leaders from President Nasser downwards (and the British before them) was to divert the Nile into the New Valley – the desert wadi system that contains the three major oases of the Egyptian desert.

There is some evidence that millions of years ago, before the Nile was formed, river systems crossed the Sahara in a number of places. One was the so-called Uweinat river – which is now covered by the Libyan–Egyptian Great Sand Sea. Such knowledge encouraged the idea that a new river could be built, a canal, carrying water, waste water if you like, from its holding tank in Lake Nasser into the desert. In the 1990s the project was hailed as saving Egypt. By 2010 you hardly heard a word about it. The canalisation around Toshka has produced far fewer acres of agricultural land than even the most pessimistic observers imagined. And salination is a constant problem that appears insoluble. Making the desert bloom has been a costly mistake.

Which makes the fact of the Nile – the sole river to cross the Sahara – even more remarkable. It does what no man has been able to imitate in his great works. Pyramids may mimic small mountains, but we have yet to build a river like the Nile. The Nile, as a living river, moving faster than any man-made canal, survives what kills all water in hot places: evaporation.

Horses sweat, men perspire, women glow and rivers evaporate – as long as they move slowly enough and widely enough. As the Nile does when it traverses the infamous Sudd swamp.

The Sudd swamp is remarkable because it is so flat. Indeed its flatness spreads so far it is hard to imagine how the river ever manages to leave. In 250 miles the slope is a meagre 0.01 per cent. Just enough to allow the river to dribble downhill to the Mediterranean 3,000 miles north.

Being so flat and slow moving, the Sudd drinks water. Willcocks and his team decided that a canal would solve the evaporation problem. But even a canal is subject to the sun's merciless rays. Even with a canal carrying water in a straight line across the swamp, the increase in the river's flow would only be a measly 5 per cent (or 7 per cent if you read other more optimistic reports).

Any way you cut it, in a hot dry climate vast quantities of water are lost through evaporation. And when the Nile reaches the desert zone in the Sudan and then flows through Egypt, evaporation is further increased. Corralled in Lake Nasser before pushing through the turbines of the Aswan dam, the Nile loses 10 per cent of its volume each year as it sits in the lake. Naturally this is a very approximate figure. When you go looking for how evaporation is calculated you realise a lot of estimation is being used. For a start you have to guess the size of the storage container – be it lake or river bank. Then you have to reckon losses by other means.

It is quite obvious water is lost through evaporation, and when the water is shallow and the wind hot, then those losses can be very great indeed. People are concerned. One nutty plan suggests spreading a network of huge plastic sheets over Lake Nasser to curtail evaporation.

We have suggested that evaporation is to rivers what perspiration is to humans. Some sweat more than others. Some lose their entire strength through evaporation; others are scarcely troubled by it. The Nile spends the last 2,000 miles of its journey to the sea winding through the world's largest desert. It loses so much through evaporation that despite its great drainage basin – over 10 per cent of Africa drains into the Nile basin – it enters the sea at Rosetta looking like a respectable European river and without the veritable lake-like width achieved by the jungle rivers of Asia and South America. The Nile sweats badly, and what it doesn't lose through the sun it loses in the swamps of the Sudd.

The Nile loses most water in July in Egypt. In Sudan it loses more in April. In the south, in Uganda and southern Sudan, due to the summer rains, the minimum evaporation is in July and August.

Just as a sweaty man will leave a salty rime on his shirt, so the Nile deposits salts as it sweats its way through the deserts of Egypt and Sudan. Those salts accumulate rather more than they did, because the yearly flood, before the Aswan dam was built, used to sluice them away. Now the sweated shirt is never washed and the side canals are saltier. And now that silt is no longer laid down each year to dilute the effect of salt, the ground becomes less fertile, more in need of fertiliser, which leaches into the river and again raises its salt level.

But we have become diverted – natural enough when one considers that irrigation is the art of diversion. It is time to return to another Nile source, the source of all that is romantic and mysterious about Egypt – it's ancient pharaonic past.

Part Two

ANCIENT NILE

Famine, pestilence and a severed penis

1 · The red and the black

The water jar wanted to test the river's stones and broke itself.
Sudanese proverb

Red and black are the colours of ancient Egypt, and of earlier, pre-dynastic Egypt. In the potsherds one finds in the desert, red and black ware predominates in the oldest Neolithic pot fragments lying on the dunes. Red and black are easy colours to make – red from iron oxide – rust – or from red ochre, and black from charcoal or pitch, carbon essentially. Egypt was known as 'the black land' because of its fertile soil. *Kemi* means 'black' in ancient Egyptian, which, once Arabised, becomes *al-kemi* – which in turn becomes 'alchemy', the Egyptian magic that medieval Europeans sought to co-opt into their dreams of wealth or enlightenment. The red was the land of the desert and the water of the Nile. Red and black are still the colours of Egypt, still the colours of the national flag.

Red is the colour of revolution, radical politics, change – or the aspiration to change. The river changes, is never the same yet is always the same. To find the answers about the Nile follow the red.

Raymond Roussel, the French avant-garde writer, used to compose his poetry using a method in which mishearings and puns would suggest the subject matter. It is hardly less daring to suggest following a colour to reveal truths about a subject. And yet one needs to start somewhere.

One of my earliest questions, when reading about the Nile, had been: how did the ancients know so much about the Nile without visiting it? And by ancients I mean primarily the ancient Egyptians. This knowledge was later passed down through the priestly elect to such travellers as Herodotus, who dutifully recorded what they had been told. How did the ancient Egyptian know that the White Nile rose in the Mountains of the Moon? Since we know that any traveller going south would have to traverse the world's largest swamp, the Sudd, and since we know that the Sudd defeated two legionaries sent by Emperor Nero to investigate Nilotic origins, we have every reason to believe that it would have defeated any Egyptian who might have travelled earlier.

Follow the red – in this case, perhaps, the evidence of the red-earthed desert. In 2007 Mark Borda and Mahmoud Marais discovered Egyptian hieroglyphics deep in the Sahara – deeper than any other known inscriptions have been found. Previous hieroglyphs found some forty miles into the desert near the oasis of Dakhla – getting on for 200 miles from the Nile – were thought to mark the furthest the Egyptians had ventured into the desert. Yet we know that in the earlier dynasties, more than 4,000 years ago, which is when these inscriptions date from, the climate was far less dry than it is now. The inscription deep in the desert, though miles from an oasis, was very near the mountain of Uweinat, a stopping-off point until half a century ago of nomadic Tebu tribesmen – until they, too, found it too inhospitable. The inscription relates a meeting between an Egyptian traveller called Tekhebet and someone from the land of Yam bringing incense. This suggests a quite normal trade route independent of the Nile that stretched deep into central Africa, the source perhaps of the aromatic woods used as incense at that time. If this trade route existed as far back as 3000 BC or earlier, which seems likely, we have a way into Africa that pre-dates anything previously considered. Supporting evidence comes from the account of Harkhuf, a pharaonic prince of the Sixth Dynasty, around 2300 BC, who recorded that he had started for the land of Yam along 'the oasis road'. This was thought to mean that he then went back to the Nile from his oasis starting point. We now know that is not the case, that his reported four journeys to Yam – each taking seven months – must have been via the deep desert and further into sub-Saharan Africa, possibly via Chad. Harkhuf inscribed on his tomb details of his travels: 'I returned with three hundred donkeys burdened with incense, ebony, hekenu perfume, grain, panther skins, elephant tusks, many boomerangs, all kinds of beautiful and good presents.' He also talks of pygmies – who inhabit a region just below the source of the White Nile. This is extraordinarily accurate, since pygmies remained a myth until the first modern explorer – Stanley in 1887–8 – 'discovered' them in the Ituri Forest region during the ill-fated Emin Pasha relief expedition.

Uweinat, at the border of Libya, Sudan and Egypt, is home to numerous caves containing rock art that pre-dates, or perhaps coincides with, the journey of Harkhuf. The inscription found in 2007 lies on a boulder about forty miles south of Gebel Uweinat, the tallest mountain in mainland Egypt – only 6,345 feet high – but it rises directly from the desert which lies less than a thousand feet above sea level.

That an inscription should be found 300 miles from the nearest modern oasis is the strongest possible evidence that the Sahara was relatively fertile until only a few thousand years ago. There were no camels in Egypt then – they were introduced around 500 BC by invading Persians – so the only form of desert transport was the donkey. The German explorer Carlo Bergmann has found harnesses, pots and other evidence of pharaonic donkey travel along the route to Uweinat, confirming this mode of transport.

Other mysteries find their solution. In 1998 it was discovered that Tutankhamen's chest pendant, a transparent scarab set in gold, was not as previously believed made of quartz. It was glass. But not man-made glass. This scarab was carved from natural silica glass, known as tektite, found in a remote region of the Great Sand Sea about 150 miles north of Uweinat. Tektites are natural glasses, formed in this case by a meteorite crashing into a proto-Sahara millions of years ago and fusing the sand into glass. But the fact that the glass, which is found in a small area 200 miles from an oasis, could be transported to the Nile is evidence again that the Sahara was not as arid or hard to travel across as it is today. Only the coming of the camel made travel possible in this region during the current dry era; it would not be practicable to travel there with donkeys now.

So, we have donkey trains stretching deep into the red land of the desert, circumventing the marshes of the Sudd, dropping through what is now the Central African Republic and the Congo to rejoin the Nile at Lake Albert, perhaps using the Mountains of the Moon to navigate.

Mark Borda's discovery is one more link in the chain that confirms ancient knowledge of the Nile's source. This knowledge was lost, mangled, reworked and ignored in the following millennia, surfacing now and again – in Roman maps, or in the oral traditions of the nomadic tribes of the Sahara.

I once asked a Bedouin in the Egyptian Sahara where the sand came from. He picked up one of the fossilised oyster shells that are common on the edge of the Great Sand Sea. 'This is when the sea was here, then the sea went back leaving the beach.' Modern thinking, knowing as we now do about the massive movement of the Mediterranean, tends to concur: the Sahara is the giant beach left behind after millions of years of seawater coming and going over North Africa.

2 · Paper and lead

The day it wishes death, the goat licks the nose of the leopard.
Ethiopian proverb

In the desert, rocks were used to paint and carve on, but it was the gift of the Nile – papyrus – that would allow writing to become private, efficient and capable of movement. With orders and instructions written on paper it was possible to control more than one city. Though there is reasonable evidence that ancient Mesopotamia was home to the first city state, it was ancient Egypt that invented the first nation state. And papyrus was the key. (Ironically, the papyrus plant had become extinct in Egypt by the 1950s and had to be reintroduced from the upper Nile by the archaeologist Dr Hassan Ragab, founder of the extraordinary theme park in Cairo, Dr Ragab's Pharaonic Village – not to be missed!)

When papyrus, a tall African grass, was chopped, pounded, drenched and laid out to dry in the sun it was found to make paper, but this was discovered only when the desert tribes started to move towards the Nile as the rains began to fail.

As we have seen, 7,000 years ago the Saharan desert was full of wildlife and had a good sufficiency of water. The Nile was a swamp, a place to be avoided. Then the weather changed and the desert dwellers found the river their salvation. The life-giving river became the inspiration for an entire mythology.

The mythology could be written down on papyrus, this miracle plant they had found growing along the banks of the river. And the stories, these earliest stories, were full of the fears of the desert dweller – the fear of drowning, the fear of being overwhelmed by this watery force of nature.

In the earliest Egyptian stories, it is the tears of Isis for her husband Osiris which form the flood that gives life to the Nile. Osiris was the wise ruler of mythological ancient Egypt and Isis was his twin sister and wife. Together they formed a perfect pair. They had a perfect son, too, called Horus.

But they also had a perfectly nasty brother, Set or Seth. Set is depicted as the god of the desert and sand storms. He undoubtedly represents the new river dwellers' distaste for and rejection of the harsh place that the desert had become. The newly recognised bounty of the river was represented by the 'good' gods – Isis and Osiris and Horus. We may note the curious way that Set is depicted, with the oversized ears of a fennec fox and the snout of an aardvark – both of them desert/savannah dwellers at that time. Later, and in keeping with the main mode of desert travel, Set is represented as a donkey.

Bad boy Set was jealous of all the love and attention his brother was getting as Lord and Ruler of the new and prosperous river kingdom of Egypt. Out in the badlands, out in the desert, he started to plot his revenge. One of the things these new river dwellers had done was, when someone died, to use a box as a coffin and dig tombs instead of the caves and stones they had employed in the desert. Indeed, the river folk seemed to have become rather too obsessed with death. Set had his plan.

In what was probably the earliest version of the Cinderella 'if the shoe fits' story, Set attended a party of the gods with a huge lead coffin. Gods are eccentric like that. He asked everyone to lie down in it and test it for size. The winner would get a nice new metal coffin all ready for when he shuffled off his (im)mortal coil (unlike most gods, Egyptian gods can die). In some versions the lead coffin is simply a stone sarcophagus lined with lead, perhaps to make it air-, and water-, tight.

Naturally, Set had taken his brother's measurements secretly and made the coffin himself out in the desert where he lived all alone. He was pleasantly surprised when the urbane guests agreed readily to his game of taking turns to lie down in a sarcophagus trimmed with lead, to see who the coffin most closely fitted. When Osiris lay in it, jealous Set conspiring with the Queen of Ethiopia (almost certainly an ancient coded reference to Ethiopia being the source of the flood) slammed the lid shut, rushed with it past the astonished guests and dropped it in the Nile.

Could ancient Egyptians swim? We know that early explorers remarked on the incredible swimming ability of Nubians, inhabitants of much of the territory of the southern end of ancient Egypt, so it seems almost certain that the ancients could swim. There are pools in palace ruins that were probably used for swimming and there are plenty of tomb-wall illustrations of people swimming. Desert-dwelling Set surely feared the water more than Osiris or Isis did.

Even if Osiris could swim, he wasn't Houdini; so, trapped in his lead coffin, he drowned. Isis found him, but very carelessly left the coffin in marshland (strangely prefiguring the Moses story). What was she thinking? Set, like the Bedouin who would replace him, was always hanging around the water margins waiting to strike at hapless settled folk.

So, while she was away, Set, out hunting, found the coffin. Using his best sword he prised open the lid. And being something of a psychopath, and no doubt aware of the god's regenerative powers, he dismembered the body into fourteen parts.

Dim but faithful Isis returned to the scene of carnage. It was essential that Osiris, like some early-day Captain Marvel, be reassembled so he could live again – in the underworld. Traipsing about, tears falling in grief, Isis found thirteen of the fourteen bloody body parts. She wept for forty days and nights looking for the fourteenth – which was, of course, Osiris' penis.

And the Nile flooded. From all the tears.

Meanwhile it wasn't surprising that teary Isis hadn't found the missing penis since it had been eaten by a hungry Oxyrhynchus fish. It seems likely that the desert town of Oxyrhynchus that borders the Nile is named after the fish; strangely, it is also the place where thousands of pieces of papyrus have been found buried under the sand. This preserved them perfectly and much of our knowledge of ancient Egypt, including versions of this myth, comes from this desiccated papyrus.

Pretty unlucky, eh? Having your tool eaten by a fish, not to mention being split into fourteen bits. But, this being the world of the gods, Isis, after fashioning a golden replacement phallus, managed to sing Osiris back to life so that he could have a proper burial. He was still dead, though. However, he was able to command a top post in the underworld, eventually becoming its king.

And this is the place whence the Nile flowed.

As a curious endnote it is related in the *Targum* (an Aramaic translation of the Hebrew Bible) that Joseph was buried in the Nile and his coffin was rediscovered by Moses lying on marshy ground. Though no dismemberment was involved it provides a strange echo of Isis finding the coffin of Osiris.

3 · Homosexual love on the ancient Nile

Where one spends the night is more important than where one spends the day. Nubian proverb

The ancient Egyptian god Set or Seth was the bad guy. Not just a fox and a donkey, but also sometimes portrayed as a scorpion and a pig – unclean beasts. And not content with killing his good brother, Set embarked on a career as a would-be rapist, trying to violate both Isis and Horus, though Horus did manage to tear one of his testicles off.

Unlike the rather straight versions of our origins depicted in the great monotheisms, ancient Egypt's was distinctly racy. In possibly the first literary representation of anal sex, Set forces Horus to have homosexual relations with him. To nullify the indignity of this rape Horus gets his revenge by getting Seth to eat a sperm-impregnated lettuce (one that Horus wiped his own sperm upon).

Given that Set represented much of what was condemned, it is not surprising that religious texts of the Old Kingdom (the Third to the Sixth Dynasties around 4,100–4,600 years ago) regard homosexual sex as an unlawful way of slaking one's sexual appetites. Things did not change much in the ensuing thousand years leading to the New Kingdom period (the Eighteenth to the Twentieth Dynasty around 3100–3600 BC): when relating the bad things a man has *not* done (as a way of appearing good in the eyes of the gods), a chapter of *The Book of the Dead* (a collection of Egyptian funerary texts) has the recital 'and I have not had relations with a man, nor practised self-abuse in any of the sacred places'. It's a pretty novel idea. Imagine Christian prayers including an injunction not to masturbate while up at the altar.

In the *Coffin Texts* (which pre-date *The Book of the Dead*) we learn: 'Atum has no power over the deceased, rather, the deceased impregnates his buttocks.' In the legends of Horus, sex with another man is seen as one man achieving superiority over another, not as an act of love – the same morality can be found today in prison in the US. The active partner could even take pride in the act, whereas the passive partner whose 'buttocks were impregnated' was regarded as shamed and disgraced. The determining factor was not homosexual activity, which was considered morally neutral, but the fact of the seed of another man entering his body. Hence Horus getting revenge by sneakily getting his sperm into Set's body – albeit from the other end.

In ancient Egyptian texts the sperm, in homosexual activity, is considered a kind of venom or poison to the violated one. Mythological homosexual rapes are alluded to in magic spells designed to protect against poisonous animal bites. Set, out on another criminal spree, male-rapes the goddess Anat (who conveniently, or maybe perversely, chooses to appear in male form). This little episode is used in a spell that protects against scorpion bites.

In an ancient Memphite hymn it is related that the brother gods Shu and Tefnut were deeply fearful of the paedophilic emisions of their father Atum – one of the most important gods. It was Atum who would lift the dead pharaoh from his tomb and up to the stars. So despite the injunctions against homosexuality it seems the gods are doing it, and throwing incest into the equation of shame too.

An Old Kingdom literary text illustrates, without pictures, corruption and decline with a tale of homosexual relations between King Nefekare and the general Sisenet. Interestingly, there is almost no pictorial representation of unusual sexual practices, apart from a series of obscene sketches by artists and artisans, perhaps for humorous purposes, on the walls of several New Kingdom (the period from the sixteenth to eleventh century BC – it contains the Eighteenth, Nineteenth and Twentieth Dynasties) Theban tombs. The ancient Egyptians, despite their rude tales, were not pornographically inclined.

They were also tolerant of unusual living arrangements. The tomb of the 'two friends', which dates from the Fifth Dynasty, around 2500 BC, is considered to be evidence that a gay relationship was sanctioned at the highest level, because both men, Niankhkhnum and Khnumhotep (try repeating those names quickly), were members of the innermost circle of the Pharaoh. The men were courtiers with the job title 'overseers of manicurists of the Great House', which some conservative theorists see as further evidence of their sexual orientation. Yep – the King's manicurist was a queer. That two friends should share the same tomb could, on the other hand, just be a sign of a non-neurotic society accepting and honouring two good pals.

Most of the evidence suggests that, in keeping with the utter disdain Set is held in, the only behaviour that was censured was male rape and the casual contact with *hemti-tjay*, or, literally, rent boys. Paedophilia, too, was scorned, and in this shame-based society the worst crime of all was fomenting scandal and offence through sexual acts carried out in public. We're back to those temple tosspots again. That ancient Egyptians had to be cautioned so strongly against doing it in public suggests that they had a bit of a thing about open-air sex. Dogging in the desert perhaps.

On lesbianism the ancient Egyptians remain quiet. There is one sentence in *The Book of the Dead* where a deceased woman recites her virtues, one being 'I did not couple with a masculine woman', but that still leaves the field fairly wide open.

4 · The Pyramids and the mysterious Menes

The dog of the family of a seer is considered a seer. Egyptian proverb

The Pyramids stand on a bluff that overlooks Cairo. From the car park in front of the Great Pyramid you mentally gird yourself against the onslaught of papyrus and postcard sellers (even with the new 'security' fence encircling the Pyramids, there are still plenty of hawkers and pedlars). As you lock your car or climb from the sweaty microbus you are drawn not so much to the incredible size and lumpy majesty of the Pyramids themselves as to the incredible prospect of a town out of control, threatening to climb up the bluff and overwhelm even this greatest of monuments: the Pyramid of Cheops, the last surviving of the seven ancient wonders of the world, built, it is reckoned, in the Fourth Dynasty around 4,500 years ago.

Now look back, if you will, at Cairo, with its layered smog, honking madness, simmering heat haze over tottering dead-eyed slum blocks (they have windows but no glass). These blocks, red and grey, built from grey concrete beams infilled with the laziest of red-brick curtain walling (lean against one of those walls and it'll collapse like a curtain, or so I always think), are built on prime farmland, illegally, because people are flooding into Cairo in a way that, before, only the Nile did.

Where these huddled masses swarm was, until the first Aswan dam, a series of highly fertile flood basins which filled up every summer as the Nile flooded. They then gradually subsided into paddy fields of rice and wheat. In fact only the rising bluff, known as the Giza Plateau, or previously the Libyan Hills, which signals the start of the Sahara

Desert, stood in the way of an endless spreading of the Nile's summer inundation.

Which is one reason why the Pyramids were built here. It is the first solid ground high up when you travel from the Nile in Cairo to the Sahara. About twenty miles east, in the opposite direction, is another bluff – the Moqattam Hills, where much of the original stone covering of the Pyramids was quarried.

The Nile was how they moved the stone. Think about it – you have no wheeled vehicles (chariots did not appear until the Middle Kingdom, roughly 2000–1600 BC, the Eleventh to Thirteenth Dynasties, introduced, it is thought, by the Hyksos, west Asian invaders of Egypt) and you need hundreds of stone blocks a day shifted from one side of the river to another.

You use the flood. Not only is there now a hugely widened river, you also have lots of basins and canals to extend the reach of the Nile even further. The stone can be lifted on to rafts of papyrus and floated across to the western side where it is needed. And, since the flood happens during the hottest period when no work is being done, you have a workforce available to help during the manoeuvre.

And for exotic granites, porphyries and basalts coming from Upper Egypt, the barges can also use the Nile to descend the river and then the floodwaters to get close to the Pyramids.

There is no question in my mind that the Pyramids and the Sphinx are an idealised artificial rendition of the desert home of the first Egyptians. They are rather like the lifelike pirate ship in Las Vegas, there to remind you of something alien and different but still somehow compelling and essential. It is as if the first Egyptians were saying, Now we have quit the desert we must not forget where we came from.

Herodotus states that the first Pharaoh, known as Menes in later accounts though no contemporary record of this name exists, built the city of Memphis, the first capital of ancient Egypt, after he had united the kingdoms of Upper and Lower Egypt. He chose Memphis (only a few kilometres south of modern Cairo), situated just below the delta where the Nile split into two main channels, because this was the start of Upper Egypt (Lower Egypt being the fertile regions of the delta to the north).

The fertile regions of the delta. Or were they, at that time? Menes, Herodotus tells us, drained the marshy regions of the Nile to create the terrain for Memphis. He did so by building the first dam on the

River Nile. It was the marshy regions that had kept early Egyptians in the desert in the first place. The desert at this time, as we have seen, was perfectly capable of supporting life and not the barren waste it gradually became. So it is quite likely that Menes and his people chose Memphis because, though marshy, it was a lot less boggy than the delta of 5,000 years ago. It was the closest inhabitable spot to the Mediterranean sea.

And even then it wasn't that habitable. Menes still needed to build a dam, or dams, to divert the river. The standard reason given is that he wanted to build on the western side of the Nile, but in those days the Nile's path ran right under the Libyan Hills. Handy for delivering stone but inconvenient as a place to build lower down. So Menes supposedly diverted the Nile higher up at Kosheish a dozen miles upstream – that is, south – of Memphis. This dam was made of cut stone, we are told, and was fify feet high and 1,500 feet wide.

The only way such a small dam could have worked against the immense power of the Nile would have been if the river had already split into several streams, and Menes' dam was simply a way of diverting one stream into another. In all likelihood the Nile at that stage was already splitting into branches; Menes merely postponed such development until the delta. On the reclaimed land he built Memphis.

Where is Memphis now? Under the new path of the Nile? Destroyed to build later versions of Cairo? Subsumed under the silt of ages? Perhaps a little of all of these three. As the Old Kingdom capital perhaps it wasn't anything like as huge as that of the New Kingdom – Thebes, now present-day Luxor (whose name comes from the Arabic for 'the palaces' – Al-Uxor).

We know that up until the high dam in Aswan was constructed – when the silt was much reduced in quantity (the first Aswan dam in 1902 let through the flood specifically to avoid the problem of silt retention) – the Nile valley increased five inches every hundred years. So a little over four feet every thousand years – so twenty feet have been added since Memphis was built 5,000 years ago. Whatever remains of the city will have to be dug out of ground that will become instantly waterlogged, requiring, as much archaeology in the delta also does, constant and costly pumping operations.

How would Menes have diverted the Nile with no heavy diggers and pumps? Willcocks gives us a clue when he speaks of the corvée, the indentured nineteenth-century labour force of fellahin, peasants of the delta, forced by the ruler of Egypt to dig canals and build levees against the flood. He observed thousands of men working with their bare hands and transporting mud on their backs. If they had tools they worked more efficiently, to be sure, but the lack of tools did not deter them from extremes of effort, often under the lash of harsh overseers. Willcocks also speaks of hundreds of men filling a channel through the use of the *shadouf*, the traditional method of shifting water into a higher ditch. The *shadouf* is really a bucket on a long lever; weighted at one end, it is swung into the lower stream and dumps water into the higher. Willcocks writes, 'They lifted water with over a hundred shadoofs working side by side. Each shadoof had four men, who worked incessantly night and day in rotation so that the shadoof never stopped for a minute. In addition to this each shadoof had four boys who worked by rotation ... helping the weight as the bucket ascended ... The life and animation of the scene I have never seen surpassed; while the resulting stream of water could not have been lifted by the largest portable engine.' There are parts of Egypt where things have not changed since pharaonic times. We can assume that the ability to work in unison in vast numbers, seen as late as the nineteenth century, was very similar to that which enabled men like Menes, thousands of years ago, to change a river's course and, of course, build the Pyramids.

5 · The Nile pump

When the marsh dries, the smell gets worse. Sudanese proverb

That Menes went to so much trouble was no more mysterious than the Pyramids themselves. But it becomes more understandable when we consider that the ancient Egyptians had already learnt to control the Nile through the use of Lake Moeris, what is now known as Lake Qarun in the Fayoum oasis.

Lake Qarun, when you turn off the highway from Fayoum, looks like the sea. There are big waves lapping the shore and fishermen standing up to their waists throwing nets.

But the lake is dying, or at least getting saltier by the year. This can be directly related to the damming of the Nile at Aswan. In 1902 when the first dam was built using William Willcocks' plans the Nile was tamed. With the high dam in 1970 the Nile was neutered. The salinity began its increase around the beginning of the twentieth century due to the reduction in the yearly flush of the inundation. With a flood of reduced impact the canals that ran from the Nile to Lake Qarun were no longer filled at the same rate. The lake began to grow more saline. By the time of the second dam no water was getting into the lake. Its fate was sealed when the fertilisers used around the lake began to re-enter the water as run-off – the need for fertiliser being a direct result of the end of basin irrigation, which relied on Nile silt, and the beginning of dammed perennial irrigation when fertiliser was added to the constant water source.

That Lake Qarun, or Moeris, waxed and waned in size I discovered for myself when I visited Qasr el-Sagha with my good friend the explorer Tahir Shah. Qasr el-Sagha is an Old Kingdom temple (though often confusingly listed as New Kingdom) which stands a good mile or more from the modern edge of Lake Qarun. It is surrounded by gritty, almost sandless desert. Behind it rise layers of escarpment that contain the caves of later Christian hermits and monks. Why build here unless the lake lapped this far inland?

We know that the shore had receded massively by later Ptolemaic times because of the abandoned city of Dimeh which lies much closer to the lake's edge, a few miles from Qasr el-Sagha. Dimeh is filled with broken Roman pottery, and the walls are mud brick. Three thousand years earlier the builders of Qasr el-Sagha used massive masonry blocks cut unevenly yet fitting together perfectly – the same construction technique can be seen in the walls of Cuzco in Peru and in the Sphinx temple in Giza.

My own interest in Qasr el-Sagha was not only because of its situation at the edge of the original Nile reservoir. It also derived from its connection to both Schweinfurth and Willcocks – men whose combined knowledge of the Nile is probably unsurpassed. They were friends and, when in Cairo, used to walk out together around Wadi Digla, a place now favoured by mountain-bikers and hikers. Schweinfurth had been second fiddle on the expedition made by Gerhard Rohlfs in 1873 across the Sahara. I had replicated this journey in 2010, finding that Schweinfurth had exaggerated the difficulties of the terrain. Strangely this made me feel more not less sympathy for him; when an expedition has been paid for by the public one feels duty bound to make it sound heroic. What was indeed heroic was his later journey into the heart of Africa to the fabled land of Bongo, where he meticulously recorded the habits of the cannibal Azande people. But more of this later.

Schweinfurth had been the original discoverer of the mysterious Qasr el-Sagha, which consists of a large inner room with what look like seven bays for statues. There are also several mysterious rooms which can be entered only through a hole near the floor the size of a large cat-flap. But what Schweinfurth and all subsequent archaeologists have missed, though I am sure Willcocks didn't, was that Qasr el-Sagha is an oracle temple – similar to that found in Siwa where Alexander the Great went to discover the cause of the Nile's flood (and to find out whether he would rule the world, if the geographer Strabo's account is to be believed). At Siwa, where Schweinfurth ended up after his desert journey, is the oracle of Ammon. It sits on top of a fifty-foot-high rock plug and is a rudely made series of rooms, interesting mainly because of their connection to antiquity, but also because they reveal the simple cunning in the practice of oracular arts. High up in the walls there are holes, there by design. Alongside the wall runs a narrow room or corridor from which one could overhear what was said within the room. Or perhaps one could intone a prophecy from within the corridor and the words would emerge as if magically spoken. If the walls were hung with tapestries or wooden panels, as they would have been, the communicating holes would be hidden, operating like a ship's secret telegraph system.

The same set-up is visible at Qasr el-Sagha, and was pointed out to me by Justin Majzub: a secret corridor running within the outer wall with a small hole at one end in the entrance wall of the temple. The entrance to the secret corridor is easy to miss – it's a slim door in the outer wall – and was no doubt concealed in earlier times, as the listening or speaking hole in the grander main entrance would have been.

What is remarkable is not that Schweinfurth missed the similarity but that not a single archaeological description of Qasr el-Sagha refers to its obvious oracle function. One can safely assume that its position was connected somehow to the function of Lake Qarun/Moeris as the regulating reservoir of the Nile. One may speculate that the oracle might furnish advance information on the extent of the flood and how large a supply might be caught within the ambit of the lake. Such information would be of crucial use. Perhaps the rate at which the lake filled would have some bearing on the size of the flood; perhaps other key

indicators were used rather as today commodity speculators use complicated cross-indicators of weather and natural disasters to compute
the future price of a trade.

The entrance to Lake Moeris was a diversionary canal known for centuries as Joseph's Canal. Willcocks, the ever present water engineer of
the Nile, suggested that a close reading of Genesis indicates that Joseph
controlled Lake Moeris at a crucial stage in biblical history.

That the original dams remain is not in question – vast dam-like
edifices of cut stone lie by the Pyramid of Hawara (where the Egyptologist Flinders Petrie also unearthed a papyrus roll that comprised books
one and two of Homer's *Iliad*). Joseph's Canal still passes within thirty
yards of the Pyramid, and due to increased winter river levels floods the
Pyramid entrance.

But control of Lake Moeris pre-dates Joseph by hundreds of years.
When the system eventually decayed, perhaps during one of the many
periods of unrest between dynasties, the Fayoum oasis blossomed in
the old lake bed. The lake shrank to its old size; we know this because
of prehistoric stone tools found all around its current edge. Yet further
up, much further, near Qasr el-Sagha we find the remains of Nile shell-
fish – a sure sign that the lake's size has not been constant. On the far
side the land is mainly low except where it rises on the bluff at the artist
colony of Tunis. This low land – all prime agricultural acreage – would
have been under water for half the year as the lake operated as a giant
regulator for the ebb and flow of the Nile.

With such control of the Nile the delta could have been better
irrigated throughout the year. The Nile – according to records stretching back over a thousand years – never has two low floods one after
another. If one year is low the next will always be normal or high. The
idea that low floods in succession cause famines cannot be supported;
just as in Ethiopia and the Sudan in the present era, famine is the
result of a natural disaster magnified greatly by political inaction or
unrest. So, it seems, with the lake operating as a reservoir protecting
against the possibility of a low flood, Egypt was the first country in
the world to wrest control of its own food supply from the lap of the
gods.

At night the sun sets across the sea-like extent of Lake Qarun and
you see the tail lights of fishermen returning home, two-up on cheap
Chinese-made motorbikes. They have been beating the water all day
just as their ancestors did for 5,000 or more years. Now that there is no

more flood to recharge the lake with fresh water, it is gradually turning to salt. There is even some talk of stocking it with sea bass and bream. But not much serious talk. In a few years the lake will be too saline for any kind of edible fish. In fact it will resemble the vast lakes around Siwa. The two ancient oracles are now silent and facing the lapping sound of dead waters.

6 · Sex lives and crumbling papyrus

If one speaks about everything the heart remains empty.
Ethiopian proverb

In this biography of the Red Nile we must not shrink from revealing all. The silent desert culture that gave way to the prolific riverine one is, thanks to the drawings of the Turin Erotic Papyrus (dubbed the 'world's earliest men's mag' with pictures of different sexual positions), and from the evidence of ancient lyric poetry, one where a great deal can be known about the intimate life of ordinary people.

In the myth Isis was grovelling around in the marsh searching for her husband's penis. In reality, it seems that, in sexual matters, the ancient Egyptian woman dominated the male, was rather exacting and certainly not weak willed.

Contrary to the practice in later, more sexist civilisations, Egyptian men were taught from an early age to respect women. The mores of the time strongly inclined everyone to a sexual temperance restricted to marital cohabitation. Despite, or maybe because of, the respect they earned from men, more sexual restraint was expected of women than of men. The reason was simple: the age-old concern about the legitimacy or otherwise of the progeny.

The Nile's flood was a flood of tears. Professional weepers were employed at religious ceremonies to cry copiously, cry me a river indeed. These women (of varying ages – crying being a skill not reserved solely for the young), who assumed the roles of the female deities Isis and her sister Nephthys in religious ceremonies, were required to be sexually abstinent for certain periods.

It was even tougher being a female temple servant – one of the 'gods' wives'. A lifelong preservation of virginity was required of them. Almost

certainly the austere practices of Christian monasticism, which arose in
the Egyptian desert while the old religions faded away, were influenced
by this requirement for sexual abstinence. The priests of Apis in Memphis were also denied any form of sexual relations.

For the rest of the populace things were not too restrictive. Young
men could marry at thirteen. Teenage sex was OK, as long as it was
within marriage. There was no civil or religious ceremony – the only
contracts drawn up concerned property rights in the case of death and
divorce, and sometimes these were drafted long after the marriage had
started.

The goal of marriage was producing children. For the blight of
infertility various treatments were available, some aphrodisiacal.
Lettuce was highly thought of in this regard, which adds another
spin to Set munching on the sperm-impregnated salad he was handed
by Horus. Another plant supposedly guaranteed to aid procreation
is known to us only by its unpronounceable name *mnhp*; this was
depicted with a hieroglyphic ending with the unmistakable image of
a phallus.

For those who were not trying to produce babies, and were perhaps
even cavorting illegally in public places, there were some widely known
methods for avoiding conception. An unusual though popular prophylactic was dung. One recipe recommended inserting into the vagina,
before sex, a compote of crocodile dung, honey and/or resin. Another
suggests inserting the tips of acacia twigs (which contain gum arabic),
dates and honey. Try fighting your way through that lot. One imagines
that the prophylaxis lies more in the obstruction to entry than in the
spermicidal qualities of the medicine.

The numerous mummies of mothers and children interred together
indicate the risks of childbirth. Those that survived were breastfed
until the age of three. Mothers' milk was in high demand – not just for
its intended purpose, but also as a cure for colds, diseases of the eye,
eczema, burns and even bed wetting. Though it is hard to see how milk
could benefit people other than babies, the suggestive list of things it
could cure seems taken from the ailments it prevents or inhibits in the
young. In other words the ancient Egyptians had observed the benefits
to the young immune system conferred by human milk, benefits that
modern science is only now confirming.

What else was going on along that great river 4,500 years or more
ago? Much that was passed on to later religions, as we have seen. Boys

were circumcised, though late, about their twelfth birthday. A scene at Saqqara depicts a priest squatting in front of a boy about to perform the act using a piece of flint, the traditional tool – no doubt a remnant of their desert-dwelling days. And, like the ceramic knives used by today's surgeons, nothing cuts cleaner than a sharp piece of stone.

It is interesting to note that circumcision was the norm but not universal for Egyptian men until uncircumcised Libyans began to mingle with the populace. Only then does circumcision become a necessity for religious purity. Almost certainly the borrowing of circumcision by the other Semitic religions, and its similar justification as a means of delineating the *other*, started with the influence of ancient Egypt.

All Egyptians were prohibited from having sex on those days when, according to the religious calendar, the gods were themselves so engaged. This was fewer than fifty days a year – the gods only getting to do it about once a week, maybe on Saturday night.

As we have hinted, in ancient Egyptian marriages the woman was considered the equal of the man. This is highly unusual, taking a global historical perspective, and a sign, surely, of the sophistication of the culture. As the Nile explorer Richard Burton (not the one married to Cleopatra – Liz Taylor – but the other one) remarked, 'the sign of an advanced culture is simple: the relative equality of men and women'. Four thousand years ago on the banks of the Nile there were even marriages where the status of the woman was quite clearly higher than that of her spouse. One account records a wealthy woman marrying a younger common soldier. Another woman marrying first a scribe and then an artisan.

Higher up the social scale incestuous marriages designed to protect dynasties were common. Keep it in the family in every sense. Ramses II married three of his daughters. Mythology supported the concept of incest, with Osiris marrying his sister Isis, and Set, despite his predatory predilections, marrying his sister Nephthys. However, it's important to realise that incest wasn't as common in ancient Egypt as was once thought. On legal documents concerning marriage a man and a woman may be referred to as 'brother and sister', and this has led to confusion. In such an instance this is a legal formula indicating they are both equal in the marriage, not that they are siblings.

But it is a strong indication of the relative fairness of this ancient marriage institution that the parties are referred to as brother and sister and not as master and servant as they were in the West until recently.

Prenuptial agreements have even been discovered from the Ptolemaic period, often putting a time limit into a marriage contract by which point, if the parties weren't happy, it could be dissolved. In one papyrus record it was stated that a gooseherd had a nine-month clause inserted, after which his wife would receive a special payment, perhaps for becoming pregnant.

Divorce, like marriage, was neither a civil nor a religious matter; it was, rather sensibly, personal. Foreshadowing modern times, many women were better off financially after divorce and many men reduced in circumstances. The causes of divorce were age old and familiar: infidelity, infertility, incompatibility or simply the desire to enter into marriage with another person. Though there was complete freedom to divorce, those that did so without substantive cause met with considerable social condemnation. From the evidence available, however, the majority of Egyptian marriages were long lasting.

7 · Enter Moses and the red plague

The god of old women is 'old women'. Nubian proverb

These gentle Nile dwellers, with their equal marriages and their tendency to perform obscene acts in sacred places, were also the enemy – when seen from another perspective, that of the ancient dwellers of Israel. The Nile dwellers, the Egyptians, are the enslavers of the Israelites, and yet in this cauldron of oppression the Mosaic religion comes into existence. So, in a sense, the enemy were also the cause of enlightenment and ultimately of freedom.

The Egyptian can be distinguished from other African religions by its movement towards the light. Instead of focusing on snake and crocodile worship (though these did feature as aspects of the central deity), the ancient Egyptian religion took a step towards the abstract by worshipping light: the life-giving sun itself. Whereas the worship of dangerous animals seems motivated by fear, the worship of the sun appears to be driven by gratitude and by a better scientific understanding of the wellsprings of life.

But it is Moses and his laws that take us to the next step in the evolution of our conception of a deity. Moses is the first figure to announce that God is abstract, that there will be no graven images made of him. He goes up the mountain and comes back laden with stone tablets on which are inscribed the laws of the new religion. (Many now think the tablets were actually of clay, which for the cuneiform lingua franca of the time would have been the usual method of recording words.)

But Moses didn't reformulate the ancient religion of the Jews in isolation; he also lived a life inextricably linked with the Nile.

Josephus, the Jewish historian writing in AD 94, claimed that the name Moses was derived from the ancient Egyptian and, later, Coptic language: *mo* meaning 'water', and *uses* meaning 'saved from'. So Moses, saved from death by being cast in a basket on the Nile, is in effect saved by the river itself (probably because of its uniquely irresistible blend of kitsch and entertainment, a rather effective tableau of this event is enacted complete with a baby doll in a basket at the Nileside theme park in Cairo – the redoubtable Dr Ragab's Pharaonic Village which I have already mentioned).

As the Nile was, effectively, the source of all water in Egypt we can see that Moses, who was saved from the water, is nominally an offspring of the river. The cause of his 'rebirth' via the river was, we learn in the Book of Exodus, that the Pharaoh of the time had decreed that all children under a certain age who were of Hebrew origin should be drowned in the Nile. Certainly it would be a quick and obvious way to despatch a large number of unwanted toddlers. (Later, a superstition grew up that anyone who drowned in the Nile would return as a ghost to haunt the living. Perhaps it was the result of so much judicial murder. By the time Caesar won the battle of the Nile in 47 BC, when he installed Cleopatra as queen, the river was no longer a place to have people killed; when he eliminated an opponent he was careful the victim was not drowned or seen as drowned in case he acquired ghostly status among the populace.)

Moses, we know, however, owed his life to the Nile because his mother, Jochebed, constructed a basket of reeds waterproofed with pitch and cleverly sent him downstream to land where the Pharaoh's daughter was bathing. Miriam, Moses' sister, asked the smitten daughter of the Pharaoh if she needed a skilled nurse to bring up the child. The answer being yes, Jochebed was introduced as the ideal nurse. So Moses, from being on the Pharaoh's hit list, gets to be brought up by his own mother in the luxurious high-status environment of the royal court. *Result!* one is tempted to shout. By cheating the Nile of his death he doesn't just cling on to life, he is rewarded by becoming a prince.

Earlier in the Bible, in Genesis, Moses is spoken of as being of the second generation of Israelites born in Egypt, descended from Jacob, who had entered Egypt because of a drought in the land of Canaan. One of Moses' ancestors was Joseph, the eleventh of Jacob's twelve sons, he of the coat of many colours, who had risen to become the Pharaoh's right hand because of his ability to interpret dreams. With this background of the royal involvement of the Jews, the stratagem of placing Moses in the royal fold does not seem so unlikely.

However, living as an impostor had its effect on Moses and he became acutely sensitive to the plight of the Jews – who were treated, then, as second-class citizens in Egypt. In one case Moses was so angered by an Egyptian who had beaten a Jew that he killed the Egyptian and then hid the body (thus breaking one of his later commandments). When word got out Moses fled into the Sinai Desert and hid as a shepherd. Here he lived for forty years until God sent him a sign: the burning bush at the foot of Mount Sinai (which can still be seen growing in the delightful grounds of the Christian monastery there today, though, in the absence of any prophets, steadfastly refusing to reignite). Having got Moses' attention via the flaming foliage, God commanded him to deliver the Hebrews from their bondage in Egypt.

Ask and ye shall receive. But when Moses asked, the Pharaoh refused. After all, this was a useful workforce he would be losing. Moses asked God for help and God didn't muck around: he sent a plague of blood – turning the waters of the Nile into blood just to scare the Pharaoh. The exact phrasing is useful because it gives an indication of what the 'plague of blood' might really have been. Moses relates that God has told him to do the following: 'With this staff strike the water of the Nile and it will be changed into blood. The fish in the Nile will die, and the river will stink and thus the Egyptians will not be able to drink its water' (Exodus 7: 17–18).

Pharaoh wouldn't agree to Moses' demands so the prophet Aaron, with his staff and under his brother Moses' guidance, struck the Nile and turned it into a river of blood. Sure enough the river could not be used as water, the fish died and all was calamity. The blood plague on the river lasted for seven days.

Coincidentally the Ipuwer Papyrus from the Eighteenth Dynasty (1550–1300 BC) – Tutankhamen was an Eighteenth Dynasty king – contains some striking parallels to this period of the plagues of Egypt, especially the plague of blood. In the papyrus it states: 'plague is throughout the land. Blood is everywhere. The river is blood. People shrink from tasting.' This is one of the few cases where one tradition corroborates the experience of the other.

The papyrus also states that this was a time of upheavals, of servants revolting against their masters. It is not hard to see a parallel with the Hebraic text. Given the needs of oral storytelling and the mythologising required to turn the no doubt confusing events in Egypt into a viral narrative capable of surviving centuries of repetition, it seems perfectly plausible that these events really did occur. Trying to prove that the plagues really happened is usually a nice exercise in creative thinking, yet recent scientific evidence rather suggests that the story is grounded in truth. So if Egypt did suffer ten plagues, what is the first, the blood-red river?

Some have suggested an algal bloom, something similar to the Red Tide of algae seen in the Gulf of Mexico. While the parallels between a harmful algal bloom and a 'blood river' are compelling – both of them lower oxygen levels so that fish and plants die – there may be another explanation. Just as the Nile becomes red with silt when the Blue Nile joins the White Nile in the Sudan, so, in the days before any dams were built, an excessive Nile inundation would have seen a blood-red tide sweeping downstream. That the plague of blood lasted only seven days is suggestive of such a one-off flood. The stench left behind after floods have receded – leaving fish stranded and river mud everywhere – also corresponds with the stench reported in the biblical account.

Pharaoh did not give in to the demands of Moses because, apparently, his own magicians could also turn water into blood – perhaps by just mixing a lot of red-coloured silt into it. That the next plague was a plague of frogs confirms the big-flood theory. Frog plagues are, or were until the high dam was built at Aswan, fairly common in Egypt. And they occurred at the time of the Nile inundation in the summer. So after the excessive flood came a huge number of frogs to plague the inhabitants of the Red Nile still more.

We've seen that the plague of blood and the plague of frogs could have a natural explanation. But what about the rest? It took ten plagues of increasing severity to persuade the Pharaoh to let Moses and his people go.

Plague three was a plague of lice. Some scientists have rather arrogantly concluded that ancient Egyptians would have been unable to distinguish between lice and 'invisible' biters such as ticks and midges and small mosquitoes. Having spent time with illiterate Bedouin who were well aware of the differences, I think it highly improbable that lice meant anything other than lice. Lice are spread by contact. Perhaps in the confusion engendered by the plagues people neglected normal hygiene and lice prospered.

Plague four was a plague of flies – quite possibly mosquitoes or disease-spreading flies of some kind such as midges or sandflies. If the fish had rotted and died on the banks of the river a plague of flies may have resulted. Egypt is relatively fly free compared to other parts of Africa, so a plague of flies would have been unusual and vexatious. Fortunately for the Jews, Goshen, a place in the Egyptian delta where they lived, was beyond the area where sandflies live.

Plague five was a plague of animal deaths. The account in Exodus states that donkeys and camels were killed but not pigs or goats. This curious anomaly has led scientists to conclude that this was a plague of African horse sickness or bluetongue, viral diseases spread by the midges of the fourth plague. These diseases affect the animals mentioned in the Bible but not those omitted, swine and goats.

You'd think the Pharaoh would have had enough by now, what with his camels and donkeys keeling over. But no – he still refused to let Moses and his people leave. So another plague it was. Plague six was a plague of boils. This could well have been an outbreak of cutaneous anthrax, typically contracted by handling the corpses of infected carriers. Since anthrax can be passively carried by camels and donkeys, perhaps the surfeit of dead ones lying around caused an outbreak. Cutaneous anthrax, which produces unsightly purple boils, is rarely fatal, though it can lead to blood toxaemia and death in certain circumstances.

Plague seven was a plague of hail. In the winter, visitors to Egypt are shocked at how chilly it can get. I've been in a hailstorm in the Western Desert – a place where it isn't even supposed to rain (though it does). It has snowed once in Cairo in the last century and probably hailed a dozen times. So this 'plague', which would accompany a particularly cold winter, though unusual, even somewhat freakish, is perfectly believable, even in the hot climate we expect of Egypt.

Still no joy from Pharaoh. And let's face it, hail isn't that scary. So for plague eight God decided to get really mean: plague eight was a plague of locusts. In any country in the Middle East locusts swarming can mean everything is eaten and famine is certain. People are genuinely scared by such things. Again, during a residence of seven years in Egypt, I was present during two locust scares – both originating in the upper Nile and heading north. In one, a plague of locusts flew up the Nile munching most of what got in their way, only stopping a few miles from the outskirts of Cairo. For weeks afterwards I found windblown locusts dying in the sandy wadis on the eastern side of Cairo. A plague of locusts, in an era without pesticides or early-warning systems and aerial observation, is very believable. The Israelites, living in Goshen – now the eastern delta region – being north of Memphis (present-day Cairo), would have been the last to be affected by the locusts, which, by then, may have ceased to swarm. Once all the crops of the Egyptians had been eaten they would have been reduced to eating old supplies of grain – which led, many believe, to the tenth and final plague.

But before that was plague nine: a plague of darkness. Despite there being evidence that the Santorini volcanic explosion of 1652 BC distributed vast amounts of ash in the Nile and delta regions it is less easy to connect this with the plague of darkness (and the plague of blood), as some have tried to do. The argument here is that the eruption caused the darkness as the ash obscured the sky, and then it entered the river, making it turn blood red. If we are to allow the sequence any validity, then the plague of darkness would have come first and the plague of blood later. But setting that aside, a far more reasonable explanation of the plague of darkness is something I've experienced myself in Cairo: a *khamsin*, or duststorm. The fact that the plague of darkness lasts three days is also suggestive – sandstorms (really duststorms, as pure sandstorms do not rise more than ten feet off the ground) can easily block out the sun for several days. The arrival of a sudden and severe *khamsin* after a prediction of darkness would have a huge impact on those who experienced it.

The final plague is the most intriguing in a way, and the hardest to explain. The tenth plague was a death plague on firstborn sons. Very nasty in a patriarchal society where the firstborn son tends to get all the love and attention. But herein lies the clue: the firstborn are the most dominant – in any patriarchal society. After the collapse of agriculture following the preceding plagues there would have been acute food shortages. Secret stores of grain would have been worth a fortune

– and available only to those who were dominant: the firstborn sons. But grain stored for too long is subject to mycotoxins, surface-growing fungi, a potential cause of rapid death. It has been proposed that a group of the most dominant citizens – largely firstborn sons – helped themselves to a last supply of grain that was infected by mycotoxins. These can kill through mere inhalation. When they all died, the rumour that there was a plague on firstborn sons would have spread rapidly.

The Jews themselves were spared: by virtue of their eating the Passover meal, the angel of death ignored them. But this meal – of newborn lamb and unleavened bread – was available to the Jews because they still had some food, the locusts having left them alone. Thus, unaffected by the previous plagues, they were not reduced to raiding old grain stores. In a sense the Passover was symptomatic of their survival rather than a cause of it.

No leader can stand by and watch all the firstborn sons perish; the Pharaoh wilted and allowed Moses to leave. But being a bad old Pharaoh, he naturally changed his mind just as they set out on their journey. Jumping into their chariots, the Egyptian army sped north to stop the Jews escaping into the Sinai and home to Canaan.

8 · Moses crosses the Red *Nile*

A fool and water follow where they are led. Egyptian proverb

The chariots jostled and fought their way along the dusty roads to the delta. The Jews, fleeing with all their baggage and herds and belongings, could see the dust rising far behind them. Time for Moses to call a friend. Or at least pull a new trick out of the bag. The obvious way to the Sinai would have involved following the coastal route of the Mediterranean – and this is where things become confusing, since there is no Red Sea around – just the Med on one side and the Gulf of Suez on the other – the Red Sea doesn't start until you are some way down the Egyptian coast. So the identity of the sea that parts is the first problem. Then, did the Pharaoh's troops get swept away to their deaths? It seems such a singular occurrence one suspects it has some basis in truth, though exaggerated to make it memorable at a time when stories were there to be told and not read.

In the Hebrew version of Exodus the sea is known as Yam Suph, *suph* also being used to mean reeds in other parts of the Old Testament. So, bizarrely – since it works in English as well as Hebrew – the Red Sea might actually be the Reed Sea. As early as the eleventh century AD, the French Talmudic scholar Rashi wrote that the Red Sea should be known as the Sea of Reeds.

There is no doubt, too, as one notes when one studies Herodotus, who came many centuries after Moses' time, that the Nile delta has always been subject to change – as one would expect after 3,000 years of heavy floods and silting up. A no longer extant branch of the Nile, the so-called Pelusian arm (from the Greek *pelous* meaning 'silty' or 'muddy'), also known as 'the brook of Egypt', extended further to the north and west than the existing Suez Canal. What was known as the Lake of Tanis may well have been an extensive muddy lake fed by this branch of the Nile and occupying the area now bisected by the Suez Canal.

In Exodus we read, 'The Lord caused the sea to go back with a strong east wind.' If we were talking about the real Red Sea, or even the Gulf of Suez, an east wind would simply have caused massive waves to break on the eastern shore of Egypt – hardly a great escape route. However, a lake lying on an east–west axis would be denuded of water by a high easterly wind. Carl Drews, of the National Center for Atmospheric Research in Colorado, in 2010 designed a computer model of such a lake to find out whether a wind could expose underlying mudflats. He discovered that a 63mph wind, less powerful than the hurricane-force winds of 1987 in the UK – in fact merely a very strong gale – would be capable of blowing back the water of such a river-filled lake and leaving the bed exposed.

The 'Reed Sea' blocked the escape route of the Israelites because it lay between the marshy coastline and the desert further inland. It would also have been a direct route from Memphis to the Sinai. Perhaps a strong wind did open up a way across the mudflats of the Red Nile, a route that the hasty and blood-seeking Pharaoh's army were unable to follow ... or perhaps they did. At which point the wind mysteriously died and a wave of water engulfed the unlucky seekers of vengeance.

9 · The Moses mystery

When they hit a fool, a wise person sitting nearby learns. Nubian proverb

Moses, watching the water engulf his enemies, escapes to the Sinai Desert. Here he goes up Mount Sinai and receives the ten commandments from God. He and the tribe then wander for forty years and eventually make it to the banks of the Jordan – the promised land. Moses is forbidden to enter the promised land because of an earlier transgression, so it is up to his brother Aaron to lead them in.

Back to the Nile. Just who was the Pharaoh either washed away or left behind fuming on the bank? This is where it gets tricky. In the Bible only one Pharaoh is named – Shishaq. He sacks Jerusalem and generally does battle in the land now known as Israel. For many years it was assumed that Shishaq was the leader whom the Egyptians called Shoshenq, a pharaoh who invaded Canaan – where the Jews lived. The similarity in name and the battles recorded make a pretty good case, though not everyone agrees. But he was not the Pharaoh of the exodus.

Any pharaoh with 'Moses' or something similar-sounding in their name – Tuthmoses, Ra-moses – has been drafted in as a potential pharaoh of Moses' time. Again there is little to back this up.

Sceptics have pointed to the lack of Egyptian literature documenting the ten plagues. Yet without the theological imperative provided by the Moses story there is little reason for the Egyptians to consider the plagues as anything more than plain bad luck – so why write about them as a special case? The so-called Famine Stele refers to a seven-year period of famine in the Third Dynasty (roughly 2685–2615 BC) long before Moses' time, yet this stele, inscribed in granite on an island in the Nile near Aswan, was actually carved much later – around 300 BC. It is therefore probably tapping into the wide Middle Eastern mythology of seven-year famines, which occur in the *Epic of Gilgamesh* (at 3,800 years old, one of the oldest literary works discovered) as well as the Bible. Mythological famines were something worth writing about in the mystico-religious hieroglyphic language; real ones probably weren't. So the misfortunes, including floods and famines, would all have been part of the experience of life along the Egyptian Nile when Moses was alive.

Most students of archaeology have plumped for Ramses II as the

Pharaoh who went head to head with Moses. This is because of his prominence and because of his ambitious building programme mentioned at the beginning of the Book of Exodus. A more compelling case, however, can be made for the Pharaoh Khaneferre, whose name is unique in the list of kings compiled by Menetho – unlike Ramses, of which there are many. Why is this an important point? Because Khaneferre is referred to as Moses' adopted father in the writings of the Jewish historian Artapanus. More compellingly, Artapanus compiled his work in the third century BC, when there would have been many more original records available in Egyptian temples and in the library in Alexandria, the greatest library of the ancient world, started around 300 BC in the city created by Alexander the Great. If Artapanus was simply making up a yarn, why choose such an obscure pharaoh? Why not go for an obvious one such as Ramses II? And, if he was operating at random, statistically an obscure name like Khaneferre is less likely to be chosen than the several versions of Ramses.

Does Khaneferre appear as a significant builder to corroborate the 'great works' referred to in Exodus? Yes, there are several colossal black granite statues of Khaneferre found at Tanis in the eastern Nile delta. If we accept that the chronology has some flexibility in it – which we must, given that the periods between the established rules of Pharaohs can never be known with pinpoint accuracy – then it looks as if the exodus occurred during the Thirteenth Dynasty (roughly 1800 BC to 1650 BC) rule of Pharaoh Khaneferre.

Supporting this is the first mention, anywhere, of the name Israel – on a stele inscribed by Mineptah, the son of Ramses II. On it occurs the phrase 'Israel is laid waste, his seed is not.' The other nations listed as subdued by the Pharaohs include Gezer, Canaan and Hurru (Palestine). Now if the Israelites had fled in the reign of his father – and were almost certainly still wandering – why would they be listed as a nation subdued? They would not even exist as a nation. Ramses II is the Nineteenth Dynasty (1300 BC to 1185 BC); if we have a much earlier exodus it makes sense that the Israelites would be a recognisable nation by this time, and so worthy of a mention.

But the Jewish historians say more about Moses. Both Artapanus and the later Josephus speak of Moses leading an expedition against the people of Kush – the Ethiopians – who inhabit the region beyond the second cataract, the area that became Nubia. There is one reference to a Thirteenth Dynasty Egyptian military operation in Upper Nubia, on a stele in the British Museum. The cartouche on the stele is none other than that of Khaneferre.

One final piece seems to tie this story together. The area of Upper Nubia invaded would have centred on the town of Kerma in present-day Sudan. A hundred years ago, on the island of Agro, just south of Kerma, there was found a headless lifesize statue of a pharaoh – identified from the inscription on the statue as Khaneferre, the Pharaoh who refused to free the Jews and suffered the mighty flood of the Nile as his punishment.

10 · A Starving interlude

The madman says, 'Everything is mine!' Ethiopian proverb

'From flood to famine' is a common mythological trope. We have already seen how the Famine Stele, set symbolically midstream in the Nile, spoke of seven years when the flood failed to come and the people starved: 'grain was scant, kernels were dried up, every man robbed his twin'. The Book of Genesis, too, provides us with several stories of famine in Egypt. Indeed it has become a country associated with famine, or the idea of it, until the building of the two great dams on the Nile at Aswan. One wonders, though, if famine was as frequent as the proponents of that dam suggest. Visiting in 1840 James Augustus St John remarks, 'these fearful visitations are, perhaps, less frequent in Egypt than in any other country'. Certainly the great European famine of 1315–17, with many stricken areas not recovering until 1322, was as grave as anything experienced in Egypt. And there were more English famines in 1351 and 1369.

The Famine Stele is somewhat lacking in detail, the misery of the Egyptians stated rather than shown. One needs to go forward in history to the Islamic period to get a more substantial view of what might occur in a famine. Leaving for a moment the ancient period for AD 1032–6, there was a great famine in Egypt initiated perhaps by a failure of the flood, but exacerbated by Berber attacks on the canal system and the greed of Egypt's Turkish rulers. Things became so bad that a small measure of wheat fetched two gold dinars (when the Sultan Saladin died he bequeathed only one gold dinar and a few pieces of silver in his will), and in modern currency this would be several hundred pounds sterling. When all the usual items had been consumed, the starving people turned to eating the flesh of rats, dogs, the bodies of the newly deceased. The dogs that remained, driven insane with hunger, broke into town houses and devoured children before their parents' eyes, parents too weak to defend their offspring. Twenty houses of the highest quality in Cairo, valued at over 20,000 dinars, were sold for a small quantity of bread. A contemporary observer, Ben Aljouzi, relates that a lady of great wealth and distinction, taking four great handfuls of jewels with her, went out into the street and exclaimed, 'Who will give me corn for these gems?' No one attended to her cries, so in despair she threw them down saying, 'Since you cannot aid me in my distress, what use are you?' And there the jewels lay since no person cared to stir and get them, so afflicted were they with hunger. In AD 1296, there was a famine in which the usual recourse of eating dogs and dead bodies was adopted before things grew even more desperate. The governor of Cairo, wandering around in a state of hunger, came across three ruffians seated around the body of a small child they were seasoning with salt, fresh chopped onion and vinegar. (Where did they get that onion?) On being apprehended they confessed that they had been 'subsisting on the flesh of infants' for many weeks, eating a child a day. They were executed and their bodies hung on the city gate at Zawiet; but, during the night, they were taken down and eaten by the famished people, all turned, at last, to cannibalism.

11 · The Red Pharaoh

A mad person is clever inside. Sudanese proverb

The spectre of cannibalism recedes as we flash backwards again in time, though not place, to the Seventeenth Dynasty (roughly 1580–1550 BC) of ancient Egypt. Like H. G. Wells' Time Traveller we return to a place utterly changed. Moses has left, Tutankhamen is in the wings, but the man of the moment is Pharaoh Seqenenre Tao II. He is truly the Red Pharaoh, as he is the only one we know for sure met a truly bloody end.

His mummy is one of the very few with healed fighting wounds. Unlike, say, the recovered skeletons of crusader kings, which are racked with healed and half-healed injuries, the mummies of most Pharaohs indicate a life without injury.

The injured mummy of Seqenenre Tao II therefore provides a unique insight into the warring world of ancient Egypt – or, rather, into the odd moments when war occurred in a culture defined more by stability and continuity than by bellicose change.

As a study of war effects, Tao's wounds provide plenty to analyse. Unlike the superficial trauma suffered by Tutankhamen's mummy, Seqenenre's wounds (breaks to skull and jaw) were obviously fatal, so the results are less speculative and more illuminating.

One problem of Egyptology, the mentionable unmentionable problem, is that there isn't enough evidence to say what really happened. Of course one can speculate, and Egyptologists have been speculating for a century or more, examining the contents of tombs and translating wall engravings and papyrus and ostraka (pottery and stone fragments with writing), but there are grave problems when one goes beyond the grave, so to speak, and attempts to describe with any semblance of accuracy the details of ancient Egypt. Why so? Because, quite simply, this was not a people who set any store by realistic reportage for the sake of it. Everything carved in stone had a symbolic or religious meaning that far outweighed its practical everyday meaning or significance. In wall paintings that describe 'everyday life' we see many things, but not a single picture of men building pyramids. In friezes that show war, the king is depicted as killing an entire army. Despite a wish to credit the ancient Egyptians with magical skills beyond even those possessed by shamans and wonder workers of any age, it is simply not possible to believe that this is an accurate representation of what happened. Not only is it slightly inaccurate, a king who defeats an army singlehandedly has no connection with reality at all. But still, even the most egregious liar or fantasist provides clues. If we look at the lovely painted casket depicting Tutankhamen crushing the Assyrians, we can be reasonably sure that that is what a chariot looked like (the young King is riding on one), that a war horse had an armoured coat, probably of copper scales, and that if war was conducted from chariots bows and arrows were used and we can see what they looked like. We can get a picture of the people, the clothes they wore, the weapons they used, but we cannot get a picture of the reality of any situation described. The trivial is apparent but the meaning of the whole eludes us. How much did religion intrude into daily life? How big were the wars described? And, most of all, what was understood literally and what was understood metaphorically?

Take the much repeated imagery of the Pharaoh smiting his enemies – indeed, smiting seems to be the fate for pretty much anyone with the temerity to oppose him. In the smiting pictures the Pharaoh is drawn large and the smitten small. Yet can we believe that a king would actually go round, hippo-hide whip in hand, smiting all day long? Surely the first luxury of kingship is to employ your own smiter?

Of course once one doubts the literal significance of such imagery the whole field is wide open. One route is to use what we know about symbolism and mysticism from other fields to unlock the mysteries of ancient Egypt. It's a perilous path, especially for the academic.

Dr Garry Shaw takes another route. In his 2008 work on royal authority in Egypt's Eighteenth Dynasty, he is forced to conclude, after marshalling all the evidence, that one can say very little for certain about the Pharaohs:

> ... it is clear that a true detailed 'history' of the Pharaoh's role as an individual in government cannot be written for this period. Any scholar who states that a certain event occurred, or that 'the king did x' is making assumptions about the evidence. There is no unbiased view of this evidence, no objective commentator from whom a view of the system from the outside can be gleaned. The evidence is a closed system, coherent within itself, but which does not translate into historical reality as there is no way to know whether the presentation can be trusted. Others may be correct in saying that the king could do as he liked, but the evidence from Egypt cannot be used to prove this assertion.

There is a welcome humility in such conclusions, since for too long assertions about life in ancient Egypt have been made on the basis of too little evidence.

Shaw does, however, admit that some conclusions can be drawn, for example when analysing the physical remains of kings preserved as mummies. Just as a CSI team can draw a great many conclusions from a corpse, the well-preserved remains of kings is one of the surer prizes of Egyptology.

Let's return briefly, though, to what we can know of the lives of kings. For one thing it is unlikely that they fought at the head of their army. Tutankhamen, who died at the age of nineteen, is depicted routing an army, yet it is unlikely that such a willowy young man would have been given command of an entire battle.

But not all mummies were wimps! There is one that has always been held up as a possible example of kingly battling, and that is the remains of the Seventeenth Dynasty Pharaoh Seqenenre Tao II. This mummy, with its attendant head injuries, has long been thought to be the body of a king killed fighting alongside his troops. But is that really the case? Garry Shaw, in the manner of a forensic detective, set out to discover the truth behind the mysterious corpse of the Red Pharaoh.

Before we follow his investigation it is worth seeing what we know about war in the time of the first nation to be established on the Nile. Indeed Egypt was the first nation anywhere, so war of a new kind was being pioneered – not war between tribes but war waged by a unified nation on whatever loose affiliation of tribes, city states and groups faced it.

We know, too, that somewhat ignominiously Pharaoh's army transported itself by donkey. Not horse and certainly not camel. Donkey bridles and saddles have been found from the earliest Egyptian eras, but camels are not depicted or even mentioned until the Persian invasions of the fifth century BC. Naturally there were horses as well as donkeys, but the donkey, with its staying power and ability to function in a dry climate, would have been the backbone of the army when it came to transporting baggage and personal effects.

We know that soldiers on campaign lived in tents erected with earthworks for protection. The king's tent, we can assume, stood in the centre of the camp with a shrine to Amun, the chief New Kingdom god. It is from the name Amun that the prayer-ending 'amen' originated, almost certainly entering ancient Hebrew and then Arabic and Greek. The accommodation was not bad on military expeditions that sought to defend the Nile against attack, or even push the borders further north. An officer's tent might have two or more rooms and a folding camp bed and folding stool, not unlike the kind of campaign furniture still in use today.

A man who had served as a soldier might be eligible for a land grant. A veteran who distinguished himself in battle might be awarded medals: a golden lion seems obvious, but there was also the order of the golden fly – what might that have rewarded? Sticking to one's target and refusing to be swatted? Khety, a scribe writing in the New

Kingdom, painted an unpleasant and therefore temptingly realistic picture of life in the army. He described rounds of brutal training, constant quarrels in camp, drunkenness, gambling, physical disablement
after battle, hunger, thirst, and ... flies. Perhaps the golden fly went to
the man who could ignore them the longest.

Though Egyptian swords have been recovered, with copper and
bronze blades and sometimes a hilt made of gold, it is almost certain
that the main weapons in those days would be clubs, lances and bows
and arrows. Just as most men who died in medieval battles suffered
broken limbs, a sword, with its propensity to stick in body fat, is not
the most efficient of killing weapons in a chaotic battle. Something
that will knock men down and keep them down is far faster; a cudgel
or mace is the preferred weapon, and if men can be levelled from a distance by using spears or arrows, so much the better.

Soldiers would march with all their gear up to a dozen miles a day
over desert terrain. Discipline appeared to be good since precise tactical manoeuvres were used in battle, using trumpets to signal the command. But was the king there directing the battle from the front? Let us
return to Pharaoh Seqenenre to find out.

His mummy was recovered, probably in its original coffin, in 1881
from Deir el-Bahri, a complex of mortuary temples on the west bank of
the Nile near modern-day Luxor. In 1997 this was the spot where fifty-
eight tourists and four Egyptians were murdered by Islamic jihadists,
turning the area once again into a place of death.

But in 1881 tourism was still in its infancy and Egyptology hardly
developed at all. The mummies were discovered by the grave-robbing
Abd al-Russul family who started their career burrowing out from
their houses in Qurna to find them. Two of the family, brothers, confessed under torture to what they had found. The mummies were then
removed to Cairo. It was Gaston Maspero, the great French archaeologist, who pursued the al-Russul brothers, though one imagines the
torture was something the local police added on their own. Maspero,
who had wanted to study dance originally only for his father to forbid
it, unwrapped Seqenenre's mummy in June 1886. It must have been
boiling hot at that time, so the fact that the mummy was rotting and
giving off a foul odour would have made the task still less agreeable.
The outer shroud was greasy to the touch and odoriferous and was
stuck to the skin beneath. Maspero immediately noticed three injuries
to the King's head (there are in fact five). These were surrounded by

whitish material presumed to be leaking brain matter. The injuries were first a large wound above the right eyebrow; secondly a mace or battle-axe blow to the left cheek that had broken the bottom jaw; and thirdly a wound, hidden by the King's hair to some extent, at the top of the head in the form of a slit – made, it was surmised, by an axe. From this slit brains had leaked.

Maspero's report indicates that Seqenenre's ears had disappeared, that his mouth was full of healthy teeth between which the tongue had been gripped. He surmises that decomposition had begun even before the embalmers began their work. The mummification process was also irregular and hastily done. No natron (a natural form of soda ash used for making soap, as an antiseptic and for preserving mummies) had been used; only fragments of spicy wood had been sprinkled over the body. The brain had not been removed. The mummy shrouds were penetrated by beetles and worms, with beetle larvae shells in the King's hair. Maspero guessed Seqenenre to have been about forty when he died and that he had shaved on the day of his death.

Later investigators noted there were no injuries to the arms or any other part of the body. For Garry Shaw this became an important clue. The massacres of the Tutsi by the Hutu in 1994 have left forensic anthropologists with much grisly evidence of the kind of injuries sustained in battles involving primitive weapons – typically clubs made from iron bars and wood and machetes. In other words, very similar to the weapons of the Egyptian battlefield of 3,000 years ago. Those same bodies that floated out into Lake Victoria from the Nile-source Kagera river bore similar injuries to those killed thousands of years earlier in battles at the other end of the Nile, just as it reached the sea, as if that seed of destruction had taken all of 'civilisation's' time on the planet to reach its furthest extent.

From the evidence of modern machete and club attacks we can surmise that in any form of open combat it is almost impossible to receive blows to the head without also receiving injuries to the arms and the body. And multiple blows to the head always involve arm injuries as the victim tries to protect himself – and has the time to do so between the individual, but not immediately fatal, attacks. This suggested to Shaw that the King had not been killed on the battlefield. He had no other injuries apart from the well-aimed and precise ones to his head.

Shaw used statistical studies of bas-relief depictions of battle that were anatomically accurate. These made the assumption that the type of wounds depicted would reflect their likelihood in battle. He found that head and neck injuries accounted for only 17.1 per cent of those depicted as dying whereas chest injuries were 70 per cent. In 'camp' scenes in Luxor temple only 12.5 per cent have head injuries alone. This further shows how the head, as a smaller target, is less likely to be injured than other more exposed and larger parts of the body.

Could it not be that armour had protected the rest of the body? There is no evidence, however, that soldiers of the Old and Middle Kingdoms wore armour. We first see its appearance in the Eighteenth Dynasty where tightly packed bronze scales were riveted to knee-length linen or leather garments. It is thought that helmets and body armour developed alongside the chariot, which was used as a mobile platform for archers rather than a personal speed wagon in the Ben-Hur tradition. In any case there were no chariots in use in the time of Seqenenre, so again it seems unlikely that this Pharaoh died in battle.

And who would he have been fighting at this time? The mysterious Hyksos, who Josephus, the first-century Jewish historian, believed were synonymous with the Israelites who were expelled during the exodus. He called them 'Shepherd Kings', his own translation of the Egyptian Hyksos. Modern scholars now believe the correct translation is 'rulers of foreign lands'. It sounds far less convincing. The shepherd kings were driven out to Canaan, which again is suggestive of them being Israelites. Josephus gets this idea from the Egyptian historian Manetho who in the third century BC wrote a history of Egypt, which along with Herodotus is the source of much that we know about the ancient Egyptians. Manetho's own name is derived supposedly from 'lover or gift of Thoth'. Though earlier beliefs about the Hyksos had them attacking Egypt as a horde, more current accounts have them peaceably infiltrating the Lower Egypt area of the delta – the area where Joseph and the Israelites settled.

We know from bas-reliefs and textual evidence that the King did not lack a bodyguard. This contradicts to some extent the fanciful narrative tradition of the King vanquishing an entire army alone and single handed, but it ties in with every observed military tradition: the killing of a leader, especially a royal leader, has a huge impact on morale. Therefore he must be protected at all costs. That a protected king could be assailed and killed by blows to the head only, while surrounded by a bodyguard, is unlikely. Increasingly it looks as if Seqenenre Tao did not die in battle.

Back to the forensics. Maspero concluded that the inept and hasty mummification was performed on the battlefield, or at least far from the capital, Thebes. The decomposition was the result of this hurried treatment and not the result of delaying mummification, since a proper embalmer of that period would have been able to halt any rot in the full process of creating a mummy. In any case, in a hot climate like Egypt, putrefaction begins almost immediately.

In the late 1960s, X-rays of the body showed that though the skeleton was disarticulated (as a result of mummification) no bones had been broken except those in the skull. It looked as if the King had been executed or, as some suggested, murdered while asleep. There was no healed skin over any of the wounds, which tells us that poor Seqenenre did not survive the attack, whatever form it took.

Was he asleep, or perhaps having a meal when an assassin sneaked up and belaboured him to death?

There has been in the past strong support for the assassination case. However, a king when assassinated is not spared a full ceremony of mummification. If Seqenenre had been killed in his own palace or even his own camp there would have been no reason to mummify him in such a partial and clumsy way.

Another point against assassination is the mixture of weapons used against him. From the several wounds to his head it has been noted that they were made by both Egyptian and Hyksos-type weaponry. Two of the wounds are consistent with a Palestinian bronze battle-axe, a weapon only found in the Hyksos region of the north-eastern delta. Other blows are more in keeping with an Egyptian handaxe or hatchet. It would seem unusual for an assassination to use such mixed equipment. However, the Hyksos had Egyptian vassal warriors fighting for them, so on a battlefield both types of weaponry would have been available, which would lend some credence to death happening in such a place – even if, as we have seen earlier, it was not actually during the battle that he died.

If Seqenenre was not assassinated and did not die fighting, how did he die? The other possibility is an execution of some kind. When people are executed by machete and club, their hands having been secured, we see similar injuries (though even here it is not uncommon to see shoulder-blade and collar-bone wounds where the executioner misses his target even in this controlled situation).

When I spoke to Dr Garry Shaw he explained that Seqenenre was probably kneeling when he was executed, on or near the battlefield. He also suggested that both sides of a weapon – the cutting edge of the axe and the blunt club-like balancing side – were used to despatch the King. After the killing his body was given a rudimentary mummification before being sent back to Thebes and its final resting place.

It is fascinating that none of the bodies of kings in ancient Egypt have anything like the damage found on a European king of, say, crusader times. Alexander the Great, contemporary accounts reveal, was covered in healed injuries. One of the most revered warrior kings was Ahmose, Seqenenre's son, who finally drove the Hyksos invaders from Egypt. Yet Ahmose had the kind of undeveloped body you might find on someone who had done nothing physically demanding in their life. He was literally too frail to have been the kind of sword-wielding hero the friezes and bas-reliefs and textual evidence reveal. Garry Shaw, when examining the relevant texts, found there was genre shift whenever a king's name was mentioned. From being a prosaic and unemotional account there is a sudden lurch into hyperbole. One is reminded of the great list of works and heroic discoveries that Kim Il Sung, Mao and Stalin were, according to their publicists, supposed to have made during their rule.

Seqenenre, the Red Pharaoh, seems to contradict the evidence that Egyptian kings kept far from the bloodshed. Yet we can now see that he was simply unlucky – being captured and killed in a manner almost as brutal as one might expect in the midst of battle itself.

12 · A classical river that rises in the Mountains of the Moon

A solution to a problem is to its possessor as a road is to the traveller.
Ethiopian proverb

The exploits of men like the Red Pharaoh spread Egypt's fame all round the Mediterranean. But it wasn't just war. Trade or gift goods from ancient Egypt have been found in Tunisia and Turkey. When in the first millennium BC the Greek Empire rose, its leaders and scholars turned to Egypt as a source of learning. And what they discovered was the Nile.

The Nile is *the* classical river. I mean, it is owned in some way by the classical references to it. Of course it is central to the ancient Egyptians and the Jews, but it was the Greeks who gave it some kind of extra glamour, lifting it out of the Middle East and into the European realm.

The current name 'Nile' comes from the Greek Neilios – which means, appropriately, 'river'. Neilios is almost certainly derived from the ancient Semitic word *nahar* or *nahal* that survives in the Arabic word *nahar*, meaning 'river', and the Hebrew word *nachal* for a smaller stream.

Homer, writing for eighth-century BC readers, described the world as bounded by an encircling ocean. The Nile was like its plughole, a drainhole reaching down through Libya to the further oceans beyond. At its source pygmies were to be found; and that is true, as pygmies inhabit the dark Ituri Forest abutting the Mountains of the Moon, the Ruwenzori range, source of much of the White Nile's water. Sceptical readers had for centuries doubted the existence of these moon mountains and of these little people, thinking they had the same reality as Homer's Cyclops.

I first heard the expression 'mountains of the moon' when I was eighteen. I knew it had vaguely classical overtones, that Caesar had written about these mountains and that they were in Africa somewhere. Beyond that I merely liked the sound of their name. Years later, when researching a book about a rare species of deer discovered by Père Armand David, I discovered that one of his students had been the Duke of Abruzzi, the first man to explore the Mountains of the Moon systematically, in 1906. This expedition had been prompted by a suggestion made by Stanley (of Livingstone and Stanley fame) – Stanley being the first European to glimpse them. The Duke scaled all the major peaks.

The Duke went on to have an interesting career, attempting to climb K2 and importing the first armoured tank into Ethiopia where it helped put down the coup of 1928. He was, at first, unlucky in love. He had been persuaded against his first choice in marriage (to a commoner), but he made up for it later by marrying a Somali peasant woman he had taken up with while setting up an experimental agricultural community in Somalia. During his time in Ethiopia he travelled to Lake Tana at the start of the Blue Nile, thus joining that select band of people who have double-sourced the river.

The Duke was really at the end of a long line of explorers searching for the Mountains of the Moon and the source of the Nile. Herodotus, the Greek historian and the world's first travel writer, was at the very beginning of this line. Herodotus still defines much of what we know about ancient Egypt and the Nile. His explanations about the Pyramids and mummification are still the accepted basis of our knowledge on these subjects. When he arrived in Egypt in 457 BC it was in decline, but it was still *ancient Egypt*, a place where practices and language had not altered in thousands of years. He was a skilful questioner and had a wonderful eye for what the *Sun* newspaper later called the 'Hey, Gladys' factor – any piece of information sufficiently intriguing to make a housewife shout over her fence to Gladys. At random: 'The Egyptians are the most healthy of all men apart from the Libyans ... on account of purging their bodies through emetics and clysters for three days every month.' Or 'Each physician is a physician of one disease only, one for the eyes, one for the head, one for the teeth and even more obscure ailments.' Or 'Whenever a household has lost a man the women plaster over their whole heads with mud.' True or not, it is certainly memorable.

Herodotus travelled up the Nile as far as Elephantine Island near Aswan in southern Egypt. It's a respectable journey of over 600 miles. A few hundred years later Eratosthenes would pay men expert in walking at an even pace to measure the exact distance. From this he would correctly calculate the earth's circumference. Elephantine is known for its ivory and its slaves, a blood island if ever there was one. Thousands of years later by some strange twist of irony a small island next to Elephantine became the gift of the grateful Egyptian government to Lord Kitchener, architect of the bloody River War. This war, fought in 1898, resulted in the slaughter of 11,000 Sudanese by machine gun and exploding shell. Only forty-seven English soldiers were killed. This bloodletting occurred at the point where the White and Blue Nile meet. (Yet another reason to name the subsequent river the Red Nile.) Today there is a fine garden on Kitchener's island and a hotel of extraordinary ugliness dominating one side of Elephantine. It bears a passing resemblance to a huge air vent.

Herodotus tells us scornfully that a priest suggested to him that the Nile rises between Aswan and Elephantine between two mountains known as Crophi and Mophi, in a fountain of unfathomable depth. Herodotus suspects the source lies far away in Africa, hence his scorn. We might scorn this priest's suggestion too, unless we read the story as a garbled version of reality, a mythological rendering of the truth.

What if the priest was relating the correct details of the real source, but in the wrong general location? Rather like giving someone a correct map of London but telling them it was a map of New York. By translating the details from Aswan to central Africa it all suddenly makes sense: we now know that the two most northerly of the snowy peaks of the Ruwenzori, Emin and Gessi, have lying between them a deep lake. This lake is the source of the Ruamuli river, a major source for Lake Albert and therefore of the White Nile. Perhaps this is the way a lot of knowledge in Egypt retained its accuracy while remaining 'secret'.

Aristotle refers to the Nile's source as a silver mountain – an allusion again, one suspects, to the snow-capped Ruwenzoris. He calls them by their classical name, of course – the Mountains of the Moon.

It is fascinating to discover that in a convoluted sense these mountains and the lake they supply – Lake Albert – are the real source of the Nile. The argument is that water flowing into the top of Lake Albert is equal in quantity to that leaving Lake Victoria. Therefore there has been no increase. And a true source from a hydrological point of view is the point when a river begins to increase in volume of flow. Lake Albert is still (as it was 12,500 years ago before Lake Victoria burst its banks) the start of the Nile's useful life; it is the place from which the river stops merely maintaining its size and starts a continual increase as it heads towards the sea.

For those, such as myself, who like to think that the ancients had it all nailed, there is further loose evidence that the Mountains of the Moon really are the source – even without invoking obscure hydrological definitions. Suggestively, the Ruwenzoris also join up with the rift-formed chain of hills that includes the upland area where the current 'real source', the Kagera river, rises.

When Strabo appeared some 300 years later in 63 BC he turned his attention to Ethiopia and the Blue Nile's source. For the first time in literature the Nile's flood is laid bare: 'Now the ancients depended mostly on conjecture, but the men of later times, having become eye-witnesses, perceived that the Nile was filled by summer rains when Upper Ethiopia was flooded, and particularly in the region of its furthermost mountains, and that when the rains ceased, the inundation gradually ceased.'

Which was about right. He also spoke of another source where the arum and the stalks of staphylini were twelve cubits high (about eighteen feet) – which sounds like the outsize and superabundant vegetation in the high Ruwenzoris. That is more loose evidence that everything worth knowing has always been known in some way.

While pursuing this agreeable fantasy one should not ignore the later religions. One hadith, or saying, of the Prophet Muhammad is 'The Nile comes out of the Garden of Paradise, and if you were to examine it when it comes out, you would find in it leaves of Paradise.' This could easily refer to the entangled vegetation of the immense swamp of the Sudd, but, more suggestively, the exuberant, giant, dripping flora of the Ruwenzoris comes to mind – a place of botanical strangeness unrivalled in its primitive grandeur.

From 7,500 feet upwards the bamboo towers to more than fifty feet high, only diminishing when the altitude creeps past 10,000 feet. At this height you enter the alpine zone where heather can be expected – but *Erica arborea* and *Philippia johnstonii* are no ordinary heathers – they grow to forty or fifty feet in height with trunks several feet in diameter. In the Ruwenzoris all year round it is the growing season; there is perpetual dampness but also exceptional quantities of ultraviolet light. What better place to identify as Eden?

At around 6,500 feet one encounters the giant lobelias – thirty-foot plants are not so uncommon, and many are over twenty feet high. The petals form dense flowers often ten feet in length. These plants have been seeded and can be grown, if treated with care, in England's cool damp climate. Protected against frost inside a greenhouse they may reach heights of four or five feet in two years of growing. Out of Eden everything is diminished, a pale copy.

Another giant, *Lobelia wollastonii*, has a whole flower spike, often fifteen feet in length, pale-blue woolly bracts covering a delicate powder-blue flower. That such vigorous growth is possible at such high altitude is amazing. When transported to Europe, however, the plant almost invariably fails to thrive and soon perishes.

More Moon Mountain madness: Stanley, in *In Darkest Africa* (incidentally in this book revealing himself to be someone far more interesting than the conventionally accepted gung-ho caricature), explained that he had found an ancient manuscript while travelling through Egypt. Oh, what images that conjures up: the Victorian explorer resplendent in his special 'explorer's uniform' (Stanley invented and popularised such a thing) wending through the labyrinthine souk. A hiss and a whisper alert him to some old wizened pedlar of antiquities. The man's shop is loaded with dusty treasures, but it is the ancient book that Stanley buys, for a Marie-Thérèse dollar he has hidden in his special 'gold bearing' explorer's belt.

Back at Shepheard's Hotel, making sure no one can see him, he peruses the manuscript which he has had translated by a bespectacled schoolmaster down on his luck. It appears to be a copy of an even older text. This was also in Arabic, and was known as *The Explorer's Desire* and was said to date from around the time of Saladin, the eleventh century. Stanley was so impressed he quoted at length from this long-lost book:

> Abu El Fadel, son of Kadama, wrote: 'As for the Nile it starts from the mountains of Gumr [almost certainly derived from *kamar* meaning 'moon'] beyond the equator, from a source from which ten rivers flow, every five of these flowing into a separate lake, then from each one of these two lakes, two rivers flow out; then all four of these rivers flow into a great lake and from this great lake flows the Nile.'

As Stanley confirmed Lake Victoria as the source of the White Nile, one can see that this text supports his findings. The ancient book continues: 'It is said that a certain king sent an expedition to discover the Nile sources, and they reached the copper mountains, and when the sun rose the rays reflected were so strong that they were burnt.'

It is interesting to note that in the 1930s, long after Stanley had died, the rich copper mines of Kilembe were found at the foot of the snowy Ruwenzoris. The Mountains of the Moon were rich in everything: water and mystery and now money.

13 · Powerstories: Aesop the Ethiopian

Two sharp edges do not cut each other. Ethiopian proverb

If there is one defining characteristic that separates the ancient and traditional from the modern, it is the store set by storypower. Though businessmen and scientists are rediscovering traditional stories as structures of advanced and subtle thought, this has yet to enter the mainstream of 'official' thinking. To traditional man, stories are the lifeblood of communication. To the modern man stories are, well, just stories.

Herodotus' text, like the Bible, Homer and *Don Quixote*, is just one story after another; indeed this was the form of all books until the modern era. One can see that the novel as an art form arises precisely when story begins to lose its official place and is being replaced by reasoned argument, logic, vaguely scientific opinion, politics, progress. The novel – as entertainment – is a suitable place for the story to retire to. And yet stories refuse to go away.

In telling the story of the Red Nile I haven't just happened on a mass of stories; it is as if the Nile itself is intimately associated with the generation of stories throughout history. It seems to attract the great story originators. One of these was Aesop.

I had made most of my journeys into the lower parts of the White Nile, but I ensured I did not ignore Ethiopia – the source of the Blue Nile, the place where the fountain of youth is supposed to be situated. It may well also have been the birthplace of Aesop. Though some traditions place him as a Greek slave, the African animals in his stories and the happy etymology of his name – Aesop/Aethiope – have led many to conclude that the stories are of Ethiopian origin, and the Greekness of the tales (and the language in which they were written) merely the nationality of the reteller or even scribe.

The Nile connects everything up: connections were appearing that I could not have predicted. Many commentators consider that the original source of Aesop's fables was a set of tales ascribed to a mythical African known as Luqman, a slave of Ethiopian origin. Delving further into orally supported traditions we discover that Luqman, the *hakim* or wise one as he was known, originated in Nubia, in a village on the Nile.

Luqman was captured by Greek marauders around 200 BC and taken back to Greece to work as a carpenter and boat builder – trades he had acquired in Africa. Most African slaves of Nile origin were known as Ethiopians, and when he started telling his fables and wise proverbs the collection became known as the Ethiopian's/Aesop's fables. A traditional tale has it that his rehabilitation to freedom and renown began when his master asked him to slaughter a sheep and bring him the 'best' pieces of the animal as well as the worst. Perhaps his owner planned to patronise Luqman by offering him the classy food in contradistinction to the inedible. Whatever the motive, Luqman carried out the task and arrived with a plate containing only the heart and the tongue. The slave owner was taken aback but kept his own counsel. He did not want a mere slave to get the better of him. However, the next day Luqman's intrigued master asked him to slaughter another sheep – and Luqman arrived with the heart and the tongue again. 'But how', asked his Greek owner, 'can these be both the best and the worst parts?' Luqman replied, 'In a sincere person the heart and the tongue are the best part of him, but in a hypocrite – the heart and the tongue are his worst parts.'

This somehow connected with his master's thoughts. The Greek was delighted and Luqman soon acquired a reputation for passing on stories which people wanted to retell. Eventually he was granted his freedom – to be able to wander and tell stories wherever he chose. When Luqman was asked how he had acquired his knowledge he replied, 'By observing the ignorant.' On another occasion he said, 'By speaking the truth and avoiding that which does not concern me.'

Many people, weary of the idea that such simple stories are merely for children, are naturally attracted to the Arabic tradition which states that Aesop's fables often have the opposite meaning to their stated 'moral'. The moral was the morsel needed to throw to the populace, and to kids, but that really each fable had a more useful, less obvious, more growth-inspiring meaning. Take the fox and the grapes story. A fox jumps and jumps to reach some grapes. Eventually he turns away disappointed and says, 'They were most likely sour anyway.' The standard moral is 'sour grapes' – we deride what we can't reach. But the inner yarn has it that the fox, a creature who kills for curiosity, stands for the merely curious part of ourselves, the part that wants to know things just for the sake of knowing them. Instead of avoiding what does not concern us, as Luqman counsels, we plunge headlong into things which may indeed harm us. And this frame of mind means any attempt at real enquiry goes off half cocked, since we have taught ourselves, like the fox, to give up easily.

Unlike a 'moral' tale, this reading of Aesop allows for any number of meanings. We have seen that it admits of a warning against casual, uncommitted interest. If we want real enlightenment – and grapes and wine turn up time and again in traditional tales as symbols of enlightenment – then we must relinquish something. This can also mean giving up on using 'reason' to create a justifying argument when things have not gone the way one wanted – giving up on a 'sour grapes' justification. By making up such comforting after-the-event arguments we insulate ourselves from the reality – which in this case is simply a failure to jump high enough. A really enlightened response is not the therapeutic use of argument but a practical response: go and get a ladder to reach the grapes. Get some assistance – a teacher, perhaps.

The fox, unlike Luqman, is interested in things that cannot benefit him. Until he learns to pay attention to that which concerns him and ignore that which doesn't, the benefit will remain out of his grasp.

Naturally, in writing about such matters I had to consider my own conduct. Wasn't I, on a more mundane level, acting out the worst kind of casual curiosity as I pursued endless leads that promised me enlightenment about the Nile? Perhaps. Yet I could not shake off the conviction, and it was only a conviction, that the Nile was the river of stories just as much as it was the river of history.

14 · The last will and testament of Eratosthenes, 194 BC

A hater hates even honey. Nubian proverb

A story. Eratosthenes, his voice carried by his breath, not distinct from it, rising and falling, dictates to a patient scribe whose face he has never seen.

'I am blind and I am old, and have been both for long enough to know these conditions as no more limiting than any other. Man is limited in his life, he carries his dreams of escape to his death. Now I have decided that the end is near enough: I will not eat again, to die by my own hand is of no interest to me, but to cease eating and to cease to be *that way*, is my way of leaving this life with some shred of dignity intact. The Library of Alexandria is where I shall continue to live – in my works – there shall the young meet me as their teacher when I am gone.

'What did I manage? I have shown the truth about the Nile, stripped it of all its ugly superstition. I have shown the truth about the world, its size and extent. The distance of the sun and the moon – all these I have shown, correctly and for the first time. Will this knowledge ever be lost again? Not as long as the Library of Alexandria exists.

'The Egyptian peasant still worships Amun, the sun, without knowing that the sun is impossibly distant. Nor does the peasant know, nor I, why the moon, which is so much closer and smaller, occupies in the skies a shape the same size – when seen from earth. Hence the moon can block the sun and the sun can block the moon – neither one nor the other can claim supremacy of size. It is as if the gods planned it that way. But the distances I know. There is no magic in that.

'To find the true course of the Nile, which I have shown a thousand times more accurately than Herodotus the old liar, is derived from my famous journeying to Syene to see for myself the sun overhead and casting no shadow to left or right. I had with me four trained pacers – who would walk at the same step for a hundred or a thousand paces. They marched only in a straight line, unless a bend of the river made that impossible. I measured the angle and course of any deviation and thus found the distance from Alexandria to Syene in Upper Egypt. It was knowing this that meant I could find the circumference of the earth.

'In Syene I was lowered down a deep odoriferous well, swinging on a rope until I could check *for myself* that there was no shadow – the sun was truly overhead.

'In Alexandria I had earlier measured the angle of the sun at noon as 7 degrees 12 minutes. The difference told me, along with the distance along the Nile I had travelled, that the world was round, was 252,000 stadia in circumference.

'In Syene I questioned all who would profess some knowledge of the river and its mysteries – why it should flood in summer and not in winter when every other river does. The answer was clear – the waters rise in mountains that trap the summer rains; in Ethiopia there are such mountains that receive the rains charged with water from the sea between Africa and India. It is said that Alexander himself did not know this and desired to – it is sad I was never at his service to relieve his ignorance.

'So it is my time too. It is strange, when one has studied the world one arrives somehow, also, at knowledge of oneself. Such knowledge tells me it is my time to die. I will not eat, instead I will rely on the light of the sun to nourish me. I have a feeling it may be longer than I planned. Perhaps I will live for ever.

'I have looked too long and too often at the sun, I am told. That is why, in my eighty-second year I am a blind man dependent on a boy's shoulder on which I rest my hand as he leads me around. But better to have at least glanced at the sun than to have hidden from its enlightening rays all one's life.'

15 · Carry on Cleo

One does not climb a tree to welcome the rain. Sudanese proverb

Eratosthenes measured the Nile and then the world. And, at that point, 194 BC, the intellectual centre of the world was probably wherever Eratosthenes cared to lay his hat, even if it was down a deep smelly well. A hundred years later, things had moved inexorably away from Alexandria and towards Rome, the high Greek Egyptian culture he knew in Alexandria in decline. It is thought that casual pillaging had begun to reduce the stocks of the library. So much so that by the time the library was burned (by whom, it is not entirely clear – Arabs blame Christians, Christians Arabs) there were hardly any books left at all.

But all that was in the future. In the time of Caesar and Cleopatra in the first century BC the city of Alexandria was still a great centre of the ancient world. It has come down a notch or two since then, as has the whole north coast of Egypt.

The much developed north coast is where I am, and right now I am swimming in Cleopatra's bath. No milk in this one – it is the outdoor version, where she disported herself with Mark Antony in 40 BC. It is hewn from the rocks but is recognisably rectangular and man-made and very near to the beautiful white-sand beaches of Mersa Matruh (where Field Marshal Erwin Rommel had his HQ in the cliff caves overlooking the town during the Second World War; in the little museum there they have his full-length leather coat donated by his son Manfred). Cleo would never have dreamed of swimming in the bright sun as I am – it would have destroyed her famous light complexion. In her day the pool would have been ringed with a hundred candles guttering in the sea breeze. There are no candles here today and no people except me. The water is chilly; it is all rather thrilling. The waves are still able to come in, and they fill the bath as the tide rises. The water is heavy, moving like a lazy body rising, salty, not really bathlike. In Roman times this natural harbour was called Paraetonium. It's 150 miles from Alexandria, so for Cleopatra and Antony to have used the bath they most probably did so during one of their many sea voyages along the coast.

Carry on Cleo: Cleo was a murderer, Cleo was a tart, when Tony lost to Gussy boy, she ran and broke his heart. When Cleo married Jules she did it to save the realm, when Cleo married Tony she was loath to leave the helm. Cleo was a murderer, she topped her dearest bro, and had her sister poisoned, the poor old Arsinoe. Cleo was a tart, she even slept with Herod, he fancied her so much he refused to leave her bed. Cleo was a ruler, the lastest Pharaoh ever, more beautiful than anyone and almost twice as clever.

Cleopatra VII was the last Egyptian Pharaoh. After her death in 30 BC the country was ruled by invaders of one sort or another until Gamel Abdul Nasser seized power on behalf of the army and the people in 1952. Cleo was the last Queen of the Nile who was proud to be known as an Egyptian ruler.

Not that Egypt hadn't been going downhill for a while. After Alexander had invaded in 332 BC and installed his own rulers, the Ptolemy family, there was a natural movement towards Greece. For a century at least the Ptolemys refused to speak Egyptian, preferring Greek – which is why the Rosetta Stone was written in both hieroglyphics and Greek (and was thus, much later, able to be used by European scholars to decipher hieroglyphics). But Cleo spoke Egyptian (which later survived as Coptic and in loan words to Egyptian Arabic). She was proud to walk like an Egyptian, and beautiful enough to carry it off with style.

The Romans had already landed, offering their services as security for Cleo's father Ptolemy XII. In order to ingratiate himself with Caesar, Ptolemy executed Caesar's enemy Pompey. Instead Caesar saw this as impudence and would have annexed the whole country to Rome after his successful battle of the Nile if it hadn't been for a twenty-one-year-old woman who charmed him so much he decided to live in Egypt with her for two years. And to let her rule instead. Imagine if Saddam had been a woman, so devastatingly beautiful that she was capable of persuading George W. to live in Baghdad and father a few more nippers? One suspects that the only way ever really to pacify a country is to marry into the ruling family ...

When Cleopatra and Julius Caesar visited Italy for the first time together, he fifty-four, she still only twenty-three, he had a brilliant golden statue made of her, set shiningly in the temple of Venus in Rome. She donated the Nile Mosaic, which is still in the temple of Isis in Pompeii. That Isis, an Egyptian god whose tears caused the Nile flood, should be venerated in Rome shows how influential in the ancient world Egypt was. In this extraordinary mosaic, it is quite apparent how the Nile is the lifeblood of Egypt, how the river's current and counter-winds make it the most efficient transport system in the ancient world. Yet Cleopatra, though drawn into the Roman world, was happy enough to desert it from time to time for Alexandria and the idyllic azure waters of Paraetonium and its outdoor bath. Her balancing act, a necessary one to keep Egypt from invasion, became in the end simply a delaying of the inevitable.

It was inevitable when Caesar, soft enough to give Cleo her own country, was not soft enough to give her his empire. Their son, Caesarion, was not named by Caesar as his successor (not a carte blanche to rulership but a distinct help nonetheless). Instead Caesar named his great-nephew Octavian, later to be known as Caesar Augustus.

Octavian knew enough to understand that there could be only one Caesar. After the murder of his great-uncle he eventually became allied with Mark Antony. Mark Antony, like Caesar, sought to rule Egypt – which, after Rome, was the richest prize in the ancient world at that time. But Cleo again proved seductive. Time, however, was running out. Octavian wanted everything for himself. He defeated Mark Antony at Actium and Cleo ran away – some said. Eventually both of them were run to earth in Alexandria, which only a year earlier had been the scene of such amazing feats of debauchery and dining the world still thrills to hear the details. But Cleo's time was up.

One might say that when Cleopatra deserted the Nile she lost everything, even her man. By living it up in Alexandria and abroad she forgot that rulers need ships and navies of greater strength than their enemies'. Perhaps she thought she could charm Octavian too. Not a chance; he preferred killing to loving.

Caesar, a greater warrior by far than Mark Antony, understood the need to remain connected to the Nile. When he entered Alexandria and was seduced by Cleopatra he did not resist, as Mark Antony later did, her suggestion of a triumphal cruise up the Nile to Memphis. It was a journey rich in symbolism and a natural act of unification in Egypt, where the Nile was the communication link, the transport artery and the source of all wealth in the form of the summer flood of silt and water. Three harvests a year made Egypt the richest domain in the Roman world. Cleopatra's wealth was legendary. She intended to hang on to it by using her extraordinary powers of guile.

And poison. One thing we can say about Cleopatra is that she knew rather too much about poison for comfort. It unnerved even her most ardent lover, Antony. When he took to employing his own tasters at the Alexandrian palace Cleopatra dipped her crown of flowers in poison and offered it to him to eat. As he was about to eat she snatched it away and threw the flowers to a prisoner, held in waiting for this purpose. As the condemned man writhed in agony on the floor, Mark Antony got the message: if she ever wanted to get rid of him she would – whatever precautions he might take.

Not that Antony was a nice man, either. When he lost the battle of Seleucas he asked Cleopatra if he might execute the general in charge of the Egyptian forces who had lost the battle on his behalf. And the general's family too. And their horses. The intrigue, the poison, the execution of foes and the families of foes recall the demented last acts of Hitler's Third Reich.

History remains fascinated by Cleopatra because she seems so unlike us. With her banquets that lasted until dawn and her extravagant actions she seems more like Elizabeth Taylor than a world leader. It's fitting somehow that Taylor played her in the quintessential 1963 movie.

The Cobra Queen had children by both Caesar and Mark Antony. At thirty-nine she was dead, by her own hand. In life she and Mark Antony had partied hard, very hard. They had formed a society, the Order of Inimitable Life. As the end approached they formed another: the Order of the Inseparable in Death. Somehow one is reminded more of Kurt Cobain and Courtney Love than the rulers of a great country.

The whole death scene is the final act of a melodrama. Or is it? Cleopatra would do anything to save Egypt. Two thousand years later and you see something similar in that modern Egyptian pharaoh, President Anwar Sadat. Someone who so completely identifies with their nation that they see no separation between it and themselves. And in that state of identification these people employ the personal as well as the political to achieve their own ends. This doesn't mean they subjugate their personal wishes to the needs of the country. It just means the personal desires have the imperative of political decisions that affect thousands, and that the repertoire of techniques to 'save the country' includes the intensely personal such as having an affair or prostrating yourself before another leader (as Sadat effectively did when he made the pilgrimage to Jerusalem to solve the Sinai problem for Egypt).

Cleopatra used her obvious attractions to get what she wanted. But that didn't mean she was someone who did not also fall in love and have some semblance of loyalty. She knew, though, that she was doomed in her alliance with Mark Antony: she could not simply desert him. However, he had to go. He'd become an encumbrance. She loved him, but that love would not diminish if he died. This is to strip it of the sentimental vein developed by Plutarch in his account of their romance, and brought to a fine conclusion by Shakespeare; yet, given all her actions, one is forced to conclude that Cleopatra would rather live to fight another day than die in the arms of her lover. And yet she loved him enough not to murder him. She wasn't a female Herod. She needed a way to force him to kill himself. At the same time, she dreaded being paraded through the streets of Rome as war booty if she were defeated. But would Octavian have done this? Surely he would have cut her a deal of some kind – this would have been her line of thinking, and yet his would have been – Do I need this troublesome woman?

Cleopatra was not yet forty, and perhaps still fantasised about charming Octavian. But for that to happen the first part of her plan needed to come off.

She had always made a great deal about poisons, her mastery of poisons, her ability to detect them. She had experimented on men condemned to death, and some who were not condemned who also died. Poison is the weapon of choice for those who have not the power to face down opponents openly. It is the weapon of court intrigues par excellence.

Though Plutarch, in his telling of the tale, makes much of her experiments with poison, it was a way of holding her own in the company of men. Mark Antony might challenge Octavian to man-to-man combat with any favourite warrior of his choice, while Cleopatra would lovingly finger her cobra or a phial of belladonna or wolfsbane extract. She knew precisely her bargaining chips: she had amassed great wealth in Egypt – indeed, as Egypt's Pharaoh, one can see that her rule was the turning point of Egypt's fortunes. It was the wealthiest country in the world at the time. Alexandria was a more impressive city than Rome. Octavian desired to mulct the Egyptians of all their wealth, their grain for sure but also their gold, their jewels, amassed over countless centuries of mining and trading with Africa and the East. That treasure hoard was the goal, and Octavian, being in debt in Rome, needed it. Did he need a queen? He did not, but he needed what she had. Cleopatra knew that this game would be played to the hilt – hence her mausoleum, which was, in effect, a bunker. It was built so strongly and cleverly that once someone was inside it was impossible for anyone to break down the doors. But there was a window high up, restricting entry to a manageable scramble of one, allowing some communication, but not much.

In the final scene, we have Antony, deserted by Cleopatra's navy and devastated, beaten by Octavian because he had tried to fight both on land and at sea. Octavian's navy was the better, and Cleopatra's sixty triremes soon turned tail and fled when the fighting went against them. As they had in previous battles. Cleo was a lover not a fighter. Antony knew this, and yet vanity led him to fight on Octavian's terms rather than his own. If he had kept to a land battle alone, if he had resisted Cleo's urge to help, history might have been very different: Egypt might have kept its wealth, largely as India and China did. There is every reason to believe that the Roman rule of Egypt, from 45 BC until the arrival of the Arabs in the seventh century, was an effective pillaging of the country from which it never really recovered. One might compare it to the delicate irrigation systems of Balkh, in northern Afghanistan, that supported a rich urban culture, destroyed by Genghis Khan and forever after condemning that land to a hand-to-mouth nomadic existence. Long waves in history, cause and effect, echoing down the centuries to the present day.

So, the treasure. And balance against that the children. Cleopatra's children, half Roman, half of the esteemed blood of Caesar himself, great-uncle of Octavian, these children she naturally wanted to protect. The eldest, Caesarion, was the most at risk. She sent him with a great fortune to India, to establish some sort of trading nation in its own right, a sort of government in exile. Her other children she would bargain for, using the treasure, the main chip, but also – and this was the eastern part of her, understanding how to realise its worth – showing just how much trouble she might be, both dead and alive. If she could play both those chips her children, and Egypt, might survive. Was she concerned for herself? It seems apparent that Cleopatra had the kind of monstrous ego that would not tolerate the insult and degradation of being treated as a slave and captive in Rome. Why, she had been celebrated there as a queen; to be dragged through those streets in chains was more shame than she could bear. But here the cunning began to show. The people of Rome were fickle. They appreciated courage in their enemies, and they had a fickle but real sense of justice. Cleopatra wanted to buy time so that Octavian would realise the dangers of parading her through the streets in a degraded state. She needed time for some kind of deal to be worked out. A better deal than him simply killing her.

Meanwhile he was bribing everyone, and Cleopatra did not excite complete loyalty. Antony's son Antyllus had a tutor who knew that the boy wore under his tunic a gigantic gem worth – well, worth more than his life. Betrayed, the boy was executed, but not before the tutor had made off with the gem. He was caught and Octavian saw that he was crucified. A double betrayal deserved such treatment: that was the message he wanted to send.

Now Antony had decided to throw his tunic over his head and kill himself. The Roman way. His exquisitely worked sword, his gladius, from which we get the word 'gladiator', was quite up to the job if he had done the deed correctly. Instead he missed his heart, which was the aim of the Roman method of falling on one's sword, and performed what the Japanese call *seppuku*, rupturing his belly in what must have been a ghastly and painful experience.

But, finding himself not dead, he forced his men to cart him over to Cleopatra's mausoleum where, initially, he believed she was incarcerated and dead herself. Except she wasn't. Hiding perhaps until she knew what to do next. Poor lovestruck Antony was unable to get Cleopatra to open the mausoleum from the inside. She claimed it was impossible. That it would be shut to the outside world as well as barred on the inside is not very plausible. To have constructed the tomb as a last resting place with no escape doesn't fit with the rest of the story. Anyway, in a moment of tragic comedy Antony used the last of his strength to manhandle himself through the high window only to crash to the floor inside. He asked for some wine, told Cleopatra she should trust Proculeius, the servant of Octavian, and died.

Next, Proculeius tried to get into the mausoleum. He too had to take the undignified window route. There is an unavoidable element of farce in all this, this extended death at the very end of the Nile. And yet this endgame is also the endgame of Egypt as a power in its own right. Finally Cleopatra was persuaded to meet Octavian, perhaps her plan all along (and certainly giving the lie to the supposedly escape-proof tomb, unless she crawled out of the window herself). In the version I prefer she put on a last-ditch attempt to seduce him. When this failed she knew that she would be paraded as a captured queen through Rome, which would be utterly shaming. Remember, this is a woman who played for the highest stakes all her life. She had already decided it would be utter triumph in life or death. Given that she could not succeed in winning over Octavian, she knew she would have to die in a way that would send a message through the ages. Some have argued that the asp that killed her, which would have been a cobra from the detailed description of her death, and was a snake used in state executions, would have been too big to smuggle in in a basket of figs. There are perfectly deadly green cobras three feet long. Cooled in an amphora of water to make it sluggish, such a snake could easily be coiled in the base of a basket of figs.

The symbol, one symbol, of Egypt is the cobra or asp. It adorned the headpiece of the Pharaoh. Like a snake the river coils through the country. Even today those who suffer a cobra bite are thought to have some sort of special blessing – if they survive. As recently as the 1940s peasants in the Fayoum would inflict a cobra bite on the earlobe of a twelve-year-old boy (after forcing the snake to bite on the carcass of a chicken). The lack of blood vessels in the region and the limited quantity of venom meant the boy would survive and almost gain a measure of immunity. In ancient times a bite was thought to confer immortality.

Yet, in Roman Egypt, the cobra was used for state executions. Prisoners were bitten on a raised vein on the trunk or leg. Or poison was collected and smeared as ointment into an open cut. We know that the asp was a cobra from the simple descriptions of death by an asp bite. Primarily neurotoxic, the venom causes the victim to suffer numbness of the mouth, tingling and paralysis of the limbs, a heavy weight upon the chest that grows into an asphyxiating torment, tendon spasms, coma and death. Unlike that of the other poisonous Egyptian snake, the horned viper, cobra venom can take effect in as little as six minutes. The viper's venom affects the blood vessels, causing internal haemorrhaging, and takes longer – sometimes up to twenty hours.

Cleopatra, as has been said, knew her poisons. In the final scene she smuggled a cobra into her chamber. All her entreaties to win over the victorious Octavian had failed. He wanted the Nile, he wanted the wealth of Egypt. After he was rid of Cleopatra, who had hung on to her possessions through her manipulation of Mark Antony, Egypt would have no more rulers. Rome wanted the Nile and would keep it.

The asp bit. Plutarch tells us that Cleopatra had two bites or incisions in her arm. We know that she tested her poisons on condemned prisoners, so she would have known that the asp was her best bet. Fast acting, the venom would do for her and both her maids too – a cobra carries up to one grain (sixty milligrams) of venom and only 0.18 of a grain is needed to kill a human. The venom is forty times more power-ful than the man-made substitute tubocurarine. Hemlock and other plant poisons have nothing on cobra venom, yet Cleopatra chose it for another reason. Mindful of the way a symbol will travel through his-tory without distortion, she showed that her death was at the hands of the one true god of Egypt: the twisting immortal River Nile.

Cleopatra was accorded a burial of some magnificence. She was laid to rest by the side of her beloved Antony, as much the cause of his undoing as he was of hers. They would certainly have been mummi-fied, it being the tradition until well into Christian times some five centuries hence. Plutarch implies that the tomb was in the centre of Alexandria; it has never been found. There have been searches as far afield as Siwa. A current favourite is Tposiris Magna, a desert outpost some twenty miles from Alexandria.

Cleopatra dead, after twenty-two years of rule – ten years more than Alexander the Great, who had started the Ptolemaic dynasty 300 years earlier – and now the dynasty was at an end, Egypt swallowed at last by the Roman Empire. Is there a modern comparison to bring home the enormity of this? America swallowing the formerly independent islands of Hawaii? No comparison. The British Empire swallowing India – closer. In any case there were still loose ends. Octavian was a cold-hearted and efficient emperor. He dispensed with the triumvirate, the tripartite rulership of Rome, as effectively as Napoleon disposed of the three-man Consulate, and was more successful in his Egyptian ventures than that later invader. Octavian knew the ways of Eastern kingship: kill all the contenders, especially those related to you. Double that if they have an auspicious name. Poor seventeen-year-old Caesarion, son of Caesar and Cleopatra – what a combination: if only his tutor, entrusted with the boy's life, had not sold him out somewhere on the Red Sea coast of Egypt on his way to Ethiopia or India. He persuaded the lad to return to Alexandria. Probably the pair had been scared and fleeced of their wealth, and the prospect of starting a new empire in India didn't look nearly as promising as a fat sinecure from the Emperor. Being no one is always hard when you have been someone since birth; maybe even being someone at risk is better than being no one living free. The boy obviously lacked the sense of self-preservation his parents had in spades. Whatever happened, Rhodon his tutor persuaded the boy he would be given Egypt to rule once Octavian had spent a little time there. On the way back to Alexandria Caesarion met the men Octavian had set to capture him. Far from getting to rule Egypt, Octavian's young cousin was tortured and then murdered. It is not recorded why or how he was tortured, but illegitimate murders are often dressed up as righteous and justifiable and perhaps the torture proved it, proved the lad was guilty of fomenting an imaginary revolt.

Cleopatra's other kids, the ones by Antony, were no threat as they were not fully grown and didn't have the Caesarian blood. They were taken to Rome and brought up as Octavian's by his sister. Cleopatra's daughter, also Cleopatra, was eventually married to the ruler of ancient Mauretania (located somewhat confusingly in modern Algeria). She had coins minted in her likeness, looking just like her mother, the Last Pharaoh of Egypt; but these coins were inscribed in Greek, not hieroglyphics.

16 · Herod on river duty

When his life is almost over the lazy person starts to be prosperous.
Egyptian proverb

The Nile connects everything to everything. Sooner rather than later. From Cleopatra we move, smoothly in fact, to the infant Jesus. The Nile is part of both their lives, but what links them initially is Herod, bad old King Herod, who had sided, in his youth, with Antony and Cleopatra against Octavian (who became, as we have seen, the mighty Caesar Augustus). Herod was friends with Antony, good friends it seems, and remained loyal to him even in the latter's defeat. Politically, though, he was a Roman. In all his quarrels, despite his Arab background, he sided with Rome (his mother was a Nabataean from Petra, his father was an Idumean – an Arab tribe that were forced to become Jewish on pain of death around 135 BC; this made Herod a Jew, though culturally he was Greek and had a Greek name and spoke Greek). When he had to face Caesar Augustus he removed his crown and openly admitted his previous support and continuing friendship, even after death, for Antony. Caesar admired loyalty and told him to put his crown back on again.

As a young man Herod was good looking, strong and decisive, but he aged badly. He married ten women and grew increasingly unstable and paranoid. His favourite wife, Mariamne, he had put to death because he doubted her political loyalty. After that he took to wandering through the palace calling her name and asking his servants to bring her when she didn't come. When they failed to return with her he had them beaten mercilessly.

He suffered from continual pains in his colon, intolerable itching all over the surface of his body, gout, swollen testes and 'putrefaction of his privy member that produced worms'. He also had a problem breathing and had to sleep, as best he could, sitting upright. Diviners said these diseases were a punishment both for what he had done and for what he would do in the future. Modern physicians have concluded that he had chronic kidney disease complicated by genital gangrene. Nasty. Certainly the great physical pain he was in did not help his delusions. He had his eldest son, the Crown Prince, locked up for treason. In ever greater pain, Herod tried to commit suicide but a local (and foolish, it must be said) retainer stopped him. In all the confusion the Crown Prince cried out from his gaol cell to be released so that he could take over the country. When Herod heard this he had him executed for treason ... and then died himself five days later, writhing with regret that he had killed his own son.

At what point Herod decided to have all the baby boys born in Bethlehem murdered we do not know – only that it was entirely in keeping with his deranged character.

Jesus, Mary and Joseph fled through the Sinai, or perhaps took a ship, to Egypt, a Roman-ruled country where Jews were also living. It was here they made their journey up the Nile, so legend holds. The Coptic Church has made much of the Holy Family's visit over the years; close to where I live in Maadi is a Coptic monastery which lies right between the Nile and the notoriously busy Corniche road. There is a kind of slipway down to the Nile and a few steps to the side mark one place where the Holy Family alighted. They only stopped for a rest break, so to speak, rather as if Keele services on the M6 had become honoured because Prince William stopped there on his way home from university one year. There are numerous other rest stops all the way to Asyut in the south. At some places the Virgin Mary has been seen. In a country that is around 10 per cent Christian it is by no means only that religion that is invigorated by reports of these sightings. Many Muslims too claim to have seen her themselves. But this is in a country where religious words are frequently discovered written in the seed patterns inside watermelons and eggplants. There is not much solid evidence of Jesus' journey through Egypt – he was still, after all, a tiny unknown baby at the time, and there was certainly no reason for Joseph and Mary to broadcast the fact that they had a prophet for a son, given that they had only just escaped his death in Israel.

However, there is a solid body of non-canonical gospel evidence and oral legend that supports the idea that Jesus visited Egypt at some point during his life. It's certainly possible – and Egypt was a centre of mystical teaching at that time.

What is certain is that Egypt was, from the earliest times, the heartland of the newly formed Christian communities that ringed the Middle East. The discovery, in the cliffs above the Nile at Nag Hammadi, in 1945, of the papyrus Gospel of St Thomas undermined New Testament certainties about the early days of Christianity. Nag Hammadi is about fifty miles downstream from Luxor. The farmers who found the cache of thirteen leather-bound papyrus codices burned one and the cover of a second, for reasons that remain obscure. They probably thought they were magical texts. The codices date back to the second century AD, to within only a hundred or so years of Christ's death. The only complete copy of the Gospel of St Thomas remains the one found at Nag Hammadi. Other texts contained within the remaining twelve codices include the so-called Gospel of the Egyptians, a fragment of Plato's *Republic*, some pages of Asclepius, the Apocalypse of Peter and the Second Treatise of the Great Seth (not the Egyptian Set but the Old Testament brother of Cain and Abel), a text in which Jesus accuses the prophets before him, in the way they have been represented, of being a laughing stock. It is believed that the Gospel of St Thomas pre-dates the canonical gospels; certainly its sayings of Jesus are worthy of as much reverence as those in Matthew, Mark, Luke and John.

There are many places where Jesus and Mary landed on their journey. Some have been the location of later sightings; almost all feature the Virgin Mary. For some reason she gets seen a lot more than Jesus, and Joseph is almost never seen. Within a short subway journey of my house there was somewhere important in this way, so I decided to check out one of the places that Jesus had been to during his flight from Egypt. This was in the fairly poor Cairo neighbourhood of Zeitoun. It's only five stops on the metro from me and easy to get to.

Strangely I also knew the name not because of what happened 2,000 years ago but from my reading of recent Egyptian history – Zeitoun had a prison where Sadat was held after his part in an assassination plot against a high-ranking Egyptian politician in 1948. Later, of course, Sadat himself would be assassinated.

I took the subway there and wandered the narrow streets that lead off the wide main street. I was surprised to see posters on shops depicting the Virgin Mary – usually such imagery is kept off walls other than those of churches. There was some tension in the air and people asked me if I was a journalist. I said no, I was a tourist. In 2009 a bomb went off outside a church during a wedding. No one was killed. It was another attempt to destroy the fragile but workable relationship between Muslims and Christians in Egypt. Picking on St Mary's Church was highly symbolic as it was here that both Muslims and Christians witnessed something very strange. Even Nasser made a pilgrimage to the spot.

I walked on amid the swirling traffic of battered black and white Lada taxis, boys with great square metal plates of bread stacked ten or fifteen high in a pyramid on their heads as they weave on bicycles through the jammed cars, donkey carts loaded with scrap and men carrying a knife-sharpening wheel, always accompanied by a child; all this is part of the attraction of Zeitoun. Oh yes, and the Virgin Mary appeared there in 1968.

A Muslim bus mechanic, Farouk Mohamed Atwa, was the first to see something strange on 2 April 1968. Then two more men guarding a parking lot agreed that there was a young woman on the roof opposite trying to commit suicide. The lot was just across the street from the church in Tamambay Street. The woman was on the domed roof. As the men shouted to her a crowd began to gather. It got larger and larger – as crowds quickly do in Cairo. Then someone noticed that the dome was far too steep for someone to walk upon. At that point the shouts of concern gave way to veneration and awe. 'It's the Virgin Mary!' No one knows who was the first to say it, but instantly the crowd knew it to be the truth.

Farouk Atwa went into hospital the next day for surgery. Some time previously he had been diagnosed with gangrene (of the foot, not the Herodian variety). After examining him the doctors were amazed to find that the gangrene had gone into remission. No surgery was now needed. Overnight the church became the spiritual healing centre of Egypt. People took photographs. TV crews filmed. You can see the pictures for yourself on the net. Strange lights and silhouettes, haloes – it all looks real enough; one of the best pictures is of a vaporous woman hovering over the church. No one could explain it. Even the most sceptical said they saw 'flashing lights'. For a while the Virgin would appear two or three times a week. In mid-May Nasser made a visit. He was at a real low point, having lost the 1967 Six Day War with Israel, and had offered his resignation. He had worsening diabetes and was taking painkillers, it was said, continuously. He went incognito and visited several times a week, staying in the car park until the Virgin appeared. In a twist only Nasser would have thought of, he brought a member of the Muslim Brotherhood with him as a witness. After a week of such visits Nasser and his man both saw the Virgin. It was even more official than when Jimmy Carter saw a UFO in 1969. The government put out a statement: 'Official investigations have been carried out with the result that it has been considered an undeniable fact that the Blessed Virgin Mary has been appearing on Zeitoun Church in a clear and luminous body seen by all present in front of the church whether Christians or Muslims.'

Nasser was so impressed he ordered the parking lot to be sold and a new church built there – an enormous structure with the tallest steeple in Cairo. It had been impossible to build a new church in Egypt during his rule, so this was extraordinary indeed. The Egyptian people did not accept his resignation, and, though not cured, he lived another three years.

Science took an interest in the pictures. Michael Persinger of Laurentian University in Sudbury, Canada, wrote a paper in the *Perceptual and Motor Skills* journal in 1989. He concluded that 'The characteristics of these luminous phenomena strongly suggested the existence of tectonic strain within the area. According to the hypothesis of tectonic strain, anomalous luminous phenomena are generated by brief, local changes in strain that precede earthquakes within the region. Psychological factors determine more elaborate details of the experiences because there are both direct stimulations of the observer's brain as well as indirect contributions from reinforcement history.'

He had discovered that 250 miles away there had been some unprecedented seismic activity which may have caused the strange lights.

One of the most curious stories involves the man who took many of the best pictures – Wagih Rizk, a professional photographer handicapped by a paralysed left arm caused by a car accident in 1967. He described the Virgin as he saw her on 13 April 1968: 'I saw her in the form of radiating light like clouds ... the light was very strong, so strong that the eye couldn't bear it and was seen near the cross over the small eastern dome. The apparition was awesome. Reverence and fear filled me like an electric shock.'

The following night he set up his camera on the roof of a garage. That first night he was too stunned by the vision even to push the shutter. But the next night he did, and took several pictures. Then he realised he was taking the pictures with his left hand. 'Five doctors, some of them the most famous surgeons in Egypt, told me it was hopeless and my hand would never move again. But the Virgin Mary miraculously cured me.'

Oral traditions in Egypt convey a different picture from conventional Christianity. Jesus is supposed to have been married and did not die on the cross. He is credited with many sayings, some collected in the Gospel of St Thomas, some still handed down as oral tradition by Muslims and Christians. There is even one tradition that he studied ancient magic in Egypt.

Egypt was the place where Christian monasticism first arose, where the desert bordering the Nile was chosen as a place to consider oneself dead to all life except the service of God; and from Egypt monasticism spread to the West, eventually dominating the culture of the Western world. But before that happened Ptolemy had to give us his map of the world. Ptolemy was not one of Cleo's clan but a Roman assuming her illustrious name. It is no surprise that at the centre of his map of the known world is the mighty River Nile.

17 · Ptolemy's forte

Rather than resembling one's father, resembling the times is better.
Ethiopian proverb

Claudius Ptolemeus, known to us as Ptolemy, was a Roman with a Greek name who lived all his life, as far as we know, in the Egyptian city of Alexandria – then under Roman domination – from AD 90 to 168. He was a scholar, famous for his works on astronomy and optics (greatly influencing Ibn al-Haytham, the first man who thought he could dam the Nile and who invented the camera obscura instead). Ptolemy also wrote copiously on astrology, but he is best known for his geographical work and especially his map of the world. He admitted that he was ignorant of the entire world, and his knowledge of the world's real size is inferior to that of his predecessor – his fellow Alexandrian Eratosthenes, the man who marched to Aswan and went down a well to look at the sun.

However, Ptolemy's map, and especially the section dealing with Africa and the Nile, was still in use 1,700 years after its completion, featuring in Richard Burton's book *The Nile Basin* as an exhibit supporting his contention that there was a second lake source for the Nile, which he erroneously thought was Lake Tanganyika (rather than Lake Albert, as we now know).

The map is surprisingly accurate; to last 1,700 years it had to be. Now that we know ancient Egyptians were penetrating through the Sahara and into Chad during the wetter period of the early dynasties, it is almost certainly true that such knowledge of the geography of Africa and the upper Nile was passed down in oral traditions among the nomadic peoples of the region. They might have been one source for Ptolemy. But wherever he got the information, his map correctly positions the four major source regions: the Atbara and the Blue Nile (with the Blue Nile correctly shown rising in Lake Tana) and the Albert and Victoria Niles.

Ptolemy is said to have relied partly on a Greek merchant called Diogenes who had travelled inland from Rhapta – which was probably an Indian Ocean port on the current Tanzanian–Kenyan border. Diogenes claimed that twenty-five days' march from the coast one came across the source of the Nile, whose waters flowed from the snow-capped Mountains of the Moon, the Lunae Montes, so named because of their white peaks which glowed even in the moonlight.

On Ptolemy's map the Lunae Montes lie lengthways and somewhat south of the two lakes that are the sources of the White Nile. This means they could conceivably be Kilimanjaro and Mount Kenya – neither of which has anything to do with the source of the Nile – though they are snow covered year round. Both are giant stratovolcanoes and not mountain ranges, which again makes them less likely as candidates since the Lunae Montes were characterised as a range. Finally, because they are volcanic, they are not associated with a rift-valley formation, necessary as a reservoir for the Nile's source. Given that Ptolemy is right

on every other detail it makes sense instead to ascribe the Mountains
of the Moon to the true sources of the Albert Nile: the Ruwenzoris – as
we have already tried to do in the earlier section devoted to this. The
Ruwenzoris fulfil all the criteria of being a true mountain range, snow
covered – the only mountains in Africa (apart from Kilimanjaro and
Mount Kenya) to be snow covered year round – and part of the same
rift formation that generated Lake Albert and Lake Edward. It is extraordinary to think that this information, almost 2,000 years old, was
only finally verified as correct by Henry Morton Stanley in 1879 when
he explored the Ruwenzoris for the first time in written history. It was,
as they say, a very good map.

18 · Christian mob murder attractive female philosopher

*A camel that was lost in the morning is not found by looking in the
evening.* Bedouin proverb

Jesus had been and gone. Within a hundred years his followers were
everywhere in the eastern Mediterranean. Religions competed – Mith-
raism and Christianity going head to head. It's nice to imagine that
Ptolemy's map was consulted by early Christians seeking places further and further removed from Roman persecution, since it was not
long after the time of Ptolemy that Christianity arrived in Alexandria –
Egypt being one of the first countries where this new religion took root.
    Christianity flourished as Rome declined. Monasticism, which fol-
lowed an ancient Egyptian mystical tradition of seeking solitude in the
desert, became the ascetic answer to the bloated excess of the Roman
Empire. Eventually this turning away from corruption became the
engine of the Western world's new order, and for six centuries the
dominant religion in Egypt before the Arab invasions of the seventh
century.
    Christians were at first persecuted by Rome, fed to lions and cruci-
fied. It does not seem so surprising that when the Christians gained the
upper hand things did not change so very much.
    In Alexandria, in AD 453, Greek learning had continued to prosper
under the Romans, but time for this old-world culture was running out.
Just as the culture was reaching a highpoint of intellectual freedom it

fell victim to the young, vigorous and bigoted new religion of Christianity. It is a mark of how evolved the city of Alexandria had become that the leading mathematician and philosopher was not a man but a woman, Hypatia.

Hypatia was brainy, beautiful, original and somewhat unusual. When she was approached by a suitor she drove him away waving a blood-soaked menstrual rag. 'There is nothing beautiful about carnal desire,' she shouted after his rapidly disappearing form. Not surprisingly, with tactics such as this, she managed to remain a virgin all her life. According to the early Christian historian Socrates Scholasticus, 'on account of the self-possession and ease of manner she had acquired in consequence of the cultivation of her mind, she not infrequently appeared in public in the presence of the magistrates. Neither did she feel abashed in going to an assembly of men. For all men on account of her extraordinary dignity and virtue admired her the more.'

Hypatia studied Plato and Plotinus and mathematics under her father, the philosopher Theon. She was known as not only the cleverest woman in town but also the best-informed person on matters to do with philosophy and mathematics. Was she an early sufferer of Asperger's syndrome?

Perhaps it was her uncompromising rationality together with a lack of understanding of social nuances, a feature of Asperger's, that led to her persecution. Her ostensible crime was to have pointed out logical inconsistencies in a rapprochement between the Governor Orestes and the Bishop of Alexandria.

A mob of lay Christians led by a hirsute rabble-rouser known only as 'Peter the Bigot' waylaid her chariot. Hypatia protested and tried to debate with them in a manner fitting to a top philosopher. But amid shouts of 'witch and pagan unbeliever' she was dragged out, and stripped naked as a further humiliation. Naked she was driven through the streets to the newly Christianised cathedral that had formerly been the Roman Caesareum. Here she was killed by having her entire skin scraped off with pieces of shell and broken potsherds. The bloody remains were taken to the gates of the town and burned. Socrates Scholasticus is fair enough to see that this was all mightily unjust, and he calls Peter someone driven 'by a fierce and bigoted zeal'.

Times change. A mere two centuries later and Hypatia had begun the slow descent into becoming demonised. The seventh-century writer John of Nikiu wrote that Hypatia 'was devoted at all times to magic, astrolabes and music and beguiled many people with her satanic wiles'. In this later account Peter has gone from being a murderous bigot to 'Peter the Magistrate'. And Hypatia, it now seems, got what she deserved.

Truth is resilient. Over the centuries Hypatia has refused to go away. She has instead become, in a way, canonised. She has inspired hundreds of fictional and non-fictional accounts, an Adobe typeface (Hypatia Sans Pro), a lunar crater and an asteroid belt, been portrayed by Rachel Weisz in the movie *Agora* and given her name to *Hypatia: A Journal of Feminist Philosophy* published by the University of Washington.

Strangely, Peter the Bigot remains an obscure footnote.

Part Three

RIVER OF THE BELIEVERS

Madness and mystics

1 · Mad kings and mad dams on the Nile

The day one becomes rich and the day one becomes bald are not known in advance. Sudanese proverb

The name Ibn al-Haytham, outside the rather specialised field of optical physics, is not well known. Many more will have heard of Roger Bacon, the English scholar usually credited with founding experimental science. Yet it was Ibn al-Haytham, in the tenth century AD in Cairo, who really laid out what we now call scientific method. It was he, centuries before Roger Bacon, who first outlined the modern scientific method of experimentation and drawing conclusions from hard evidence. He was also the father of modern optics, inventor of the camera obscura, a philosopher, hydrologist – a true polymath. He also said he could dam the Nile. And that was the cause of his downfall.

Ah, so where are we exactly here? We've had the Greeks and the Romans and poor old Hypatia. The Eastern Roman Empire, which would continue as the Byzantine Empire until 1453, was centred on Constantinople but spread its tentacles into the Levant, Greece, Turkey and parts of north Africa. The Byzantines embraced the Greek language rather than Latin and were Orthodox Christians. The split with the Western Roman Empire had happened early, in AD 380, followed shortly afterwards by the downfall and conquering of Rome by the Germanic tribes in the fifth century. The Byzantines, who were in power when Hypatia was killed, controlled much of Egypt and the Nile until, in the seventh century, new stirrings in the Arabian Desert brought forth an invasion army the like of which had never been seen: Islam was on the move.

The first Arabs in Egypt were true Bedouin – they disdained the great city of Memphis and lived instead in the fields of Fustat (now in central Cairo) in their tents. This alone shows their strength of purpose, their will, compared to the effete Byzantines and their glorious wealth.

But the Arabs then were no Taliban force of shark-faced dictators. They espoused tolerance and humour and believed greatly in the spread of learning. Indeed it is now a commonplace to state that it was the Arabs who reinjected Greek learning into the West through the great encyclopaedias and learned translations of Aristotle written by their scholars.

As the Arab empire grew to encompass Afghanistan in the East and Spain in the West, a huge revival in learning occurred, a true renaissance. It was in this tradition that Ibn al-Haytham was brought up. Without visiting Egypt he wrote a book on civil engineering in which he claimed he could build a dam and a series of canals and levees to control the annual flooding of the Nile. He wrote, 'Had I been in Egypt, I could have done something to regulate the Nile so that people could derive benefit at its ebb and flow.' Living in Basra, in what is now Iraq, he probably felt this theoretical pronouncement would never be tested. But he had reckoned without the madness of Caliph Hakim of Egypt.

Hakim's 'eccentricities' were legendary. He once had all the dogs of Cairo executed because their barking was driving him mad. Or maybe madder. (Having seen the feral-dog problem of Cairo first hand, I can offer a smidgin of sympathy here.) But it gets worse. Hakim persecuted not only Christians, but also Jews and Muslims – equally. He destroyed the ancient city of Fustat, the original Arab capital of Cairo, because its orientation 'displeased him'. He built a great library in Cairo to rival the House of Wisdom in Baghdad; then he sacked the Church of the Resurrection in Jerusalem. At night he would wander in disguise in the hills of Moqattam, said to be the haunt of mystics and madmen.

Ibn al-Haytham can't have been too thrilled when, comfortably sitting in Basra teaching the sons of the wealthy, he received a letter. His next job offer – dam the Nile. Only, it was less of an offer and more of an order, an order from a notoriously unstable ruler. But the engineer in him ignored all that and jumped at the chance to prove his theories right. He travelled to Cairo in 1011 to survey the task. Though the Pharaoh Menes, around 3000 BC, built many canals and desired to dam the Nile, no one had attempted such an undertaking until Caliph Hakim ordered Ibn al-Haytham to do so.

Ibn al-Haytham must have known that this monumental assignment would probably take the rest of his life. But the forty-seven-year-old philosopher and scientist probably did not suspect that it would cost him his life, or might do. But once he had met Hakim and started work it became increasingly obvious that turning down the job would result in his becoming another of Hakim's victims.

When he arrived in Egypt Hakim was so excited at the news that he rushed to the village of Khandaq to meet Ibn al-Haytham in person. Ibn al-Haytham, who was lodging there in a small caravanserai, was on his way to Cairo. The mad Caliph was so pleased with Ibn al-Haytham's plans that he pledged his entire treasury to complete the project.

Somewhat unnerved by his sponsor's intensity, Ibn al-Haytham now began the long task of travelling up the Nile to find the right place to make the dam. He found it at Janadil, a village near Aswan. As they passed the Pyramids and great temples along the way Ibn al-Haytham began to get his first feelings of disquiet. He remarked on the astonishing precision and workmanship and drew the worrying conclusion that these incredible engineers, who could build the highest buildings in the world, had chosen not to dam the Nile. There must have been a reason.

At Janadil Ibn al-Haytham saw that the high granite banks would be perfect for a dam. Then he measured the opening, which owing to the disparity between the actual river banks and the granite cliffs, looked less than it was. The banks were only 1,800 feet apart. Only. But the granite was 3,200 feet apart at ground level. At a point 360 feet above the river, the granite cliffs were 12,000 feet apart. More than two miles. Sixteen times the width of the Great Pyramid.

Unfortunately he was 900 years too early. He'd found the right spot, and years later this was where the Aswan dam was built.

When Ibn al-Haytham finished his measuring he knew he was in deep trouble. Without any form of mechanical assistance he'd need a million men to complete the dam, and even then it would take one or two hundred years. It would be folly to continue. It would be folly to return.

Reluctantly he travelled to Cairo to break the news to Hakim. If Ibn al-Haytham expected to be reprimanded, punished or even killed he was wrong. Hakim, as unpredictable as ever, offered him a plum job as an adviser in his inner court. Ibn al-Haytham accepted, again out of fear. He knew about such tactics. You lull a man into a false sense of security, you invite him into your tent and shazam – you strangle him with the silken cord of his own dressing gown. The Caliph Hakim was, Ibn al-Haytham now saw, a sly man, a feared man. Sooner or later he would turn on Ibn al-Haytham, the man who had said he could dam the Nile and didn't.

Ibn al-Haytham then pulled a master stroke out of the bag. He pretended to be mad.

Now, convincing a mad monarch that you are madder than he is takes some doing. The genuinely mad are very often gifted with a sixth sense for sniffing out the genuinely sane. It would have to be a class act. So Ibn al-Haytham went overboard: he ate foul beans off the floor – which he had placed in a bucket to look like nightsoil. He refused to answer questions except by singing answers. He insisted on wearing a mask when he left the house. He claimed it was the mask that did his talking as he had lost that power.

The ruse worked, kind of. Hakim had him removed from government and there was no question of Ibn al-Haytham being executed for failing to dam the Nile. Under Islamic law the insane have a protected status, they are untouchable. However, Hakim still had his suspicions, so he imprisoned Ibn al-Haytham in two rooms in Cairo for months, months that stretched into years. Strangely this may have been exactly the chance the scholar needed.

Imprisoned in his darkened rooms, Ibn al-Haytham began to think about light and vision. He invented the camera obscura – not surprisingly he felt as if he were trapped within one – and the camera obscura is the basis of all cameras that ever followed. He devised the first scientific thought experiments – because he had no chance of testing things in practice. He was the first to realise that the ancient Greeks were wrong about sight – we do not send out rays from our eyes that see things. Rather, light reflects off objects and that makes them visible. That he was imprisoned is obvious from his science: of the dozens of experiments he describes, only one requires the use of an assistant.

So, Ibn al-Haytham, imprisoned in Cairo for failing to dam the Nile, had much time to contemplate not just the scientific but also the mundane, the mystical and the plain insane. He pondered deeply on how to rid the world of the benighted evil of Hakim.

2 · Hakim goes out too much

Islam arrived as a stranger and will depart as a stranger.
Hadith of the Prophet Muhammad

The power behind the Egyptian throne at that time was not a man but Sitt al-Mulk, 'the lady of power'. We will see that she was not the first or last female ruler of Egypt. Her brother, and the reason she was able to rule at all, was the mad Caliph Hakim. His rule was so bad that she was welcomed as an alternative. Compared to his excesses, a woman was no madness at all.

Hakim started his problematic rule by *going out too much*. This was something no caliph should do, unless wearing a workable disguise. Hakim, on one memorable Saturday, made no fewer than six appearances. One on horseback, one riding a donkey, a third in a litter hoisted on high by a retinue of Nubian porters. At the fourth appearance he was seen on the Nile in a boat not wearing a turban. After this disgrace the fifth and sixth appearances almost failed to register.

Hakim was only eleven when his forty-two-year-old father died in the bath, as a result of taking dangerous medication after a freak accident (his foot had slipped off a carriage wheel and been twisted and snapped by the rotating spokes – he was in the process of whipping a servant at the time). It was hot weather and the body of the old Caliph needed to be buried. Hakim's father, like Hakim himself when he grew up, was a very tall man and it is reported that no coffin would fit him. He was carried to his grave in a box with the end knocked out and his bare feet poking out.

Hakim's sister, Sitt al-Mulk, who was sixteen years his senior, found her brother increasingly intolerable. He was obsessed with her apparent infidelities. And he hated the sound of barking dogs. There have always been stray dogs – the earliest travellers record their presence as something unpleasant but inevitable. But so terrified of Hakim were the people that they vied to complete the order for the dogs' destruction. One breed was rendered extinct. If a dog appeared at the head of an alley, day or night, it would be chased down and killed, stoned or beaten to death immediately. To try and kill them all, which Hakim nearly managed, shows just how insane he was.

People were terrified of his random malignancies. Hakim once walked past a butcher's shop, took a liking to the enormous cleaver stuck in a block, pulled it out and swung at the astonished butcher, cutting his head in two. He then carried on with his ramble through the city as if nothing had happened, holding the dripping cleaver by his side. Onlookers were so stunned that the butcher remained unburied, lying in his shop until three days later Hakim ordered a magnificent shroud to be sent to cover his putrefying remains.

Hakim developed a preference for nocturnal walks around the city.

Dressed in sumptuous clothes, bejewelled and wrapped in furs in winter, he and his retinue demanded that the shops be open at all hours of the night when they chose to visit them. The city became inured to this reversal of ordinary life. Indeed, as any modern visitor to Cairo will attest during the month of Ramadan, Cairenes adjust very easily to living by night. But once the city had become addicted to living at night Hakim changed his mind and decreed that no one should appear on the streets between dusk and dawn. All public amusements were banned. Wine, even for Christians, was forbidden. Gallons of wine were tipped into the Nile at Roda, turning it as red as blood. The entire grape crop was also dumped in the river, where it fermented at the bank, turning the Nile briefly into a river of alcohol. Even *mulukhiyya*, a national dish, was made illegal. (This would be like banning something like potato crisps in the UK.) Then Hakim ordered that no women should appear on the streets. Christians were forced to wear a heavy wooden cross at all times, Jews a tiny bell around their necks to warn of their arrival. Donkeys rather than horses were to be ridden by those of these religions – and this despite the Islamic ruling that Christians and Jews as 'People of the Book' were entitled to protection under the Caliphate.

The final descent into madness, and its resolution, were caused by the Nile itself. A persistent drought had meant food shortages. Hakim called forth his advisers and rebuked them for failing to solve the problem of the drought. Bread prices rose as grain grew ever scarcer. Bread is a sensitive issue to all Egyptians. There were bread riots in the 1970s that almost toppled Sadat. Hakim decided to tax it in order to dissuade people from buying too much. Instead the people revolted and bread riots spread through the city. It was a merciful release from all the restrictions they had been labouring under.

The increasingly lonely and ascetic Hakim took to wandering in a simple woollen robe among the hills of Moqattam. One day he disappeared. His sister ordered the hills from Moqattam to Helwan to be combed and all they found was a donkey with its leg gashed. It was said that this beast belonged to the mad Caliph. It was clear, to most Cairenes, that his sister, who would go on to rule for the next four years (using her infant nephew as a proxy and excuse), had killed Hakim. Allowing her to rule was not a problem. Hakim had been so hated that the person – man or woman – who removed him deserved to rule.

Yet Sitt al-Mulk had seemed genuinely upset by her brother's death.

Rumours abounded about how he had really died. It was claimed the real killer was a member of the Beni Husayn tribe who had killed the Caliph with three other men. This man was captured and interrogated. 'This is how I did it,' he announced, shoving a previously hidden stiletto blade between his own ribs and dying in front of his inquisitors.

3 · The strange confession of Ibn al-Haytham

One does not learn fully from one's host by remaining a guest.
Ethiopian proverb

'For ten years I have been under house arrest. It has been a fruitful time for me but I grew weary of the solitude. My single window, from which I could see the palace and the Moqattam Hills behind, was my sole joy for many months. The light that entered through this window was life to me. When the light ceased it was as if I were dead. The fellow who brought my food, and later his son, were contemptuous of me at first. I was known as the madman. But they brought me paper and ink, I was allowed to work. Using shadows cast by various engines and contrivances I made I was able to calculate all the distances outside my window. I knew, for example, that the Caliph left from a door 560 cubits from my window. That he passed under an arch on his nocturnal visits to the Moqattam at exactly 879 cubits. That he entered a cave exactly 17,987 cubits from the arch. This last was discovered by the warder's son who became my unwitting accomplice. I am getting ahead of myself. First I needed to demonstrate my use to them. I was mad, yes, but I had the power of seeing into the future, the power of curing all ills. The boy suffered from a partially severed finger. The stench of it was appalling but sheer ignorance and fear allowed the infected digit to remain, hanging on by little more than a thread of skin. He began to sicken and I saw that infection would set in and he would die. The father agreed to hold the boy down. I severed the finger using a barber's razor cleansed in a flame. Then I applied a poultice of honey and myrrh. The hand, and the boy, recovered quickly and I was now their physician. I took care to treat only the obviously curable. If they brought a relative who would be impossible to improve I would go into a trance, roll my eyes and pronounce them incompatible with

my peculiar talents. Over time I had sufficiently few of such cases to
win their trust – knowing that many of those I cured were going to get
better anyway.

'The warder's son, on my instructions, paced out the required distances into the Moqattam Hills and left two polished flat-bottomed
pots at locations I informed him of. When the sun was high the reflec-
tions off these pots could be calculated as angles with a quadrant device
I fashioned. I instructed the boy to scatter lentils across the paths at regular distances beyond the copper pots. Each day he reported whether
the lines of lentils had been disturbed. Quite soon I obtained a detailed
account of where my former lord and master took himself off to in the
lonely hills. There were rumours he belonged to a strange sect who
promised power in the other world … It was no concern of mine. I was
busy at the time constructing light boxes that contained one or more
candles. With these I proved that light beams that are separated by
holes in a screen do not merge when they cross over. Light must therefore be composed of particles of some sort that interact, but not in the
way, for example, particles of a liquid interact.

'I adapted one of these boxes so that a precisely directed sunray could
be captured by a curved mirror and then ignite a candle into flame.
Here I drew on the experiments written about in my book *On parabolic
burning mirrors*. This sun-powered device was placed in the wilderness,
its position noted on the quadrant. I ought to say that the area of the
hills his majesty entered was always checked and emptied of people
by a squadron of his trusted troops. My royal tormentor would, when
his troops had gone, then head towards the cave of his sect of fellow
idiots. This place was lit by a single flickering candle which served like
the lighthouse in Alexandria, to draw him in. With my device located
on the opposite side of a perilous ravine I waited for a moonless night.
Reflecting the rays of the setting sun with a mirror, I directed a light
stream at the capturing mirror in the device. I kept my burning mirror
still, using a heavy blacksmith's vice that held the quadrant with the
mirror attached. I had to trust that the candle was now alight, though,
as it was still daylight, I could not tell.

'The sun set in layers of glowing yellow and red, making the hills look
wonderfully wholesome. The squadron were completing their inspec-
tion. Night fell. Yes! I could see my little candle flickering, some way
ahead of the second candle that indicated the cave. I knew, though,
that the second candle would not be visible until it was a little too late.

'The following morning the blood-stained clothes of the Caliph Hakim were found at the bottom of the rocky wadi. He had fallen and his body was taken away by whoever wished to profit by such a manoeuvre. In my own case I was released a few days later and took ship to Basra without further incident.'

The disappearance of Hakim, who was missed by very few, caused great consternation nevertheless. A caliph, God's representative on earth, does not just disappear. The conundrum led to one of the major tenets of a religion still with us today. The Druze are the remnant cult of those who believe that Hakim will return. They had been formed from an Ismaili sect by an itinerant astrologer who had wormed his way into the confidence of the mad Caliph. Hamza ibn Ali told Hakim what he most wanted to hear: that he would never die because he was actually God himself. In a mystical sense this might have been true, but Hamza went one further and announced that Hakim would one day return in person, a statement that qualified him in the eyes of the Cairene populace as being just as mad as Hakim. The Druze were driven out of Egypt for their unorthodox views, finally taking up their current residence in the mountains of Lebanon.

4 · Ibn al-Haytham and the student

The road and an argument end when one wants them to end.
Nubian proverb

Ibn al-Haytham was free to get home to Basra, which he did. In his later years all the knowledge of his scientific exploits joined with the years of contemplation: he became known as a wise man, someone to be consulted, someone from whom one could learn what life was really about. It was said that by talking to Ibn al-Haytham one's best course in life would be revealed twenty years earlier than if one relied on the natural abrasions of life experience. If you listened, he could save you time.

Naturally this made him popular. He took measures to be hard to reach and sometimes did his old trick of acting mad to dissuade the unsuitable from bothering him for advice they would never take. But some, a minority, he was able to help.

Surkhab, a rich nobleman, asked to study with Ibn al-Haytham. 'Of course,' said the scientist. 'But you must pay me.'

'How much?' asked the bemused Surkhab, for in all honesty he had thought the bearded one would have been pleased to have a student, so pleased that he would teach him for free – for is it not written that 'wisdom cannot be bought or sold'?

Ibn al-Haytham still had the reputation of being mad. Or being struck down from time to time by bouts of madness. Surkhab knew this but he also trusted his own judgement. He was thirty-five years old and had seen enough of life to know these things:

1 A rude man can be more helpful that a 'helpful' man.
2 Real insight is rare. Mostly people repeat what they have just heard, or heard from their father.
3 Real insight is as slippery as a recently caught fish, and its reality as fragile as the scales of that fish reflecting the sun in all its glory in the moments after it has been caught, but dead and falling off after only half an hour in the basket on the bank.
4 Depending on circumstances, the opposite of the accepted truth can be the real truth.

Surkhab had mixed travel with pleasure, riding on his fine horse searching for men of wisdom and knowledge. He was interested in science, but he was equally interested in what men called the 'higher science', the science of how men could perceive God more clearly, know the future and live in greater harmony with themselves and others. By observing Ibn al-Haytham, covertly, over a few months' residence in Cairo, he saw that he was smiling, never ill-humoured, spoke well of people, yet was considered eccentric, possibly a little mad. He saw that Ibn al-Haytham knew about far more than he did; more to the point, he had a different perspective on what he knew. It was as if that perspective sharpened his interactions in daily life rather than, as he had seen with many learned men, muted or blunted them.

But he did not expect to have to pay money. Probably he thought to himself, This is a nominal amount enabling Ibn al-Haytham to 'prove' to his student that the learning was worth something. But calmly the wise man asked for 100 dinars a month. That is the equivalent of about £450 at present prices. Things were cheaper then because Ibn al-Haytham was supposed to live off copying one set each of Euclid's *Elements* and Ptolemy's *Almagest*, together with Euclid's *Data, Optics* and *Phenomena*. He earned 150 dinars for this – about £675 at current calculations. And we can safely say that 100 dinars a month was a surprisingly large sum for the young seeker to have to pay. He could afford it, but that wasn't the point. 'I'll have to think about it,' he told Ibn al-Haytham.

'As you wish,' said the scientist, 'though of course I may not be here next time you seek me.'

Surkhab finally decided to say yes, and pay the money.

He studied with Ibn al-Haytham for three years. When it was time to go Ibn al-Haytham gave him 3,600 dinars. 'You deserve this money all the more for having trusted your intuition that I had something to give. I, in turn, wished to test your sincerity. But when I saw that for the sake of learning you cared little for money I devoted full attention to your education. Do remember that in any righteous cause it is not good to accept a return, a bribe or a gift.'

5 · The grandmaster of the Assassins

Introducing oneself does not insult another. Sudanese proverb

Everything connects. The Druze, remnants of the cult of Hakim, had started life as Ismailis – that is, one of the two branches of Shiaism, itself a schismatic sect within Islam. Ismailis, or one significant branch of that sect, took up living in the mountains of Lebanon not so far from the Druze, whom they naturally disagreed with on many issues. But on one issue they agreed, and that was the elimination of the unbeliever. For the Druze this meant ardent fighting against the new menace from the West: Frankish crusaders. For the Ismailis it meant cutting out the rotting heart of Islam itself, by assassinating Islamic leaders. And from then on their name changed and they became known as the Assassins.

One hundred years after Ibn al-Haytham, the Islamic renaissance that encompassed the River Nile was already under attack. From roughly the twelfth to the fourteenth century, crude violent men from the West who called themselves crusaders sought to gain control of the Holy Land. It was related that these Franks did not even know soap or perfume and had lost contact with the advanced learning of the Greeks. All this they had to relearn from the Arabs, having forgotten everything except monastic rites after the downfall of the Roman Empire. They even indulged in cannibalism during their heroic attacks on Jerusalem.

The crusades were a holy jihad – by Europeans, whipped into a frenzy by the monastic-based culture of Europe, who feared that Christian access to Jerusalem would be barred for ever. Because they were rooted in primitive notions of revenge and 'rewards in heaven' rather than intermarriage and cultural assimilation, the crusades were characterised by acts of cruelty and strategic folly – in many but not all cases. By some law of unintended consequences, the crusaders and their enemies both learnt to appreciate the qualities of the other, and took such understanding home with them. But such judgements were far from the minds of the native people of the Middle East, including the Christians who already lived there.

Into this turmoil stepped a Kurd born in Syria: Saladin. He promised to free the Nile of the Frankish invaders and their allies. Unfortunately he had other enemies apart from freebooting European knights – the Assassins were after him. Some dispute the origin of the name. Did it derive from their use of hashish – still an export of the Lebanese valleys – or did it stem from the Arabic *assass*, which means 'foundation', and *assassyoun*, which means 'he who is most faithful to the foundation'?

Either way they tried to kill Saladin three times before he captured the Nile and stopped the Franks in their headlong invasion. The Assassins were sent from the clifftop eyrie of Hassan al-Sabah, the old man of the mountain, an impregnable fortress naturally called 'the eagle's nest'. Hassan al-Sabah, the Osama bin Laden of his time, commanded absolute loyalty. His motivation was simply to seek power for his Ismaili Shia sect – the Assassins – a sect that would eventually become known as the sole inheritor of the Ismaili mantle. They continue to this day, currently headed by the Aga Khan dynasty. Strange to think that a reference to the playboy Aga Khan in a 1960s pop song – 'Where Do You Go To (My Lovely)' by Peter Sarstedt – connects to the Assassins of the eleventh century. The Nile connection remains: the playboy Aga Khan's father, Aga Khan III, was buried in 1957 at Aswan, his favourite wintering spot (and also François Mitterrand's). Remember, Aswan is where Herodotus foolishly claimed that the Nile started and where Eratosthenes first measured the world from down the bottom of a dark well.

Back to the crusades. Little is written about Saladin's appearance: he was small and frail, it is said, with a short neat beard. Some accounts say it was red. More mention is made of his pensive, almost melancholy face, which would light up with a comforting smile to put people who were talking to him at their ease. He was always generous with visitors, urging them to stay and eat even if they were infidels; he would satisfy all their requests, accord them full honours. He could not bear to let people depart his house disappointed, and of course there were many who took advantage of this. Baha al-Din reveals that his generosity was legendary. Once a Frank called Brins of Antioch arrived unexpectedly at his tent and asked for territory that had been taken by Saladin four years earlier. Saladin promptly gave it back. His treasurers always kept a portion of the royal hoard hidden from their master, because if he knew of it he would spend it immediately. 'There are people', said Saladin, 'for whom money is less important than sand. If you are such a person it is foolish to pretend otherwise.' He had no taste for finery. When the fabulous palaces of the Fatimid caliphs fell to him, he gave them to his emirs, saying he was better suited to a vizier's lodgings than a grand palace. Besides, he liked a good siege tent best of all.

He had two aims: to unify the Arab world and to reconquer Jerusalem from the European invaders. The Assassins thought differently. At first they were driven by their own warped notions of Islamic purity. Then the logic of assassination soon became justification enough – they had perfected the means to kill, therefore they were always available to kill, perhaps for the leanest reason. The crusaders had taken Jerusalem, now the ultimate prize of the Nile awaited them – if they could stop Saladin. The Assassins would be their weapon, guns for hire in the Middle East.

The first attacker appeared at Saladin's tent door in 1175 during the siege of Aleppo. We can only imagine he didn't announce his presence like an Avon door-to-door saleswoman. He would have been stealthy. The stealthiest. But still, Saladin was surrounded by the best in the way of associate warriors. An emir sensed that this intruder was not who he pretended to be, a court insider, and barred his way.

There was no verbal confrontation – standard operating procedure among the hashish-using Assassins was utter silence. They were the Trappists of Terminal Prejudice. The answer to a fool is silence ... or in this case a scything dagger blow to the arm. The knife was sharp, made of Damascus steel. Even now its exact structural strength is a mystery to metallurgists, but this super-sharp steel was the preferred weapon of the Assassins. Often the blade had an inlaid groove – for poison. Assassins specialised in the use of poisoned knife blades: even if the stab did not kill, the poison would do its insidious work. The venom of a horned viper was commonly used, promising a hideous death by destruction of the blood system. Only quick action and application of an ammonia solution (or plain urine if that was not available) allowed an increased chance of survival. So, exit one emir looking for someone to pee on his cut arm. But exit also the Assassin. The emir, though cut, had managed to bring out his scimitar and in one blow cleave the attacker from clavicle to waist.

In 1176, when Saladin was again campaigning in Aleppo, there came a second attack. This time the Assassin burst into Saladin's tent and attempted to stab him in the head. By now the warrior leader was prepared. He had under his fez a chainmail head-covering. The attacker went for his neck, but here Saladin was wearing a high mail collar attached to a thick tunic. Saladin's guards arrived just as a second and a third Assassin burst in upon him. His reputation as divinely protected only increased when he miraculously escaped any injury from this concerted attempt to get rid of him.

Saladin received a message from the eagle's nest, from Sinan, the new Master of the Assassins. The messenger asked to speak in private to Saladin. The Sultan dismissed his guard apart from two Mamluks, slave soldiers from eastern Europe known for their fighting abilities, and their loyalty.

The messenger insisted he could not deliver his message unless they were alone. 'These men are like my sons,' said Saladin. 'They and I are as one.' At this the messenger turned to the two and said, 'If I ordered you in the name of my master to kill this Sultan, would you do so?' They drew their swords and said in unison, 'Command us as you wish.' The messenger then left with the two Mamluks, having delivered his message all too clearly: even your closest ones can be got to. No one can be trusted.

Derren Brown, the well-known stage hypnotist, has shown conclusively that it is not very difficult to implant a suggestion that can result in an attempted assassination. Perhaps this story reflects the fact that this ability was used by the Assassins. It has certainly been suggested before that hypnotism was one of the many tricks they used in their nefarious quest for total power.

Naturally Saladin was getting a little perturbed, if not annoyed, by all this attention. No more Mr Nice Guy. He decided to attack the eyrie-like fortress in Masyaf. Sinan, the Master of the Assassins, was absent at the time. When he heard about the siege he asked for another interview with Saladin at the top of a nearby mountain. Believing he had the Master within his power, Saladin sent troops to arrest him. But such was the power of suggestion surrounding Sinan that the troops returned shamefaced saying their limbs had been attacked by some strange force impeding their ability to attack.

Such suggestion worked on Saladin's mind too. Protecting himself with a ring around his tent of lime and ashes (a guard against both snakes and demons), he lay down to uneasy sleep. He ordered lights to be lit surrounding the whole camp and the guard to be relieved every half-hour. No one attacked and next morning there were no footprints in the ashes. Yet, next to his bed lay some scones, still hot, lying in a shape peculiar to the Assassins – a circle with a zigzag line, a snake across the ring of Solomon. There was also a note, which read: 'By the Majesty of the Kingdom! What you possess will escape you, in spite of all, but ultimate victory remains to us: understand that we hold you, and that we reserve you till your reckoning be paid.'

Saladin gave a terrible cry and his guard appeared instantly. Never one to be foolishly proud, the Sultan realised that he would be killed unless he lifted the siege of Masyaf. Which he did, departing so hastily that he left some of his artillery behind. At the bridge of Munkidh, his withdrawal noted, he received a safe-conduct from the Master of the Assassins.

Saladin prided himself on never being too proud. So he decided to try a different approach – conciliation. If the Franks could pay the killers he would pay more, and he would pay them with compliments. His combination of money and flattery worked. He successfully wooed them away from their old employers, one of whom was Amalric the Frankish King.

Saladin fought many battles and succeeded in ending the hundred-year occupation of the Holy Land by European immigrants. He also kept the Nile from becoming a Christian river, so to speak, five centuries after the Arabs had wrested it from the first Christians.

Saladin was old now, and tired from all his troubles. He passed his last days surrounded by his family. He had always suffered poor health but now, at fifty-five, he seemed prematurely aged. He died soon afterwards. His personal wealth at the time of his death was one dinar of

Tyre gold and forty-seven dirhems of silver. He owned no property, no
goods, and even his horse had been given away before he died.

6 · Moses of the Nile no. 2

One is not afraid to hold a snake in someone else's hand.
Egyptian proverb

Saladin's great adviser in matters concerning Egypt and the Nile was
the Jewish polymath Moses Maimonides. In the twelfth century the
Jews much preferred Muslim rule to that of the intolerant Franks. Many
migrated from Christian kingdoms to live in Muslim lands. Alexandria
then had over 3,000 Jews. Cairo had a Jewish population of 2,000. In
Muslim Morocco Jews were not harmed but one had to hide one's religion; not so in Saladin's Egypt, where Jews could practise openly and
hold high office in government.

Maimonides was born in Muslim Spain and then settled in Palestine,
which was then under crusader rule. But he found living under the
Europeans so wretched that he moved to Cairo. He was a lawgiver and
a physician as well as a wise man whose counsel was sought on every
subject. In Egypt he wrote his philosophical masterpiece – still in print
today – entitled *The Guide for the Perplexed*. Could there be a better
title for a philosophical work? It was said that Richard I 'the Lionheart'
(1157–99) was so impressed by Maimonides that he offered him the
position of vizier in his own court. In fact it was probably Amalric I, the
French-descended crusader King of Jerusalem, who was interested in
Maimonides. But wisely the sage declined. He correctly predicted that
any pact between the Europeans and the Egyptians (there were several
short-lived ones) would quickly be over, leaving any physician to the
Franks stranded with the enemy. So he restricted himself to helping
Saladin and his family.

Saladin suffered from malaria, endemic along the banks of the Nile,
but his health was never good; he used to take medicines of all kinds.
Maimonides had a different view. He counselled that minor ailments
should not be medicated, because that makes the body grow passive in
its ability to fight infection. He believed mainly in a healthy regimen as
a way of avoiding illness in the first place – a view in tune with current

theories about boosting the immune system rather than relying on intrusive pharmacological solutions. Maimonides quoted Hippocrates, 'Nature cures diseases.' He told Saladin, 'I have warned you, advised you and urged you to rely on nature as it is quite adequate in most cases if left alone and undisturbed.'

When Saladin's nephew, Taqi, who surrounded himself with a bevy of maidens, became impotent, he asked Maimonides for ways to 'enhance his ardour' as his over-exertions in the bedroom had left him emaciated, febrile, light headed and weak. Maimonides set to work and wrote a book for the prince entitled *On Sexual Intercourse*. (He had a knack for book titles.) He prescribed aphrodisiacal treatments and methods, yet also strongly counselled temperance in erotic pursuits. Maimonides denounced concupiscence in eating, drinking and copulation; sexual intercourse, though apparently energy enhancing, was really, like drinking, a form of disinhibition – which if it went too far resulted in spending all one's energies. As with drinking if one imbibes with friends, in a happy atmosphere with much laughter, the emotion will influence the intercourse in a positive way. But negative emotions such as anxiety, sorrow and aversion only work to reverse the palliative effects of intercourse. He counselled against intercourse with unattractive women, those with dark hearts and no laughter. He also considered women that were too young or too old a strain on the erotic energies of the Prince.

He prescribed black pepper imported from India to improve the sex drive. Hot spices mimic the sweating and rising blood rate of an intimate encounter. Maimonides saw them as a way to trick the body into sexual compliance. Honey water and a little wine were also recommended, though an excess of alcohol, anticipating Shakespeare, stimulated a desire that could not be matched by the performance. In between several learned quotations Maimonides says he will reveal a 'wondrous secret never before revealed'. This is one of the marvels of medieval Islamic literature – the utter flexibility of content from the obscene to the religious within a page. Maimonides says the Prince must mix some oils with saffron-coloured ants and use the blend to massage the penis for two or three hours before sexual intimacy. The resulting erection, the sage confides, remains even after the act. Medieval Viagra, or a treatment guaranteed to wean the Prince off sex for life? No doubt the formic acid in the ant-bite venom had some effect; it is interesting to note that formic acid is often used in the leather-tanning process.

He suggests making an infusion of alcohol with the herbal plant known as oxtongue. Oxtongue was used in Roman times as an elixir to dispel melancholy. Indeed European herbalists used it for this purpose, giving the herb the name 'borage'. This was the same succulent as the nepenthe remarked on by Homer. This, according to Pliny, was a drug that left one with absolute forgetfulness – medieval Rohypnol by the sound of it. Maimonides advises the Prince to inhale aromatics, myrrh and nutmeg especially. He ends his sex treatise with a blessing: 'May the Lord lengthen your days with pleasures, and may those delights be attached to eternal delights for the sake of God's kindness and goodness.'

7 · The well of Joseph

Breasts are two but the milk is the same. Sudanese proverb

Cairo was watered by the Nile and by a series of wells, not very deep, which reached below the Nile to the shallow water table beneath. But the Nile was no place to defend the Nile. Saladin needed a fortress. There was nowhere better than the site of Ibn al-Haytham's imprisonment a century before: the edge of the Moqattam Hills. It was high, dry and rocky, with the vast quarries of the Pharaohs still in evidence.

Here on the bluff Saladin built an immense fortress, the Citadel. The only problem was, it had no water. So near to the source of all water in Egypt, yet so far. This time he turned to his other sage and Mr Fixit – Karakush.

Sadly, Karakush has been traduced by history. Karakush has had his name ruined. Imagine a great man, imagine a great builder, turned into a figure of popular fun, something so low as to have his name synonymous with Mr Punch in children's puppet shows. Such is the name Karakush. In the East it was turned by one indefatigable enemy into a name to be ridiculed and lampooned. And this has obscured the real achievements of Karakush, eunuch and chief adviser to Saladin, builder of the Citadel and indeed the architect of the inclusive Cairo we see today.

In the twelfth century the Nile lapped the edge of Abbasid Cairo. The

Abbasids were the Sunni Caliphs of Islam whose capital was in Baghdad. Saladin was loyal to them rather than the Shia Fatamid Caliphs.
The Abbasid part of modern Cairo is known for Khan al-Khalili souk
and the Al-Azhar mosque. The Nile then bent westwards just above Old
Cairo, which is where the Coptic churches were; only years later was
this land above Old Cairo gradually reclaimed from the river. Where
the British and American embassies now stand would have been under
water most of the year in those days.

Between Old Cairo and Islamic Cairo lay Fustat, the place where the
first Arab invaders made their city of tents. Karakush joined all of these
places to create the Cairo we know today – and linked them with the
great fortress he built on the hills overlooking Cairo: the Citadel. Years
later, it would be at the foot of the Citadel that the body of Egypt's
second female ruler would be found. And it would be at the Citadel
that the Mamluks who had murdered Shajarat al-Durr, the Sultana of
Egypt, would themselves be murdered by the Albanian brigand and
future ruler of Egypt Muhammad Ali.

But first Karakush had to build the place. There was no shortage
of building materials in Cairo. Then. The old city of Memphis still
had temples and pyramids. These are now long gone and Memphis
is simply a string of villages on the west bank of the Nile – almost
opposite my home in the Cairo suburb of Maadi. The stones of these
monuments were used to build dykes, walls and palaces. But before the
Citadel could be built to protect the new and greater extent of Cairo,
stretching now from the Nile to the hills behind, a new source of water
needed to be found.

Smirkers imagine that eunuchs were weaklings, lithesome boy-men
who would run hither and thither, perhaps good at cleaning and cooking. Far from it. A man made into a eunuch after he has reached puberty
is like a clock with a lighter weight – it just keeps going. Eunuchs were
often the biggest and strongest men in the palace, and Karakush was
no exception. He towered over the diminutive red-headed Saladin like
a great dark eagle, which is what his name meant: Black Bird.

Karakush could not build the Citadel, perched as it was in the ideal
position on the edge of the Moqattam Hills, without water. Many had
seen the defensive advantages of the Moqattam ridge but none had
dared build there. Without water, and a lot of it, no castle is secure.
Saladin even doubted if a castle could be built there, but Karakush
was adamant: 'Where is the Nile? If the Nile is not five leagues away

then there must be water!' Not only was there the Nile, there was also the water that made the city of Cairo possible – an aquifer some sixty feet down that allowed so many wells to be dug in the city, making it unnecessary to go each day to the river to collect water in times of attack. Karakush knew he just had to dig. But where?

Karakush was aware that a well dug only a few yards from another can produce twice as much or half as much as its neighbour. It was all luck, or God's will. But Karakush favoured the old saying, 'Trust in God, but tie your camel first.'

God speaks through the world, thought Karakush, and employed a dowser to find the right place to dig. There have been dowsing rods found in ancient Egyptian tombs; cave paintings in the Sahara show men apparently divining with a wand of some kind; Herodotus wrote about the Scythians using a willow stick to dowse for gold; both Solomon with his staff and the Queen of Sheba were reputed dowsers for water and gold. But any kind of witchcraft was frowned upon by Saladin. Fortunately dowsing could be done at night, by the light of an oil lamp.

The dowser came fully wrapped in a robe; it was a windy night and the lamp flickered over the bare rock of the Moqattam Hills. He withdrew an ancient stick of myrtle wood, the origin of the magic wand used by magicians in the popular imagination. He sensed Karakush's agitation and raised a hand to still his impatience.

'Every mistake in this field is a mistake of greed: greed to discover, or greed to discover quickly – they are the same thing. We will take as many nights as we require to find what may be here.'

The dowser held the wand lightly in his fingers, explaining that the spirit of the water would speak to his own vitality and that would cause the wand to waver.

Back and forth he marched over the entire area of the proposed Citadel. Nothing.

'There is no water here?' asked Karakush. 'Not anywhere?'

'Oh, there is water, but it is too deep. Over two hundred feet or more.'

Karakush laughed. 'I will dig, just as my Lord has fought. We fight the easiest battles first and by the time the hard ones appear we have so much force behind us we will win.'

The dowser rubbed his scraggly beard and covered his chest against the cold wind. 'I will walk again, searching to any depth.'

Within a few minutes he had found the spot. 'Here is the most water, it is 250 feet down – not a foot more, not a foot less.'

'How much water?'

'How wide will the well be?'

'As wide as it needs to be.'

'I think eighty bushels a day for a six-foot shaft.'

'Not enough. For a twenty-foot shaft?

'450 bushels ...'

'That will suffice.'

The dowser accepted his money without looking to count. Without a word he had turned and gone.

The next day they started to dig. The workers were not the most motivated in the land. There were, as the historian Jubayr noted, more Europeans building Cairo than Arabs. These were prisoners from the crusades – put to work in destroying the Pyramids of Memphis and building the wonders of Karakush's Cairo. Twenty burly Franks manned the drilling tortoise. This was a giant jig made of palm wood which held drilling rods in place – two men taking it in turns to hammer while a third turned the drill swiftly by hand, moving himself out of the way in case of a missed blow to the drill base.

Karakush looked down one day to see men idling at their crowbars and picks. The hole was wide enough for twenty men to work side by side, breaking the limestone – but slowly, ever so slowly, as raising and lowering the tortoise to clear the stone took time. It was while walking in the vast ancient quarries of Moqattam, the quarries that gave the Pharaohs their stone for the Pyramids, that Karakush evolved the idea of using a step principle to excavate the rock. Narrow shafts were pushed through the rock and then linked by drilling sideways. The drill was simply an iron rod pounded and turned and pounded again. In the Moqattam quarries one could see how wedges of wood had been used to split the rock. It was into these drilled horizontal shafts that porous cedar was introduced, then watered. As it expanded, fissures opened up across the shaft enabling whole blocks to be lifted out with a crane made of palm trunks. Joseph's well got deeper and deeper. The name came from Saladin's own first name, Yusuf. Over time the place became confused by some travellers with another well, in Gallilee, supposedly built by the biblical Joseph.

Saladin came to inspect when the well was seventy feet deep. 'Still dry,' he remarked.

Karakush smiled, 'We are a third of the way down, perhaps less.'

Saladin looked thoughtful. 'If it is dry we will say nothing about it ever again.'

At a hundred feet it was beginning to get dark at the bottom of the hole. Karakush installed a giant, highly polished, tinned-copper mirror at the wellhead. One man was instructed to reflect the sunrays down the hole, providing light and a little warmth to the labouring men.

At 130 feet down Saladin heard a whisper. 'He has the place wrong. He is moving the well.' He said nothing to Karakush, he knew better than to question his most trusted aide. If one lost trust everything fell apart. But he did, a few days later, go and inspect the well, making his way at dawn down the spiral path half carved into steps that encircled and descended deeply downwards.

At the bottom a cave of sorts had been excavated, was being excavated, from the oolitic limestone. Some thirty feet from the shaft, in a westerly direction, tools discarded indicated a new and slightly narrower hole. So the rumour was right. Confounded, Karakush had been reduced to drilling in another place.

Still Saladin said nothing to his deputy.

The work continued. Month after month they dug and chiselled and split rock deeper and deeper. An ingenious second mirror was set up at the foot of the first shaft. This reflected light a short distance to a third mirror above the second shaft.

Finally at 250 feet down Karakush began to lose faith. The hole was completely dry.

At 260 feet he called the water diviner. Saladin heard and asked if the well was dry. He asked also why they had started a second shaft.

Karakush answered carefully. 'The second shaft is directly below the place indicated by the water ... expert. The first shaft is deliberately thirty feet east of the right spot. Halfway down that cave you refer to is a reservoir, since I calculate it will take too long to bring water to the surface by a single bucket chain 250 feet long.'

Saladin nodded and Karakush understood this to be an apology for having questioned him. The diviner could not, however, explain why the hole was still dry. It was a principle of Saladin's to pursue the same goal whatever the opposition, as long as the original reasons for embarking on that course of action remained. Karakush saw no reason to stop digging.

At 270 feet they finished work for the day in a dry hole. The next day, by some miracle, it was full of water to a depth of ten feet. It has never been empty since.

In 1976 the well was closed to the public as the steps had worn into a slope that was tricky and dangerous. I came across a poem that gave some indication of what it was like to descend the old well five centuries after it had been built (though the depth is wrong by a factor of ten – the well is eighty-five metres or 280 feet deep).

> We entered by the broken door,
> atop the high hill
> surrounded by strong walls,
> to keep the city safe.
> Full eight hundred metres deep
> we must descend;
> clinging to the creviced wall,
> down slippery ramp.
> Black abyss on our right.
> I dare not look down.
> Wrapt in silence,
> candles flickering,
> we delved those inner depths
> with unknown steps,
> down until there seemed no more
> way, and uncounted ages had passed.
> But wait,
> one bush, and into its tangled branches
> we must slide, ever down
> to that clear pool beneath
> where the coins shine.
> So many before us
> had ventured here?
> And from how long ago?
> *Giza El Aala, 1973–4*

8 · Shajarat al-Durr, shadow warrioress

The lower lip despises the upper lip. Ethiopian proverb

The long era of Islamic rule over the Nile continued. Many of the Sultans were bad and quite a few mad – but only one was a woman. In AD 1250 Shajarat al-Durr became the first and only Sultana of Egypt. Her life is even more venomous and convoluted than Cleopatra's, whom she perhaps rivalled in looks, as she certainly did in ambition. Shajarat's life was seriously complicated: she ruled after the death of her first husband, then murdered her second husband (she was his second but most important wife), but then she was killed by a slave woman owned by the first wife ... of the second husband!

They said Shajarat al-Durr was born more beautiful than the moon when it is just reappearing as a sliver of light in the night sky. They said she was as a young woman more exquisite than the remembered flight of doves in the wilderness. She was called the 'Tree of Pearls' because she was like a willow adorned with the greatest treasures of mankind. She had a voice so low and seductive, they said, that milk never curdled in a place where she could speak or sing. Shajarat al-Durr had green eyes, blonde hair and skin as white as mare's milk. Though she was born in Turkmenistan she came from a tribe whose ancestors had migrated west thousands of years earlier, one of the anomalous groups of the white-skinned and blonde-haired that exist in the world. In her life she was quiet and pious and known for never being deceitful.

She also murdered her way to becoming the ruler of Egypt.

Shajarat al-Durr started her career as a bondmaid to a rich man. What would she be today? A talented personal assistant? Someone ready of course to sleep their way to the very top. How she made it to the Levant we do not know, but it was there, as a slave, that she was bought and entered the life of Ayyub Salih, an Arab warlord of high standing. But Ayyub's luck took a turn for the worse, and in 1249 she loyally accompanied him to prison. Not very surprisingly, despite the presence of his mistress turned fourth wife, Ayyub's health seriously weakened while he was incarcerated. That she, alone of his wives, had accompanied him to his gaol was a sign of her loyalty, and of her steely character.

A year later everything had changed. Ayyub had recovered his health, stage-managed his release and was Sultan of Egypt – which was now under attack again. The Nile was in danger of being over-run by King Louis IX of France. It was the Mamluks who would defeat him.

Who were the Mamluks? Recall the loyal slaves of Saladin – Mamluks were slaves from eastern Europe and central Asia who main-tained their own extraordinary non-hereditary caste of warriors whose sole purpose was to serve the Islamic Caliphate. They were born as infi-dels (no Muslim can enslave another) and then offered the chance to make their fame and fortune as mercenaries. In Egypt their base was the fortress on Roda Island, symbolically in the middle of the River Nile in Cairo. Used by the Sultans of Egypt, they gradually achieved such power as to eclipse their nominal slavers.

> They care only about raiding, hunting, horsemanship, skirmishing with rival chieftains, taking booty and invading other countries. Their efforts are all directed towards these activities ... In this way they have acquired mastery of these skills, which for them take the place of craftsmanship and commerce and constitute their only pleas-ure, their glory and the subject of all their conversation. Thus they have become in warfare what the Greeks are in philosophy ...

The key is in the reference to horsemanship. The Mamluks were, in fact, the mirror image of their one-time oppressors, the Mongols. Many were recruited from the Kipchaks, a Kazakh tribe, some of whom had been driven west by the Mongols to settle in parts of Europe. They were far from the illiterate hooligans certain crusader chronicles have por-trayed them as: there is a considerable indigenous Kipchak literature, understandable even now using the *Codex Cumanicus*, a dictionary compiled by later Christian missionaries. The Kipchaks later absorbed their Mongol neighbours, and also provided the first Mamluk rulers of Egypt – Baiburs and Qalawun. Not that all Mamluks were Kipchaks; even before the later reliance on blond Circassians, Albanians and Balkan slaves there were Prussian Mamluks. Any sufficiently warlike tribe seemed able to convert to the military meritocracy practised by the Mamluks.

It has long puzzled historians, the wave after wave of warlike tribes rushing westwards from the Eurasian steppes. The answer is simple enough when you pause to consider it: horses. The steppes, like the American West during its brief tenure under the Plains Indians, were

perfect horse country. The steppe tribes were able to leverage their natural warlike tendencies a hundredfold through mounted assaults on
the largely foot-bound western peoples. The Mongols and, in sincere
imitation, the Mamluks were masters not only of the mounted attack
but also of the mounted attack by massed archers. The methods of controlling a battle were simple – banners carried by each war group were
visible to the commander, who could, at a glance, tell how his troops
were performing. Add to that a small manual of tactics that revolved
around superior horsepower and you have a virtually unbeatable force.
The tactics added vastly to the possibilities of battle. Outflanking is easy
if your men are so used to fighting on horses that can outrace anyone
over any terrain. The fake retreat can even derive from a real retreat
when the enemy is being stretched in pursuit, so you never suffer the
psychological difficulty of stopping a retreat turning into a rout – that
age-old military problem. If you can retreat faster than they can attack,
you can regroup and counter-attack when they are slogging up the hill
to meet you.

Mongol tactics all derived from the incredible familiarity they had
with their horses and their ability to strike from horseback at long
range and with great accuracy using their powerful bone, wood and
leather bows. Only with the coming of heavy artillery did the Mongol
methods finally lose their overwhelming superiority. To find a modern
equivalent one might look at how the development of the aeroplane
changed every conflict in the second half of the twentieth century.
Without air superiority no land battle could be won, whatever the size
of the army on the ground.

So, with these military masterminds at Shajarat's command, she
ruled, not easily, but through clever negotiation – for, at that time, large
parts of the Arab world would not willingly submit to being ruled by a
slave. Bedouin, famously, baulked at such authority, and this required
any Mamluk, however powerful, to cloak his abilities in the authority
of the Caliphate, the equivalent in some senses to the role played by
the Pope in medieval Europe. So even though Mamluk warriors under
the supremely efficient leadership of Baiburs and others managed to
secure the defeat of Louis IX at Mansoura on the Nile, they could not
immediately claim the throne.

In fact they would not have wanted to, since they believed that the
Sultan Ayyub was still alive. History really is 'his' story when it comes
to Shajarat al-Durr, since many of the historians who document the

period are keen to play down the effectiveness of this extraordinary woman and former slave.

Perhaps one should say something about the nature of slavery in those days and in that part of the world. The term had yet to acquire the extreme pejorative nature that developed after the experiences of Afro-Americans in the eighteenth and nineteenth centuries. Employment, as we know it today with all its securities, pensions, health benefits, did not exist. To some extent, slavery, at least for a military or administrative slave, was something similar to employment – providing lifelong security in an uncertain world. One might argue that the slave did not elect to become a vassal; the same argument might be used to explain the powerful social forces that encourage people to seek employment rather than run their own business. Even today, among Bedouin and tribal peoples of the Middle East it is a cause of some shame 'to sell one's hours', employment taking on the same negative overtones as slavery.

These überslaves, the Mamluks, who later would usurp their slavers, could be compared perhaps to the paid executives of a giant multi-national, who with their huge salaries and bonuses are eventually able to take a stake in the company themselves; they may start as the office boy but they may end as the owner of at least part of the company.

It is necessary to explain this in order to avoid the errors made in popular literature, where the Mamluks are portrayed as brutalised slaves in the modern sense of the word, avenging themselves on a 'free' world of Christians and Mongols. In fact the feudal nature of Christian Frankish life allowed far less social mobility for those of talent than the comparable systems in the Middle East. Indeed only the monasteries allowed talent to flourish, whereas in the East religious universities encouraged native academic talent and Mamluk orders nurtured those with military and administrative gifts.

As a woman, Shajarat al-Durr needed to be very cunning in order not to lose power when her husband died. He was ill when the French invaded and, Shajarat al-Durr knew, could not last long. As he lay dying the Sultan's hand was guided by his wife's as he signed over a thousand blank sheets of paper – for orders that Shajarat al-Durr planned to give. As soon as he had died, she exploited the traditions of mummification to ensure that he was embalmed and looked alive, if, one suspects, not quite his usual self. In a scene reminiscent of *Psycho*, Shajarat al-Durr and her two commanders who were in on the deception visited

and tended to the dead and embalmed Ayyub daily. Showing the same
nerves of steel that she would later use to hold on to the power she
had wrested from her dead husband, Shajarat al-Durr spent each night
alone with the embalmed man, sleeping on a couch at the foot of his
huge bed. What dreams she must have had! What waking nightmares
perhaps? But this was nothing compared to what was to come. Imagine
a Lady Macbeth who didn't go mad.

Her inner circle did not, purposely, include the militarily powerful
Mamluks. They could not be trusted to do more at this stage than fight
her battles. Her confidants were Fakhr al-Din, the Arab commander of
the Egyptian army (a free man), the Vizier, and the chief eunuch, who
had authority over the Mamluks.

Of course, word eventually did get out. This brought Turanshah,
Ayyub's eldest son, scuttling over from Syria to claim his throne, but
by then plans had been laid. Meanwhile Fakhr al-Din had been killed
resisting the ongoing crusader attack that was stopped by the Mamluks
at Mansoura. Louis IX was captured and was heard to mention, shortly
before this event, in tones of hubris, perhaps, that all he desired now
was to have the heart of Turanshah, preferably still beating, brought
into his presence. This pronouncement was made when things were
going well for the crusaders during the early taking of Mansoura by
Robert of Artois.

Shajarat al-Durr's general, the 'Bloody' Baiburs, laid a trap for the
French. By leaving Mansoura open he encouraged the crusaders to
enter a city they thought they could secure. Of course, Baiburs prepared
several secret ways to enter the city after dark. The surprised invaders
were driven to the river's edge and slaughtered, row after row of them,
falling 'like ripe corn' into the Nile. From here to the sea it was said
the Nile was red with the blood of the slain Frenchmen. Further Bahri
Mamluk attacks turned into a rout of the French across the wetlands of
the delta. Louis IX would live to eat his words.

Bahri Mamluks were so called from *bahr*, meaning 'river' or 'sea'.
These were the Nile-based Mamluks whose headquarters were in Cairo
on Roda Island. Roda is the site of the Nilometer, a stone-built structure
from where one can measure the height of the Nile's flood. Records
have been kept continuously at Roda since early Islamic times when
the job of recording was taken over from the Byzantines, the Romans
and before that the ancient Egyptians. Since information about the
flood's extent was essential for knowing when to break the levees and

allow water to flood the fields, the Nilometer was a strategically vital place in Egypt (there were other Nilometers further upstream, but the Roda Nilometer was the most important). It was no accident that the Bahri 'River' Mamluks chose as their base this centre of power for the Nile.

But though they occupied a power base, the Mamluks had yet to seize power for themselves. Turanshah, elbowing aside his stepmother Shajarat al-Durr, scooped up the lands and Mamluk soldiers indentured to Fakhr al-Din. The Bahri Mamluks grew nervous. Turanshah, like any CEO aiming to make his mark, promoted a new black eunuch as head of the royal household and another was made master of the Royal Guard. The white eunuchs and the Mamluks took note – though there is little evidence that such racial discrimination meant anything more than a preference by Turanshah.

The new ruler was said to be impetuous and of low intelligence. He also liked to drink – some said this was to control the nervous twitch that enveloped his left shoulder and face whenever he was contradicted by someone he feared. It was during a palmwine-soaked evening that he drew out his scimitar of Damascene steel and started lopping the tops off the line of giant tallow candles that illuminated the great tent in Mansoura. 'So shall I deal with the Bahris!' he shouted. The scimitar was so sharp it cut the metal holders in two when his sloppy aim missed the candles.

But such sharp weaponry would not keep him from his stepmother and the Mamluks, whom she informed of his vile intentions. To add insult to injury Turanshah demanded back the jewels his late father had given to his stepmother. His death sentence was only a matter of time.

In a master stroke Shajarat al-Durr sought to use the Bahri Mamluks; some said it was Baiburs himself who was behind the attempt. Nevertheless, in a scene similar to the death of Rasputin, Turanshah did not die easily. The first junior Mamluk assailant managed only to chop into his shoulder blade as the youthful Sultan slashed his way out of his tent. Here he met a solid ring of determined Mamluks. When the body of Turanshah fell senseless to the ground the still-beating heart was hacked out of its shell. With macabre humour this heart was presented to that other loser in the story – King Louis IX. Indeed it is recorded that this was done to cheer up Louis, who had been complaining that the ransom demanded for him by Turanshah was too high. The Mamluks cut a deal and Louis went home. On his deathbed, Turanshah's father, the Sultan Ayyub, had written to his son advising him to stay off the alcohol and treat the Bahri Mamluks with respect. Good advice, unheeded.

In the resulting vacuum Shajarat al-Durr offered herself as the only possible leader. One can sense the Mamluks as being slightly bemused but willing to take a chance on this, the closest power had ever come to them. Shajarat al-Durr minted coins in her own name. They claimed her authority as Queen of the Muslims by virtue of her being the mother of Ayyub's son Prince Khalil – though Khalil had died in childhood during his father's reign. In other words it was a transparent attempt to persuade the public of her authority. The Bahri Mamluks were not sure which way to go. On the one hand, she was a woman, and surely a woman could be easily controlled. On the other hand, despite her credentials connecting her to the former Sultan it was unlikely that the Abbasid Caliphate would endorse her rule. Shajarat al-Durr was not to be dissuaded in her mission. She needed a man to legitimise her rule. But not a powerful man, merely an acceptable one. A man she could control. We know she succeeded because for the next seven years coins were minted in both their names. In a society where women tradition-ally hid behind veils and *mashrabiya* screens, this was quite an achieve-ment, though not as unusual as might be imagined, as we have seen in the case of mad Caliph Hakim's sister, Sitt al-Mulk.

The man she chose was not an eminent Mamluk, not even a Bahri Mamluk, but he had been important in her previous husband's life. His name was Aybak al-Turkomani and he was the old Sultan's poison taster. He was also married, but such details had never stood in Shajarat al-Durr's way before.

9 · Bloody Baiburs' letter

The person who has a tongue has sins. Egyptian proverb

If there is a figure who encapsulates the sheer bloodiness of the Nile and the people who have lived there, it must be the leader of the Mam-luks, Bloody Baiburs. As an ally of Shajarat al-Durr, Baiburs had saved Mansoura during the Seventh Crusade and imprisoned there Louis IX.

Baiburs was born in Crimea into the Kazakh tribe of the Kipchaks. Then he was captured by the Mongols and sold as a slave in
Syria. There are similarities with the rise of Shajarat al-Durr. We are
taught that the past was impermeable to meritocratic ascent, that it
is only in the modern world that the poor man gets ahead. But here
we have the world being carved up by people lower than the poor
– slaves.

Baiburs wasn't even good looking. His first master, the Emir of
Hama, feared this fair-skinned short, energetic man with his single
occluded eye, a cast covering the green, an evil eye no doubt, and sold
him to the Ayyubid rulers of Egypt (for a profit: when Baiburs had first
been bought he had the insultingly low price of 800 dirhems, owing to
his imperfect face). Despite his odd eye, Baiburs was known for never
blinking. He made up for his looks by his fearlessness and his skill at
fighting. He soon became the Sultan Ayyub's main bodyguard.

Baiburs' tribe were crushed by the Mongols, but later it was Baiburs
who exacted the first defeat on the ever expanding Mongol horde. He
commanded the Mamluks under Shajarat al-Durr and then under her
killer, Qufuz, and ten years later at the battle of Ain Jalat he faced his
Mongol enslavers and beat them. All Baiburs asked for was to be made
Governor of Aleppo. But the Caliph Qufuz feared him and denied him
any reward. Baiburs then had his ruler killed while out hunting. Two
men broke the Caliph's neck and secured him upon his horse, slapped
the horse and sent it home. It was an insult to the intelligent, a transparent deceit – how could a man with a broken neck remount and ride
home? A hunting accident, everyone was told.

Now Baiburs was the Sultan of Egypt. He ruled from the saddle or
the military encampment and never went hunting with men he
couldn't kill quicker than they could kill him. He was truly paranoid.
A sultan in his palace is a sultan waiting to be attacked. At night he
slept badly and had nightmares. His stomach was reputedly 'not
strong' and he preferred soups and palliative dishes over the immense
feasts his contemporaries enjoyed. On moonlit evenings, when he
couldn't sleep, like Haroun al-Raschid (an earlier ruler whose behaviour
was mythologised in *The Thousand and One Nights*), he would patrol
the streets in deep disguise, listening for rumours and conspiracies,
unmasking spies.

He was known for the swift despatch of his methods. During a
siege he would promise everything to the inhabitants – a full pardon,

freedom, unlimited food and drink – if only they opened the front door
to him. They always cracked, sooner rather than later, and then he
would renege on all his promises and massacre all of them. Hitler used
similar tactics; the end always justifies the means. But Baiburs wasn't
as bloodthirsty as later Circassian Mamluk rulers of the Nile. He might
order a crucifixion or even a bisection, but only if no other course was
open to him. Though the Mamluks would later excel at siege warfare
they were not skilled at first in the use of war engines. Instead, Baiburs
anticipated the total war of later centuries and destroyed crops and
orchards around fortress towns in order to weaken their defenders eco-
nomically. If he could get his way without killing, then he preferred
that – as long as it was swiftly achieved.

In 1266 he was after the Mongols again, this time their vassal states
of Antioch and Tripoli, ruled by the Christian Prince Bohemond VI.
When Antioch fell Bohemond, who had not been present, retreated to
Tripoli. Baiburs sent an extraordinary letter detailing the massacre at
Antioch 'because their ruler had been absent'. He told Bohemond that
the same fate would befall Tripoli. In truth Baiburs knew that his own
generals did not want another lengthy campaign north of Egypt. They
wanted to return to the Nile and enjoy their plunder. Baiburs hoped
this letter would change history, by expelling the last of the crusader
kingdoms in the Middle East into the sea:

'It is a pity when the commander cannot witness the sacrifice his
people make on his behalf. And a beaten commander cannot rely on
the words of his friends. They seek only to reassure him. Rather he
should be strong enough to rely on the words of his enemy; these he
can always trust.

'When our men entered the eastern gate they marked their displeasure at being stoned from above by imaginative use of the hand cannon.
[Baiburs' use of the hand cannon in the turning-point battle of Ain
Jalat is the first recorded use of firearms in a battle.] Our men took the
Christian defenders and removed each one from his shirt of mail. The
hand cannon was loaded with rough projectiles made of granite. These
are not good at distance. The captured man was made to repudiate his
unbeliever's religion but refused. The hand cannon was manoeuvred
so that it would fire vertically and remove, at a shot, the captive's manhood. This was achieved on no less than seven occasions. In every case
no trace of the captive's equipment could be found.

'Many hundreds were treated to a Mongol staghunt. This in honour of your Mongol lords. For there in their steppe they hunt a deer by not killing it but by wounding it deliberately and allowing it to slow down its family. More deer are shot and wounded with spears and arrows in their legs and hindquarters. The hunt now takes the form of herding the deer sometimes over a cliff, or to a wadi with one end blocked. There all are killed. In the same way our men, using the sword and lance as clubs, broke the legs of those enemies who would fight and allowed them to escape into a street blocked at one end. All were killed by blows to the head as my men complained that the human fat spilled by so much killing had blunted their swords and what is more the blade would stick in the fat making this form of killing too slow.

'One amusement for our men was to boil duck eggs for half an hour until they were as solid as rock. These fine objects kept their heat well as they were introduced into the fundament of the city's best defenders. These men, unable to use their bound arms, were burned on the insides by this interesting method of dispatch.

'Many who were not killed were deprived of their noses and ears, which I believe you received some while ago. Thinking they were now free my men allowed themselves a small joke by capturing again these deformed ones and drowning them in several barrels full of mares' milk, which turned red with the blood from their burst lungs.

'Naturally the women and children did not escape. Many were killed together. The women with the most spirit of defiance were herded to the top of high buildings and urged at lance point to jump. None survived except one, whose head was crushed by a watching halberdier. No children survived. They were encouraged at sword point into the latrines of the city and caused to be drowned in excrement.

'This will be your fate and the fate of all your people if you do not surrender. Your red flags have been replaced everywhere by our yellow flags, your bells are now silenced by the cry of Allah Akhbar! Called from every mosque.'

True or not, the letter had the desired effect and Bohemond decided not to fight. It was a masterful stroke; the letter was so bloodcurdling that Bohemond agreed to a truce, sparing Baiburs the need to commit real bloodshed.

10 · The heart is where the home is

Something troubling one's legs is better than something troubling the heart.
Nubian proverb

The Red Nile: it is a river that has turned red with the blood of invading armies, red with the colour of silt, red with the colour of ancient plagues; on this river it is wildly appropriate that the innermost secrets of blood should be discovered.

Mansoura is a town on the Nile. It is north of Cairo in the delta, where the Nile forks to run its last miles into the Mediterranean. Formed by several million years of silt, the delta is the most prosperous part of Egypt. It is also, as we have heard, the place where Baiburs stopped the crusader advance into Egypt and imprisoned Louis IX. And it is where Baiburs' most trusted friend, the physician Ibn al-Nafis, started the Al-Nassri hospital and wrote many of his medical works.

Not that he did much anatomy – Al-Nafis said he loved animals too much to dissect them for the sake of science, an unusually enlightened approach. What he learnt about the body must have come from studying humans rather than animals. But what he did discover was extraordinary – he wrote over eighty volumes on medical topics alone. He wrote just as much on theological, legal and general subjects. His philosophical novel *Theologicus Autodidacticus* is credited with being the first sci-fi novel. And 400 years before William Harvey, he discovered how the blood circulated in the body.

Until Al-Nafis, it was the second-century BC Greek, Galen, who was the accepted authority on the mechanisms of the human body. Galen's theory, which had been accepted by the great polymath Avicenna (on whom Al-Nafis would write a commentary dealing with the function of the heart and lungs), was that a plethora of invisible pores perforated the cardiac septum allowing air somehow to enter the bloodstream. He postulated that the venous and the arterial blood systems were entirely separate. Until recently it has been a medical orthodoxy, playing to the Western sense of self-importance when it comes to scientific discovery, that the world was ignorant of the way the blood circulated until Harvey, anatomy lecturer and physician extraordinary to James I. It seems an odd sort of historical symmetry that both of these discoverers of the secrets of blood circulation should have been favoured physicians of their particular monarch. Harvey, though, was a cutter. In his anatomy lectures he made it a rule 'to cut up as much as may be in the sight of the audience'. But we now know that he was not the first. In 1924, while rootling through the vast archives of the Prussian State Library in Berlin, an Egyptian doctor named Muhyi al-Din al-Tatawi came across Al-Nafis' *Commentary on Anatomy in Avicenna's Canon* (1242). Al-Nafis had been twenty-nine when he wrote it. Towards the end of the fifteenth century the Venetian scholar and diplomat Andrea Alpago had translated another of Al-Nafis' works – a compendium of drugs used in the Arab world – and in a side-note mentioned Al-Nafis' disagreement with Galen about the circulation of the blood. Alpago's nephew published this book in 1547 – and it was reprinted in 1556, 1562, 1582 and 1595. Harvey studied medicine in Padua from 1599 to 1602 when he graduated as a doctor. Almost certainly he read or heard mention of Al-Nafis' ideas at that time.

Al-Nafis wrote:

the blood from the right chamber of the heart must arrive at the left chamber but there is no direct pathway between them. The thick septum of the heart is not perforated and does not have visible pores as some people thought or invisible pores as Galen thought. The blood from the right chamber must flow through the vena arteriosa to the lungs, spread through its substances, be mingled there with air, pass through the arteria venosa to reach the left chamber of the heart.

Perhaps Al-Nafis, who was born in Damascus and came to Cairo in 1236, was inspired by the ebb and flood of the Nile in his description of how the heart worked. Galen could not see how the vastly dissimilar-seeming venous and arterial systems could be the same. But the Nile in flood is vastly different from the Nile in ebb, as different as the extravagant bounty of arterial blood compared to the thin offerings of a vein.

The need of the lungs for the vena arteriosa is to transport to it the blood that has been thinned and warmed in the heart, so that what seeps through the pores of the branches of this vessel into the alveoli of the lungs may mix with what there is of air therein and combine with it, the resultant composite becoming fit to be spirit, when this mixing takes place in the left cavity of the heart.

Al-Nafis states his position unequivocally:

> The heart has only two ventricles ... and between these two there is
> absolutely no opening. Also dissection gives this lie to what they said,
> as the septum between these two cavities is much thicker than else-
> where. The benefit of this blood (that is in the right cavity) is to go up
> to the lungs, mix with what is in the lungs of air, then pass through
> the arteria venosa to the left cavity of the two cavities of the heart ...

The flood of the Nile brings nourishment to the land in the form of
waterborne silt. Al-Nafis might have had this in mind when writing:

> again his [Avicenna's] statement that the blood that is in the right
> side is to nourish the heart is not true at all, for the nourishment to
> the heart is from the blood that goes through the vessels that perme-
> ate the body of the heart.

That one of the most bloodcurdling of rulers should have the discoverer of the circulation of the blood as his personal physician seems
appropriate. Yet I like to think it was the Nile that provided him with
the answers, not the vast numbers of corpses his ruler made available
to the world.

It is reported that Al-Nafis, when not working, loved the spectacle
of fireworks (which must have arrived from China along with Baiburs'
hand cannon), great bonfires, jugglers, tumblers and conjurors of every
stripe.

11 · The poison taster's wife

When a woman is pregnant she is equal to all other pregnant women.
Ethiopian proverb

Many of the roles of modern government originated in apparently
menial servant chores, chores which, however, required great loyalty.
And all regimes are built on loyalty ahead of intelligence, competence
and flair, for without loyalty the enemy assassin could strike at any
time – as Saladin knew. The chamberlain was originally the master

of the bedchamber. The chancellor was the doorkeeper to the ruler's quarters, but doorkeeper can be a very powerful job when government becomes established and bureaucratic. Men who occupied these posts could expect promotion, perhaps to the key position of sultan. However, in the case of Ayyub it was none of the more prominent Mamluks who became sultan. Shajarat al-Durr, fully intending to keep her position as ruler, required someone connected to the former ruler, acceptable to Bahri Mamluks but not one of them – because that would grant them too much power. Such a person was Aybak, Ayyub's former poison taster.

In a culture as paranoid and unhealthy as that of the Mamluk court, poison taster was a key job. Not only absolute loyalty was required, but also courage, and competence – since the key requirement was managing the kitchens in such a way that poison could not be introduced at any stage in the proceedings from kitchen to dining room. And even employing only chefs from the village of Manial Shiha, which Aybak did, as this was a place not only where good cooking could be found but where all were related and bound by a similar bond of loyalty – and all knew that if the ruler was poisoned they too would be killed (bisection with a razor-sharp sabre being the usual death a poisoner could expect). Still, even with a spotless and systemised kitchen secure from interlopers and with a loyal staff, there was the possibility of a rogue element entering the equation. For this the poison taster needed to be able to spot a poisoned dish – even when he was half asleep, last thing at night or first thing in the morning. Such knowledge also, naturally, made him expert in the art of poisoning and therefore not wholly trusted by the paranoid Mamluk court. It was not an easy job.

Belladonna, ratsbane, the potato bug, vitriol; laurel water, wood-ash lye, monkshood and antimonial wine; thorn apple, Jamestown weed, ink cap and lead vinegar – all had their own signature, their own telltale signs. Hellebore, Indian poke, hemlock and henbane – you had to be careful: mistake one for another and the antidote would exacerbate the damage. The antidote was the last line of self-defence. One did not, after all, want to die doing this job. Naturally the poison taster always had a tame doctor at hand in case of emergencies.

At the first sign that poison was present, one induced vomiting – the best method being an emetic of ground mustard or powdered alum in a syrup of molasses. If hemlock is suspected – known by a dryness to the throat, tremors and dizziness – then the stomach must be fully emptied, using ammonia, if necessary, to complete the job.

Indian-poke poisoning produces symptoms of violent vomiting and bloody stools. The vomiting need only be speeded up through the intake of draughts of warm water and molasses. Oily purgatives and clysters of strong coffee, camomile and opium will all help counter this pernicious plant poison.

For a mineral poison such as oil of vitriol, bloody vomiting may precede excessive thirst, convulsions and death, with the mouth and lips excoriated, shrivelled white and yellow. Calcined magnesia mixed with milk to the consistency of cream, if taken immediately, may be remedy enough. When the poison is got rid of, slippery elm tea and flaxseed gruel will aid recovery.

Aconite or wolfsbane poisoning leads to numbness and tingling in the mouth, and bit by bit all regions of the body likewise submit. It was used in ancient times to poison wells, as well as for tipping arrows and spears used on a lion hunt. A form of aconite is present in the common buttercup; it is very unwise to put its leaves and petals in the mouth. Should aconite poisoning be suspected, a strong emetic is needed straight away followed by a tiny measure of ammonia every half-hour. If cold well water is available, douche the head and chest with it, though apply warmth to the extremities.

Deadly nightshade or belladonna is an old favourite of court poisoners as there is no known antidote. The plant has little odour and only a small bitterness easily concealed with molasses or honey. Belladonna poisoning causes dryness of the mouth followed by loss of vision. Since there is no cure save hopeful reliance on a prompt emetic it is best to keep stimulating the body through alcohol and opium until either the symptoms pass or death prevails.

Laurel water (the active ingredient is cyanide) in a large dose is almost instantaneously fatal. In smaller doses there is loss of control of the voluntary muscles. The odour of almonds is usually enough to alert a poison taster to this concoction. If afflicted, spirits of hartshorn largely diluted may be given, the vapour of it cautiously inhaled.

It is quite possible to murder a prince or a king with opium. The symptoms are giddiness and drowsiness at first, a feeling of wellbeing that rapidly descends with the fatal dose into stupor; the pulse slows and weakens, the pupils contract, and as death approaches the extremities become icy cold, the sphincters relax. Naturally an emetic of strong proportions must be administered. Strong coffee is also advised. In extreme cases belladonna may be used – tiny amounts every twenty minutes, the exact quantity gauged by watching for the pupils to expand. Use whatever method is available to prevent the onset of what may be the last, fatal sleep.

Nux vomica, or in modern parlance strychnine, exerts a peculiar effect on the body that is immediately noticeable: all the muscles contract and the spinal cord becomes a rigid column of bone. A profound calm soon descends followed by a second, titanic seizure, longer than the first, and during which respiration is halted. These symptoms then cease and the breathing becomes easy, leading to a stupor, followed by another attack; the titanic seizures return with increasing ferocity until the onset of death. If any part of the body is touched during a quiescent period of the poisoning it immediately sets off another seizure. Interestingly, even threatening to touch the victim can trigger a fresh titanic seizure. A purgative clyster should be taken along with a strong emetic. Oil of turpentine can be administered as an antidote after the stomach is cleared. Opium, too, has some success in extreme cases. Oils and butter taken into the emptied stomach are also useful.

Thorn apple perverts the vision and leads to vertigo. It is to be treated in the same way as belladonna poisoning.

Hemlock is known through the exquisite dizziness it causes, followed by a dry throat and a creeping paralysis of the limbs. The stomach should be emptied with mustard and then dosed with small amounts of ammonia. It may be that air needs to be blown into the victim's lungs by an attendant physician, if the breathing weakens to a dangerous extent.

But Aybak's status as the husband of Shajarat al-Durr was not enough to convince the Bahri Mamluks, so a co-reign involving six-year-old Musa, the grandson of a previous Ayyubid sultan, became the front for a curious three-handed regime.

Under the Turks, a rule, the harsh rule of the wolf pack, endured. The man who kills the ruler is the only one fit to rule. Those who served with obedience and competence but did not wish to despatch the ruler when the time was mysteriously right, perhaps when he had begun to lose his power, luck or abilities, such people did not deserve to rule. This ideology, brutal but effective, reached its apogee in the behaviour of Turkish princes murdering their siblings to ensure that they had no obvious rivals for the throne.

Aybak became cocky. He managed to oust the Mamluks behind little

Musa and proclaimed himself the sole ruler, omitting Shajarat al-Durr's name from newly minted coinage. He went one step too far, though, and sought to marry the daughter of the Emir of Mosul. It was purely political – you can imagine him explaining that to his enraged wife back in Cairo. In any case the decision would cost him dear. As he reclined in the harem in his ornate tiled bath, with rose water being poured over his head, he was seized by the bath attendants, slaves loyal first to Shajarat al-Durr, and his throat was cut, so deeply that his head almost fell off, filling the bath with arterial blood.

But Shajarat al-Durr had miscalculated her power. The Mamluks realised that their time had come. In some versions of the story the Mamluks encouraged Aybak's former wife to avenge herself on the woman who had supplanted her in his affections, before arresting her for murder.

Shajarat al-Durr locked herself in the Red Tower of the Citadel to escape capture. Growing weaker and weaker from lack of food, she spent her days grinding her jewels on a flat granite stone used by Bedouin in the desert for crushing grain. Determined that no woman would ever wear her finery, she managed to destroy an enormous amount of her wealth. In one version of the story she even, in her final delirium, ate the powdered jewels because she was so hungry. Eventually, utterly starving, she opened the door. Dragged out by the other female members of her dead husband's harem she was beaten to death with clogs and her body discarded in the ditch surrounding the Citadel. In this ditch, 500 years later, the last of the Mamluks would meet his doom at the hands of the Albanian brigand Muhammad Ali.

And what of Baiburs, who would soon take over the throne from the ill-used Shajarat al-Durr and her poison-tasting husband? He would lead the Arabs to great victories over the Mongols and the Christians, securing the Middle East for several centuries. He would die aged sixty-four in 1277 from drinking *kumiss*, fermented mares' milk, a favourite drink of the Kipchaks and Mongols. Baiburs, who had become increasingly paranoid and was afraid that he would be killed, insisted that the mares' milk used be coloured with his colour – saffron yellow – so that he knew it came from his safe stock. Baiburs' paranoia was fed by other ailments – poor digestion and a failing memory. Food and drink sometimes turned up under the pillows where he rested. If left too long, *kumiss* turns into a deadly poison; it seems that Baiburs may have poisoned himself.

12 · Baiburs' city

Do not buy the swift strong horse, buy the one already tamed.
Egyptian proverb

The best time to see Old Cairo, the Cairo of Baiburs and Al-Nafis, is around 6 or 6.30 on a Saturday morning. No one is around. The sun has just risen and is catching all the great mosques and walls and palaces in its rosy-fingered glow. If you're on a motorbike you can get down any number of narrow alleys and overhung streets; walking works too, but somehow having wheels multiplies the grandeur of the place, as you can take more in more intensely. And you can zoom past dogs. Hire a taxi and just drive around.

Of course I only rarely follow my own advice. Often I used to be driving through the old city last thing at night, its ancientness illuminated by green mosque lights and the stuttering glow of a street arc welder.

Once, out later than usual, I stopped at a café with *shishas* (waterpipes or hookahs) just below the Citadel, not far from the City of the Dead cemetery. Two boys, maybe fifteen or sixteen years old, were performing for the small audience, who were, I must say, only mildly interested. Not me. These boys were the real thing, thin as wire in their grubby tracksuits and dusty sandals, armed with just a Baraka water bottle full of gasoline, a small bucket brazier filled with glowing charcoal and a few rags. While the older one ate fire, the other, who had dyed his hair on top an odd light-brown colour, juggled with it, thin sticks each wrapped with a cotton wad soaked in petrol. When they saw I was interested the tricks got better. The fire eater took a length of metal – iron or steel, I guessed – and heated it until it glowed red from the brazier. Very slowly, but with little other ceremony, he bit off the end and spat it into a water glass where it hissed and sizzled most convincingly.

The other handed him some grubby sponges quickly doused in petrol. He held them in the *meshi*, the tongs used to tend a waterpipe. Then he lit each one with a concealed lighter and tossed it high into the night sky. He caught each burning sponge in his mouth as it came down – yet at the end his mouth was empty. I alone applauded this, though two other old gaffers were watching with amusement. I knew I would be the one paying, but it was worth it.

The last trick was almost the most impressive. With no warning and none of the fandango of a 'real' magician, almost in fact as an after-thought, the boy picked up with a fork a piece of charcoal from the red-hot glowing brazier. With no pause for it to cool he popped it in his mouth. Then another, and another. One, two, three, four – down they went, and all he did was smile. He showed his empty white-toothed mouth – the red-hot charcoal all swallowed, it seemed.

I gave them money, about four pounds, which was a lot for that kind of place, and took the older boy's mobile number, explaining that I wanted to take some pictures of the act. Two days later I was waiting in the same place at four in the afternoon but they didn't turn up – and after answering my first call they did not return my calls or pick up when I phoned. The owner of the café, a man with a cast in one eye, remembered me and asked what I was doing as he riffled through an immense wad of grubby currency. He told me that the magician boys were homeless and the phone was probably stolen. They had got scared. 'But he can tell you how they do those tricks.' He gestured at an incredibly thin man in a grey *galabiya* sucking on a waterpipe with what looked like a toothless mouth. It wasn't – the man smiled and revealed a couple of blackened stumps. He beckoned me over, patting the plastic chair next to him. He was keen to talk, wired on tea and *shisha*. He told me he knew about these tricks from years of watching. 'Only watching.' Judging by the condition of his teeth he looked like he'd done his share of fire eating too.

'So why do you think they always come here?' he asked.

'Why?'

'Because this spot is famous for such fire acts since the time of the first Arabs, even before, since the fire-eating Persian priests came to Egypt. I tell you I learnt as a boy all those tricks – though those lads are good. Take the fire eating – that's easy as long as you exhale all the time, not too strong or people can see. Then when you shut your mouth on the flame it goes out instantly. As long as the gasoline isn't dripping it won't hurt – and you keep your mouth wet drinking water and yoghurt beforehand, all day in fact.'

'What about biting off the steel?'

'That was iron, not steel. They get it from old barrels. Beforehand he's bent that iron back and forth a hundred times to weaken it so that it will drop off almost if you touch it. Granted, it's red hot when he grips it in his teeth, but if you don't touch the lips or gums the teeth can hold something very hot for a second or two. When he spits it out he is really just dropping it from his mouth with a little extra force by swinging his head. Easy to make a mistake on that one though, I would say.'

'But the burning coals – how was that done?'

'Without you seeing, he's dropped some pieces of soft pine in among the coals. It burns up and goes as black as charcoal but remains soft – that's why he uses a fork. The only one that he can stick the fork into is a piece of black pine. Unlike charcoal it loses heat very quickly and you can chew it up and swallow it easily. But there's one they didn't do which I always like. If you see someone drinking boiling lead this is how they do it – they add bismuth [same word in Arabic] and tin to the lead – this makes it melt at less than the boiling point of water. So they cast a spoon from this metal and produce it as an ordinary teaspoon. They demonstrate by stirring some tea with it (which it will just about stand). Then the showman melts the spoon into a ladle over the brazier and pretends this is white hot. Then he takes the molten metal into his mouth where it cools and hardens again.'

'Isn't it poisonous?'

He laughed. 'These boys don't care about such things as long as they get a pound for it. The older one is ill anyway, he has bilharzia.'

One of the customers, who was listening in, raised his lips from his waterpipe to say: 'When he was a boy he played with water too much, now he plays with fire.'

Part Four

THE NILE EXTENDED

Raw steak and Napoleon

1 • The Fountain of Eternal Youth

A deer goes to the clever hunter and a woman goes to the man who waits.
Nubian proverb

Herodotus mentions, quite casually, in his *Histories* that the Fountain of Eternal Youth is in Ethiopia and attributes to it the extreme longevity of the Ethiopian people. Is it any surprise that one source of the Nile, the Blue Nile, is also in Ethiopia?

The Blue Nile feeds the White Nile. We've seen how it creates the lower Nile through the massive influx of summer floodwater. In an image central to this book, it backs up the river near Khartoum for five miles or more, reversing the current of the White Nile and spewing out sediment – turning the White Nile red.

So the Blue Nile is just as much the 'source of the Nile' as the White Nile is. Much of the confusion in ancient times stems from not knowing that there were two equally important sources. True information about both was seen as contradictory rather than equally true.

But the Blue Nile as the water of life? There are rivers such as the Ganges that have endemic microbial infestations that actually aid healing or at least stop one from becoming ill from drinking their otherwise dirty waters. The Nile is something like this. Swift flowing, when not dammed, there is evidence of a mild antiseptic effect.

However, nothing suggested that the 'Little Blue Nile', the river which feeds Lake Tana which in turn becomes the Blue Nile proper, was anything more than another spring. I naturally approached it with high hopes but little real conviction. The water of eternal youth is a persistent myth across many cultures. It appears in the *Alexander Romance*, a collection of legends about Alexander the Great, where the mysterious guide to Moses, Khidr, who also appears in the Koran and in much oral storytelling material in the East, knows the way to the fabulous fountain.

The hunt for eternal youth shifted to the New World with the discovery of the Americas, where Juan Ponce de León was sure he had found it. Bimini in the Caribbean became associated with the fountain of youth and even David Copperfield, the magician, has recently got in on the act, claiming that scientists are testing the waters in his Caribbean mini-archipelago (which cost him $50 million) that are supposedly capable of rejuvenating ... leaves. But then David Copperfield is the man who paid Claudia Schiffer $100,000 to say she was engaged to him.

That the Fountain of Eternal Youth is a useful symbol, a mythical thought experiment, and is not meant to be taken literally doesn't occur to otherwise intelligent folk as often as it should.

Eternal life is often cited as a mixed blessing. The tattered old crow who drinks from the fountain and cannot die though he wishes to. The cursed sailors who rampage around the earth with no peace – most lately in *Pirates of the Caribbean 4* – are new examples of the myth's fecundity.

The Tis Abay is actually the waterfall (also called the Tissisat Falls) usually taken to be the start of the Blue Nile. Now its thunder has been stolen by another hydroelectric plant, and only on odd Sundays and when foreign dignitaries arrive do they turn on the water to make the falls smoke as they did when the early Jesuit explorers first reported them.

Interestingly, Gish Abay – the 'calf Nile' – competes as the real source of the Blue Nile as it fills Lake Tana, from which the Blue Nile exits. However, there is no discernible current across the lake from the outlet of the 'calf Nile' to the start of the Blue Nile, which for many rules it out (recall the Kagera's current successfully crossing Lake Victoria). The Gish Abay, or 'little Abay', spring waters are associated with healing. If mythology is a cartoon version of reality designed to burn into our cultural retina, what better way to ensure that a spring with healing powers remains unviolated than to credit it with being the source of eternal life?

The sacred spring of Gish Abay, which is about twenty-two miles from Lake Tana near the town of Sekala, lies in the grounds of a monastery. I had been warned at the guesthouse that I should not eat that day. The thin, serious man at reception who sat over his huge bookings tome like a man reading a great Bible wagged his skinny finger and said, 'Go early, for they will not believe you have not eaten if you come after noon.'

Something in me, the same kind of silliness that makes me put false information on the pointless forms you have to fill in for joining video-rental clubs and the like, drove me to avoid breakfast – in case of spies – but to munch secretly and joyously on a Cadbury's hazelnut bar before I set off. How could those monks know?

It was a long walk along dusty ways to reach the fabled, rather dilapidated monastery. I arrived at 8 a.m. but there was already a microbus disgorging some irritable Germans – who were no doubt missing their morning coffee. I felt pretty good myself because as I walked I had kept up my spirits with some winegums and another chocolate bar.

I was relieved of several hundred birr at the entrance to the monastery and more money at the wooden fence by the marsh that signified the source of the Blue Nile. I could see the baptismal pool where I planned to swim later. The spring itself emerged from a rusty pipe, about an inch in diameter. It was housed in a stone dwelling with a low wooden door. There was a cheerful guard on the door – a monk with a Bible.

'Pure?' he asked.

'Yes.'

'You understand no food?'

'Yes, no food.'

He looked away. '300 birr.'

'But I've already paid!'

'Perhaps you have already eaten too!'

He knew. Maybe I had chocolate stains on my teeth.

'I just want to take some water for luck.' I showed him my French lemonade bottle with its wire-bound pop cork.

The hard, Bible-holding hand barred my way. I paid and ducked in.

The water looked clean enough as it dribbled into the bottle. As the guard wasn't looking I took a swig, without siphoning it. It had to be clean, this high up the food chain. And moving water is usually fine as long as it has no floating matter in it; it's the stagnant water that gets you. This is what I always tell myself when I'm thirsty. Still, the water had a slight seaweedy smell, somewhat iodine-like too.

Then I stripped off behind some white-and-green-robed Ethiopian pilgrims who were about to be baptised. The stone steps were slippy, slimy. The water was cold. Cold! It was, I thought, markedly different too from the White Nile water. It wasn't the clarity of the water so much as the air around me, the atmosphere. Probably the altitude contributed, but I felt energised, revitalised. Yes, healthy. I could see my limbs distorted in the water, I had the feeling I was suddenly tiny, floating on the amniotic fluid of the Nile, a child about to be reborn.

2 · The lands of Prester John

A camel resembles the land where it lives. Somali proverb

We have seen how the Islamic world consolidated its grip on the Nile through Egypt – going both up the Nile and in from the Red Sea coast from the seventh century onwards. Christianity was now on the run. Coptic Christianity had made its way before Islam, or was driven ahead of Islam. In Ethiopia it found a stronghold. Monks lived in caves high up on cliff faces, hauled themselves up in baskets banging against a rock wall 200 feet above the ground. Churches were carved from rock. This was the land of Prester John, the mythical Christian king of the East. Here the Copts would be safe, or so they thought.

In the sixteenth century Europe woke up. It decided to go looking for things. Africa was an obvious choice, as was America. Mythical rulers were as attractive as lost cities. Raleigh gave his life looking for El Dorado. Others searched for Prester John. What they found was almost stranger than the myth.

I first came across the Prester John myth, as many do, in T. S. Eliot's poem 'Conversation Galante'. Then there was the John Buchan novel *Prester John* – though it was set in South Africa, not Ethiopia, the traditional location of this mythical king. Rumours of a Christian king in the East undoubtedly spread from the Coptic Church's presence in Ethiopia, perhaps magnified by the distorting echo provided by the conversion to Islam of all the surrounding lands.

But it was the Portuguese explorers of the sixteenth century who believed, when they encountered the Christian kings of Abyssinia, that they were in fact meeting the royal family of Prester John. In Francisco Álvarez's 1540 work *Ho Preste Joam das Indias. Verdadera informacam das terras do Preste Joam* we discover that before they die the sons of Prester John are 'shut up in a mountain and heard of no more'. Burial alive? Certainly, for in Ethiopia Europeans would find a culture far odder than they could imagine.

These Portuguese explorers, burning with a missionary purpose, had entered Ethiopia from the Red Sea. Unable to penetrate the upper Nile through Islamic Egypt, Europeans now attempted to reach the land of its source from the Indian Ocean coast of Africa. As we have discovered, though the White Nile is the longer river, the Blue Nile supplies 85 per cent of the water in the high flood of summer, the flood on which Egyptian agriculture depended. So, in the hunt for mythical sources, the source of the floodwater was found.

During these great bursts of exploratory activity, in the sixteenth and seventeenth centuries, the obsession arose that there was a Christian kingdom hidden in the East. In a sense there was – Ethiopia – which followed the same Coptic religion as the Christians in Egypt. In 1621, expecting to find Prester John, Pedro Páez, a Jesuit missionary, found instead one source of the Nile, that of the Blue Nile. He also encountered a Christian people who wore the entrails of cows as ornaments, who carried on their spears a fragment of red cloth bearing the testicles of the men they had killed, who put out the eyes of their captives before any interrogation. One source of the Red Nile had certainly been found.

The Portuguese, under Vasco da Gama, had circumnavigated Africa and found their way to Abyssinia in the closing months of the fourteenth century. They then began the task of establishing a trading presence on the Red Sea coast. This coincided with a Muslim invasion in 1527 from Danakil country led by the imam Ahmed Gran, 'the Left-Handed', who with 10,000 men turned what was possibly a looting expedition into a religious war. The Abyssinian King, in his desperation, called for help from the only other Christian nation he knew of, the Portuguese, who in 1541 sent 400 musketeers under Cristóvão da Gama. By the time the men with guns arrived the Abyssinian King, Lebna Dengal, had perished as a fugitive and all seemed lost to the Islamic world. As many ancient manuscripts dating back to the first arrival of Coptic priests in the fifth and sixth centuries were destroyed by Gran's invasion, we can be sure that the Portuguese arrival probably saved a good deal of the cultural artefacts of the Ethiopian Church.

Cristóvão da Gama, whom Richard Burton called 'the most chivalrous man of a chivalrous age', was the son of the explorer Vasco da Gama. When Ahmed Gran heard of his intentions, he sent a messenger to da Gama with instructions to quit Ethiopia or submit to his rule. The message came with a present – a monk's habit. What kind of insult was that? Perhaps the implication was that da Gama was no warrior and would be better off praying for deliverance like the other monks in Ethiopia. Da Gama was up to this game, however, and sent back a refusal, a counter-suggestion that Gran leave or submit, and the gift of a large mirror and a pair of tweezers – the implication being that Gran was a woman who needed his eyebrows plucking.

Gran was far from pleased with this message and sent for a thousand musketeers from southern Arabia courtesy of the Ottoman Empire. Vastly outnumbered and outgunned, da Gama's men fought on, only to discover that Lebna Dengal's son and successor King Gelawdewos had only sixty men to his name and was still in hiding up in the hills.

After skirmishes and small battles the Portuguese managed a major confrontation with Gran. Here the valiant da Gama was shot, his arm broken, and he was captured by the 'Left-Handed' warrior Ahmed Gran. The dreaded tweezers were produced and Gran pulled out every one of da Gama's beard hairs. This did not have the desired effect, so worse torture was applied: he was strung up by his broken arm which was agitated until it tore apart; he was gashed and mutilated and his tongue removed. Still he did not recant or change religion. Finally his head was removed and thrown in a spring, which according to legend thereafter provided health to the sick. Hearing about the reputation of the spring Ahmed, with an unerring sense of the despicable, ordered a dead dog to be thrown into it and a large rock placed on top to block it up.

That done, Ahmed Gran felt rather pleased with himself and assumed that the war was over. He sent home all but 200 of his Arabian musketeers and retired to Lake Tana to enjoy the relative calm of the rainy season.

It seems appropriate that the source of the Nile should be the scene of a bloody battle, one that determined the precise extent of the religious map of Africa.

Queen Sabla Wangel and her son Gelawdewos, encouraged by the remaining Portuguese and by the stock of arms they still carried, rallied and went to do battle. It was fiercely fought on both sides with many falling. There is a persistent story that one Portuguese warrior was so intent on avenging the hideous mauling of da Gama that he rode with his loaded arquebus right through Ahmed's front line until he could fire at almost point-blank range on the Muslim leader. The wounded imam fell and his troops turned and fled.

One account of the battle states that a champion Ottoman fighter refused to run away with the others. Once he saw that

> the Moors were giving way, he determined to die; with bared arms, and a long broadsword in his hand, he swept a great space in front of him; he fought like a valiant cavalier, for five Abyssinian horsemen were on him, who could neither make him yield nor slay him. One of them attacked him with a javelin; he wrenched it from his hand, he houghed [hamstrung] another's horse, and none dared approach him. There came up a Portuguese horseman, by name Gonçalo Fernandes, who charged him spear in hand and wounded him sorely; the Turk grasped it [the spear] so firmly that before he could disengage himself the Moor gave him a great cut above the knee that severed all the sinews and crippled him; finding himself wounded, he drew his sword and killed him.

By 1543 the Arab-backed invaders had been repulsed and Ethiopia remained a Coptic anomaly in a Muslim east Africa. Prester John had triumphed.

3 · A kind of Blue

The morning is for work; the rest of the day depends on the person.
Ethiopian proverb

James Bruce was an explorer whose name is firmly associated with the Blue Nile. He claimed he was the first European to visit its source, though this was not true.

We have heard how the Blue Nile, or Abay as it is called in Ethiopia, has its source in the mountains at Sekala, a fact that was known for many centuries before Bruce explored Ethiopia. Baltazar Téllez, writing in the seventeenth century about the Jesuit missionaries who visited Ethiopia, wrote, 'It was said of Alexander the Great that the first question he asked when he came to Jupiter Ammon [the oracle at Siwa] was where the Nile has its rise, and we know he sent explorers throughout Ethiopia without being able to find out this source.' Earlier, the Persian invader King Cambyses, who later lost an army in the Sahara on its way to sack the same oracle that was visited by Alexander, also sent troops in search of the Nile's source in Ethiopia.

Neither of these efforts came close to succeeding. Though the general area was known, the exact spot wasn't, and it wasn't until the arrival of Pedro Páez in 1613 that the source of the Blue Nile was seen by a European. There is some controversy over this, given James Bruce's claim that he was the first European to get to the Blue Nile's source when he traipsed there from the Red Sea coast in 1769–71. That Bruce of Kinnaird's journey was epic and extraordinary no one could contend; it was also the first to entail travel from the Blue Nile to the White – but without following the cataract-laden length of the Blue Nile. The honours, however, must go to Páez. His description of the spring where the Blue Nile rises is so accurate that he must have seen it. It does Bruce no credit that he tried to muddy the water surrounding Páez's claim; later, when he returned to Britain and had his own, perfectly true revelations about Ethiopia ridiculed by Dr Johnson among many others, one feels an element of poetic justice at work.

James Bruce visited the sacred spring in 1770. Emperor Takla Haimanot II said, 'I do give the village of Gish and those fountains he is so fond of to Yagoube [Bruce] and his posterity for ever, never to appear under another name in the deftar [register] and never to be taken from him or exchanged.' The church at the source is dedicated to St Michael and Zarabruk. When Major R. E. Cheesman was British consul in northwest Ethiopia in 1925, he enquired about the origin of Zarabruk. The priests said he was a saint, but knew no more (though it can also take the meaning 'blessed seed' in Amharic). Yet when Bruce was there the place had the single name St Michael Gish. It has been suggested that 'Zarabruk' is a corruption of the explorer's name, so it might be that Bruce's legacy lives on as commanded.

At Wigtown literary festival in Scotland I met a direct descendant of Bruce. He worked for a whisky distillery. As Bruce had married the daughter of a wine merchant, it seemed appropriate. Alex Bruce, the descendant, lived on an estate in Scotland. However, he had no idea that his family owned land abroad, fabulously strange and mythical land too: the source of the Blue Nile.

4 • James Bruce – the 'liar' of the Nile

Truthful speech is short; a lie is long. Ethiopian proverb

James Bruce, a distant relative of Robert the Bruce and the Earls of Elgin, was, on the face of it, the most ideally equipped explorer ever to search for the Nile's secrets. Like Samuel Baker who we met at the Murchison Falls, he was big and strong – six foot four with red hair and a muscular frame. Like Burton, he mastered languages – Arabic, Coptic and Amharic. Like Stanley, he was fearless and aggressive in pursuing his aims. Like Schweinfurth, he was a natural scientist who took a wide and informed interest in all he saw. And yet, for many years, he was most remembered as a liar, a thin-skinned boaster, an ineffective bully and a nasty cheapskate. Oh, and he was fat too, at the end, so gross that his carriage wobbled uncontrollably when he mounted it, and when he fell down some stairs his enormous weight proved the death of him, crushing his once strong frame. Just what had gone wrong?

Bruce brought back news of the Nile, of its source, that people just didn't want to hear. He spoke of farmers removing a steak from a living cow, eating it raw, then sewing up the skin and letting the creature live to graze another day. But this was merely the alibi for his ridicule, the thing Dr Johnson and others latched on to when they found this overbearing, overweening Scot unbearable in his boasting, lack of generosity and above all humourlessness. It is interesting that in France Bruce commanded respect and was given an influential hearing. In England he received merely ridicule. Only someone defective in a sense of humour would have presented the cow/live-steak information in anything other than a circumspect and comical format. He would have realised that he would be disbelieved and would have moved on to other topics. Here's how Bruce dealt with it: when a guest expressed disbelief in his story he cut a raw steak and would not let the man leave the table until he had eaten it. That's a guest in his own house. Imagine how he reacted when literary London found his stories a little ... unusual. No, Bruce is a singular example of how an unspeakable man, however impeccable his achievements, can end up being largely ignored.

Bruce started life in Scotland, was educated at Harrow and spent two years as a consul in Tunis. He was brave even then, standing his ground in court while another petitioner was strangled in his presence. He was also an originator. Before Mungo Park, the first European to go up the River Niger, Africa had been largely ignored by land-based explorers (it is interesting that four of the world's greatest explorers were Scottish: Mungo Park, Alexander Mackenzie (the first across North America), James Bruce and David Livingstone). It took more guts to go inland through unknown tribes than to sail the globe in a man-of-war, and Bruce was the first to show it was possible. He was determined to solve the problem of the Nile and he did. Before everyone laughed at him.

Strangely it was not in his outward journey that he was a trail blazer, merely his homeward trek. Getting to the source of the Blue Nile, he had attempted to travel upstream from Cairo but had soon abandoned the river for the Red Sea route that brought him to Wassawa. Here he was following in the footsteps of generations of Portuguese, and he landed with an Italian who agreed to accompany him to the source. The Italian, Luigi Balugani, was a fine artist who would die in Ethiopia. Bruce, ever the pragmatist, acquired his drawings and gave them to George III, passing them off as his own. And in his memoirs, written seventeen years later, Balugani gets not a single mention. In this we see the seeds of what made him disliked. What kind of man would travel with another who died prematurely, steal his only contribution, his legacy, and never mention his name?

When Bruce gets to the source he is 150 years late. His real journey, his significant journey, has yet to start, except he thinks it has already ended. At Lake Tana he accuses Pedro Páez, the first European to the source of the Blue Nile, of lying, of never having been there. When R. E. Cheesman, the last of the great explorers of the Nile (he mapped much of the Blue Nile for the first time in the 1920s and 1930s), visited the sites visited by Páez he realised that the Jesuit had really been to the source and Bruce had deliberately misled the world in order to make it appear that an Anglo-Saxon, and an anti-papist, was the first.

To avoid the conniving and rapacious inhabitants of Massawa on the Red Sea, Bruce went home by following, at least some of the way, the Blue Nile to where it joined the White Nile in Sudan. Understandably subdued by the view of that great river extending away south into Africa, he pretended it didn't exist, or didn't count. He couldn't even bring himself to name it, calling it by the local name Abiad instead, which means 'white' in Arabic.

From here he went downstream past strange obelisks and steep pyramids, and was the first to note, perspicaciously, 'It is impossible to avoid risking a guess that this is the ancient city of Meroe,' referring to a site near Shendy in present-day Sudan. He kissed the hand of the Queen of Shendy – whereupon she drew back utterly shocked, exclaiming that no one had ever dared do such a thing before. True to his polymathic nature he observed that Venus was peculiarly bright at that time: 'it appeared shining with undiminished light all day, in defiance of the brightest sun'. In that year Venus was indeed at its closest to the earth for 243 years.

He then crossed the Nubian Desert by the famed Forty Days Road, taking only eighteen days and crippling his feet in the process. He arrived at Aswan and bathed them in the Nile, stating with typical spikiness that he would never be back. In Cairo he rested some months to allow his feet to recover, then he returned via Italy where he challenged to a duel the Italian husband of a former love (she had gone twelve years without so much as a letter). The Italian Count apologised profusely and claimed ignorance of the whole affair. Bruce slouched towards London where his stories rather quickly became a byword for invention of the most ludicrous kind. He fell foul of Dr Johnson who had, in his first publishing endeavour forty years earlier, translated an account by Father Jerome Lobo (a comrade of Téllez) of the Jesuits in Ethiopia. Here came Bruce saying it was all lies. It didn't help that James Boswell was a near-contemporary and disliked Bruce too. Fanny Burney, who also met Bruce, added to the slyly derisive note familiar to all who have been mocked by the English: 'Mr Bruce's grand air, gigantic height, and forbidding brow awed everybody. He is the tallest man you ever saw *gratis*.'

He retired to his estate in Scotland in high dudgeon and refused to write the story of his adventures. Fifteen years passed and he softened somewhat and employed a pastor in the Moravian church in Fetter Lane (how did he find *him*?) who would act as an amanuensis. Dr Johnson gets Boswell and Mr Bruce gets B. H. Latrobe, who wrote, 'I had once or twice the misfortune to offend him in endeavouring to expunge a few grammatical errors.' Latrobe worked long and hard, taking down five volumes of memoirs. True to form, Bruce didn't pay him, so Latrobe resorted to sending pleading letters. Bruce replied, 'I never really thought you put yourself on the footing of payment, nor do I well know for what, for it has been of no use to me . . .' In the end he paid Latrobe five guineas for his work.

The books appeared and the laughter had not died in the interven-
ing years. Horace Walpole pronounced the lengthy volumes 'dull and
dear'. Others took up again the theme of lying. A 1792 sequel to *Baron
Munchausen*, published in London, was pointedly dedicated to James
Bruce. It is the fate of some explorers who lie to be believed, the fate of
other truth tellers to be doubted. Most explorers are truth stretchers –
they do amazing things but then they have to add a bit extra. Maybe
that is what drives them.

But the Nile was not just attracting explorers. Tourists and even ath-
letes were soon to come looking at the world's greatest river.

5 · Running the Nile

Don't try to run in front of a river in flood. Ethiopian proverb

Mensen Ernst was the world's first professional athlete, bar a few prize-
fighters and jockeys; he was Norwegian and he was born to run in 1795.
He made his money slyly, by making bets with people about distances
no one could possibly run, then he'd run them. He was the world's
second marathon runner and the world's first ultra-marathoner. He
once ran from Paris to Moscow in fourteen days, did a day's sightseeing
and then ran back again. In 1836 the East India Company bet him £250
he couldn't run from Constantinople to Calcutta – he did it in four
weeks. After three days' rest, and perhaps a quick curry, he ran back
again. The total journey, there and back, took fifty-nine days, averaging
eighty-seven miles a day.

Ernst was fearless, operating on the theory that he could outrun any
potential attacker, even those mounted on horseback. To prove his
point he once outran a racehorse – not in initial speed but in endurance: the racehorse collapsed exhausted after a mere seventy miles.
Ernst was only getting his second wind by then.

In 1842 he decided to run all the way to the source of the White
Nile. Never mind that it had not yet been found, never mind that
Nero's centurions, plodders rather than runners, had disappeared centuries earlier in the great suppurating swamp of the Sudd. What was
he planning – to walk on water? Nevertheless, the earnest Ernst set out
running from Cairo in very fine fettle in December, the best month to

start (he had already run from Prussia via Jerusalem to get there). He drank Nile water and he pronounced it 'invigorating'. He ran upwards of fifty miles a day, holding himself back for the big desert crossing. In Aswan, he rested for a moment under a tree, and died. His body was found several days later, quite dried out. According to a contemporary German biographer, Ernst's motto was 'Motion is life. Stagnation is death'. This seems curiously true about rivers as well as men.

Sadly, the world's first ultra-marathoner is thought to have succumbed to dysentery and heat exhaustion. The stones marking the site of his burial were buried by the construction of the Aswan dam, the building of which made the canals of Egypt stagnant.

Word of the Nile was spreading. With the establishment of publishing houses and an increasingly informed readership, attention turned to all that was exotic. One avid reader of anything about the East, and about the country of the mighty Nile, was a young Corsican artillery officer, Napoleon Bonaparte.

6 · Queen of the Nile

A weak person loves the weakness of the strong. Nubian proverb

Europe had not forgotten the Nile – there is a steady stream of travelogues appearing throughout the eighteenth century by the likes of James Bruce, Jan Potocki and Richard Pococke. It took Napoleon, however, to bring the Nile fully back into the European mind. He wanted to be Alexander the Great, only Greater, and Alexander had conquered Egypt and the Nile before turning his attention to India. Napoleon would do better; he aimed to take Egypt, then the Levant, and finally wrest India from the calculating British.

Napoleon saw the river as the lifeblood of Egypt. He said, 'If I were to govern this country not one drop of water would be lost to the sea.' This same quotation was used 150 years later by the Greek Egyptian engineer Adrian Daninos to support construction of the Aswan high dam – one lasting impact of Napoleon's short-lived invasion of Egypt. This quixotic expedition also led to the birth of the Egyptology we know today, dragging Egypt from its long slumbers under Ottoman rule. Napoleon's soldiers uncovered the Rosetta Stone, thus starting the process of finally decoding hieroglyphics; and the influx of French *savants* led to a scientific interest in the Nile, the first barrage across the river and ultimately to the Suez Canal.

And Napoleon did it all without his beloved Josephine. When he went to Egypt to conquer the Nile in 1799 he imagined he would be there with Josephine. They had tried for a child but none was forthcoming. The cunning Josephine suggested that a cure at the spa of La Plombières might aid conception rather better than a fifty-four-day journey by sea to Alexandria. Napoleon was very unhappy about this but grudgingly allowed her to remain in Europe.

Josephine, however, had no intention of taking a rest cure in the Vosges Mountains; not even the famous *glaces Plombières* could tempt her. Instead she stayed in Paris and continued having an affair with a young man called Hippolyte Charles. Napoleon, who up to this point had never been unfaithful to Josephine, was grief stricken by the news. And it wasn't the first time. In Italy he had threatened to kill Josephine when he discovered her affair with a young adjutant called ... Hippolyte Charles. He had Charles dismissed from the army. Now it seemed that she had been spotted in a private box in the theatre with Charles, that that charming Charlie had given her a little dog and had even been seen in her carriage. Not that Napoleon believed any of this at first. As a successful general he was surprisingly trusting, but his friend and long associate General Junot assured him most forcibly that it was true. Bonaparte was furious and sad and then furious again: 'Josephine! You should have told me. To have been so fooled. I will exterminate that race of jackanapes and dandies. As for her – divorce! A blazing public divorce!'

Instead he conquered Egypt. Call it being in denial. To take his mind off things still further, Napoleon intended to do a lot of reading during his campaign. The camp library he insisted on taking with him included his favourite poets such as Ossian and Tasso, forty 'English Novels', Homer, Ariosto, Plutarch, works on geography, travel and history such as Fontenelle's *Worlds* and Cook's *Voyages*, treatises on fortifications and fireworks (their more deadly variants, one assumes), Voltaire, Goethe and, listed in his own hand under 'Politics': the Bible, the New Testament, Koran, Vedan (sic) [the Vedantas], Mythology, Montesquieu's *De l'esprit des lois*.

Was it prescience that led him to list works of religion, once he had headed east, to their very source, as works of politics; or perhaps in his messianic drive religion was more use to him than the endless arguments that pass for much of politics? When leaving France he remarked to his secretary, Louis de Bourrienne, 'Europe is a molehill. There have never been great empires and revolutions except in the East.' On arrival he wrote to his brother Joseph, 'Egypt is richer than any other country in the world in corn, rice, vegetables and cattle.' His ambitions were clear when he was asked how long he would stay: 'A few months or six years; all depends on circumstances ... if all goes well, it will enable me to get to India.'

Meanwhile he had his books. Often he preferred to be read to: his secretary reported, 'if I read poetry he would fall asleep; but when he asked for the "Life of Cromwell" I counted on sitting up pretty late'.

We have travelled from Islamic Cairo to the source of the Blue Nile, then with Bruce we have found ourselves back in Cairo, where the River Mamluks were still in power, albeit now under the auspices of the Ottoman Turks, who had conquered them in 1517. (Egypt would remain somewhat nominally an Ottoman state until 5 November 1914.) With their antique weapons and ancient tactics the Mamluk rulers of Egypt were soon to be outgunned. Napoleon fought his way from Alexandria to Cairo and there his army squatted, starved of entertainment and women.

A young accompanying officer, Niello Sargy, who later wrote up his experiences in Egypt, recalled: 'The common women were horrible. But the Beys, the prominent Mamluks of the country, had left behind some pretty Armenians and Georgians, whom the generals grabbed for the so-called good of the nation.' Napoleon, spurned by Josephine – who continued to refuse to accompany him east – may well have been sensitive to the notion that an Eastern potentate must have a harem. He knew now, thanks to his confidant General Junot, that Josephine was serially unfaithful not just with Charles, but also with his own powerful friends. While it has often been true that an Eastern potentate would have the right to annex any woman, this was far from always being the case. Rulers such as Saladin often married the widows of friends or relatives to provide security for these women in old age – and in any case their first boast would be of children rather than their wives. Napoleon was a European and not so self-assured – he wanted a trophy wife. Perhaps, too, he was thinking of the last European conqueror of Egypt – Julius Caesar. He needed his own Cleopatra. The highest-status women were the Caucasian mistresses of the deposed Ottoman rulers. Napoleon 'relaxed at first with some of the women of the beys and Mamluks. But finding with these beautiful Georgian women neither reciprocity nor any charm of society, he smelled a void in all of them, and missed all the more the lascivious Italian and friendly French women.' Did the abandoned women of the beys really give Napoleon the cold shoulder? Or did he, with his generals cavorting with the locals, desire to go one better and get a *bona fide* French woman?

The beys' wives were certainly smarter than their deposed husbands, or one was. Ibrahim Bey, the Egyptian ruler under the Ottomans, had all the Europeans in Cairo imprisoned in his island palace on the Nile when Napoleon landed. This was the same palace on Roda that centuries earlier had been the headquarters of the River Mamluks (whose descendants, in a few years, would meet a grisly end).

Ibrahim Bey then gave the order for the Europeans to be executed. His wife, Zuleyha Hanem, intervened with the argument that a saying of the Prophet had predicted that the French would seize Egypt. She then hid the captives on her side of the palace until such time as they could escape to safety. Bonaparte, to his credit, did not attempt to seduce her as a reward – he awarded her with a writ of safe conduct and a personal guard. Wily to the last, Zuleyha used her writ to slip out of Egypt and join her husband in Syria.

In his drive to find a woman, Napoleon tried once again – sending out an order that the six most attractive women in Cairo be brought to Alfi Bey's former palace, which he had commandeered. According to de Bourrienne, 'their ungraceful obesity displeased him and they were immediately dismissed'. His tastes, perhaps, had been spoilt by Paris.

In Paris, revolution in fashion had followed the overthrow of the monarchy. It was the period of 'naked fashions', which even Jane Austen noted in faraway Hampshire in 1801, remarking in a letter upon a 'Mrs Powlett [who] was at once expensively and nakedly dress'd'. The nakedness referred to the almost transparent muslin dresses that mimicked, in their unornamented simplicity, the garb of women in the Greek city states of ancient times. Gone were the corsets, false breasts, padded bottoms; gone was the hair daubed in 'extraneous matter'. In was the 'snow-white drapery', though as one contemporary observer put it, 'some thoughtless females indulge in the licence of freedom rather too far, and show their persons in a manner offensive to modesty'.

Such a woman was Pauline Fourès, born Pauline Bellisle on 15 March 1778, admirably suited to demonstrating the latest Parisian fashions as she was a dressmaker and milliner by trade; by birth she was the daughter of a cook and a clockmaker. She was also an adventuress who looked good in a uniform. When her honeymoon with Lieutenant Jean-Noël Fourès was interrupted by his call-up for the impending invasion of Egypt, she vowed to join him and, dressed in his Chasseurs jacket, stowed away on board *La Lucette* bound for Alexandria with the French fleet – along with, well dispersed on sister ships, the 300 other women who were supposedly not allowed. But 300 women don't go far among 25,000 soldiers ...

Once in Cairo Pauline reverted to female dress. She would not have worn much lingerie – in its original meaning of fine linen collars, cuffs, fichus, frills; she would have relied on her own figure with insubstantial pink underclothes showing through her white muslin dresses, slit at the side so that a glimpse of pink stocking could be caught by any passing world-conquering general. The dresses would be cinched under the bosom, to show off the breasts to greater effect, with a lowered neckline. Indeed some Parisian beauties were known to dispense with any breast covering at all. Pauline Fourès, certainly at first, would not have gone that far.

It was her husband, the crudely ambitious Lieutenant Fourès, who insisted that Pauline attend the officers' parties that were happening all over Cairo. The 300 real French women looked rather mannish since, as Sargy observed, to get on board ship to Cairo 'only a few who dressed up as men got through'. These rough-handed ladies, many of whom were cooks and laundresses, now 'shone in the midst of the army'. Pauline must have outshone them all. She was twenty years old, brown haired and dark eyed. She was described as petite, kind, a little plump (but evidently not obese), spiritual. She had enough education to speak easily, to supply the flirtation and wit the French soldiery so missed.

After Pauline had agreed, in order to advance her husband's prospects, to attend an officers' party, it was not long before she was in high demand. Lieutenant Fourès couldn't believe his luck. He began to receive invitations to the gala balls intended for the highest ranks, the most favoured commanders. Pauline danced with everyone. It was what her husband had ordered. What was the point of her having stowed away in a dark damp cabin if not to be of some use to her husband? She told him, 'I came here only because I love you.' Eventually, inevitably, she attracted Napoleon's attentions. He asked for a dance. He complimented her on her bonnet. She had made it herself? Her hair, too, he admired, so free of the unguents and potions favoured by the Circassian women. Hardly the chat-up lines of a master seducer, but, as befitted a world leader, he allowed one of his generals to complete the operation. Junot cornered Pauline and told her, 'You would have to be very cruel and insensitive to refuse the gift of his heart.' Junot, who apparently had never been quite right after receiving a head wound in Napoleon's Italian campaign a couple of years earlier, then said that her husband could expect a great promotion if she acceded to Napoleon's desires. Pauline refused, admirably expostulating that she would be contemptible in her own eyes if she agreed to such a thing. Besides, such a rapid promotion would be embarrassing and obvious to everyone.

Junot smiled his slightly damaged smile and reported back to his master: 'It's not going to be easy.'

Napoleon was now 'inflamed and dreaming of means to possess the object of his desires'. The new ruler of the Red Nile desired a companion with all the passion that that river inspires.

Napoleon invited Lieutenant Fourès and his wife to lunch at Alfi Bey's old palace. There were five places set; Junot was already present. A trumpet fanfare announced the arrival of the new ruler of all Egypt, together with General Berthier. Napoleon engaged the young lieutenant (who was around the same age as himself, twenty-nine) in polite chat about his career, making a rather forced attempt to be friendly. Towards the end of the meal Napoleon placed his hands to his brow. This was the agreed signal. Junot leant across Pauline and deliberately knocked a demi-tasse of coffee down her brilliant white dress. Making a great fuss of her, Junot suggested she change clothes in a neighbouring room. She demurred. 'There is water there, you can at least save the dress,' he suggested in a kindly tone. He showed her the way and returned to the table. Apparently tired, Napoleon now took his leave with Berthier, while Junot opened a bottle of brandy and began talking intimately and amusingly with the flattered lieutenant. Meanwhile Napoleon had made his way swiftly into Pauline's room by another door. He wasn't a master strategist for nothing.

Napoleon threw himself down on his knees to announce his

love, but Pauline, 'realising immediately what he wanted of her, resisted the conqueror, broke out in tears, and seemed not at all interested in him'.

Lieutenant Fourès was in a tricky position. His attempt to get in his superior's good books had gone rather too well. One can imagine the conversation in the carriage home:

Her: 'He tried to seduce me!'

Him: 'Are you sure?'

Her: 'Sure?'

Him: 'Well. He's a man.'

Her: 'Is that all you can say? He tried to force me.'

Him: 'All right. He's a monster!'

Her: 'I said as much. I said I would never be unfaithful. Whatever happened.'

Him: 'What did he say? Did he mention me?'

Her: 'No.'

Him: 'Not at all?'

Her: 'No. But what about your prospects? Your promotion? I feel bad.'

Him: 'To hell with them. We will return to France and live as paupers. With our honour intact.'

Her: 'That is what I said to him exactly!'

Him: 'You did?'

Her: 'And I said if you found out you would most likely ask for satisfaction ...'

Him: 'You suggested to the commander of the army in Egypt that I would challenge him to a duel?'

Her: 'Yes, I did.'

At this point Lieutenant Fourès probably leant forward, cradled his head in his arms and whimpered for mercy.

Bonaparte was touched by her innocence but kept up the attack. A stream of love letters and fine gifts found their way to her. Many more heated conversations must have followed in the Fourès household. After a lengthy siege, Pauline Fourès relented and became Napoleon's mistress.

7 · The stone

'The land of my fathers!' said the louse remaining on the bald head.
Sudanese proverb

Meanwhile at the very end of the Nile, in the town of Rashid on the
right-hand channel that drains with little ceremony into the Mediterranean, the influence of Napoleon was being felt. In Rashid, better
known to us as Rosetta, the local Turkish fort, built in the fifteenth
century, was being improved and better fortified. All kinds of stone,
any that could be found lying around, was used to strengthen walls.
Recycling the stone of former buildings had always happened in Egypt.
Memphis, it is said, was used to build Roman Cairo; and the cover
stones of the Pyramids provided Islamic Cairo with some of its best
stone. In the ground of Rosetta a stone with three kinds of script was
about to be rammed into the wall of the fort when a young lieutenant
of engineers noted its singular appearance. He reported it quite casually
to his commanding officer, who knew at once its importance and sent
it to Cairo strapped to the back of a camel (the roads were generally too
poor for carts, though Napoleon improved them, of course). One of
Napoleon's 167 *savants*, the men who had accompanied the invader to
study every aspect of Egypt (so igniting the new subject of Egyptology),
Michel Ange Lancret, studied it in detail as the mysterious rock, a piece
of diorite (it was thought later to be basalt, a mistake made because of
the wax coating it was soon to receive), lay in state in a palace in the
Ezbekiya area of Cairo.

   Let's muse on that side of Napoleon for a moment and get back to
the stone later. Have there been any other invaders in history who
insisted on studying the people and place they were invading? Though
some argue that the effect of Napoleon was purely destructive, his
desire for knowledge, for its beneficial increase, cannot be questioned.
Most invader types think they know it all already. Cromwell wasn't
about to start learning Gaelic when he started rampaging round Ireland. Hitler didn't go into the Ukraine with a microscope and a butterfly net. The only ones who did, that spring readily to mind, were
those other Nile invaders the Arabs, who brought with them a culture
that would, through the translation of Aristotle and a new openness in
enquiry, kick-start the Renaissance. Interestingly it was an Arab scholar

who, nearly a thousand years before the Rosetta Stone was decoded by a Frenchman, would discover the meaning of the majority of the ancient Egyptian hieroglyphs, knowledge that would be lost in the West until the nineteenth century.

By bringing his *savants*, it was almost as if Napoleon sensed that the Nile required more respect than a mere ragtag invasion. His interest is not commercial, it is military – he wishes to conquer the East and strike at England's power in India. His eye is on glory. But to justify such action he needed also to increase knowledge. In the same way, an explorer justifies his love of adventure by bringing back news and scientific data from places that are dangerous to visit. Perhaps it is no surprise that Napoleon's scholarly invasion of the Nile should have had far more lasting effect than his military one. The desire to control, it seems, always defeats itself in some way, whereas the desire to understand can lead to greater alignment with events and with nature, ensuring prolonged usefulness.

Napoleon's scholar who first saw the stone recovered at Rosetta knew it was extraordinary. It was decided that the thing would be best shipped to France to be studied in the Academy.

8 · The great Cairo balloon fiasco

The fool thinks that wherever he sleeps is home. Egyptian proverb

The Rosetta Stone was fated, though, to move in a mysterious way. Part of it involved Nicolas-Jacques Conté, the inventor of the modern pencil, the Conté crayon, and several rather unsuccessful balloons.

Any modern visitor to Luxor has the chance to see the Nile and the fabulous temples from the privileged position of a balloon, usually at sunrise. These are giant hot-air machines, with a booster pack of propane roaring their blue flames upwards from within the twenty-five-person basket. From up there the temples look like smashed cake decorations, lightly dusted with corrosive sand. Your fellow passengers get slightly hilarious, perhaps anticipating the promised cold Luxor beer at the end of the flight. Some, like me, might be hiding their nerves – in 2009 one of these monsters hit a mobile-phone mast and crashed, seriously injuring sixteen people. When the burners are switched off the silence is palpable. Gradually, as the novelty wears off, sound creeps to your ears; you notice the rustle and creak of the cables, the squeak of the canopy above. Someone asks if they can smoke – as a joke – and they are told it's fine, go ahead: bluff called, no one tries it.

As the sun rises it cracks the horizon, like some elemental wink, and floods everywhere with light and warmth. You cannot miss the Nile, as the fast-moving sunlight reveals its perfectly looped bends. The intense green band of palm trees higher up on the west bank contrasts with bright yellow sand and the faint grey-green of the river. It looks like a loose rope that has been half buried in nature, needs tightening, pulling clear of the enfolding ground. Thankfully the balloon doesn't burst. Even before the 2009 accident, they haven't all been as safe. The very first balloon attempt was at the hands of Conté, army officer, favourite of Napoleon, artist, inventor and the man who covered the Rosetta Stone in wax. This was after Napoleon and Pauline had made a special visit to see it.

Napoleon said of Conté, 'he is a universal man, with taste, understanding and genius, capable of creating the arts of France in the middle of the Arabian Desert'. Conté had dabbled in both hydrogen and hot-air balloons in France. He was eager in Egypt to overawe the locals with the magic of the occident. Napoleon had already tried this with his *savant* Claude Berthollet, who demonstrated the latest experiments in magnetism and chemistry to a group of Islamic scholars. They remained impressively unimpressed. When they were asked for their comments, Sheikh El-Bekri said, 'Can he make me be in Morocco and here at the same time?' Berthollet replied that he couldn't. 'Oh, then, he is not even half a sorcerer!'

The balloon, it was intended, should restore the wow factor to French techno-superiority. Conté worked day and night to get his apparatus ready, though he was distracted by another project that Napoleon had pressed upon him: to produce an exact copy of the script on the Rosetta Stone. Conté was unsure how to do this and focused instead on what he did know about – balloons. He ordered the printing of notices publicising the event. They read: 'On Friday 21st we intend to fly a vessel (balloon) over al-Ezbekiya lake by means of a device belonging to the French people.'

On the appointed day in front of 100,000 people in Ezbekiya Place the contraption was readied. The envelope of the balloon Conté was extremely proud of – he had arranged for it to be made in red, white and blue by the skilled tailors who worked in the tent bazaar in Cairo. This envelope was held open by the use of a stout pole. Suspended beneath was a cylindrical basket containing a large cauldron filled with oil. From this a giant wick extended. With much hurrahing and noise of trumpets the wick was lit.

Abd al-Rahman Al-Jabarti, the Arab scholar who chronicled Napoleon's invasion of Egypt, wrote, 'The smoke sought to rise to its centre but finding no escape, so it drew the apparatus aloft with itself. They cut the ropes and it soared into the air ... then it began to sail with the wind for a very little while.'

But disaster was at hand. Just as an earlier experiment had led to a balloon catching fire in the desert, this time the heat from the huge wick had burned through the ropes securing it in place. Al-Jabarti continued, 'the bowl fell with the wick and the cloth sail followed suit. The French were embarrassed by its fall. Their claim that this apparatus is like a vessel in which people sit and travel to other countries in order to discover news and other falsifications did not appear to be true. On the contrary it is like the kites which household servants build for festivals and other happy occasions.'

Another own goal for the boastful Gauls.

Conté turned his attention to the mysterious stone and how to record its message most perfectly. His experience of printing made it obvious – the stone, with its graven words and images, could be used as a printing block. Daubed in wax (which remained until 1999 when it was finally cleaned up), the stone was set in a clever invention of the irrepressible Conté. Using the great weight of the stone (over fifteen hundredweight), he set it in a frame so that it could be tilted on to a sheet of paper. Inking the stone with a roller, the weight pressed down on the paper causing an image to be printed. Large numbers of copies were made and distributed, enabling anyone to have a go at cracking the secret of the stone.

The Rosetta Stone was famous – and was shifted to Alexandria to be shipped to France at the first opportunity.

9 · How the British got the Rosetta Stone

'There is no hill we did not fart at,' said the donkeys. Ethiopian proverb

It is well attested that Napoleon, coming from Corsica, which the British under Nelson invaded in 1794, had, in his youth, wished to join the Royal Navy. The Royal Navy was then, as it would remain, despite Napoleon's efforts, the greatest naval force in the world. Did he apply? It seems he petitioned an uncle to try and get him some kind of introduction. But after a few weeks at military school he saw that the future was in artillery and his naval ambitions waned.

If Napoleon had joined the Royal Navy the world would have been saved a lot of bother. Maybe he would have served under Nelson instead of fighting him. But he didn't, and so these two mighty warriors were destined to meet in Egypt – where else? But what if the real and lasting result was not that France lost and England won – round one at least – but that incidentally Britain got hold of the Rosetta Stone by beating the French? That the main thing of value going on then and there was not all the bloodshed and rallying of ships but a simple transfer of booty? Let's pretend so anyway.

The British dominated the Atlantic but hadn't entered the Mediterranean in a year, owing to French supremacy there. Once word escaped that Napoleon had invaded Egypt their fleet swept through Gibraltar's straits looking for action.

It wasn't easy to find the French. Nelson stopped in Sicily and even did a little sightseeing at Syracuse. (After the impending battle he would meet here for the first time Lady Hamilton, wife of the English Ambassador, later establishing a ménage à trois with them.) Even when they found the French and were hastening to do battle before the sun set, Nelson dined well with his officers. The French, meanwhile, were dining a little too well. They were still aboard Admiral Brueys' flagship at a briefing dinner when the British hove into view.

Where are we? At the extreme left-hand exit of the Nile just before Alexandria. But in the sea, not the river. The French fleet had pole position – defending any ingress into Egypt and up the Nile. Nelson, who did not realise that his sole purpose here was to capture a stone with a bit of ancient scribble gouged into it, drew closer and closer to the moored French fleet.

Many of the French were on land and sailors had to be parcelled out to man boats they usually did not serve aboard. The British slowed to fix spring anchors, a device to help them moor alongside French vessels and blast the hell out of them. Much has been made of the English decision to get between the French ships and the land, Nelson and his officers reasoning that there must be enough space to manoeuvre, otherwise they would not have moored there. But it seems this tactic was not decisive; that was almost certainly the element of surprise and Nelson's ability to press home an attack fiercely.

The Reverend Cooper Willyams was the chaplain aboard HMS *Swiftsure* and he recorded his experience of the battle:

> The enemy's line presented a most formidable appearance: it was anchored in close order, and apparently near the shore; flanked with gun boats, mortar vessels, and four large frigates; with a battery of guns and mortars, on an island near which we must pass. This posture gave the most decided advantage to the French, whose well known perfection and skill in the use of artillery, has so often secured to them the splendid victories on the shore: to that they were now to look for success; for each ship being at anchor, became a fixed battery.

The British plan was to fire at night from two sides on the disoriented French. Nelson ordered each ship to carry four lights at its crosstrees, and a white ensign illuminated by an oil lamp hung in its midst. This would serve for recognition. By such arrangements the British were able to avoid shooting each other while pouring shot into the anchored French fleet.

The plan was good. Seeing through the glass that the French fleet was freely anchored and not on spring anchors that could be used to spin a ship when it was stationary, Nelson and his commanders deduced two things: that the French would be slow off the mark when attacked and, as we have seen, that there would be enough water (though it didn't look to be the case) between the moored ships and the coast.

It was imperative to strike first, while the French would be expecting them to wait, owing to the lateness of the hour. One of Nelson's watchwords was that going straight to the battle was worth more than hanging back and making a strategy; perhaps the suggestion was that one's strategy should already be in place to take advantage of whatever luck goes one's way. So the British attacked. The French had not foreseen such a bold move and though there were gunners ashore there were no land-based guns pointing out to sea to cover the inside piece of water between the French fleet and the land. The attack was further helped by the fact that the French officers were at the briefing dinner with Admiral Brueys; in all the confusion of being fired upon they had to be rowed back to their respective ships. Some did not make it. The French fought for the most part with much reduced troops, with sailors doubling as gunners, with not enough of either to allow them to set sail and fight at the same time.

Red-hot cannonballs were fired into the sails of the French ships. They burst into flame. Masts came crashing down. Admiral Brueys, an aristocrat who had survived the Revolution and seen half his family killed, was wounded twice and almost cut in half by a cannonball. He died at his command post around 9 p.m., expiating his tactical errors by this great display of fortitude.

Little did he know that he had already lost the stone.

Nelson felt something strike his head and his good eye was suddenly blinded by blood and a hanging flap of flesh. Shrapnel had opened a three-inch wound that exposed part of his skull. Nelson, who went into battle prepared to die, was carried off the deck crying that he was done for (apparently he had predicted his demise like this before, and would again) and to be sure to tell his wife this, mark this – but before he could say what, the sawbones had sewn up the flap of skin and staunched the bleeding. 'It is, sir, what they call a flesh wound hereabouts.' Nelson was back on deck and giving orders again in under twenty minutes. Though it appeared to be an injury of little account, it was a long while healing and gave him pain for the rest of his life – another seven years.

The battle raged on through the night and into the morning. It looked as if the British had won. By controlling the entrance to the Nile they controlled Egypt. When the country was finally surrendered to the British, however, Napoleon through his generals who remained in Egypt was able to negotiate that all the treasures accumulated in Cairo should be sent to the Louvre. Thus began the glorious ascendance of French Egyptological studies. Or it would have, if the surrender hadn't noted that all goods already in transit at Alexandria were now the property of the British. And that's how the stone, which was sitting in a wooden box at the docks, ended up in Britain. Which turned out to be a good thing because, though it was a Frenchman who ultimately translated the stone, it was an Englishman who helped him get there. And if the stone, by pure chance, had not ended up in London the English-man in question, the polymath Thomas Young, would never have tried to crack its code. We might still be puzzling over hieroglyphics even now, as we are with the Indus Valley script, Olmec, and the still untranslated Minoan language, Linear A.

10 · Women shed blood at the battle of the Nile

Because the brave one is absent, the battle will not be postponed.
Nubian proverb

In a story about the Red Nile, all the battles it occasions serve further to redden its flow. We have seen crusaders and Arabs slaughtered to pre-serve the Nile for one ruler or another. But Nelson's battle was probably the first in which women and children took part.

It puts into perspective the French women, like Pauline Fourès, who stowed away to follow the French fleet. It is hard to believe that 300 or more women could really be hidden, and of course they weren't – both the French and the British navies turning a blind eye to such things, inconceivable though it is to us, used to what are in some ways the more draconian modern navies. (In the US Navy, for example, the old liberality with beer has been replaced by one beer every fifty days when at sea. Of course, people compensate: on big aircraft carriers it is common knowledge that many of the men get high sniffing solvent used for cleaning the planes.)

However, in Nelson's time there was plenty of alcohol, and, it seems, plenty of women and children too. John Nicol, who served with the British during the battle of the Nile on board HMS *Goliath* and was one of the very few ordinary seamen who wrote diaries, noted, 'I saw little of this action ... Any information we got came from the women and children carrying the powder.' The magazine, whence the powder came, was the centre of the action during a battle, so it shows how integrated into the ship's life the families of the common sailors were. Nicol wrote:

the women behaved as well as the men and got a present for their
bravery from the Captain ... I was much indebted to the gunner's
wife, who gave her husband and me a drink of wine every now and
then, which lessened our fatigue much. There were some of the
women wounded, and one woman from Leith died of her wounds
... One woman bore a son in the heat of the action; she came from
Edinburgh.

The seeming strangeness of giving birth was not so uncommon –
the heat and noise of battle induced labour. There were twenty-three
women and twenty children aboard ships during the earlier battle
of Cape St Vincent, and there may well have been more during the
battle of the Nile. We know of one woman, Ann Hopping, the wife of
a gunner, who was employed as a seamstress until the 'clear for action'
signal came; then she carried powder and assisted the surgeon as he
routinely removed the shattered limbs of fallen sailors. There were at
least five women on the *Goliath*; four of them lost husbands and Captain Foley took the unusual step of entering their names in the muster
book which entitled them to both small pay and victuals. One woman
who was aboard the *Majestic* later wrote to Nelson telling him how she
had served on board by attending to the sick. Her husband had been
killed and she sought compensation.

Modern notions suggest that women and children get in the way
of the fearsome emotions needed for battle. We are led to believe that
men will try and protect the women (and children) from injury and so
shirk their duty. Evidence from the past suggests otherwise. Ann Hopping attended the arm amputation (with rum the only anaesthetic) of
a thirteen-year-old midshipman: 'During the operation the poor child
never uttered a groan, and when it was finished he turned his head
towards [me] and said, "Have I not borne it like a man?" These words
were scarcely uttered when a cold shiver seized him, and in an instant
his young soul had entered the land of immortal life.'

With Admiral Brueys' death the French began to lose their way. By
morning their fleet was sunk and those not sinking were burning in the
early-morning sun's rays. Control of the sea had been an imperative for
success. It seemed Napoleon's big adventure was all over before it had
begun. Bonaparte, when he heard the news, is reputed to have said,
'Unfortunate Brueys – what have you done?' But he quickly recovered.
'So, gentlemen, we are called upon to do great things. Seas of which we

are not master lie between us and our country, but there are no seas between us and Africa, or Asia!'

The troops rallied and there were other incentives as well as fine speeches: officers who muttered that it was time to quit Egypt were threatened with being shot; Arabs who seditiously spoke against the French would have their tongues cut out. But it would do no good. Napoleon had lost control of the Nile.

Back to the more important matter of the mysterious stone of Rosetta: 46 inches by 30 inches by 12 and ... *bloody heavy*. Even an amateur like Napoleon could see it was a key to ancient Egyptian; the problem was all in the details – and the lack of them. Of the fifty-four Greek lines the last twenty-six were damaged – as were the last fourteen lines of hieroglyphics. And of the thirty-four lines of demotic (a quick version of hieroglyphics) the first fourteen lines were badly damaged. It was going to take a lot of very inspired guesswork.

11 · Cracking the stone

No matter how much one loves one's dog, one does not circumcise it.
Sudanese proverb

The stone, of course, would speak of the Nile – you could almost have predicted that – but how to find out? Well, we will find out, but first let us divert into the Egyptian desert.

I was there, in Dakhla Oasis, to look at the Roman-period temple of Deir el-Hagha. It was here that the explorer Schweinfurth had carved his name into a stone column in 1873. Like looking for Arne Saknussemm's leads in Jules Verne's *Journey to the Centre of the Earth* I always love hunting down clues left by earlier explorers. In the case of the column I discovered just how fast hieroglyphs had been replaced by Coptic. In one part of the temple we have carved hieroglyphs, in another, in a niche pointed out to me by the temple's guardian after I had slipped him a few Egyptian pounds, was a rough mural featuring imagery of the cross and words written in Greek and demotic characters – Coptic.

The collapse in the use of hieroglyphics occurred in a generation. The last inscription was made in AD 394 in Philae. Demotic graffiti continued for another fifty years, and then nothing but Coptic. Since the old religion was banned by the new cult of Christianity its sacred language must be outlawed too.

But one has to ask – what did people speak? You can't change a spoken language in a generation. Coptic had to come from somewhere. It was of course the language of ancient Egypt – but now written in Greek, the sanctified script in which the New Testament was recorded. Since there were sounds in ancient Egyptian you couldn't make in Greek, four symbols from demotic were added, the last heritage of the Pharaohs.

When the Arabs arrived in the seventh century they started the slow change to Arabic. By the eleventh century Coptic was used only by Christians. By the fifteenth century it had become a dead language, used only in church services, though there were dictionaries available translating Coptic into Latin.

But the crucial Coptic connection went unnoticed in Europe. They were too mesmerised by the stone. One of Conté's printings had reached Thomas Young, the English polymath. When he heard that the Rosetta Stone itself was now in London he took himself off to look at it. Meanwhile in France a young obsessive called Jean-François Champollion had vowed, aged ten, that he and only he would be the man to crack the secret of hieroglyphics. Both were highly intelligent and very good at languages. Before he was fourteen Young had studied Latin, Greek, French, Italian, Hebrew, Chaldean, Syriac, Samaritan, Arabic, Persian, Turkish and Ethiopic. Even if his knowledge was, say, only at GCSE level it was all pretty darn impressive. At Cambridge 'Phenomenon Young', as he was called, blossomed into a serious scientist. He became in a way the inheritor of Ibn al-Haytham – studying light and the eye and describing the way light must be a wave, using slit experiments reminiscent of Ibn al-Haytham with his camera obscura. On his annual holiday in Worthing – Young was evidently more adventurous in thought than action – he decided to crack the Rosetta code. It was 1814. In another holiday resort – the island of Elba – the man who had set all this in motion, Napoleon, was slipping away in darkness to the mainland to make his last stand.

And in Paris the obsessive Champollion was really no closer to solving the problem, despite having learnt before he was fourteen Latin, Greek, Sanskrit, Zend, Pahlavi, Arabic, Chaldean, Persian and Chinese. Oh, and he had become so obsessed by Coptic that he had recorded diary entries in this language as a teenager. We'll get back to that later. But despite all this linguistic artillery Champollion was really nowhere. In fact he spent most of his time in displacement activity learning new languages (OK, I think some of that list he learned *after* he was fourteen – Chinese must have taken a while, surely?) that would prepare him for the great task ahead.

Unfortunately the problem had already been solved eight centuries earlier by the Arab scholar Ibn Wahshiya. This is the finding of Dr Okasha El-Daly, an Egyptologist working at University College London who is also able to read ancient Arabic manuscripts – something both Young and Champollion were supposed to be able to do but evidently never did. Dr Okasha produces firm evidence – in fact Ibn Wahshiya's book is online – that by the ninth century, which was when Ibn Wahshiya was living in Cairo, he had cracked the phonetic nature of hieroglyphs, and that the language was very similar to Coptic – so similar he called hieroglyphs 'old Coptic' and Coptic written in Greek letters 'new Coptic'. He had also mastered the various determinatives and endings used in hieroglyphs. However, his purpose was practical. Having cracked the code he used it to investigate ancient Egyptian manuscripts to discover any scientific knowledge they might have had. It is only just coming to light, but the explosion of scholarship under the Arabs was undoctrinaire and interested in *everything*. It was part of the same movement that brought us Maimonides and Ibn al-Haytham. Yet the prejudice against the language of the heathen – after the crusades – meant that many Arab works of science are untranslated to this day.

But Ibn Wahshiya was luckier. His book was translated – albeit eight centuries later – by the wonderfully named Joseph von Hammer-Purgstall (who also wrote a history of the Assassins). In 1806 he published Ibn Wahshiya's work as *Ancient Alphabets and Hieroglyphic Characters Explained*. This raises intriguing possibilities. The book was certainly known to Champollion's colleague Baron Silvestre de Sacy and surely he must have mentioned it to Champollion.

But Champollion was, like many obsessed men, peculiarly stupid in his own way. When he heard that someone had actually cracked the code – in 1808 – he fainted out of sheer unadulterated envy. It turned out to be a vicious rumour – Champollion was still in the running. But for ten years all he seems to have done is study obsessively his Zend, his Ethiopic, his Pahlavi. Making no progress at all.

Not even using that Coptic he was supposed to know already.

Young, without any Coptic, and calling it 'the amusement of a few leisure hours' really broke the back of translating hieroglyphics – and it was very impressive compared to the *fourteen years* Champollion had so far wasted.

Young worked out that the encircled characters, or cartouches, were real names and that the hieroglyphs had phonetic values, and he got most of these right for the hieroglyphs he translated – such as those for 'Ptolemy' and 'Berenice'. Unfortunately his knowledge of Chinese undid him. In Chinese, foreign words and names are spelt phonetically; the rest are represented by pictogram characters. And in Chinese a special mark, similar to the encircling of a name cartouche in hieroglyphics, indicates a foreign word. Young gave up the struggle, and moved his butterfly mind to something else – publishing his findings in the 1819 *Encyclopaedia Britannica*.

Which Champollion most surely must have read, though he never acknowledged his debt to Young – who in the true, even-handed and rational spirit of academe denounced Champollion's work as error prone, misguided and plain wrong. Translation: I want a name-check please.

Armed with Young's insights Champollion broke new ground. He studied hieroglyphs from older times with cartouches that could not have been foreign. His huge breakthrough (which occasioned another fainting fit) was to work out that the symbol ☉ which looked like the sun (as in Chinese, which was helpful this time) might be pronounced Ra, as this was the Coptic word for 'sun'. This gave him Ramses – the name of the greatest Pharaohs in ancient Egypt. From then on, using Coptic and cryptic analysis, he worked out in two years the whole hieroglyphic language.

The fact that Coptic was written using Greek characters plus four demotic characters for sounds not in Greek must surely have been a big clue that demotic and Coptic were very similar. And since demotic was demonstrably a simpler version of hieroglyphics, why did it take so long for a supposed fluent speaker of Coptic to work out the connection? Young took a few hours and Champollion many years to arrive at similar conclusions. It was only when Champollion used Coptic that real progress was made. I suspect that he learned his Coptic rather later than he claimed, perhaps after he had read Ibn Wahshiya's groundbreaking ninth-century text.

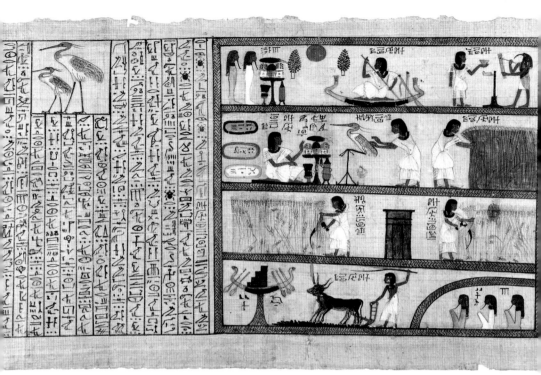

Papyrus survives even to this day buried in the sands at Oxyrhynchus near the Nile. A piece of papyrus from the Book of the Dead, Late Eighteenth Dynasty, 1350–1300 BC.

Croc skin is reinforced with bony osteoderms, making it the original armour. Back view of a crocodile-skin suit of armour discovered near Manfalut, third century AD.

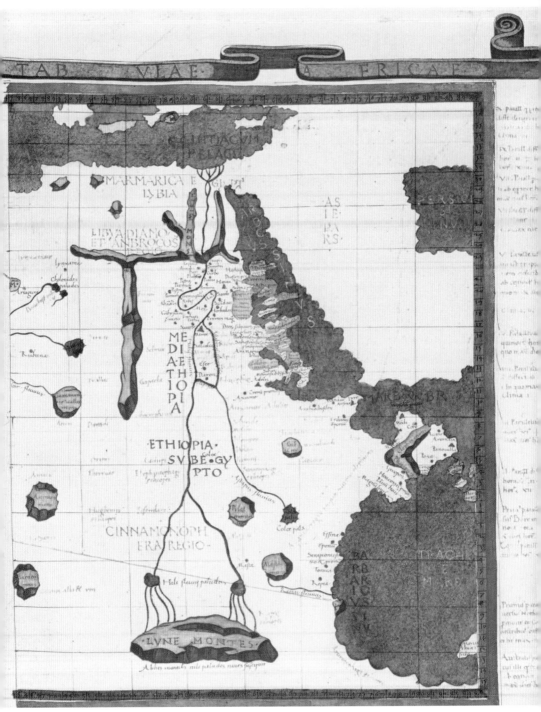

A 2,000-year-old map that is still substantially correct. A fifteenth-century version of Ptolemy's Map with the Mountains of the Moon indicated as the source of the Nile.

The Nile's flood was used to float blocks used to the build the pyramids: the Great Pyramid of Cheops reflected in the Nile overflow.

The brainchild of William Willcocks, fitness fanatic and religious scholar: the first Aswan Dam, looking north, c.1936.

The seventh crusade made the Nile, seen here in the background, run red with Frankish blood; from *Les Grandes Chroniques de France*, fifteenth-century French illumination.

The central pillar of the Nilometer on Rhoda Island measured the Nile's flood throughout the artistic splendour of the Islamic period.

Nelson 1; Napoleon 0. The Battle of the Nile, 1 August 1798 at 10 p.m., as depicted by Thomas Luny, 1834.

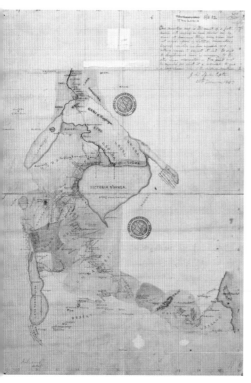

The unspeakable Speke's final triumph: Speke and Grant's map of their route from Zanzibar to the Nile.

The Tissisat Falls sees the source of the mighty Blue Nile.

The sole picture of the
photosensitive Flaubert in Cairo.

The epitome of romance, from
Flaubert to Agatha Christie: a late
nineteenth-century *dahabiya* in Cairo.

The best river swimmers in the world.
Boys shooting the rapids of the Nile
on logs. c.1901.

The inundation: a scene you'll never
see today now the Nile is dammed.
Cairo, c.1898.

Gordon had many chances to leave. Finally, it was just too late. *General Gordon's Last Stand*, by George William Joy.

Sadat tried shouting at them to stop ... Egyptian soldiers fire at President Anwar Al-Sadat while reviewing a military parade on 6 October 1981.

At the Murchison Falls the whole Nile is forced through a six-metre gap, falling a height of only forty-three metres.

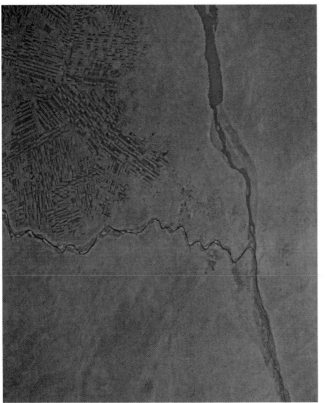

When not in flood the Blue Nile is dwarfed by the White Nile. In flood, this is where the Red Nile begins. Aerial photograph of the confluence of the Blue and White Nile, taken from the Columbia space shuttle.

12 · Battle of the Nile *deux*

Evil neighbours hold against each other the number of times the spade was borrowed. Nubian proverb

Not another battle! Since we have, in a kind of Borgesian conceit, decided that the only real result of Napoleon's invasion was the discovery of the Rosetta Stone, it seems a little much to have another battle of the Nile. But this is a book of bloody encounters, so perforce we must tell the tale. Those who don't like descriptions of fire and cannonade, skip to the next section.

Nelson may have effectively sealed the fate of the French expedition to Egypt almost before the invasion had really begun. But that did not mean Napoleon couldn't turn the tables later. Indeed he very nearly succeeded in breaking out of the Middle East during his Syrian campaign. If he had, it might have been a French Empire in India, not a British one.

But before he could do this there was another battle of the Nile to be fought. Napoleon was advancing on Cairo from Alexandria and it was decided by the ruling Ottoman elite that a stand should be made on the Nile on the west bank opposite Bulaq in central Cairo. Yes, we forget that though he was fighting the British, or they were fighting him, Egypt was under Ottoman rule, or rather Mamluk rule under Ottoman dispensation. Napoleon had to beat the Turkish Egyptian forces first.

Meanwhile the rest of the French army were marauding their way up the side of the Nile from the delta. At every village and town they met opposition. In one hamlet an aide-de-camp got too far ahead of the supporting troops. A woman carrying a baby in her arms, perhaps to distract attention, got close enough to put both his eyes out with a pair of dressmaking shears she had concealed beneath her veil. General Berthier was so incensed by this display of cunning that he had her shot on the spot, the baby handed to a bewildered peasant bystander.

One of Napoleon's tenets of invasion, and how he managed to run such enormous armies, was the principle that soldiers must feed themselves by living off the land they passed through, or by taxing the food of the native land they were invading. Either way his principle was never to pay unless it was expedient to do so. In the early part of the campaign it was easier to buy wheat than steal it, though in one village an army storekeeper and his servant were attacked by Egyptian Bedouin who burned their bodies, having tied them to a tree. A furious Napoleon, rather in the manner of the Nazis at Oradour in his native France 140 years later, ordered that the whole village be razed and the people executed by shooting or the sword. It was especially irrational as the fellahin villagers would have seen themselves as different to, and not responsible for, the action of the nomadic Bedouin.

When a priest attached to the army was asked to look at some manuscripts cached in a pigeon loft he pronounced them 'books of magic'. This may have been the case, as such things did exist, but his subsequent order to torch the lot was hardly in keeping with Napoleon's stated mission to learn everything he could about this strange land.

Naturally such behaviour was deeply unpopular with the Egyptian fellahin, a people notorious for their obstinacy and close guardianship of their land and its produce. In any case, when they did try to trade, the French often found their money useless, and they had no Egyptian money yet, but quickly discovered that the buttons on their uniforms were preferable to coins. The notion spread and soon every soldier had denuded his coat of buttons. François Bernoyer, the former tailor turned quartermaster, wrote that it was with some disappointment that only the uniforms of artillerymen and carabiniers yielded acceptable currency; these had polished brass and copper buttons, while the chasseurs and infantrymen had wood.

By the time the army reached Cairo in July 1798 their uniforms were so ragged, and so unacceptably hot, that Napoleon ordered Bernoyer to distribute a new uniform made of cotton: an indigo *habit-veste* that buttoned straight down the front and unbleached linen trousers, dyed blue for the infantry. In September cotton greatcoats were also issued in anticipation of cooler nights ahead. Everything was made by local craftsmen, including a novel headdress – a peaked helmet made of sheep's hide dyed black with folding flaps to protect the ears and neck – later to be made popular by the Foreign Legion. On top of this rather warm headgear was a woollen crest dyed in different colours for each brigade. When the army went to Syria these hats came into their own as protection against the cold mountain winds.

The French army was deployed along the western bank of the river while the river boats fought the decisive part of the action midstream. Things were going against the French. Rear Admiral Perrée, chief of the flotilla, reported that 'The Turks were doing more harm than we were doing them ... our ammunition would soon be exhausted.' The army was still too far inland to be of much help. The Turks, or Ottoman Egyptians, wrote Bourrienne, seized the most powerful of the French brigs and 'massacred the crews before our eyes. And with barbarous ferocity showed us the heads of the fallen men.' Perrée sent a message to Napoleon begging for help. That moment, in a stroke of luck of the kind enjoyed by the young Bonaparte, the sail of the Turkish flagship commanded by Commodore Kürdlü caught fire. The generous fore and aft mainsail rippled with flame, fragments of burning shrouds even setting fire to Nileside palm trees. The fire reached the main magazine and a double boom of immense volume, followed by a veritable waterspout, signified that the main magazine, stuffed full of gunpowder, had detonated – killing all the crew and the Commodore himself. This was a great psychological blow to the Turks, who had rallied and were gaining at that moment. In confusion they lessened their attack and took stock of the situation.

At the moment of this accidental hiatus Napoleon's land-based troops arrived after their long wearying journey from the sea. Forsaking a pincer action that would have captured all the Mamluk slave troops, Bonaparte drove straight towards the Nile to save his flotilla. When the Turkish sailors saw the advancing army they upped anchor and departed hastily across the river to Cairo. The defeat was decisive – it was only a matter of days before the whole occupying army of Mamluk slaves and Ottoman Turkish beys, who had controlled Egypt since 1517 (the Mamluks serving various leaders since the ninth century), would be ousted by the twenty-nine-year-old Frenchman.

13 · The end of the affair

Truth, even a snake comes to it. Egyptian proverb

The effect of the French occupation on the women of Cairo was evident first of all in the clothes they wore. It was reported at the time, 'The French would bring out Muslim women and girls barefaced in the streets and it became widely known that wine was being drunk and sold to the troops.' The outrage was a little misplaced. Certainly women were throwing aside the veil, but early nineteenth-century Cairo was no hotbed of virtue even before the French arrived. According to the contemporary commentator Al-Jabarti, Frenchmen sought to please their women and avoided contradicting them even if the women cursed or struck them. No doubt he was annoyed to see local women walking and laughing in the streets protected by French soldiers. Even more disgruntled, he adds, 'women order and forbid, laying down the law'. Cairo, known for centuries as a pleasure town, a reputation it still enjoys today among visitors from the Gulf, was in some ways in the position of Thailand during the Vietnam War: a local culture of prostitution fanned into something of an epidemic through the presence of so many French soldiers. Niello Sargy wrote that he was surprised how few brawls took place, 'despite the whoring that went on'. Close to Bonaparte's lodgings in the Alfi Bey palace, drunken French soldiers broke into a harem, the non-public part of a house. An officer went to break up the mayhem as 'already a great number of inhabitants had assembled before that mansion express-ing loudly their indignation'. Inside he discovered 'soldiers of differ-ent regiments giving themselves over to all the excess and brutality that a long privation could, while not excusing it, at least allow us to understand'. The soldiers were chased from the mansion, but even so the gang rape of the odalisques, or concubines, provoked a large public demonstration.

The problem was that prostitution in Cairo had become something of an art form, with the woman performing music, dancing and gen-erally taking as long as the man desired. This style of courtesanship continued after the French had left, a style followed by such famous characters as Kuchuk Hanem, with whom, fifty years later, the novel-ist Gustave Flaubert was much smitten. But for the time being things became rough and ugly. The printer and *savant* Antoine Galland remarked, 'One saw girls of twelve putting themselves, completely nude, in the middle of a square for a few coins.'

Meanwhile, at the other end of the scale, Pauline Fourès' hus-band had been despatched down the Nile to get him out of the way. Lieutenant Fourès got as far as the port at Rosetta but then went AWOL, returning to plead with his wife. Arriving at night in the dark-ened city he made his way to the civilian quartermaster Bernoyer's house. He was distraught to find that his wife had moved in with Bonaparte and was living in an apartment next door to his. The amiable Bernoyer, touched by the man's distress, offered to speak with one of Pauline's friends the next morning. The mission was a failure: Pauline refused to meet her husband, saying that all bonds between them had been broken – as she had predicted – by his overweening ambition. The end of their relationship was all his fault, she said; again and again he had refused to listen to her. Fourès, on receiving this news, became hysterical. Bernoyer had to restrain him from bursting in on her private apartment. He sent a message saying that Lieutenant Fourès was capable of anything – even suicide. Pauline sent by return a dry riposte: 'Calm down. I know my husband well enough to be certain he will not cause a scandal, nor will he commit any crime. He cherishes life too much to sacrifice it so lightly … he should return to his post as soon as possible, since you know that Bonaparte wants to be obeyed' – and here there was a hint of threat – 'especially when his orders concern service to his army.'

Bernoyer tried to encourage him by suggesting that back in France there were many more women he could find to replace the unfaithful Pauline. Fourès was not convinced; but, broken and slinking back to the port like a low cur, he waited to hear from his leader and usurper Napoleon Bonaparte. Perhaps Pauline had mentioned something, but Napoleon himself issued the orders for Fourès, instructing him to visit Malta, Italy and then Paris, where he was to deliver some papers to Paul Barras. This must have been his own wry way of getting his own back: Barras had cuckolded him with Josephine. But there was a reward, too, in the arrangement; he asked Fourès to pick up papers and newspapers from his brother Joseph Bonaparte – a very useful contact to be offered. And the payoff – not a few silver coins but 3,000 francs 'to defer expenses'.

With Fourès out of the picture, the affair took off. Pauline was seen covered in jewels and sumptuous clothing. She took to wearing Bonaparte's clothing, even his uniform – or else Bernoyer supplied her with one that was identical: a blue coat with a high collar embroidered with red and gold, lapels generously decorated with gold oak leaves, a black cravat over a white cretonne shirt, voluminous red sash tied gaily at one side, white riding jodhpurs and turned-over riding boots. She created quite a sensation. On her head she displayed her milliner's skill by tying a tricolore sash into a fabulous bonnet. The troops called her 'La Générale' or 'Clioupatre'. Instead of her husband getting a promotion and a new uniform (and there is no evidence from the records that he ever advanced higher than lieutenant), it was Pauline herself who was promoted. She rode an Arab stallion outfitted for her sole use and was accompanied by Bonaparte's aides-de-camp. One of these was Josephine's son, who understandably was a little put out at the way his stepfather was behaving. His annoyance reached a pitch when he was forced to ride behind a coach containing Pauline and Bonaparte as they went for an evening ride. 'Not able any longer to bear the humiliation, I went to General Berthier to ask that I be transferred to a regiment. A rather lively scene passed between my stepfather and me as a result of that action; but he ceased at that moment his rides in the coach with that lady.' Bonaparte may have retreated but he did not give up. He and Pauline were set on conceiving a child; had it happened, he would almost certainly have divorced Josephine.

But no child was forthcoming. Fourès now returned to the scene. There is some confusion about whether he made it to France or not. In one story his ship is intercepted by the English who, discovering the transparent flimsiness of his mission, unearth the fact that they have Napoleon's lover's husband on board. To confuse the great conqueror further, they sent Fourès back to Egypt. Whatever the truth, on his return Fourès was put in a rage when he discovered just how far his wife had gone, from a shy and retiring hat maker to the talk of the town. He demanded to see her and told all who would listen that he would take a *sabot* (a clog from her native Pyrenees region) to her comely backside. Pauline was not intimidated: she demanded a divorce 'to protect myself against his brutality'. In eight days, thanks to Sartelon, Napoleon's commissionaire in Egypt, the marriage was dissolved.

Pauline blossomed as a mistress of the salon. Her picnics at the Pyramids, site of Napoleon's great victory the previous year over the Mamluk army, were the gayest and most eagerly attended gatherings. She took tuition in that native lute-like instrument the *oud* and, by all accounts, was most proficient. She also learnt the harp, its calming tones so welcome to Napoleon, whose victory in Egypt was gradually looking like stagnation. Blockaded by the British, unable to defeat the Ottomans in Syria, he received word that France was itself in a dangerously vulnerable state. Telling Pauline that he was simply going 'up the delta' for a few days, he did a midnight flit back to Paris. The man who would conquer Europe and burn Moscow was too afraid of his girlfriend to tell her he was leaving her. He did write a letter explaining things, and Pauline, with her instinct for survival, installed herself as the mistress of Napoleon's successor in Egypt, General Kléber. She is said to have grown skilled at telling false diamonds from the real. When offered a diamond she would, and this must have been hard to carry off with style, let a drop of water fall on to its surface and move it around with a hat pin. If the gem was glass or paste the water spread, if a real diamond it remained as a globule.

Pauline returned to France in 1800, shortly before the French gave up their occupation of Egypt. In 1801 she married a well-placed retired officer, Henry de Ranchoup, a marriage secured through Napoleon's advice to Ranchoup. She never again met Bonaparte, except once, at a ball, in 1811, a year after he finally divorced Josephine and married Marie Louise of Austria. Probably he and Pauline did not dance on that occasion.

As a wedding present Ranchoup was given the consulship in Santander and in 1810 he was sent to Sweden. Pauline stayed in Paris, becoming one of the great salon hostesses of the time. She painted, played the harp and wrote three novels: *Lord Wenworth* (1813), *Aloïze de Mespres* (1814) and then, after a long gap – coincident with Napoleon's defeat and exile and death – *Une Châtelaine du XIIème Siècle* (1834). Of the 112 works in Napoleon's library on St Helena there were no novels by his former mistress.

Ranchoup died in 1826. To restore her fortunes Pauline went to Brazil to start a venture buying tropical hardwoods in partnership with a retired Imperial Guards officer. She succeeded, and in 1837 returned to France to live a rich and eccentric later life. She took up smoking, was notorious for bringing her lapdog into church and kept, in her orangerie, a troop of small monkeys. She died aged ninety-one, in 1869, the year the Suez Canal, the work of another Frenchman, Ferdinand de Lesseps, was finally opened.

I went searching for the palace of Alfi Bey and the apartment occupied by Pauline Fourès. It was in the Ezbekiya neighbourhood, a place now known for its enormous outdoor second-hand book market. Of the palace nothing remains – though the name lives on in the traditional restaurant Alfi Bey's, which is to be found in Alfy Street just opposite the raunchy bellydancing club the New Arizona. A little bit further along is one of my favourite hostelries, the Windsor Hotel bar;

I popped in to drink to the extraordinary career of Napoleon's Cairo mistress Pauline Fourès.

14 · Muhammad Ali – from taxman to king of the Nile

Don't ask news of an old person, ask it of a traveller. Egyptian proverb

It's 1805. Napoleon's navy is getting its final drubbing at Trafalgar where Nelson will be shot once too often and die. Meanwhile, Egypt is up for grabs. The Mamluks are still running things but their credibility has been destroyed by Napoleon's invasion. Into the vacuum steps a determined Albanian tax collector – Muhammad Ali, a man who will leave an indelible mark on the Nile from Cairo as far as the great Sudd swamp.

Muhammad Ali was, like Alexander the Great, born in Macedonia, though of Albanian parents. It is strange to think of Alexander, Napoleon and Muhammad Ali all linked not just by their overweening ambition and similarity in personality but also by the fact of Egypt being the focus of their ambitions. Without Napoleon's example and the opportunity afforded by his invasion of Egypt, Muhammad Ali would have remained a *bolukbashi*, or tax collector, in Macedonia. Though his father was a tobacco trader, Muhammad Ali was taken under the wing of his uncle, through whose connections he became first an efficient tax collector and later leader of the Kavala volunteer regiment, one of many that went to Egypt in 1801 to reoccupy the country for the Ottoman Turkish regime. In the power vacuum left by the departure of Napoleon the Ottomans did battle with the much weakened Mamluks, the military power in Egypt since the ninth century. By carefully playing for both sides but always with an eye on both the people and the sheikhs of Al-Azhar mosque, Muhammad Ali presented himself as an able ruler. So much so that by 1805 the *ulema* (Muslim scholars) asked Ahmed Khushid Pasha to stand down as *wali*, or governor, of Egypt and allow Muhammad Ali to take over.

His personality and character were suited to the great tasks ahead of him. James Augustus St John, who visited Egypt later on in Muhammad Ali's rule, spent some time with the *wali*, observing him:

Mohammed Ali is a man of middling stature, robust and stout in his make, exceedingly upright, and, for a man of sixty-five, hale and active. His features, possessing more of a Tartar cast than is usual among European Turks, are plain, if not coarse; but they are lighted up by so much intelligence, and his dark grey eyes beam so brightly, that I should not be surprised if I found persons familiar with his countenance thought him handsome.

St John reports that Muhammad Ali Pasha slept little and that Europeans who shared his tent while on a journey complained of being asked questions at all times of the night, and of his conversation going on long after they wished to sleep. He rose before daybreak and quickly rode to his divan or office where all petitions, letters and despatches awaited his opinion. These were read out to him as he paced the floor and dictated his replies. Muhammad Ali's habit of having most letters read to him gave rise to the persistent rumour, held now by many Egyptians, that a mere illiterate had gained power over them. Apart from its being a requirement for a tax collector, there is ample evidence that Muhammad Ali could read in Turkish if not in Arabic. St John states that one of his pastimes was to retire to the banks of the canal, have a carpet thrown down for him to sit on, and there while coffee was being prepared read and seal his despatches. He would then enjoy his coffee and a *shisha*, before returning to the palace. In his harem, the private part of the palace frequented by eunuchs and women alone, he read or had books read to him, or 'amused himself by conversing with the abler part of his eunuchs'. At other times of leisure he dictated his autobiography or played chess, to which he was addicted. 'In fact, his active restless temper will never suffer him to be unoccupied; and when not engaged with graver and more important affairs, he descends even to meddling.' His interest extended to the seemingly minute. An educated Egyptian teacher of mathematics, engaged in instructing a group of young officers in Alexandria, was made to give an exact account of how each one was advancing in his studies. When his fleet was being prepared he was rowed out each day to observe the shipwrights at work, urging them on by his presence. Though he would often go to bed late he would rest, or at least withdraw, from about 11 a.m. to 3 p.m. in his harem. Then he would be back at his divan dealing with business until 11 at night or even later.

The accidents of the weather never interfered with his business. Rain-fall, which most Cairenes deplore, never deterred him, and, indeed, making a journey in a torrential downpour had once caused him a very serious illness. Everywhere you see evidence of his will to initiate, pursue, complete. His movements were known to be sudden and unex-pected. He could be in Cairo and a few days later in Alexandria, arriving unannounced; it maintained the agents of government in their vigi-lance better than admonitions from the centre. Others said it was an affectation or a caprice; nevertheless it worked.

To regain his composure there was a small alcove in the Shubra Palace where the Pasha would sit at about eleven or twelve o'clock at night, sometimes for an hour, sometimes less. As St John relates, 'From this alcove two long vistas, between cypress, orange and citron trees, diverge, and extend the whole length of the grounds; and in the calm bright nights of the East, by moon or star light, when the air is per-fumed by the faint odours of the most delicate flowers, a more delicious or romantic station could hardly be found.'

Muhammad Ali had one wife, whom he treated, it is said, with pro-found respect. She was known as an energetic woman who had a great deal of influence over him. When she died he never remarried, though he did keep a number of female slaves in his harem.

John Barker, the British Consul-General in Egypt, related that at his first meeting with Muhammad Ali to present his credentials he handed over the Imperial firman, or decree, from Turkey, the nominal ruler of Egypt. The Pasha did not deign to look at the document. Instead he spoke of the fine new frigates he was building. The Pasha praised the new Consul's predecessor for never opposing his will or disrespecting his opinions. Muhammad Ali concluded, though, that this was easy as his words and actions were founded in reason and justice. 'I will tell you a story,' the ruler added.

I was born in a village in Albania [sic], and my father had ten chil-dren, besides me, who are all dead; but while living not one of them ever contradicted me. Although I left my native mountains before I attained my manhood, the principal people in the place never took any step in the business of the commune, without previously inquir-ing what was my pleasure. I came to this country an obscure adven-turer, and when I was yet a *bimbashi*, a captain, it happened one day that the commissary had to give each *bimbashi* a tent. They were all my seniors, and naturally pretended to a preference over me; but the officer said – 'Stand you all by: this youth, Mohamed Ali, shall be served first.' And I *was* served first; and I advanced step by step, as it pleased God to ordain; and now here I am.

He glanced again at the Imperial decree: 'You see, I have never had a master.'

Above all, the Pasha was a simple man. (You hear the same said about Franco and Stalin.) When St John interviewed him about his life he was treated to a long exposition on his victorious expeditions to Sennar, Nubia, Kordofan, the Hejaz and Syria. St John writes, 'I observed however, that, in the enumeration of his achievements, no mention was made of the destruction of the Mamluks. Doubtless, as he ran back over the track of memory, the recollection of that bloody day [when Muhammad Ali had 499 Mamluks killed] presented itself among his brighter reminiscences, like Satan among the sons of God; and conscience may, moreover, have whispered that his hearers also remembered the event.'

Muhammad Ali could never, however, be drawn to comment on the fate of the Mamluks. He had excised them from memory, and from history.

15 · Napoleon and Muhammad Ali

Embers, the child of fire, can also burn a person. Nubian proverb

Every Nile ruler from Cleopatra to Sadat has been fearful of poisoning. Napoleon, exiled after his defeat at Waterloo and writing feverishly in St Helena, was no exception. He believed himself the victim of poisoning, slow poisoning (there is controversial evidence from his hair that he was poisoned with arsenic). However, even while worrying about his health, he did not cease thinking of Egypt. He wrote in his prison diary, 'The day will come when work will be put in hand to dam the two branches of the Nile at the head of the delta, so that all the waters of the one branch can flow through one and then the other alternately, and the flood can be doubled.'

Muhammad Ali, sitting in Cairo, had everything written by

Napoleon translated and read to him. The Frenchman was Muhammad Ali's role model – Napoleon, after all, had not only given him Egypt, he had inspired him in his campaigns to conquer the entire region. It made sense to listen to his hydrological advice too, albeit in a simplified form. At first Muhammad Ali wanted to stop up the Rosetta branch and let it all be diverted to the other branch at Damietta. Louis Linant, his French water engineer, who would later lay the groundwork for the Suez Canal, objected on the grounds that it would deprive Alexandria of fresh water. The Pasha's next plan was to dismantle the Pyramids, which he considered a heathen distraction, and use the stone to dam both the branches of the Nile. This plan was half adopted: the dam or barrage was built, but the seventh wonder of the world was not the source of masonry for the expedient reason that it was too costly (that is, heavy and cumbersome) to transport. It gives us some idea of the feat of the ancient Egyptians that they managed to construct a monument so massive that it resisted destruction through sheer weight and bulk.

Despite plague and a war in Sudan, Muhammad Ali conscripted a corvée to build the barrage, the first of the Nile dams. In point of fact a barrage is a subspecies of dam proper in the sense that a barrage never blocks the river – its purpose is simply to raise the level of the water behind itself. There is no sense of a reservoir lake being built, something in which there is no current. A barrage simply backs the river up, slowing it down but not stopping it. By raising its level it can be drawn off for longer into the canals upstream of the barrier. The barrage, once its teething troubles had been fixed, which it has to be said took many years, was hugely successful in increasing cotton production.

The *barrage du Nil* meant that cotton could at last be grown in quantity, since cotton cannot survive inundation but needs regular watering throughout the summer. With the barrage backing up the Nile towards Cairo, with canals and pumps and syphons installed, it was possible to water a vast area of land previously allowed to be fallow in the summer.

When he was over seventy, the man who owed his reign to the invasion of Napoleon, who was inspired by Napoleon, was visited in turn by Napoleon's son, Count Walewski. One suspects that the son was jealous to maintain his father's reputation when he wrote of Muhammad Ali: 'His genius is greater in civilising than in organising. He has neither the eagle eye which sees men and things from above, nor the superior intelligence which permits a man to take decisions which at first sight seem surprising, but he has a keen intelligence, perseverance, a strong will, and astonishing dexterity. Had he been born in our country he would have become a Metternich or a Talleyrand rather than a Napoleon.'

Though Muhammad Ali was an avid reader of Napoleon's work, it was only because Napoleon demonstrated his knowledge through deeds as well as words. When Machiavelli was read to Muhammad Ali he remarked after forty pages that 'I can learn nothing from this man. And as regards cunning, I know far more about it than he.' He returned to reading, or having read to him, the works of Bonaparte.

That the student failed to outdo his master in grandiosity and sweep is evident. But Muhammad Ali lived until he was eighty, and had, quite probably, a more lasting impact on Egypt and the Nile than even Napoleon did. His legacy was certainly bloodier.

16 · The killing of the 499

They don't praise the army going to war, they praise it on returning.
Egyptian proverb

There were 500 – and 500 were called. One stayed in bed and then there were none, none except him. All 499 dead, cleaved into pieces, grapeshot and musket fire tearing their bodies to pieces, scattered in the ditches of the Citadel, where Shajarat al-Durr's body had been left, the traditional dumping ground of the Mamluks themselves.

Muhammad Ali planned a feat of treachery that not even Machiavelli would have conceived. Rightly the Albanian had little time for the Italian fox. The plan was quite simple: lure the troublesome Mamluks, who still thought they should have power, to a single spot. And then kill them all.

The River Soldiers knew their time was up, but they sought a new role with Muhammad Ali. They clung to their power, as all do, because power is the hardest thing to give up. The British, a century and a half later, would have to give up their power over the Nile and it broke the heart of Churchill, who as a young man had been in the battle of Omdurman and helped win that power.

So the Mamluks suspected but they did not suspect. The River Soldiers who still rode out with swords and armour battered by Napoleon's victories, with red and green banners, these Mamluks came from all over Egypt to be honoured by their Albanian ruler.

All 499 of them. One stayed in bed. It's like a cautionary tale in reverse. The late bird doesn't just get the worm, he gets off scot free and gets to live the rest of his life in the Levant. Which is what happened. The rest were slaughtered.

It is not an easy job to kill 499 men, mounted on fine Arabian horses, attended by servants, all trotting along the lengthy defile that runs to this day around the foot of the Citadel. You can see it as you speed past on the autostrade heading to the airport or downtown.

No machine guns. No gas. No depleted-uranium bombs to fulfil the order. Single-shot muskets and grapeshot did the job, or most of it. The worst part, hacking down the survivors and killing the wounded, was done by Anwar the Druze and his crack squad of murderous subordinates. Anwar was a giant of a man, bursting his tunic at chest and belly, huge blacksmith's arms, though in truth he had never done a day's honest work in his life. His arms were the legacy of a youth spent on smuggling ships on the Syrian coast. Now he was the trusted killer, wielding a curved sword that was soon blunt from cutting off heads. 'It is better to stab than cut,' he told his men, 'because it is quicker and blunts the sword less.' But he could not help cutting, and cutting and cutting. The ditch was soon ankle deep in the blood of horses, Mamluks and their servants.

And the one that got away? He awoke late and decided not to leave his estate in the delta. But the news reached him that not a single Mamluk had returned home. It was enough. He was slipped under cover of darkness onto a trading barge going downstream to Rosetta. From there he was smuggled on a fishing boat to Cyprus and then to Jaffa. His family lived there until 1948, when they escaped again, strangely, back to Egypt. I know this story because the sole descendant of the one who escaped told me.

17 · Death(s) on the Nile

Who learns about the leopard lives. Ethiopian proverb

Blood flowed freely – not only in the ditches of the Citadel, but on the banks of the Nile, in Egypt and Sudan. There were many funerals. Muhammad Ali craved control of the entire river; he was the first ruler to see that control of the Nile meant controlling all the wealth of Africa – slaves, ivory and gold.

Muhammad Ali made many expeditions up and down the Nile, subduing the last remnants of the Mamluks, Baiburs' descendants, outmanoeuvred by this wily Albanian who, we have seen, is said to have tricked those 499 into attending a gathering in Cairo. But others, including Muhammad Ali (but why should we trust him?), claim he was not so careless. In another story it is related that, over a few years, he picked off the Mamluk leaders one at a time all over the country. This final massacre was just the last few, a mopping-up operation. In one account it is suggested only twenty-four turned up to be killed. Whatever happened at the Citadel, Muhammad Ali had made himself undisputed ruler of Egypt. His expeditions south resulted in conquering the Upper Egyptian and Sudanese tribes; he became known as an enlightener – to some – but to many he was the bringer of death. Funerals along the Nile marked the passage of his armies.

Muhammad Ali's troops killed Christians and Muslims alike. It is a sign that the funeral service is ancient and, in essence, precedes both Islam and Christianity in that it remains, in Egypt, largely the same for each religion. But there are differences. The Christians bury in coffins, which, in accordance with a tradition of ancient Egypt, were made of stone, but in more modern times were wooden. Muslims use only a shroud, or rather several shrouds. Shortly after the Napoleonic occupation there was a case where land belonging to Copts was seized by Muslims. It was found to be a burial ground, and all of those graves, when excavated, contained coffins. As a Coptic burial ground it was returned to the Copts.

Burial in either religion must take place within twenty-four hours of death. On the way to the grave, in Christian cases hymns and chants are sung. In the case of a Muslim, a hired singer or singers of the Koran will lead.

Copts are closer to the ancients in that they are buried in their finest garments, including a few jewels. The shroud, on a rich man, is embroidered in gold and silver. If the dead man has made a pilgrimage to the River Jordan, the garments he wore may be interred with him. If he is not a pilgrim he will be clad in the robe he wore in life for receiving Holy Communion. At both Muslim and Christian funerals prayers and incense are offered up for the soul of the departed.

The ancient Egyptians chose to bury their dead on the west bank and to live on the eastern bank. Crossing the River Nile, like the Styx, was an inevitable part of the route towards one's own death. That the ancient Egyptians were obsessed by death is evident everywhere. Some of that obsession continues to this day with elaborate ceremonies performed at graves seven days, forty days, one year and seven years after someone has died. Both Muslims and Coptic Christians respect the *arbyeen*, the forty-day ceremony, meaning it is almost certainly of pharaonic origin. The Nile is still a river entwined with death, natural death and the cycles of the flood seeming to go together. But by the nineteenth century man would begin his attempt to change nature. The Nile was soon to become an unnatural river of death.

Part Five

THE NILE DAMNED

Elephants, exploration and Agatha Christie's trunk

1 · The discovery of Mougel Bey

Do not fear the person who talks much. Eritrean proverb

Napoleon long gone, Muhammad Ali slowly fulfilled the impatient Frenchman's dreams and dammed, or barraged, the Nile. The year he started operations was 1840 – and this initial barrage was not completed until twenty years later in 1860, and was not functional until 1889. It was a damn slow dam. But the act of damming the Nile was a turning point. Man, at last, knew, or thought he knew, that he could conquer the river.

The desire to dam the Nile started, as we've seen, with the Pharaohs, peaked first with the mad plans of Hakim the Caliph and Ibn al-Haytham, then receded until the arrival of Napoleon, who immediately saw the utility of damming the river, but never got round to fitting this enormous plan in with all his other enormous plans. There is a strong correlation between big dams and megalomaniacs. Just as one may conquer countries to satisfy a desire for extending the dominion of the self, so one can conquer nature, most obviously by stopping up its greatest and most powerful rivers.

That Muhammad Ali should have sought to dam the Nile is, in a way, entirely predictable. That his heir across the centuries, Gamel Abdul Nasser, should also seek to dam the Nile was also entirely unsurprising. But, to succeed, both attempts needed European help.

The barrage was the first dam across the Nile. But was it a dam or even a barrage? For its first fifty years it was neither, having failed to hold back water without ominous cracks appearing. So, reluctantly, its builders asked for its gates to be left fully open. From then until the early 1880s it served as a picturesque and very useful bridge across the Nile.

The Frenchman Linant Bey was the first European engineer enlisted to get the project off the ground. In fact it was he who saved the Pyramids as we know them. We've already alluded to this fact, but it deserves repetition: without Linant Bey there would be no existing seventh wonder of the world. Just as the Taliban put an end to the Great Buddhas, so

Muhammad Ali desired to replace the greatest works of the past with one of the present that was even greater. We can imagine his joy when he realised he could kill two birds with one stone (or many), kill off the competition provided by the Pyramids and use their stone to build something even bigger and better. But unlike the great pyramid builders he was in a hurry. Perhaps this is how megalomania always reveals itself in the end – its practitioners are always in too much of a hurry to achieve their ends. Napoleon's hurry to conquer the world resulted in a failure to build up a large enough navy – a prerequisite of world conquest in the eighteenth and nineteenth centuries. Hitler's hurry to replicate Napoleon in Russia resulted in an unwinnable war on two fronts. Though speed brings many benefits – Napoleon's rapid marches and Hitler's blitzkriegs are testament to that – in the end both of those leaders overextended themselves and ground to a halt. But the pyramid builders just worked as meticulously as ever, day in, day out, until their great monuments were finished. What a torture to build the Pyramids in a hurry! But slowly, painstakingly, that made it all possible.

Linant Bey, though eager to build the dam – actually two: one on the Rosetta Nile branch and one on the Damietta branch – was not so eager to go down in history as the man who levelled the Pyramids (though the mad Caliph Hakim came close). But Muhammad Ali ordered him to do so. Linant then did what anyone under the command of a madman does, he took the job seriously, so seriously that he felt compelled to make a comparison of the costs and time – time being the most important and persuasive factor here – involved in a pyramid demolition versus cutting the stone in an ordinary quarry closer to the Nile and floating it in the correct size downriver. The savings in time and money were so great that reluctantly Muhammad Ali agreed to keep the Pyramids.

But something of his earlier enthusiasm had left him, as if, deprived of the chance to make his mark doubly – through gigantic destruction and construction – he was depriving himself of a motivation he sorely needed. With this failing interest in the project, Linant was soon to be pensioned off and his place taken by another French enthusiast – Charles Mougel, soon to be Mougel Bey.

Mougel Bey arrived in Egypt to help extend the docks of Alexandria. His success at this job led to him taking over the dam project. Mougel Bey improved on Linant's plans and moved the barrage a fraction upstream so that both branches could be closed by the same structure.

But still he was subject to the same pressure that Linant had endured. At one point Muhammad Ali ordered that 1,300 cubic yards of concrete be poured every day – regardless of whether it be needed or not. Now that *is* the sign of a megalomaniac.

By the time Muhammad Ali died in 1849 the barrage was not completely finished, though they had been building it since 1843. Already it was showing cracks and springing leaks. Ali's successors Abbas and then Ismail could not be persuaded to renovate those parts that had been built too quickly. Utterly exhausted and impoverished, Mougel Bey had neither the money nor the inclination to move back to France. He had married and produced children, and still his barrage had never been tested. But so much time had passed that times were, indeed, changing. When Egypt defaulted on its loans in 1876, Britain assumed a new and powerful role in its affairs, ousting the influence of the French.

Egypt, under Muhammad Ali's grandson Ismail, had spent so much on building the next big thing – the Suez Canal, as well as rebuilding Cairo on European lines – that it had become bankrupted. Britain exchanged debt for control of the Suez Canal. When there was a popular uprising in 1882 that threatened British expatriates, Britain shelled Alexandria and more or less assumed control of the country.

The British already had big plans of their own for the Nile and the first of them was to dam it properly. Out with the old and in with the new; Colonel Colin Scott-Moncrieff, fresh from the Punjab, went out to the barrage to see if, as all the Egyptian staff recommended, it should be abandoned and a new system, perhaps using pumps, constructed to aid canal irrigation.

What struck Scott-Moncrieff as he gazed at the forty-year-old structure was how well it was designed and how well it was sited, and this aroused his curiosity as to why it had failed. He found one answer in the hastily constructed floor that sealed the area around the dam's base to stop seepage – all those tons of concrete had been washed clean of their lime before it had properly set, leaving a partially porous floor, the source of 'springs' in the dam further down. Iron grilles set into the base of the sluices created turbulence that further damaged the base of the dam; some of the structure leaked but could be fixed with a coffer dam. In short, there was no earthly reason not to proceed and make the barrage work properly.

It was only after he had started work that Scott-Moncrieff heard a rumour – that the creator of the dam was dying in a Cairo slum. Taking time off from regrouting the barrage and building temporary earth dams to allow access to the dam floor, the Colonel went in search of the dam's chief engineer. What he found was a sad sight: the former top engineer lying on a ratty divan in the winding streets behind Midaq Alley – the market area of Khan al-Khalili, later made famous by the novelist Naguib Mahfouz (who moved out when he was twelve). Mougel Bey was too poor to afford meat more than twice a month, his health had suffered and his eldest son was gravely ill.

It is to Scott-Moncrieff's credit that while working on the dam he tirelessly petitioned the British government in Cairo to provide Mougel Bey with a pension commensurate with his great achievement as the first man to dam the Nile. Realising that Mougel Bey also needed psychological help, Scott-Moncrieff regularly visited to ask his opinion of improvements that he might make. He was said to have treated Mougel with great deference, reporting progress on the barrage to the broken old man 'as if to his chief'.

On the day of a great test which the barrage had passed with flying colours, Sir Colin (he was knighted in 1887) hastened to the old man's alley dwelling. There he found a crowd of mourners – Mougel Bey's son had died that morning. The old man was speechless with grief, rocking back and forth in a stupor. Sir Colin went to leave but was encouraged forward to make his condolences known. When he leant towards the old man he could think of nothing to say so he whispered the latest news: 'The barrage is holding up three metres of water.'

The result was unexpected, but illuminating of the kind of man who takes on the biggest projects. Mougel Bey rose to his feet and flung his arms wide in a gesture of exultation. 'Vous entendez, mes amis!' he cried. 'Trois mètres! Trois mètres!'

2 · Important information on irrigation (which can be skipped if necessary)

Oh salt! For your own sake be tasty – or they will call you a stone and throw you away! Sudanese proverb

Since the beginning of time agriculture in Egypt largely depended on a system of basin irrigation. The land was flooded in August when the Nile inundated the land. The great lakes formed by the flood and held in position by a series of dykes and raised levees were soaked for six months, allowing the all-important sediment to manure the land. Around November the waters had largely receded and the land was sown with a winter crop of wheat, barley, beans, clover – known as *bersim* and the standard fodder of all the donkeys plodding the streets of Cairo. Fenugreek too was planted in winter, as were lentils. *Bersim*, which was fast growing, could be cropped several times, but the other winter plantings yielded only one crop a year on the flooded land.

Along the edge of the river, and needing extensive irrigation, a summer crop could be grown – rice, indigo, sugar cane and cotton were all grown in summer. Requiring an ox-powered *sakia* (waterwheel), or a swinging lever-and-bucket (*shadouf*), these crops were labour intensive with their need for constant water.

One more crop could be grown when the Nile was rising, and this also required extensive irrigation, largely through canals connected to the Nile. In the reign of Muhammad Ali one of the first steps taken to increase crop yields was through the enforced digging of more canals. The so-called corvée of forced labour was not unpaid, though it was highly unpopular. Men were taken from their families, or else their families accompanied them, living off their meagre pay of a piastre a day plus a food ration of cereals and meat twice a week. As the number of canals increased so did the requirement to maintain them, also carried out by the corvée. This habit of employing farmers to dig and dredge provided a trained and experienced workforce for when the Nile barrage and later the Suez Canal came to be built using the corvée system.

The Pyramids had been built using the same system – not slavery exactly, but not freedom either, a kind of focused effort possible only because of the holiday allowed by the Nile after its flood. Without the flood these great strivings of humanity would never have occurred, the Nile goading men to greater and greater efforts.

A corvée has the potential of an army, albeit as an organisation dedicated to construction, to do something for the common good. An army too can protect, and does something for the common good that way. But we have got ahead of ourselves. The corvée provided Muhammad Ali with a new and compelling idea. He built an army to surpass the illiterate turf cutters: he formed a gigantic robber band to go pillaging far to the south of Egypt, eating up the Nile as they went. Their announced mission: to bring peace ...

3 · Control through terror

He who refuses all advice will still take advice from Satan.
Nubian proverb

In 1820 Muhammad Ali sent his son to the Sudan to pacify the
unruly southern tribes – in reality to take control of the lucrative
African Nile trade routes. Accompanying the troops was his brother-in-
law, an administrator known as the Defterdar who was greatly feared
and loathed for his immense cruelty. Such was the barbarism of his
acts it was a relief for the people to embrace a rebel leader calling
himself the Mahdi who promised to rid Sudan of the rapacious Turk
(which would result eventually in the killing of General Gordon, the
last representative of the British–Turkish–Egyptian government of the
Sudan).

In one account, the Defterdar received a poor man whose sheep had
been stolen by a Turkish soldier and who had been verbally abused
into the bargain. Seeking redress from the Defterdar he had to wait as
the evil tyrant caught several flies, snatching them from the air; it was
his favourite pastime. After hearing the case the Defterdar exploded
with rage: 'How dare you bring such a trifling case before me? You
will go before the *kadi* for such insolence!' The poor man thought for
a moment that at last he might achieve justice, for *kadi* is the Arabic
name for a judge. But the Defterdar's *kadi* was a cannon parked behind
his divan. The man was strapped across its barrel and blown to bits for
daring to complain.

A man struck another man in the market and was brought before
the Defterdar. 'Which hand did you strike with?' he was asked. 'My
right hand.' To show what happened to people who take the law into
their own hands the Defterdar had the skin of the man's palm removed
down to the ligaments. It was done scientifically with a small machine
designed by the Defterdar himself. When the man screamed with pain
as this atrocity was committed he was held down and his tongue was
cut out for daring to rebuke the Defterdar.

On the feast day of Bairam it is customary to be given presents by
one's employer. One feast day a score of the Defterdar's grooms decided
that if they asked for something en masse they would receive it. Each
kissed their lord's hand and asked for a pair of shoes for their naked

feet. The next day each was given a pair of iron shoes which were nailed to the feet.

In the end Muhammad Ali Pasha grew weary of hearing such tales in his court. He ordered that his monstrous son-in-law be poisoned with henbane. (Symptoms: twitching, dimness of vision, stupor, intermittent pulse, coma, death. Cure: stomach pump or emetic, a tiny hit of belladonna, mustard plasters, strong coffee.) Ah, poison and the Nile – one liquid supplies life, the other certain death. The order was quickly carried out and there was not the usual manoeuvring to avoid being the one who charged the cup with death's liquid instrument.

4 · The source code

Though the hyena eats dark meat its dung is white. Ethiopian proverb

But the Nile, the whole Nile, the full Nile, the Red Nile south of Egypt had been awakened. It would never be silent again. Its call could never now be ignored. But in 1840 the dying old Albanian sent another expedition further south, in search of the source of the Nile. He had succumbed at last to the dreams he had avoided all his practical life. It was this expedition, and the subsequent book by one of its European members, Ferdinand Werne (its leader was the Circassian officer Suliman Kashef), that fired interest in solving 'the Nile problem' – in other words, to find the source, once and for all, conquer the river and so control it. Werne, a German medical doctor, and his book are mentioned in Jules Verne's 1863 book *Five Weeks in a Balloon*. Given that Verne's book was a bestseller for many years, it would be like having a travel book referenced in a book by Frederick Forsyth or even J. K. Rowling. Despite being very definitely not on the map, such references made sure that the idea of the Nile was very much on people's minds. John Petherick, Burton, Baker and others almost certainly read Werne's book. Petherick tricked natives by placing gunpowder in a pipe so that it exploded by 'magic'. He learnt this trick either from Werne's book or from the crew of Werne's boat whom he was able to meet later in Khartoum.

Werne's work, *Expedition to Discover the Sources of the White Nile*, has an even stronger vein of bigotry than is usual in nineteenth-century travel books: 'The complete depravity of the Asiatic world, even in the lifeless and powerless form of a mass dissolved in corrupt fermentation, always effervesces strongly into cruelty with the wide-spread barbarians of the East, and displays itself in bestial vices, to the disgrace of mankind and scorn of the sacred bond of nations. A truly savage nature is theirs …' But this dislike of Asia is turned as much on his Turkish companions in exploration as it is, as might be expected, on the African tribes they meet. Indeed Werne is observant and even sympathetic. Here he describes Capitan Selim (the boat's commander), distributing gifts: 'No beads are given gratis; the poor people must run, make the Turk laugh first, and give them entertainment, before it is determined to throw on shore these glass bits of paste, though Capitan Selim possesses an enormous stock of them, and then this generosity is only for the sake of seeing the bustle and noise …' When he observes some Dinka dancing he writes, 'the men shake their chests with such agility and force, as I had never witnessed in the dances of the Arabs. How inferior all our gymnastics are to the natural nimbleness, and lion and tiger-like flexibility of these freely developed limbs!'

Werne notes that among the Shilluks who inhabit the sides of the 'White River', as the Nile is known, there are some who prefer to despatch prisoners with a knobkerry or club rather than a spear: they 'beat them to death like a dog with the hassaie'. Only the King kills prisoners using a spear, which he does personally, without ceremony, while seated under a huge tree. There, we discover, he passes judgement with a heavy spear in his hand and 'assumes a very angry look'. Perhaps the look frightens them. Already the expedition is getting nervous.

Werne's expedition with Kashef and Capitan Selim is really a turning point of Nile exploration. It is the first expedition where the shock value of firearms is fully realised. Werne plans another expedition with just two assistants who, if fully armed, would be strong enough to intimidate even a vast crowd of the natives. It will be Stanley and Frederick Lugard who will finally bring this bloodthirsty dream to fruition.

Werne questions the native people about the source of the Nile. Here, at around 4 degrees North, they are told the source is thirty days away, that there are four streams and they become only ankle deep. They also hear that copper is abundant at the source, a claim made by some of the ancient authors about the Mountains of the Moon and substantiated by the copper mines opened around Lake Albert in the early twentieth century.

But it is the news of the Niam Niam that really puts fear into the explorers. The crew had long been talking about the Niam Niam, who supposedly went on all fours like dogs and ate any human who strayed into their land. They also had dogs' heads, some said, but the Dinka argued that the Niam Niam merely allowed all their teeth to remain (the Dinka and Shilluks, among whom they travelled, removed all four lower teeth for ritual reasons) – the better for gnawing on human flesh. Werne tries to be brave and speculates that the crawling on all fours is just a way of saying that they do not join combat openly but sneak in close to plunder and perhaps eat those who are most easily taken.

It is fear of the Niam Niam together with the rocky bar revealed across the river by the falling waters of the dry season that decides the men to return. Crowds of natives march alongside the boat and appear to threaten it. When Capitan Selim wakes early to pray and sees just how many native fires there are along the shore he loses his nerve and refuses to go on.

But this mixed bag of Turks and Europeans had done enough – they had shown it was possible to penetrate the heart of darkest Africa. The race for the Nile's source had truly begun.

5 · Sex tourism on the Nile

She cried for marriage, and when married she cried again.
Sudanese proverb

Muhammad Ali may have initiated the race to discover the Nile's source; he had also, inadvertently, inaugurated the world's first sex-tourism destination. Cairo had been the brothel of the East for centuries. It was no accident that the raunchy stories of *The Thousand and One Nights* (also known as *The Arabian Nights*) were collected in Cairo. The book may have been set in Baghdad but the happenings described were informed by Cairene excess and voluptuousness. Napoleon's army vastly expanded the need for prostitutes in Cairo, and this remained much the same after he left in 1801. With Muhammad Ali's embrace

of French learning and his heirs' embrace of French culture, the popu-
larisation of ancient Egypt by Napoleon's programme of listing all the
country's monuments and the building with French expertise of the
barrage, it comes as no surprise that some of the first tourists travelling
the Nile should be adventurous Frenchmen like Gustave Flaubert, lured
as much by sex as by the mystique of ancient monuments. And they
had to go up the Nile to get their full taste of it because Muhammad Ali,
in an attempt to curtail the loose legacy of Napoleon's army, in 1834
had banished the courtesans of Cairo south – to the Nileside towns of
Asyut, Esna and Luxor.

In 1840, the Nile traveller James Augustus St John reported on the
almeh or *ghawazi*, the banished courtesans of the Nile. St John wrote,
'In reality what is termed the "dance of the almé" is the opera of
the Orientals. All ranks, and both sexes, young and old, delight in the
exhibition; and the ladies of the harem, instructed in the art by the
almé themselves, perform in their own apartments, for the amusement of their families.' St John made his way to a village suburb
of Cairo where the *almeh* were living. 'They were all young; none
perhaps exceeding twenty; and the majority between ten and sixteen
years old. Some few would have been considered handsome, even in
London, but the greater number had little beside their youth and the
alluring arts of their profession to recommend them.' St John was led
to a coffee house where about a hundred dancing girls were all
intent on the enjoyment of the moment. 'Not being habituated to
wine, coffee appeared to produce in them the same excitement and
petulant gaiety to which Champagne or Burgundy sometimes gives
birth among European women.' The performance began and St John
wrote of the bellydancing, 'I fear that a company of accomplished
almé, engaged by an opera manager, would draw crowded houses in
Paris or London.' He has recourse to Greek: 'The dance, which is *porneia*
mimetic, represents a tale of love; at least, as love is understood in the
East.'

He omits any but the most oblique references to the main way the
coffee-house dancers enhance their earnings. Muhammad Ali, before
banning such girls, employed a *Pezawink bimbashi*, a Captain of the
Courtesans, to administer the vice of his country. The girls were divided
into four classes and each had to pay a special tax to the government
which the *bimbashi* had to collect along with a list of their names. St
John remarked, 'Lately this honourable personage, after a lengthened

delinquency, was convicted of the most nefarious practices, among which was that of inserting in the list of courtesans, apparently through revenge, the names of several respectable ladies: the wives and daughters of his superiors …!'

6 · Flaubert and his 'little lady'

When the river straw burned, the sieve at home made of straw cried.
Ethiopian proverb

And the sex tourists came. One of the more famous was Gustave Flaubert. Of course Flaubert, being a romantic as well as a sex addict, had other reasons for his visit to the East. In the mid-nineteenth century there was no more romantic journey than taking a *dahibiya*, a sailing houseboat, to see the great monuments of the Nile at Luxor, Kom Ombo and Aswan.

Flaubert, in search of the romance he had imagined in his first novel, *The Temptation of St Anthony*, set off up the Nile with his equally sexually active pal Maxime du Camp. It was du Camp, a pioneer photographer, who took the first photographs of the monuments of Egypt – from the Pyramids to the temple at Luxor; and it was du Camp who, after a mammoth three-day reading session, advised Flaubert to burn the *Temptation* novel. In between sleeping with prostitutes, Flaubert spent long hours musing on the beauty of the Nile cataracts, or rapids, in Aswan. His letters and diary entries suggest that it was here that Flaubert first came up with the idea for his great novel *Madame Bovary*.

I went up to Aswan in search of Flaubert. I wanted, in a kind of Alain de Botton moment of secular worship, to find the exact spot where Modern Literature was born. But instead of the black-granite rocky islands and surging currents of through-flowing water there were only the placid waters of Lake Nasser – and the giant curved concrete wall of the Aswan dam. The roaring cataracts that had mesmerised Flaubert and caused him to rethink his whole idea of literature were gone, subsumed under masses of concrete. Maybe it was a fitting tribute after all.

But what had caused this momentous idea for a starkly realistic novel about sex and love rather than the tepid romance of St Anthony? Was it Flaubert's encounter with the legendary courtesan Kuchuk Hanem a mere ten days earlier?

He and the photographer Maxime du Camp were at the furthest point south of their Nile journey, above the second cataract, now submerged by the waters of Lake Nasser. Flaubert marvelled at the river: 'The water of the Nile is quite yellow; it carries a good deal of soil. One might think of it as being weary of all the countries it has crossed, weary of endlessly murmuring the same monotonous complaint that it has travelled too far. If the Niger and the Nile are but one and the same river, where does the water come from? What has it seen? Like the ocean, this river sends our thoughts back almost incalculable distances.'

It was here at the second cataract that he decided to give up his desire to rewrite a romance about the East and instead be absolutely rigorous. It was here he decided, surrounded by all that was ancient, to write the world's first modern novel, *Madame Bovary*.

Flaubert had come to Egypt for many reasons: to escape failure, to rejuvenate his writing, to accompany his friend du Camp; but undeniably also for the simple pleasures of sun and sex. In a way he's the prototype of a kind of modern traveller – not travelling solely for sex, but motivated by it, with ruins and river journeys as nice extras.

As we have already seen, the prostitutes, banned from Cairo in 1834, had decamped up the Nile. Still, the two determined young men still managed some screwing in Cairo. After satisfying themselves Flaubert paid for his servants to pleasure themselves with local prostitutes and remarked, 'I shall never forget the brutal movement of my old donkey driver as he came down on the girl ... all in one movement laughing with his great white teeth ... the rags wrapped around the lower part of his diseased legs.' Very quickly Flaubert amalgamated his former romanticisation of the East with an eye for its harsh and often bizarre details: 'A week ago I saw a monkey jump on a donkey's back and try to jack him off – the donkey brayed and kicked, the monkey's owner shouted, the monkey itself squealed, and apart from two or three children who laughed and me who found it very funny, no one paid any attention.'

In Cairo they stayed two months at the Hôtel du Nil. The single photograph of Flaubert in his twenties was taken in the garden of this hotel. This photograph was one of the earliest taken in Egypt, a calotype, made by immersing the finest Turkey Mill drawing paper in silver iodide solution and exposing it for two minutes through the camera. Flaubert must have been standing very still. His head is covered by what looks like a black fez topping a white turban. He is bearded and beefy, bearlike.

The pose, in the hotel garden in 1850, looks very similar to that struck by a devout Muslim in the standing moments before prayer. Flaubert's eyes are fixed on the ground a few yards ahead of him. There is something black at the base of the picture, perhaps a window ledge. That's it: du Camp is inside the hotel photographing the shy Flaubert, who wrote, 'I would never allow anyone to photograph me. Max did it once, but I was in Nubian costume, standing, and seen from a considerable distance, in a garden.' (The true narcissist refuses to be photographed; he is matched only by the one who insists on being photographed continually.)

The Hôtel du Nil was Flaubert's and du Camp's permanent base in Cairo. The owners were two Frenchmen: Bouvaret and Brochier. Bouvaret was a former provincial actor, a man of dubious taste who longed to make his hotel the 'the last word in Parisianism'. Flaubert mocked him and his pretensions but stole his name, recalling it months later at the second cataract when he decided to write *Madame Bovary*.

Finally the two friends set sail up the Nile on a barge, a *cange*. Maxime du Camp made notes about their companions:

Rais Ibrahim. Captain of our boat. A handsome man of twenty-four or five ... when he was angry with the sailors he would spit at them and punch them. During the five months he was in our service he gave us not a single cause for complaint.

Hadji Ismael. Of all the sailors he was the one I liked the best. He was very sweet natured, with an ugly face, one-eyed, superb muscles.

Khalil. Former *bardash* [homosexual]. He did in fact have a charming behind, which we often saw when he jumped into the water with the other sailors.

Farghali. Old philosopher. The only one who remained as fit as ever at the end of our journey, when all the others were so exhausted as to be unrecognisable.

Mohamed, whom Gustave called Narcisse because he resembled a servant of that name he had once had. The strand of hair he let grow at his occiput was very long.

All these men, except the captain, had their right forefinger cut off
to avoid being taken for military service.

Slowly they sailed up the great grey-green river, against its constant
current but aided by the breeze, always blowing, almost always blowing
from north to south. It is this breeze, which balances and overpowers
the counter-flow of the river, that has made the Nile such a wonderful
conduit through the centuries. Flaubert loved the river with its curves
and longueurs but soon became tired of the ruins that all tourists feel
duty bound to inspect. He dreamed of the pleasures of the *ghawazi*,
the banished dancing prostitutes of Cairo. In E. W. Lane's *Manners and
Customs of the Modern Egyptians*, first published in 1836, the author
wrote: 'Egypt has long been celebrated for its public dancing-girls, the
most famous of whom are of a distinct tribe, called "Ghawazee".' They
were different from Egyptians, living apart from the general population, with separate customs, their own social structure, and perhaps
even speaking a different language.

When their boat arrived at Esna, a tumble-down town of dust and
broken stones, Kuchuk Hanem, the most famous *ghawazi* of her time,
sent her procuress, who had a pet sheep, to the river to meet Flaubert
and du Camp. The pet sheep's wool was painted with spots of yellow
henna, and it had a velvet muzzle on its nose. They were led to Kuchuk
Hanem's house where she entertained them most royally.

> ... Kuchuk Hanem is a tall, splendid creature, lighter in colouring
> than an Arab; she comes from Damascus; her skin, particularly on her
> body, is slightly coffee-coloured. When she bends, her flesh ripples
> into bronze ridges. Her eyes are dark and enormous, her eyebrows
> black, her nostrils open and wide, her shoulders heavy, full apple-
> shaped breasts. She wore a large tarboosh, ornamented on the top
> with a convex gold disc.

Flaubert was excited. He wrote, 'One learns so many things in a brothel,
and feels such sadness, and dreams so longingly of love ...'

More than one writer had fallen for Kuchuk Hanem. In the same
year that Flaubert met her, George William Curtis observed in his
long-forgotten *Nile Notes of a Howadji* (*howadji* means 'foreigner') that
Kuchuk Hanem was 'a bud no longer, yet a flower not too fully blown'.
When things hotted up he became coy, writing 'whereupon, here the

curtain falls'. Flaubert was more detailed. He wrote, 'her cunt felt like rolls of velvet as she made me come. I felt like a tiger.' In another letter he wrote, 'Towards the end there was something sad and loving in the way we embraced.'

It was at this point that Flaubert and du Camp made their way further upstream to the second cataract. Already Flaubert's writing was changing from the purple prose of *St Anthony*. Instead of describing a moon-drenched landscape he wrote, 'it was shining on my right leg and the portion of my white sock that was between my trouser and my shoe'.

Du Camp later observed of this time, 'Flaubert's future novel engrossed him. "I am obsessed by it," he would say to me. Amid African landscapes he dreamed of Norman landscapes ... on the summit of Gebel Abusir, which overlooks the Second Cataract, as we were watching the Nile dash itself against the sharp black granite rocks, he gave a cry: "I have found it! Eureka! Eureka! I will call her Emma Bovary!"'

On the journey back down the Nile, du Camp and Flaubert again stayed at the Hôtel du Nil. Perhaps it was then that the famous photograph was taken. The posture is so reminiscent of leave taking, of the sadness of parting. Flaubert wrote after his second and last meeting with Kuchuk Hanem, 'I intensely relished the bitterness of it all; that's the main thing, and I felt it in my very bowels.'

Flaubert is overshadowed in that photo by the two rundown buildings behind him. Perhaps on their roofs there might be storks nesting. The garden looks wintry, a couple of low acacia trees and a taller tree, perhaps some kind of palm, framing the right-hand side of the picture. On an occasion when Flaubert makes Madame Bovary seem the epitome of the deluded romantic fool he has her imagine herself and Rodolphe living happily in a low, flat-roofed house in the shade of a palm tree.

On his way home Flaubert wrote from Constantinople, 'Why have I a melancholy desire to return to Egypt, to sail back up the Nile and see Kuchuk Hanem? No matter: the night I spent with her is the kind one doesn't have very often, but I enjoyed it to the full.' He was still seeing prostitutes. It's not surprising that du Camp and Flaubert both contracted venereal disease – but not in Egypt, most probably in the Lebanon.

Kuchuk Hanem made such an impact on Flaubert that his account of their night, in a letter home, was turned by the poet Louis Bouillet into a poem where the courtesan is depicted as 'sad as a widow' after the departure of the virile young Flaubert (they've done it five times in about thirty-six hours). This poem made Flaubert's muse-figure and mistress Louise Colet jealous. Flaubert wrote to her, realistically one feels, 'You and I are thinking of Kuchuk Hanem, but she is certainly not thinking of us. We are weaving an aesthetic around her, whereas this particular very interesting tourist who was vouchsafed the honours of her couch has vanished from her memory completely, like many others.' In Flaubert's writing Kuchuk Hanem appears in the dance of Salome, the dance that leads to John the Baptist losing his head.

Twenty years after Flaubert's visit, his ex-mistress visited Egypt in 1869 for the opening of the Suez Canal. She felt driven to sail up the Nile in search of Kuchuk Hanem. She claimed she met an old and diseased woman of that name. The discarded lover's last revenge? Later we will follow her on this quest.

For his last novel Flaubert again reverted to Egypt for inspiration. He was still thinking about the owners of the Hôtel du Nil when he thought up Bouvard and Pécuchet, the dim-witted autodidacts in what was intended to be his masterpiece. He never finished it. A few days before his death in 1880 Flaubert wrote to his niece: 'for the past two weeks I have been gripped by the longing to see a palm tree standing out against a blue sky, and to hear a stork clacking its beak at the top of a minaret'.

I went looking for the Hôtel du Nil in downtown Cairo the other day. In Murray's 1857 guide the hotel was located across from Ezbekiya Gardens in what is now Goumraya Street. I searched up and down this street, now mainly dedicated to the sale of air compressors and mechanics' tools, for some sign. But like the second cataract the hotel is long submerged by the workings of modernity. Dodging crazy taxis and surrounded by blaring car horns, I came in the end to the conclusion that the frantic forecourt of the MISR petrol station was the former site of the garden of the Hôtel du Nil.

7 · A journey down the Nile – 2007

The eye of the guest sees cockroaches giving birth. Nubian proverb

I thought of Flaubert strolling along the Nile in Cairo and I imagined that the islands midstream, rather than the banks, would be the closest approximation to how things had looked 150 years ago. But the islands are inaccessible except by local ferry. No tourists visit them (I am talking about the islands that have no bridges to the mainland). I decided to do my own cruise through Cairo to see the islands that are inhabited midstream but are unvisited by tourists and have no cars upon them. You might see a solitary motorcycle crisscrossing the fields, more likely a donkey. These islands would have been submerged during the flood; at best they would have been swamps. But since the first dam at Aswan was built over a hundred years ago they have become permanent parts of Cairo. The largest island has both a church and a mosque; it is straddled by the huge Mounib Bridge, but there is no access to the island from the bridge. Instead you must take a small ferry that costs the equivalent of 5p. There are other, smaller islands, all given over to agriculture and a way of life that has disappeared on the mainland.

For transport I needed something inconspicuous, invisible even. Foreigners are not encouraged to take their own boats along the Nile without official protection, or that's the theory. In any case too much of a presence would result in lots of unwelcome attention. I'd been with a professional photographer in Ezbekiya book market and been warned off by bullying members of state security – I didn't want that sort of interest on my little cruise.

My Maxime du Camp was my friend D'Arcy Adrian-Vallance, who is usually up for most aquatic larks – we once paddled the fields of Oxfordshire during the worst of the floods – and who reminded me that I had once boasted that a rubber beach raft was the best way to travel on the Nile. The challenge was on. My beach raft, which cost around £20, was about nine feet long with rubber rowlocks and enough room for two – one at each end. I had two tiny oars to row with. D'Arcy was happy to keep watch and cradle our only rations – a water bottle and some biscuits. I was grateful for the water as I had something of a cracking hangover and had arrived with nothing except the boat tied to my car roof. This we inflated at a local garage in Maadi and then with a £2 tip to the nearest felluca captain we launched from the jetty next to TGI Friday's. Feluccas ply the River Nile at all the main towns. In Cairo they are limited by the bridges – their masts being too tall to fit under some of them. We would have no such difficulties.

Quickly we were midstream and travelling fast with the current. Throughout its length the Nile is never sluggish – it is a young river still, or feels it, no, that isn't right, it is a virile river, it knows its own mind. There is nothing sleepy about it.

I was always surprised and was surprised now at how little floating garbage there is in the Nile in Cairo. You'd think by now after all these miles it would be a veritable cloaca. The canals that lead off it are horrible. Those that haven't been covered over are like fly tips or open sewers. You see lads bathing horses in these canals, riding the horses in up to their withers. No, the Nile is a clean river, cleaner now that there is a sewerage system that takes city waste far out into the desert to be treated. I looked down and saw no fish, though I have seen them in shoals in the sun-heated shallows near the bank. I rowed on, feeling the sun on my dehydrated face but blissfully happy. D'Arcy dangled his fingers in the water as it streamed past, or rather as we streamed along with it, as it was the roughly 3mph current that was taking us towards the centre of Cairo.

We were at the tip of the big island known as Geziret Bahrein when children began shouting and waving to us. You never get that in the city – kids are too blasé there and there are too many foreigners walking around for it to be a novelty. We passed a little beach where women were washing giant aluminium cooking pots, and in a sort of concrete river-lapped pool they were smashing clothes against the water. Boys dived in to swim to us, but in some kind of natural etiquette they kept their distance from our ludicrous little craft, though their faces were beaming – all wet heads and white teeth. We declined all invitations to land and rowed on past an enormous two-masted dhow, a sandal, whose sides were overflowing with freshly cut reeds. It looked like an enormous floating haystack. Special boards, grey and worn-out looking, were fixed to the gunnels to raise the ship's sides. This meant the reeds reached right up to the bottom of the sails. There was no engine on the craft, perhaps the last working sailboat in Cairo – I would never have thought I'd see such a thing in the twenty-first century. The rudder was especially massive, hewn, it seemed, from timbers a foot thick with a great arching tiller arm like the bough of a tree. Men, half hidden by the high reeds, called out to us laughing. It seemed we had found the ideal way to travel into Cairo.

Not 300 yards away was the infamous Corniche, the racetrack along the Nile's bank where it is not uncommon to see a car in a tree – that is, off the ground like some Formula 1 mishap. That's how dangerous it can get. Ever been undertaken by a car going 100mph while simultaneously being overtaken by one going about 90? I'm not surprised that foreigners decide to hug the slow lane come what may, though it does put you nearer to the trees. And the river. Which is obviously the best place to be. Strangely, we were making good time. The six or so miles from TGI Friday's in Maadi to the island of Zamalek would take us just under two hours. When the traffic is really bad I've done the same journey in an hour and a half. D'Arcy and I talk excitedly about getting a power boat to move in and out of Cairo with ease. But we'll never do it; drifting with a bit of rowing is way better than blasting and bumping over the waves creating a power ripple that annoys the net-casting fishermen, even though they are so inured to insult they never show it.

We drift on past the enormous fountain base midstream beneath the rotating restaurant in the sky attached to the Grand Hyatt. The water piles past the concrete base and we noticed a small maintenance ladder which we grab hold of. In such a small craft the scale of the world seems changed, as if we are Borrowers scurrying around the giants' world.

Finally we arrive at the cultivated market gardens that stretch along one edge of Zamalek. There are similar gardens all along the Nile. Any patch of earth near a water supply gets turned into a bed growing something. When they burned the police huts down during the 2011 revolution only the gardens next to them were left unscathed. Egyptians are gardeners before anything else – I've never seen a garden that isn't tidy, artistic and good to look at. In Europe, good gardeners tend, on the whole, to be about as imaginative as petrol-station designers. The flower growers are sometimes a tad more creative than the vegetable experts, but not by much. But an Egyptian garden is at its best when it is mainly vegetables. These will be grown in an ordered but pleasing way, with a flower or two thrown in – which we now know contributes to better growth all round. When you see Egyptian gardens, market gardens and vegetable gardens, you understand how they could have built the Pyramids – a stone at a time, each one individually crafted but broadly similar, but not mechanically similar. I think that's what makes these gardens so pleasing.

We pulled the boat out. Deflated it, put it on the roof of a hailed taxi and drove back to Maadi in half an hour. It was early and the Corniche was empty.

8 · Kuchuk Hanem's fame

Trust in God, but tie your camel first. Arab proverb

Flaubert was in Egypt in 1849–50. So was Florence Nightingale and so, as we have seen, was George William Curtis, American author of *Nile Notes of a Howadji*. Curtis later became editor of *Harper's Weekly* and, like Flaubert, was more interested in the mysterious orient than in ancient antiquities. He wrote a long description of the dancing girls of Esna, and he, too, succumbed to the delights of Kuchuk Hanem, whom he took to be in her late twenties and calls, wrongly, Kushuk Arnem. For all the brilliance of Flaubert's description we are left with a woman like the statue of Memnon, her lip curled and carved in stone. Curtis, a worse writer, makes her live: 'Smiling and pantomime were our talking and one choice Italian word, she knew – buono. Ah! How much was buono that choice evening. Eyes, lips, hair, form, dress, everything that the strangers had or wore, was endlessly buono. Dancing, singing, smoking, coffee, buono, buono, buonissimo! How much work that one word will do!'

With her young associate Xenobi and an aged couple beating drums and playing a one-stringed fiddle, Kuchuk Hanem began to dance. We see immediately the expert bellydancer at work:

> Her hands were raised, clapping the castanets, and she slowly turned upon herself, her right leg the pivot, marvellously convulsing all the muscles of her body. When she had completed the circuit of the spot on which she stood, she advanced slowly, all the muscles jerking in time to the music, and in solid substantial spasms.
>
> It was a curious and wonderful gymnastic. There was no graceful dancing – once only was there the movement of dancing when she advanced – throwing one leg before the other as gypsies dance. But the rest was most voluptuous motion – not the little wooing of languid passion, but the soul of passion starting through every sense, and

quivering in every limb. It was the very intensity of motion, concentrated and constant ... Suddenly stooping, still muscularly moving, Kushuk fell upon her knees, and writhed with body, arms and head upon the floor ... it was profoundly dramatic ... it was a lyric of love which words cannot tell – profound, oriental, intense and terrible.

Poor Louise Colet hadn't a chance.

9 · Colet searches for Kuchuk Hanem

The hyena will enter at the place where a pet dog breaks through the hedge.
Ethiopian proverb

Louise Colet was ten years older than Flaubert. She died in 1876, four years before he did. It was during the interregnum of their intense eight-year affair, from 1846 to 1854, that Flaubert spent his night with Kuchuk Hanem. After he had reported it all to Louise Colet, the idea, the image, the competition, this woman, this dirty foreigner, she just wouldn't go away. It ate away at Colet and she should, of course, have let it go. Instead, in 1869, she wangled an invitation – as with her Académie Française prizes, it was said she was expert at getting influential people to intervene on her behalf – from Muhammad Ali's grandson Ismail Pasha. To celebrate the opening of the Suez Canal, Ismail was sparing no expense: a boat would sail up the Nile, quite the match for one of Cleopatra's galleys, and on board would be the greatest minds of literary Europe, the celebrities of the day, the aristocrats and the men of wealth and influence. All on one boat which would traverse the Suez Canal and then proceed up the Nile as far as Aswan, stopping, of course, at Esna, the adopted hometown of Kuchuk Hanem. By some quirk of fate, Colet and Hanem were not quite the same age – sixty years old and fifty years old, women who had shared the same man, the inventor of the modern novel, some twenty years earlier. One, a French intellectual, a poet, a salon hostess. The other, a courtesan, a prostitute perhaps, but also a marvellously skilled dancer, a musician and a singer.

   Like all intellectuals Colet was jealous of physical charms that trumped intellectual ones. Not that she hadn't been beautiful in her day, but a life spent sitting around reading books doesn't develop the body along the same lines that dancing and fornicating do. Flaubert's description of Kuchuk Hanem emphasises her broad shoulders, her powerful head and, yes, her beautiful throat that smelled of sweet turpentine.

The journey up the Nile was exactly what Colet had expected. She wrote in her diary that 'The Nile surpasses all photographs but only if you are holding your hat – it is very breezy.' She landed at Esna with one thing in mind, to find and speak with her lover's ex-love.

There was no assistant courtesan with a decorated sheep to meet Louise as there had been for Flaubert and du Camp. The ship would stay a day and two nights. Most visitors were taken in *carrotta*, donkey carts, to see the ruins at Kom Ombo. Louise walked up the hill with a dragoman from the ship leading the way. All along he tried to convince her that there was no one of that name – *kuchuk hanem* only means 'little lady' he tried to explain. In the shadows, spies were watching.

On the second night she went back again. Again Kuchuk Hanem's spies told her of this strange woman. In the end, for amusement, Kuchuk Hanem summoned the ageing French beauty to her spacious town house, built with the wealth of a thousand conquests. The women were waited upon by two giant Nubians, one with a single eye.

Hanem was older than Colet had imagined and was thick around the middle; she was watching Colet with her still powerful eyes. Her ankles were still beautiful though, her legs slim.

Yes, she was known as Kuchuk Hanem. What was that to the *how-adji*? She made a joking aside to her maid, older than she, a woman with infinitely understanding eyes and grey tresses, a black gown and arms knotty and veined with work. Every element of opposition had been rolled out of her form, perhaps by centuries of despotic rule by men and Pharaohs alike, perhaps by her life as maid to Kuchuk Hanem and others.

Hanem's eyes were huge, almond perfect, outlined in kohl enough to make each one still a precious object. She listened to the babbling story and understood it. Since Flaubert's time she had mastered not only Italian but also fluent French. Colet was insistent about one thing: 'Did she remember this man?' She proffered the photograph. Kuchuk Hanem nodded. She recalled the two men – the first photographers ever to ascend the Nile. How could she not?

Now the delicate bit: what was he like, how had their night of love been? Kuchuk Hanem roared with laughter: 'There are no nights of love! Only days when we imagine such things. Your husband was a writer, you say. It was another good story for him to tell the world, no doubt.'

Yet when Colet left, Kuchuk Hanem checked again the photograph she had been given by Flaubert, who had implored Maxime du Camp to part with this keepsake, this memento of a few hours so many years ago.

10 · The calling

The eye of the horse is the bit. Egyptian proverb

Maxime du Camp photographed grand things, or people. He resisted the urge, though the site was venerated, to take a picture of a single young lady's footprint preserved already some weeks in the sand by the infatuated tour guide in Luxor (this gives some idea of the increase in tourist volume since then: a tourist's footprint would last about three minutes in most sites in Egypt now). It was the footprint of Florence Nightingale, who, as we have already noted, was travelling up the Nile at the same time as the louche novelist.

Florence was travelling without her parents, with friends of the family. The object was to see the great ruins of the Nile, and come to some decision about marriage. She had just turned down a proposal from one of England's most eligible young bachelors, Richard Monckton Milnes – a wealthy poet, politician and friend of many in high office. He would become one of the closest friends of Richard Burton, Nile explorer and translator of *The Thousand and One Nights* (one of Florence's favourite books and, in another translation, her preferred reading on her Nile voyage). Milnes had already made his own Nile cruise with a disreputable pal who brought along a hammer and chisel to remove any 'hieroglyphic friezes' that took his fancy. They also brought panes of glass to seal the windows of the *dahabiya*, or house-boat, against the cold and the mosquitoes (you can get both in winter along the Nile). Milnes returned to England with the soubriquet 'the first Englishman to enter the harem'. It was not this that put Florence off. She loved the man. Nor was she concerned by his interest in the perverse (though she may not have been fully aware of it). The reason she had declined his hand was because she felt she had a higher purpose, a purpose she would discover in Egypt on the Nile.

That Florence Nightingale narrowly missed marrying England's most famous pornographer – as Milnes later became – is something only an inhabitant of an alternative universe can really relish. I mean, what if she had? Monckton Milnes was a gentleman and poet, a bon vivant, a great and generous entertainer, friend of the good and the great – what did it matter that he had a penchant for the Marquis de Sade, whose work occupied pride of place in his 'Aphrodisiopolis'?

That Florence did not marry a porn collector naturally only happened because she took a Nile cruise. Of course it would have been bad for nursing, thousands would have suffered and possibly died, and she did have a calling to be a nurse. But still, something perverse draws me to the idea of Florence Nightingale spending her life with a man with the greatest collection of dirty pictures in Europe. A year after her return from Egypt she would still write, 'I know that if I were to see him again ... the very thought of doing so quite overcomes me. I know that since I refused him not one day has passed without my thinking of him.'

Though Florence had said no to Milnes before she left for Egypt, he had evidently given her time to think it over. Her Nile cruise with some family friends was to help her decide, or to get over him altogether. Instead it coalesced her long-held dreams and gave them the courage to speak for themselves. Almost any life of external achievement and prominence looks inevitable in hindsight, but with Florence Nightingale the effect is absurdly noticeable. She seems destined to stand up for women's rights.

Her father William had been given the choice aged twenty-one of inheriting £100,000 – the equivalent of £7,000,000 today (the money went a lot further then because of the greater differentials in income) – as long as he changed his name from Shore to that of his childless benefactor great-uncle Peter Nightingale. The catch was: if William Nightingale had no male heir, then he had to ignore his daughters and send the money to the nearest male relative in turn.

Naturally he said yes, ditched Shore, became Nightingale and looked forward to fathering several sons. He had two daughters. One born in Naples who was called by the Greek name for that city, Parthenope, and one born in Florence who fortunately was called not Firenze but

Florence. Parthenope was Florence's elder sister, and it's just as well she had no ambitions of her own to be a nurse. Parthenope Nightingale doesn't quite sound right (how about Napoli Nightingale?). Parthenope was often ill; in fact in their youth they both were, and Florence often nursed her. Parthenope would later write with the insight of sisterhood but not its sentiment, 'I believe she has little or none of what is called charity or philanthropy, she is ambitious – very, and would like well enough to regenerate the world with a grand coup de main or some fine institution.'

The parallels with that other ambitious young person, Flaubert, travelling up the Nile at exactly the same time, has been drawn to our attention by the clever and diligent researches of the writer Anthony Sattin. Both were looking to make their mark in the world but neither had a clear idea until they had embarked on a pilgrimage up the Nile to its higher reaches. But whereas Flaubert is a clear-sighted hedonist, with all the ennui and sadness that relentless pleasure-seeking entails, Florence is a buoyant enthusiast, burning with a desire to serve and fuelled with a sense that God has plans for her. This is why her sister's analysis gives a skewed impression. Florence, though ambitious, is not shallow or conventional. In fact the impression gained from her writing is of someone very likeable.

As the journey progressed Florence realised that momentous changes were occurring in her inner life. Much of this mutation was brought on by her appreciation of the unity of ancient Egyptian religion with Christian and Islamic spirituality. With her Unitarian Church background it was probably easier for her to make that leap of connection; nevertheless it reveals her as quite beyond the literalist Christians who saw nothing but barbarity in the ancient works. Florence wrote that the image of Ramses at prayer 'taught me more than all the sermons I ever read' about the relationship between the human and the divine. At Abu Simbel she noted in a letter, 'I never thought I should have made a friend and a home for life of an Egyptian temple.' She was not the first spiritually sensitive person to have thought thus: the Sufi mystic Dhun-Nun al-Misri was known to have lived some years in an ancient Egyptian temple despite being a Muslim; reputedly he could read hieroglyphics, there still being, in the eighth century, Coptic speakers who could interpret them.

Florence had learned five languages as a child – home-schooled by her father – and now she learned to read hieroglyphic inscriptions. Her keenness is more invigorating than Flaubert's likeable response at Abu Simbel – 'How sick I am of temples.' Florence experienced something of a revelation within the temple of Seti on the west bank of Luxor – she simply noted down, 'God spoke to me again.' At Philae, in the Osiris chamber, she buried her gold cross, to symbolise the fruitful union in her mind of Osiris and Jesus.

We live in an age of scepticism and mockery, which serves its useful purpose of dealing with hypocrites and charlatans, but not all things outside our current comfort zone are false. The conventional and easy pose of the honest sceptic blinds us to those whose naive language of revelation actually relates to real events. To say that Florence had been spoken to by God is merely to state that she received an impulse whose source was mysterious to her. But here we find an inner awakening of a conviction to help others and to sacrifice all hope of a conventional married life. Monckton Milnes hadn't a chance.

But how could she turn these intuitions into action? She had long been keen on nursing the sick. Indeed during a flu epidemic in England when she was sixteen she had nursed her whole family and fifteen sick servants – it had been the 'sole real activity' of her youth. That she excelled at organising such things must have been obvious to all. But no gentlewoman ever became a nurse in the 1850s. A nurse in those days was a byword for drunkenness and promiscuity. Her parents would not even allow her to study the subject.

But back in England she did not give up. Her ambition drove her to write a novel entitled *Cassandra*, excoriating the absence of chances for women. Her later books on nursing proved she was an able writer, but this wonderful passage drawn from her Nile letters shows her talent: 'The golden sand, north, south, east, west, except where the blue Nile flowed, strewn with bright purple granite stones, the black ridges of mountains east and west, volcanic rocks, gigantic jet-black wigwam-looking hills.' Anyone who has visited south of Aswan will recognise this description at once.

Writing, however, was not enough. When it became obvious that she would pursue nursing at any cost her father settled upon her £500 per annum – more than enough for her to live an independent life without being married. Slyly he had outwitted the terms of his own sexist inheritance. Florence managed to study in Paris and Germany. A great inspiration was Elizabeth Blackwell, a young Englishwoman who found that the only place where a woman could study medicine was at the New York State Medical School. When she arrived the all-male student body took a vote on whether she should be allowed to study with them. She was, and went on to graduate top of her class. In 1853 Florence was allowed to take up a job as superintendent of a nursing home for gentlewomen in London. A year later when the Crimean War broke out she travelled as part of a group of volunteer nurses. Her dedication was unharmed by her striking good looks, and she stood out as the 'lady with the lamp'. Queen Victoria asked to meet her and Florence was able to make suggestions to alleviate the poor quality of English nursing.

Strangely, a hundred years later in Cairo, in the 1950s, nursing was still not considered among well-born Egyptian families to be a suitable profession for a young woman. The same charge of loose behaviour was levelled at the poorly paid Egyptian nurses. But the tide was turning – British-run military nursing academies brought the spirit of Florence Nightingale back to the Nile. My own mother-in-law had to battle the scepticism of her parents to become a trainee nurse in a military academy. She later rose to become the administrator of a hospital and told me that her greatest teachers were the British sisters at her first training college. No doubt the spirit of Florence united with Osiris would have approved.

11 · The island

The love of the cat and mouse: they eat each other while playing.
Nubian proverb

The stories of *The Thousand and One Nights* hang over the Nile quite as much as those of the Bible. The *Nights*, even before their definitive translation by Richard Burton, had seeped deep into the European conception of the East. In the East the stories are somewhat looked down upon. Not just because of the vulgar content of a few – the case of the masturbating hashish addict caught with an exposed erection in a Cairo bath house is hardly bedtime reading for the genteel – but because, the over-cultured and the religiously obsessed believed, *The Thousand and One Nights* were always stories for the people, entertainments for the unlettered. But that was precisely the secret of their survival, which continues to this day. The stories contain material beyond the merely amusing or even moral; they have the value, as many non-degraded traditional tales do, of providing an abstract model of human predicaments sufficiently accurate and shorn of irrelevant detail actually to be of use to the hearer. Without wanting to make the *Nights* sound like a self-help book, there is no denying that some of the stories, or the stories within the stories, are genuinely capable of stimulating insights into life that are useful in the twenty-first century. As they have been since their conception as oral tales, and since their first collation in the tenth century in Cairo.

A curious symptom of Asperger's syndrome results, for some, in the childhood sufferer hating stories. Such a child will stand in stark contrast to most children, who seem programmed at birth to love hearing any kind of story. This unusual child will take refuge in memorising lists of capitals, birds' names, 'interesting numbers'. To engage such a child ask them about 'infinity plus one'; to offer a story will cause them physical distress since they lack the ability to understand it. This seems remarkable. Surely all humans can understand stories? Surely they are the basic form of all spoken communication – be it religious, scientific or social? Not to understand a story, at its most basic level, is to lack the ability to know which parts of a story are important and which are not. To appreciate a story you must have a basic understanding of what makes people tick, human wants, desires, fears – which is why great works of literature often seem dull to undergraduates, who have yet to observe in real life similar things for themselves.

There is no doubt that a child who hates stories and prefers talking about numbers might well become an excellent engineer. In a world where, only recently, reverence for mechanical marvels has been tempered with a note of scepticism about their ultimate worth, we see a strange reversal. The child who is a freak, who hates stories, becomes the cultural icon, the trail blazer, the important man of the tribe. Storytelling, though enjoying a continuing revival since the 1970s, has yet to usurp statistics and 'testable' hypotheses as the significant game changers in our lives.

Yet remarkable people of all ages are driven by stories – the stories they are told as children, and the stories they pick up along the way. On the Nile, the guides and boatmen of Aswan tell stories to their charges that they have learnt from hearing *The Thousand and One Nights*. In the story of Anas el-Wogud they speak of the King's favourite who had the misfortune to fall in love with the Vizier's daughter, Zahr el-Warda, Blossom of the Rose. But, though a favourite of the King, Anas was not a prince, and any vizier worth his salt desires that his daughter marry into royalty.

Learning of the young courtier's affections the Vizier had his daughter confined to an island far away. But he had reckoned without the persistence of Anas el-Wogud, who travelled far and wide in search of the Vizier's daughter. Eventually he came across a desert hermit, sitting in his cave and contemplating eternity. The hermit directed Anas to the island but warned him of the multiple difficulties he could expect – not the least of which were the crocodiles infesting the water. Yet Anas found a friendly one, and lying on its back made his way under the eyes of the guards to rescue his love, who of course he married.

The island, the boatmen will tell you, is Philae, and the Osiris room there, where Florence Nightingale buried her necklace, the bridal chamber of Anas and his Rose. We know that Florence was reading probably the 1840 Lane translation of the *Nights*, which Richard Burton would call 'a sorry performance at best'. She would have thrilled perhaps to hear a dragoman of Aswan relate the local Philae version of the story, and in the room of the Anas–Zahr marriage she pledged her own marriage – to her humanitarian cause, which she saw as her 'real self' as opposed to the less significant social selves who desired an ordinary marriage and a conventional life.

The story is a love story on one level, but its real interest becomes apparent when we cast the Vizier's daughter as our potential and the faithful Anas as the mixed-up everyday person who must trick crocodiles and prison guards to identify and 'rescue' the right future for him.

12 · A murder that changed the world

Although he has no ox his bag is full of whips. Sudanese proverb

In 1854, while Florence Nightingale was busy trying to persuade her parents that she should be allowed to study nursing seriously, and while Flaubert battled away at draft after draft of *Madame Bovary*, a murder was being planned on the banks of the Nile. This would not only change the world in a figurative sense, it would literally change the world by altering its very geography.

Murder was not uncommon in the royal families of the Ottoman Empire. Like queen bees killing competing queens, Ottoman princes were used to doing away with rivals. In Egypt things were more civilised, until Abbas Pasha (another grandson of Muhammad Ali) supposedly fell foul of a Turkish aunt over an issue of inheritance. In a way that harked back to Saladin she sent him two 'loyal' Mamluk slaves (Turkish rather than Egyptian Mamluks). These men waited for their chance as they worked polishing horse brasses and restuffing mattresses in Abbas' court.

Abbas was a man who disliked Europeans. His only concession to modernity was to allow George Stephenson to build Africa's first railway from Cairo to Alexandria in 1853. Abbas had no interest in the dreams which had obsessed the French since the arrival, brief stay and departure of Napoleon – namely, the revival and excavation of a canal connecting the Nile and the Red Sea. Indeed Stephenson was a consulting engineer on an early plan to build the Suez Canal, a plan Abbas quickly scotched. If Abbas had remained in power the Suez Canal would never have been built.

The two Mamluk assassins had a hobby: collecting tail hairs from Abbas' favourite horses. Quite a collection they built up of horse hair (longer than the horse hair they used for stuffing mattresses, but easy to hide in the same place). These long hairs were for spinning by hand into a single powerful thread. When Abbas retired early to his divan on 13 July 1854, he was not alone. The horsehair garrotte ended his reign in a few violent minutes.

His successor, his uncle Muhammad Said, was quite a different man. He loved the idea of a great canal.

Four thousand years ago, in the reign of Pharaoh Sesostris I, a canal was built, according to later classical writers, which linked the Nile north of Memphis with the Red Sea. A suggestive inscription at the temple of Amon in Karnak records that the canal may well still have been in use 600 years later in 1290 BC.

Ships would have sailed up the Nile from the Mediterranean, or, more likely, would have been rowed along the eastern arm of the delta to Bubastis (close to the wonderfully named Zagazig of modern times). From Bubastis the canal cut across to the Bitter Lakes, which drained at that time into the Red Sea Gulf of Suez.

By the sixth century BC the Bitter Lakes had long been blocked by drifting sand, so the Pharaoh Necho decided to cut a new channel from the lakes to the Gulf of Suez. Herodotus tells us that this plan cost the lives of 120,000 Egyptians. This is surely an exaggeration, but it is one that lives on. In 1956 Nasser made a speech about nationalis-ing the Suez Canal. In it he claimed that 120,000 Egyptians had died while the modern canal was being built! (The real figure is considered to be between 5,000 and 10,000 – though these are still rough estimates.) A year ago I was on the subway train to Maadi and was reading a book about the Suez Canal. A middle-aged Egyptian standing next to me told me he now lived in the US and was 'visiting the Third World' for a holiday. He saw my book and assumed the aggrieved air of a national-ist – did I not realise that 120,000 Egyptians had lost their lives build-ing the Suez Canal? Had he been reading Herodotus, I asked him? He had never heard of him. I told him the actual figure and he said I was wrong. I agreed that I might be and got off the train.

An oracle warned Necho that the advantage of such a canal would be enjoyed most fully not by the Egyptians but by the barbarians. Given all the foreign manoeuvring around the Suez Canal the oracle seems strangely perceptive. Necho gave up his work, but the invading Persian king Darius completed the work about a hundred years later. The canal was a great success, was used by Alexander the Great and was later enlarged by the Roman emperor Trajan around AD 100. By the fifth century AD with the collapse of Rome the canal again silted up.

When the Arabs invaded they took an interest, and in the eighth century a navigable canal existed between Old Cairo and the Red Sea. You can still see the filled-in remains of this canal as you wing along the Corniche. According to an ancient treatise by Dicuil, an English monk called Fidelis sailed on the canal during a pilgrimage to the Holy Land in the eighth century. Though this extension of the Nile into the Red Sea was opened and closed several times until about 1000, it even-tually silted up and fell into disrepair. It took the arrival of Napoleon to change things.

The British most definitely did not want a canal through the isth-mus of Suez. Indeed they opposed it almost until the day of its open-ing ceremony. Sailing round Africa may have taken a long time, but it meant they could not be held hostage by whoever controlled the Nile – since control of the Nile would imply control of the Suez Canal and whatever trade passed through it. And the British did not control the

Nile – Napoleon did. He took great interest in looking at the remains of the old canals. In the run-down town of Suez he saw the potential for a new and illustrious port. He ordered the building of it. His chief engineer, Jean-Baptiste Lepère, drew up the plans, meanwhile, for a canal. We can marvel now at his idiocy, but it was an idiocy that held sway for fifty years. Lepère, owing to faulty measuring equipment, arrived at the astonishing idea that the Red Sea, at high tide, was thirty feet higher than the Med at low tide, so a direct canal could not be dug. He argued (and only a few clear-thinking mathematicians opposed him) that to construct such a canal would be asking for a tidal wave to sweep up the diggings and flood the Nile delta. If this had been the case then it would have happened thousands of years earlier when the ancient canals were built. His mistake was enough to kill the project until the royal murder in 1854.

But Lepère's words had an impact beyond his cancelling of the project. His published book *The Canal of the Two Seas* inspired the retired diplomat Ferdinand de Lesseps that East and West really could be joined. The mystical union of East and West was part of the philosophical agenda of the Saint-Simonian cult headed by Prosper Enfantin, who believed that the physical conjoining through Suez (and Panama) was a prerequisite to the spiritual marriage of both cultures. Enfantin spent his life – when he wasn't campaigning for the Suez Canal – looking for the symbolic perfect female 'other half' for another kind of conjoining. He dressed in a loose tunic and tight trousers with 'Le Père' emblazoned across his chest. His future partner would be forced to wear a similar get-up but with 'La Mère' across her chest (it is odd that Lepère and Le Père should both be necessary to the plot). But just as destiny did not allow Le Père the chance to meet the perfect female to balance his perfect male, so too the canal was never to be completed in his lifetime.

Enfantin was a true visionary but an obvious nut. Perhaps we'll discover, at some later date, similarly useful ideas in the words of David Icke. Perhaps not. But we'll need a practical man for the task who does not shy away from big projects. De Lesseps was the unlikely candidate. His career as a diplomat having stalled, he took Lepère and Le Père's ideas and looked for a way to make them work. When Abbas Pasha fell foul of his two slave servants and was murdered after only a brief period reigning in Egypt, de Lesseps' time had come. He had in his youth been confidant and fencing teacher of the next ruler of Egypt, Muhammad

Said. De Lesseps had also known Linant Bey, the man who had saved the Pyramids and designed the first incarnation of the barrage across the Nile. Linant would form the nucleus of engineers assigned to the technical design of the canal, something de Lesseps had no training in.

De Lesseps knew his time had come because the day he presented his idea to his friend Said Pasha there was a Saint-Simonian rainbow in the sky linking East to West. Said had not forgotten his old friend and tutor – he agreed immediately that such a canal should be made.

Without the corvée the canal could not have been built – and the corvée existed because of the Nile. But long before the problems of digging the canal appeared de Lesseps had to fight the Turks and the British to get his canal started. His correspondence offers a handbook in surmounting huge difficulties. He never doubts that he will succeed. He is willing to continue until he drops (his wife had died and he had vowed he would never marry again until he had achieved his Suez dream – and on the opening voyage through the canal which Flaubert's mistress Louise Colet joined, he married again). And he never writes anything negative. And eventually he succeeded. Fifteen years after his old pupil Said (who was now dead) had agreed to de Lesseps' plan, the canal was opened.

The canal changed the position of Egypt almost overnight. It extended the Nile east, and became the gateway to India. From being sceptical the British suddenly appreciated its worth. As we have seen, when Said's successor Ismail bankrupted Egypt through rebuilding Cairo, they assumed his debts and took over the country. From the moment Britain became the driving force in Egypt the Nile became British business. To boost the exchequer it was decided to improve irrigation and thus agricultural yield. While many hated Lord Cromer, the British proconsul in Egypt, he and his Nile irrigation experts such as Scott-Moncrieff and William Willcocks turned Egypt from a bankrupt country into one that enjoyed a commercial boom.

I got a little obsessed by de Lesseps. He seemed both so ordinary and yet so extraordinary in his efforts. In the end he went slightly mad and was sentenced to a suspended prison term for corruption over his next big scheme – the Panama Canal. He was eighty-eight at the time.

I saw in a book of black and white photographs a giant statue of de Lesseps lying in a heap of rusty cables and scrap metal in Port Said. I went looking for the statue, which I discovered had been erected at the entrance of the Suez Canal and had been sculpted by Emmanuel Frémiet.

Yet rather than the figure of de Lesseps it had nearly been the Statue of Liberty that graced the entrance. Another French sculptor, Frédéric Bartholdi, had approached the Egyptian ruler Ismail and suggested that a giant statue of an Egyptian peasant woman holding a torch should act as a lighthouse at the entrance of the Suez Canal. Sketches and models were made but the project was derailed by the Franco-Prussian War when Bartholdi's home was occupied by the Prussians.

The models and sketches found their way to America with Bartholdi, who now became obsessed with building his light-bearing statue at the entrance to New York. Slowly he gained support. The inside structure of the giant sculpture was designed by Gustav Eiffel (who incidentally also built one of the famous bridges over the Nile at Cairo). The whole was donated to the Americans as a part of the hundredth-anniversary celebrations of American independence. The committee which decided this was led by none other than Ferdinand de Lesseps, which explains all the Egyptian connections. If you have ever wondered who the Statue of Liberty was modelled on, it was actually a Nile-dwelling Egyptian peasant girl who, Bartholdi announced, symbolised 'light in the world' (though the statue also bears a certain resemblance to his mother). If you are an Egyptian visitor to the USA the sight of a fellow country-man in such a prominent place should be reassuring, though it should perhaps not be mentioned when you are given the third degree at JFK Airport ...

The imposing thirty-foot-high statue of de Lesseps that once stood guard over the Mediterranean entrance to the canal was blown off its plinth by enthusiastic Egyptian patriots in 1956, the year Nasser would also go ahead with his plans to build the Aswan dam. The dam-aged statue ended up in the scrapyard of the Suez Canal Company – where it still resides, albeit now back on its feet again in a sort of gravel viewing area surrounded by old cable drums and scrapped heavy-lifting material. De Lesseps' family paid for the little memorial patch and family members visit every year, so the supervisor at the yard told me. It was an embarrassment really, because if they reinstated the statue on the plinth nationalistic Egyptians would complain. If they sold it abroad then the publicity would be damaging. So, in a true Egyp-tian compromise, the man who brought Egypt its fourth-largest source of revenue resides in a place of oily old engines, rusty remains and broken pipes.

13 · Petherick's problems solved by a fly

Even though the flies swarm they cannot lift the lid of the pot.
Sudanese proverb

*The Nile has two special features: one is the extent of its reach since we
do not know of any other river in the inhabited world that is longer, for its
beginnings are springs that well from the Mountain of the Moon which is
purported to be 11 degrees south of the Equator; two is its increase which
takes place when others dry up for it begins to increase when the long days
start to end and reaches its maximum with the Autumn equinox when the
canals are opened to flood the lands.* Abdullah el-Baghdadi (AD 1200)

The Suez Canal was opened in 1869 – the year that Burton and Speke
would confront each other over the source of the Nile. But we must
go back a little, to the 1850s, before any of the new generation of Nile
explorers had set out. It is strange: we assume that explorers come
before tourists, but they don't in the case of the Nile. Some early tourists, such as Flaubert and Monckton Milnes, came first and may have
inspired the explorers to go further, to the uttermost ends of the river.
We know that Milnes' best friend Richard Burton must have heard
stories from him of the Nile. And though traders usually follow explorers, some seem to keep neck and neck with them, especially when it
comes to such valuable items as slaves and ivory.

The region that came to be known as Equatorial Egypt and later as
Southern Sudan was, due to the barrier of the Sudd, really the nub
of the problem. When Werne's (and Verne's) account of Muhammad
Ali's expedition was circulated in Europe, many were determined to
push further, either through Equatorial Egypt or in from the coast of
east Africa. Burton and Speke headed in west from Zanzibar and John
Petherick attacked from the north. They either followed slave routes or
opened up routes soon to be used by slavers.

The amiable Petherick, Welshman, mining engineer, not quite out
of the same drawer as Baker, Speke or even Burton, was decidedly
from the lower end of the spectrum, similar to Livingstone and Stanley.
It seems that explorers come from either end of the social scale and
rarely from the comfortable middle: either they have nothing to lose,
or they have so much that losing isn't a problem. Petherick has been
harshly treated by history. He spent years exploring the lesser-known

regions of the upper Nile, and quite unfairly was lambasted by the unstable, unreliable Speke after he had failed to be there, in person, to greet the explorer when he emerged triumphant in Gondokoro ... a year late. Missing a date by a year, I think, excuses the person stood up for being a little less than punctual. But Speke did not see it this way and did his darnedest to blacken Petherick's name to everyone and everywhere. Petherick fought back, and achieved apologies and compensation for the damage to his reputation, but the damage remained done. His books are hard to find but make admirable reading. He is every bit as brave as the more famous explorers, and a lot more inventive. In 1854, seven years before the exploration of the Nile by Burton and Speke began in earnest, Petherick was pushing further and further south in Sudan into the region of the Dinka, Nuer and Djibba tribes along the upper reaches of the Nile. The Djibba wore wrist knives: 'with the bracelet he inflicts severe blows upon his antagonist's face'. The Djibba decorated themselves with the hair of their fallen enemies, which they wove into their own hair to form 'a long tail, reaching almost to the ground'. Petherick was one of the first Europeans to proceed past the Sobat river, a tributary of the Nile that drains the lower part of Ethiopia. Forty years later, the French Marchand expedition – the first to traverse Africa from west to east – would proceed up the Sobat in a steel boat they had dragged through hundreds of miles of jungle.

Petherick was poor, and any attempt at exploration had to be funded by trading. For five years he was in the gum-arabic business at Al-Obeid, a trading town in Sudan established by the Egyptian Turks in 1821 but later destroyed by the Mahdi's army. When gum-arabic ceased to be profitable his mind turned to the Nile, the mains cable of African wealth snaking its way into the jungle. Capitan Selim, in the expedition funded by Muhammad Ali Pasha in 1840, reached 4 degrees 42 minutes North. This expedition established that the Blue Nile was definitively not the only source of the Nile – that the ancients had been right in positing a source deeper in the heart of Africa. Petherick's friend Alphonse de Malzac, an ivory trader who had been an attaché at the French Embassy in Athens, had explored some of the tribes around 7 degrees North, but he had recently died in Khartoum. There was plenty for Petherick to do, and if by chance he also found the source of the Nile, so much the better.

Petherick was tough. He reported that he suffered fevers in his first two years and then none for the next nine. Without passing judgement he describes the native cures as something that would 'kill a horse', cures such as ingesting a pound of butter on an empty stomach and, if internal pain is intense, branding with a hot iron on the skin. 'Diarrhoea, dysentery, liver-complaints and Guinea-worm are the prevailing diseases; smallpox is the most deadly, cholera and plague are very rare.' Of Guinea-worm he writes,

This fearfully distorting malady occurs only among the barefooted part of the population, and its period is confined to the rainy season. Attacking generally the foot in the first instance, the swelling extends frequently to the knee to a loathsome extent, and is accompanied by excruciating pain to the sufferer. At last a small soft spot presents itself as if suppuration were coming to a climax, into which a red hot nail is thrust; and, in nine cases out of ten, in a few days this effects a cure. Sometimes, however, two or more such places in different parts of the limb require as many firings which at last become 'too hot' for the disease. Another method, not so much practised, is to allow the spot apparently suppurating to burst, when a threadlike substance emerges. This, the real cause of so much pain and swelling, is a long and almost endless worm, perfectly white, and of the substance of a thick cotton thread. Protruding sufficiently to be laid hold of, it is wound round a piece of reed as thick as a straw, and generally extracted by turning the reed until resistance is experienced ... Each day the worm, morning and evening, is wound out of its unwelcome hiding-place; and an expert hand, in the course of a few days will succeed in extracting the entire worm, when the disease disappears. If, unfortunately, the worm is broken during extraction, it still continues to torment the patient; and causing great pain eventually reappears in another locality, when the operation of winding it out is recommenced.

Smallpox received a less successful cure: the patient was laid out, completely nude, on a bed of ashes with the juice of raw onion continuously dripped into their eyes. The cure ceased only when the ash-encrusted patient either recovered or died.

To further fund his travels, Petherick was looking to trade ivory and had with him 'some tons of glass beads, cowry shells and a variety of trifles in request by the negroes'. He had an armed escort of twenty

Maghrebis from Kordofan – North African Arabs who had settled centuries earlier in Sudan.

The party soon passed out of the area administered by the Turkish Egyptian government. Their boat traversed a maze of beautifully wooded islands, small blue monkeys bounding from tree to tree. 'Mimosa and Heglig [the desert date, like a plum with an outsize stone, whose fruit are a preventative for bilharzia] were the predominant trees; the magnificence and beauty of their rich foliages I cannot describe.' Moving upstream they encountered Shilluks, Dinka and Nuer. When a Nuer chief came aboard, the guns and knives of Petherick's men were much admired. Immediately the chief 'rose up on his knee [and], grasping my right hand and turning up the palm, he quietly spat into it; then, looking into my face, he elaborately repeated the process'. Having just been spat at (which in Egypt is a not an uncommon climax to a verbal row), Petherick wrote, 'Staggered at the man's audacity, my first impulse was to knock him down; but his features expressed such kindness that I vented my rage by returning the compliment with all possible interest. His delight seemed excessive, and returning to his seat, he expressed to his companions his conviction that I must be a great chief.'

Petherick pressed on up the Nile past 8 degrees latitude into an area of marshy lakes thick with reeds: the Sudd. Hippopotami were now more common. The river became a baffling labyrinth. Eventually they found an island and attempted a landing. From nowhere, it seemed, 'some hundreds of negroes assembled on the opposite side of the channel, and with frantic ejaculations of rage, wielding their lances and clubs on high, defied us to land on their shore ... I found not a man that would follow me, nor a sailor to man the boat ... I had no alternative but to return.'

Weaker or less adventurous men would have left it at that, but a year later, in 1854, Petherick was back, with an increased number of men, determined to push on past the hostile island, his previous 'furthest south'. Surprisingly this time there was no hostility and a small present of beads soon established cordial relations. It seems the aggressive natives had been not of the Raik, as these people were, but a party of marauding Nuer. Petherick decided to leave the Nile and investigate the interior. He then heard there were tribes with much ivory not far away.

His party travelled from tribal group to tribal group, picking up guides and porters as they went. Always, they were told, the next tribe had ivory, great stores of ivory. Petherick waited three hours for the chief of the Wadj Koing to arrive 'surrounded by the population, who, criticising and laughing at us, congratulated themselves on the rich spoil that had providentially fallen into their grasp'. The chief finally turned up and banged his club on the ground as he told Petherick they had no ivory and that he and his men must leave immediately. Petherick would not be beaten so easily. He told the chief that if he wasn't more welcoming they would sack the village and burn their huts, and his own hut would be first. After the usual display of firearms, hostility was replaced by an interest in trading food for beads. But it soon became clear that Tschol, the chief, had other plans.

Overnight the African porters were scared away and the guide disappeared. Petherick and his men now had no way of moving out unless they left behind their trade goods – which of course was Tschol's plan. Petherick enticed the chief into his own hut and said he would shoot him before sundown unless they received water: the terrified chief signalled that they be allowed to drink. For food Petherick shot game and they subsisted off meat alone. He sent out two parties, one with his donkey loaded with beads – this was their only donkey and it had been brought for Petherick to ride. It was the first time these people had seen a man riding a creature and they declared that the beast was part of him, that in some way they were one creature – a rather humble nineteenth-century centaur. It is fascinating to speculate that the mythical origin of creatures half man half horse might lie in the recorded first reactions of people to mounted invaders. But such speculations were far from Petherick's mind. His hope was that one of the two parties would encounter a hospitable tribe and, by trading beads, gain enough porters to enable them to return and rescue his property.

After two weeks of waiting it all became rather desperate. Tschol saw that Petherick was drinking brandy each night and asked for some, knowing it was alcoholic as he himself drank manioc beer. Petherick was down to his last bottle so he gave the chief a glass of vinegar instead. The requests for brandy stopped.

Every day Petherick shot game and read from the few books he had with him. The chief admitted they would have killed him long ago but for 'my mysterious dealings with the little black marks on paper'. They feared his sorcery would cause the extermination of the tribe. Petherick was inspired by this admission and, capitalising on the fact that there was a drought, he told the chief (after consulting very publicly an antiquated copy of the *Weekly Times*) that he could provide rain as long as the tribe could pass a special test.

'Despatching some men to catch half a dozen large flies, bearing some resemblance to a horse fly but larger', Petherick then trapped the flies in a bottle with a little flour. This he shook over the flies before telling the people that they had done wrong, had carried off women from neighbouring tribes, had murdered others and generally misbehaved, and until they made restitution by providing cattle to the people they had wronged the rains would not come. The people denied these charges but Petherick said he had the means to know they were lying: the fly bottle. If they could catch the flies when he released them, that would prove they were telling the truth. But if they couldn't then they would have to repent and accept that they had to pay with cattle. Somehow Petherick had caught the imagination of the tribe and all were fascinated by the flour-covered flies buzzing within the bottle.

> Hundreds of clubs and lances were poised high in the air, amidst loud shouts of 'Let them go! Let them go!' With a prayer for the safety of my flies I held up the bottle and smashing it against the barrel of my rifle, I had the satisfaction of seeing the flies in the enjoyment of their liberty. Man, woman, and child gave chase in hot pursuit ... it was not until after the sun had set that the crest-fallen stragglers returned. Their success having been limited to the capture of two flies, though several spurious ones, easily detected by the absence of the flour badge, were produced.

After a long consultation, and firmly believing in the 'fly oracle', the people agreed to make their cattle payments. But here Petherick's plan reveals its cunning: they could not agree what payments should be made or to whom and as the arguments dragged on, Petherick's own execution was stayed a few more days.

Just when he had given up all hope a long winding column of men carrying ivory appeared out of the bush. Both the parties he had sent out had been successful – not only in bartering trade with the Girwi and Ajack tribes but also in securing food and porters. Petherick became quite emotional: 'I met my men like old and dear friends rather than dependants.' He added: 'My persecutors, the Wadj Koing, seeing the Girwi and Ajack ... carry ivory, now came forward, but in small numbers, to offer themselves as porters ... affording me an opportunity of returning to my boats ... With wind and swelling current in our favour, we were not long in reaching Egyptian territory and Khartoum.'

14 · Killing an elephant

An elephant does not kill a liar; it sniffs him and passes by.
Sudanese proverb

The biggest trade was slavery, but ivory grew in importance as travel along the Nile and throughout Sudan became easier. Even then, without arming the natives, it was, thankfully, difficult and laborious to kill elephants, especially large and aggressive ones. Until the Turkish Egyptian conquest enabled the ivory trade to flourish, the hundreds of small fiefdoms in east Africa competed with each other, some hunting elephants and some not. The warriors of those that did risked injury and death for the prestige of being an elephant hunter (rather similar to being a matador) and for the enormous quantity of meat an elephant could provide to the tribe – because, until the explorers and traders arrived, it was the meat of an elephant that was desired, not its tusks.

Petherick was one of the first explorers to observe the various native methods of killing elephants without the use of a firearm. Despite being part of an ecologically sustainable system it was still a bloody business. Some especially daring types would infiltrate themselves through the close thickets to where an elephant might be browsing. With a quick slash of a native-made sword the tendons of the elephant's leg would be severed. The animal would then be tracked and killed. A variation involved the slightly safer deployment of spears or lances.

Fifty men succeeded in bringing an elephant to bay, around which they stood in a circle; whilst the furious young beast, with tusks about a foot in length, trumpeted his displeasure ... A lad, sixteen years of age, sprang into the circle towards the elephant; when within ten yards of him the lad, making one more bound forward, threw his lance and hit the elephant on the foot, a feat entitling him to the animal's tusks ... the infuriated beast withdrew the lance with his trunk, and screeching with rage, he broke it in two, and darted at

the party who had injured him. At the same time they made a simul-
taneous attack on his left side, which they pierced with their lances,
and succeeded in drawing him off towards them from the object of
his rage; this was no sooner undertaken than his right side was similarly pierced by half a dozen lances, thrown with such force that they
penetrated to the socket. The maddened animal stood for an instant
still, squirting water on his wounds from his trunk, extricating some
of the lances, and breaking them; while so engaged he was subjected
to renewed attacks, until, losing patience, he bolted off at a hard trot
with several of the lances sticking in his body. The negroes followed
at their utmost speed and succeeded in bringing him to bay a second
time ... the elephant, after repeated attacks, was overcome. Great
were the rejoicings in the village on this occasion.

Other methods that were less man-intensive included excavat-
ing pitfalls in the vicinity of waterholes and streams where the herd
were accustomed to drink. If the herd habitually went through narrow
passes or gorges this would also be a good place to dig a pitfall. One
cannot help feeling that the elephant displays as much intelligence in
his defence as the attacker in his traps. Petherick reports one elephant
being helped out of a pit by his fellow elephants using their trunks to
haul on his trunk and so rescue him. Another method, which Samuel
Baker also reported, involved a strong lance, five feet long: 'the extremity shaped like a club, about four inches in diameter, is laden with a
stone fixed to it with cords and plastered over with clay, the whole being
made as heavy as it can be managed'. The hunter then ascended a tree
that was known to overhang the noonday haunts of his prey. 'When
[an elephant] is directly under him, with all his force he sends the spear
into his back and shoulder. When the spear has been well directed the
animal bounds about for a short time, increasing the wound by the
oscillation of the spear and thereby accelerating his death.'

Petherick soon became an ivory trader himself. When he told a
reluctant chief through a translator that he wanted ivory,

the effect was electric; that they could obtain such valuables as glass
beads for useless tusks of elephants, seemed incredible. Several of
them bolted off immediately and [the chief] promised that on the
morrow an abundance of tusks would be forthcoming ... Trade of
any description was perfectly unknown in the far interior which I had

now reached ... the only use made of ivory by the Niam Niam was for ornaments, such as bracelets and necklaces; some were ingeniously cut in imitation of cowry shells; and neatly cut thin flakes, like the scales of a fish, were curiously attached to a band like a piece of ribbon, and worn by the females around the neck.

Of course, the presence of ivory traders encouraged natives to hunt far more elephants than they could eat. This hastened the sad demise of the great herds. Petherick, however, was there at the very beginning of this slaughter in the upper reaches of the Nile.

A herd of eighteen elephants was announced, by beat of tom-tom, as being in the vicinity. Old men, hags, warriors, women and children collected with the most sanguine expectations; and, anxious to witness the scene, I accompanied the hunters: a finer group of well-grown and active men I never beheld. The slaves, many of them from the Baer, but most of them from unknown tribes in the west, were all but black, and followed their more noble-looking and olive coloured masters. Two hours' march ... through magnificent bush brought us to the open plain, covered hip deep in dry grass; there were the elephants moving leisurely towards us. The negroes, about five hundred, swift as antelopes, formed a vast circle around them, and by their yells brought the huge game to a standstill. As if by magic the plain was on fire, and the elephants, in the midst of the roar and crackling of the flames, were obscured from our view by the smoke. Where I stood, and along the line as far as I could see, the grass was beaten down to prevent the outside of the circle from being seized in the conflagration; and in a short time – not more than half an hour – the fire having exhausted itself, the cloud of smoke gradually rising, again displayed the group of elephants to our view, standing as if petrified. As soon as the burning embers had become sufficiently extinct, the negroes with a whoop closed from all sides upon their prey. The fire and smoke had blinded [the elephants]; and, unable to defend themselves, they successively fell by the lances of their assailants. The sight was grand, and although their tusks proved a rich prize, I was touched at their massacre.

Before trading, Petherick had to impress a chief enough so that he wouldn't be robbed or detained. Their guns, called 'our thunder', were often the way such an impression was made, sometimes by shooting an elephant at a range impossible to spear throwers. But even a chief cowed by guns could be devious. Petherick borrowed Werne's method of appearing omniscient when he discovered the native love of tobacco, called *taab*.

> They were great smokers of tobacco, of their own growth, mixed with the rind of a banana, also indigenous to the country. To my great discomfort, after having partaken of my pipe, [the chief] expressed a liking for my tobacco; and not knowing how to refuse him, and at the same time exceedingly anxious to retain intact the small quantity remaining, I had recourse to a ruse; and, giving my instructions accordingly to my servant, he retired into the interior of the hut to fill the pipe. In the mean time I explained to Dimoo [the chief] that if any person smoked my tobacco who was not perfectly well disposed towards me, it would betray him by breaking his pipe in my presence. Not afraid of the ordeal he accepted a well-replenished pipe, whilst my servant, by a sign, acquainted me that my instructions had been carried out. Dimoo, seated opposite me in the company of some eight or ten notabilities of the place, commenced smoking vehemently, when an explosion of gunpowder in the bowl of the pipe sent it, as well as the chief and his companions, flying. Dimoo, regaining his equanimity, begged me to pardon him, and that he would never more conceal anything from me; and the only harm he meant was to detain me amongst them until they had become possessed of the whole of our riches ... After this little event, I was looked upon as something almost superhuman, and was respected accordingly.

15 · A bit more on elephants

They make a fool laugh then cunningly count his teeth.
Ethiopian proverb

But following the modern Nile, I was not here to kill elephants – unlike, say, Bob Parsons, the founder and executive chairman of internet colossus Go Daddy, whose 'vlog' features busty young women in Go Daddy tee-shirts mock-interviewing him about his self-help advice (some of which, I have to say, are pretty good: I particularly recommend his top ten business tips). Anyway, Bob was on a hunting trip in Africa when some impoverished locals asked him to kill a rogue bush elephant that was destroying their crops. This being Zimbabwe they were also starved of meat – which the elephant provided after Bob had shot it. In a stunt of dubious taste Bob posted a video of himself astride the slain elephant with locals cutting up the meat while wearing Go Daddy tee-shirts.

In parts of Africa it is true that there are too many elephants for the land they are meant to live on. In South Africa they have begun to cull elephants – not for ivory, but because there are too many. But around the Nile and its sources the opposite is becoming true – elephants are fast disappearing, victims of a Chinese-driven trade in ivory. So I wasn't here to kill anything, I was here to listen.

I was at the Murchison Falls, not so far from where elephants roamed through the forest in great herds, though I had yet to see any here. I saw Nile elephants by Lake Albert and in the Sudd, standing by the river, a small group of females undecided, it seemed, about whether to be in or out of the water. In the forest elephants make far less noise than their giant form suggests, unlike bears which are noisier than you'd expect. Seen from a river boat pushing through some giant this-tle on the bank, an elephant looks so big you wonder that there are any left at all. Needing upwards of 400 pounds of vegetable fodder a day, elephants are always on the munch. If they are undisturbed their bel-lies make the most incredible gas-powered food-processing noises, but if they catch your scent they have the strange ability to switch off the stomach rumbles immediately, leaving an ominous silence, and you are at once anticipating being charged and flattened.

That they make so much noise when digesting is no surprise – only 40 per cent of the massive amount they eat is actually digested. Then there is the water – no wonder the elephant needs the Nile, as it requires over thirty gallons a day of it, to be precise. Sleeping only two hours a night, elephants make a habit of the midnight feast, the dawn raid. 'It is the best time to see them,' said Carl Meurer, an animal-watching German whom I met at the river camp. 'Just look for the white cattle heron over the river bank – they always go where there are elephant.'

Carl's main interest was animal sounds. He had an iPod loaded with strange noises: whale music, chimp chatter and his latest find, what sounded to me like an industrial washing machine. Carl was ecstatic, 'That's what it is, this is the noise of a washing machine in a zoo next to the elephant house. And that is an elephant imitating the noise!' The resemblance was uncanny, but Carl told me that elephants in the bush now habitually make the noise of truck roar on a road, the sound of a Land Cruiser rattling into life, or a strimmer zinging through grass. They can also do natural sounds such as frogs croaking or big cats coughing.

Their super mimicry skills seem best suited to low-frequency sounds which they can emit and receive in spectra below human audibility. The trunk and even the legs enable them to hear over distances of several miles. The trunk and each foot contain many nerve endings designed to register sound in association with the auditory nerves in the ears. If it really needs to hear, an elephant will lay its trunk along the ground and raise one foot. This improbable move increases pressure on the other three feet and boosts their hearing capability.

These recently discovered skills are all part of the clever ways elephants organise themselves, both in groups and wandering alone through the savannah and forest of the upper Nile region. 'Elephants are far more intelligent than chimps,' said Carl, swigging on a Nile Gold beer. 'In fact they're more intelligent than humans.'

He told me of an experiment which had previously been designed to test the reasoning and creativity of chimps. The test required two elephants to solve a mechanical problem by pulling ropes to get food. If there was only one elephant it wouldn't work. They needed to co-operate to win. Not only did the elephants co-operate, some didn't even bother to try until the second elephant was released to help them. And one prescient pachyderm worked out how to stand on the rope and get food that way – something even the experimenters hadn't thought of.

Elephants with specially daubed marks on their faces have been paraded in front of large mirrors. In a show of intelligent awareness, or perhaps nascent vanity, the subject very ably used the mirror information to rub the mark off with its trunk. That is, when they can see the mirror clearly: elephants have notoriously poor eyesight. Hunters report being missed by an elephant they are in broad view of not six yards away. Upwind, of course, the elephant's sense of smell is capable of whiffing danger over a mile away, which along with their specially developed hearing means they are well defended.

African elephants exist in two species – forest and bush elephant. These can interbreed but rarely do so. Bush elephants are considerably larger and have one toenail fewer, a small enough difference, but enough to earn them different-species status. A large bull bush elephant can weigh up to ten tons. And the blood within him is 10 per cent of his weight. So killing an elephant can literally release a ton of blood.

Elephants use their intelligence to avoid this bloodletting in many surprising ways. Hunters report groups of female elephants protecting a large bull by forming a pack around him and moving in sympathy, this way denying the hunter a shot at the valuable ivory-bearing male (female African elephants also have tusks but they are smaller and more curved than male ones).

Modern textbooks report that African elephants live in female herds with mature males living alone or in temporary bachelor herds. But this may well be an intelligent adaptation that has occurred in the last hundred years due to the mass killing made possible by the repeating rifle. Aviatrix Beryl Markham wrote of flying in the 1920s over vast herds of elephants with several males among the females. She speculates that changing behaviour to lone males and all-female herds – which were less attractive to hunters – improved the chances of elephant survival.

One hopes they can come up with something new to defeat the latest weapon waged against them: helicopter hunting. Though the Ugandan government receives millions of dollars from the US to hunt down Lord's Resistance Army leader Joseph Kony (more on him later), there have been substantiated reports that helicopters have been used both to shoot and to transport the ivory of elephants in Uganda and southern Sudan. Kony has been accused of funding his decades-long children's army rebellion with ivory that finds its way via Khartoum to China. Certainly the recent explosion in illegal elephant killing has received an impetus from Chinese commercial involvement all over central Africa: it makes it that much easier to ship the stuff home. Workers are counselled (via Chinese websites on getting ivory) to wrap their ivory in tinfoil to thwart airport X-ray machines – in Africa rather than Beijing, one suspects. Will the African elephant go the way of the northern white rhino – whose horn sells in China for $30,000 a pound, more than the price of gold? The white rhino is virtually extinct in the wild, whereas there are said to be between 689,000 and 472,000 elephants in Africa, though of course it is hard to say exactly how many.

Hunted from helicopters, they may not stand much chance, but on the ground the elephant – it's the world's largest land animal – is a pretty dangerous beast. It can outsprint Ernst the Norwegian Nile runner, managing a good 30mph when it charges. Hit by something weighing over six tons doing thirty is like being hit by a very heavy truck, one of those low-slung vehicles carrying bottles of Coke perhaps. Every year there are deaths in zoos, at least two and often up to four a year, stretching back to when we started keeping wild elephants in zoos. Man-killing elephants are no longer executed, though they were in the past. Some were shot and some were hanged in some kind of strange anthropomorphic rite, but the most bizarre was the fate of 'Four-Paw Topsy', who stomped a visitor to death during an animal show in 1903 in America. The killer elephant was about to be hanged when Thomas Edison jumped in and offered to electrocute it, at Coney Island. His rationale was that it would show how dangerous AC current (used in electrocutions) was compared to the DC current his company supplied. Fed cyanide-laced carrots just in case Edison's machine failed, 6,000 volts and a few minutes later the creature was dead – the whole thing being filmed by the newly formed Edison Film Company. You can see a copy of this gruesome snuff movie on YouTube, though you're warned it could be disturbing to some viewers. Old and murky, it *is* disturbing.

Being thrown to the elephants was a fate for the gladiator who drew the short straw in Roman times. Josephus, never one to miss a good story, tells us that Ptolemy IV, who ruled in Egypt from 221 to 204 BC, wanted to enslave and brand all Jews dwelling along the Nile with the symbol of Dionysus. The Jews refused and were dragged into an arena full of trumpeting elephants, to be stamped to death. Josephus reports that a miracle occurred; angels intervened and the Jews were saved.

That elephants from Africa get called Jumbo or Dumbo is not surprising – their name in Swahili is *tembu*, quite unlike the Arabic which is *fil*. However, *tembu* when I heard it first used made absolute sense: the ancient Egyptian word for elephant is *yebu*, which also happens to be the name of a village on Elephantine Island in the Nile at Aswan.

16 · The island of elephants

Time is what finishes an elephant and makes its ivory expensive.
Nubian proverb

At Elephantine Island, the African Nile gives way to the Egyptian; the people are Nubian and their ancient trade was ivory. In fact the word 'ivory' is one of the few English words of ancient Egyptian origin. *Abuw* or *yebu*, just mentioned, means 'elephant' in ancient Egyptian; when the Romans arrived in Egypt this became their word for 'elephant tusk' – *ebor* – which, with the usual *b/v* equivalence, became 'ivory' in English.

Yet the multiple twistings of elephant lore don't stop there. By a kind of doctrine of signatures, Elephantine was destined to be: the island itself is curved and tusk-like. The 'new' name of Elephantine (the old one is Yebu, still reserved for the main village on the island, as we have just seen) comes from the Greek word for 'tusk' – *eliphas*. Along the shore the giant grey, rounded granite boulders look exactly like bathing elephants – so much so that a guide will tell you that this is why it is really called Elephantine Island. Add to all this that Elephantine is the last, or first, trading post before the impassable (to trading boats) cataracts and Africa – source of all ivory – and you can see why it just had to be.

It is one of the oldest continuously inhabited sites along the Nile, and 6,000 years ago would have been surrounded by elephants – specifically the now extinct, but intriguingly named, north African flaccid elephant. Perhaps it was an elephant island even before ivory started coming downriver. I had seen for myself on boulders in the desert, hundreds of miles inland from Aswan, engravings of elephants.

Elephantine is just across from Aswan; indeed Yebu used to be more important than Aswan in ancient times. Aswan is, as Eratosthenes proved, directly below the Tropic of Cancer in midsummer, which again seems mysteriously to make it the centre of something important. You begin to see why the priests told Herodotus that this was where the Nile originated. There always have been temples on Elephantine – the one to the ram-headed flood god Khnum is beautifully exact – the tawdry Mövenpick Hotel on the island has tried to emulate its design in its monstrous tower: it is a failed architectural tribute, which, as I said earlier, looks more like a giant air vent, or perhaps a theme-park garbage bin just waiting to be stuffed to its gills with burger boxes and Coke bottles.

I sat in Aswan in the Yebu Café, one of the cheapest eateries, marred only by its direct view of the Mövenpick tower. A fellow diner interested me when he tried to haggle the exceedingly low price for dinner even lower. He was a backpacker – not surprisingly – and he was French, but what his artful blond dreadlocks did not give away was that he was also an ivory trader.

The idea that a world ban on elephant-tusk trading would make it go away – after 6,000 years – was admirable but somewhat hopeful. Of course it has made a big dent, though some would argue it is habitat destruction that will end the elephant's wild tenure, not the pursuit of its tusks. No doubt they go hand in hand. It is certain, however, that once guns started to be used the elephant's days were numbered. As far back as 1831 over 4,000 elephants a year were being killed for their tusks. The craze for the pianoforte drove the need for ivory ever higher. It is thought that the utter collapse of the huge Kenyan herds in the twentieth century was caused by American keyboard demand. Despite the similarly high demand in China for pianos, the keyboards are plastic; now the Chinese want ivory for luxury items, carvings, inlays, chess sets.

My French-hippy ivory trader acquaintance told me of worse atrocities: the recent slaughter uncovered in Chad, the fact that in 2011 over thirty tons of illegal ivory were seized (requiring the deaths of 4,000 elephants). But Fabrice was unmoved by pleas of ecology or even anticruelty. 'Look,' he said, 'it will always happen. The Chinese make it happen. I don't make it happen. All I do is find people who love ivory and make the connection to poor Africans who bring ivory to sell.' He told me that several trucks a week crossed the Egyptian border from Sudan loaded with refugees. Some brought ivory with them to pay their way to Europe – in Aswan they could find buyers, like Fabrice. I did not ask how he smuggled it out. Well, I did – and I received an incredulous look of Gallic scorn. But he did tell me he always flew on Eastern European cheap flights to Luxor, and I imagined the Moldovan or Bulgarian customs were less interested in 'camel bone' artefacts than the staff at Charles de Gaulle Airport.

Fabrice spoke longingly of the so-called Schreger lines in pure ivory, which enable you to tell its provenance and worth. Camel bone – which is often passed off as ivory – has no such markings. Tusks from extinct mammoths – which, in the slowly unfreezing permafrost of Siberia, is a major source of ivory – have tightly curved Schreger lines, while those from African elephants are more rounded. 'More beautiful,' whispered Fabrice.

17 · Slavery

My slavery forbade me to speak; the truth forbade me to keep silent.
Sudanese proverb

A hundred and fifty years ago at Elephantine there would have been mountains of ivory, not the handfuls that Fabrice dealt in. And instead of tourists being herded around and sized up for their worth to the nearest penny, there would have been a sorrier human cargo: slaves.

Aswan and Elephantine are at the end of the Forty Days Road, the desert route through Sudan used to avoid the impassable cataracts on the Nile. Along the Forty Days Road were brought slaves from the regions of the upper Nile, bound for Cairo and the Ottoman Empire.

It was while walking with camels along the upper section of this route that I came across grinding-stone stations – large bowl-shaped *murhaga* stones seemingly discarded, always with a few rounded granite pebbles near by. These were for grinding corn. Very sensibly, instead of carrying such heavy items, or such messy stuff as flour, desert travellers, from ancient times until recently, have camped at such stations to grind corn for the bread they need to eat. Which would not have been much when the travellers were hunters or nomads. But when people settled, then their bread requirements increased. (The Bedouin I travelled with sometimes took the stones home to serve as knife sharpeners.)

Georg August Schweinfurth, an explorer we have met already and will meet a few times more, makes an interesting point about the proliferation of slavery in the Nile regions of Africa. The *murhaga* method of grinding corn, whereby a large flat stone works as the mortar and a smaller hand-sized stone as the pestle, can, after a day's hard labour, produce only enough meal for five or six men. When the economy moved from one based more on hunting to one based on agriculture, with the migration of Arab Sudanese to the south of Khartoum into the *seriba* territory (a *seriba* is simply the thorn fence surrounding a village, but it came to mean the settlements established by the northern migrants), the need for people to spend all day grinding corn increased. Who would do such a loathsome job? A slave. According to Schweinfurth every Nubian settler possessed around three slaves. The migrations of the nineteenth century provided reason enough to perpetuate slavery within the Sudan; it was also an entrepôt for the export of slaves to the world outside, to the Middle East and beyond.

Slavery may have increased with the settlement of the Sudan by the Arabs of the north, but it was not invented by them. Slavery in the regions of the upper White Nile is mentioned in the Greek *Periplus of the Erythraean Sea*, a first-century AD account of trade in the Red Sea complete with sailing directions. Burton speculates that African slavery in this region was the result of ancient trade with southern Arabia. Its origin, though, is 'veiled in the glooms of the past'. But by the nineteenth century slavery was almost universal in the country between the Nile and the Indian Ocean. Not all tribes exported slaves from the interior to Arab lands; many were importers and users of slaves themselves.

Arab traders initially relied on African tribes to get goods from the interior. The first travellers to these places, men like Petherick, showed them a more direct route was possible – if you were armed. Arab traders and explorers went deeper and deeper into Africa. And these traders were not only after ivory, they wanted slaves. There had been slavery since the beginning of recorded history. Slaves in ancient Egypt, though they did not build the Pyramids, were used for domestic duties and acted as concubines. Unlike the position under later Islamic rulings, the child of a slave remained a slave even if one parent was a free man. Only the child of two free people could be considered free persons in ancient Egypt. Where did the slaves come from? Since we now know that the desert was less of a barrier, certainly in the Old Kingdom, many slaves may have come directly from central Africa across the desert. The other source would have been along the Nile or possibly up the east African coast to the Red Sea ports.

During the Ptolemaic period, there was already a long-standing slave trade serving the Indian Ocean. The seaport Berbera in Somalia, known as Malao in ancient times, is reported in the *Periplus* as exporting 'myrrh, a little frankincense, the harder cinnamon, duaca, Indian copal and macir; and slaves'. Zanzibar, further down the coast, was another entrepôt of slavery, which made inroads into east Africa but left the Equatorial regions unaffected until the results were felt of the Turkish Egyptian invasion of 1820. In the northern parts of Sudan, as far as Khartoum and Obeid, slavery was controlled, after the 1820s, by the invading army of Muhammad Ali. In 1840, an English visitor to Cairo could write of the city's slave market:

The slaves, all young women and girls, were confined in a suite of wretched cells, closed in front with mats, which were thrown aside, like a curtain, when any customer presented himself ... Supposing that we were desirous of becoming purchasers, the *jellabis* [slave merchants] commanded the young women, who were all squatting on the ground when we arrived, to get up and exhibit themselves; which they did, without manifesting the slightest indication of disgust or unwillingness, though they were as nearly as might be in a state of nature. Not one was pretty, but there were several whose forms were rich and graceful ... the oldest appeared to be about sixteen, the youngest not more than eight. The highest price demanded was sixty-two dollars.

Further south, slavery was much more haphazard and, according to Petherick, endemic:

Cultivation [of crops] was well attended to, the labour being performed by slaves, of which the members of the tribe owned considerable numbers – some individuals owning them by hundreds; and in case of emergency they accompanied their masters to battle. As everywhere else in the interior of Africa [before the arrival of commercial slavers], within my knowledge, they were treated affectionately, and, generally speaking, both master and slave were proud of each other: in negro families I have often observed more attention paid to the slave than to their child. But I was assured by both free and slave negroes that a runaway slave belonging to the Niam Niam, if captured, was made an example of, by being slain and devoured. I was also informed by the Niam Niam, who seem to glory in their reputation for cannibalism, that their aged, and indeed all when supposed to be on the point of death, were given up to be murdered and eaten.

The Niam Niam recognise no superior chief; but, like the Dor, the tribe is divided into numerous chieftainships. They are all large slave-owners, and the respectability and importance of the chiefs depend on the number of slaves in their possession. These are held to add importance as retainers and labourers; and being kidnapped from their neighbours for their own especial use, are not bartered either amongst themselves or adjoining tribes. A slave merchant, therefore, is not known in the country.

Baker, coming later, wrote about the prices for slaves among the Bunyoro in western Uganda. A healthy young girl was worth a single elephant's tusk 'of the first class' or a new shirt. In other areas 'where the natives are exceedingly clever as tailors and furriers', a girl could be bought for thirteen needles. But this 'innocent traffic' was soon disrupted by such traders as Abou Saoud, who found it 'more convenient to kidnap young girls, which saved much trouble in bargaining for needles and shirts'.

After giving a 'sermon' on the evils of the slave trade, Baker tells a chief of the Sheir tribe that, sadly, his own sons are dead. The chief tells him, 'I have a son, an only son. He is a nice boy – a very good boy. I should like you to see my boy – he is very thin now; but if he should remain with you he would soon get fat. He's a really nice boy and always hungry ... You'll like him amazingly; he'll give you no trouble as long as you give him plenty to eat ... he's a good boy, my only son. I'll sell him to you for a molote! [a native iron spade].' Baker concludes: 'I simply give this anecdote as it occurred without asserting that such conduct is the rule. At the same time, there can be no doubt that among the White Nile tribes any number of male children might be purchased from their parents – especially in seasons of scarcity.'

Baker makes the distinction between the practice of slavery, which, as in Egypt and ancient Rome – where slaves could reach positions of high regard and be well rewarded – was not an unmitigated evil, and the practices of slave hunters and traders, who, from all accounts, were entirely evil. The armies of the slave hunters roamed the countryside better armed than the people they preyed upon and stealing everything they might need to survive. 'When the slave hunters sought for corn,' explained Baker, 'they were in the habit of catching the villagers and roasting their posteriors by holding them down on the mouth of a large earthen water-jar filled with glowing embers. If this torture of roasting alive did not extract the secret, they generally cut the sufferer's throat to terrify his companions, who would then divulge the position of the hidden stores to avoid a similar fate.'

Schweinfurth, travelling at the same time as Baker, in the late 1860s, bore witness to the awful depredations of the slave trade. No European traveller (apart from traders such as the Maltese Andrea De Bono) ever condoned the slave trade run by the Turks and Arabs of Khartoum, though Schweinfurth was less proactive than Sam Baker. He watches a dying slave being lashed to 'prove whether life was yet extinct'. The slavers then proceed to 'play at football with the writhing body of the still gasping victim ... He was finally dragged off into the woods where a few weeks later I found his skull, which I deposited with those of many others of his fellow sufferers in the Museum of Berlin.'

Not all slaves were equal. Those from Bongoland (the Sudd region of southern Sudan) were much prized 'as they are easily taught and are docile and faithful, and are, besides, good looking and industrious'. Female slaves from the Azande, or Niam Niam, were much sought after, 'much dearer than the best Bongo slaves, but they are so extremely rare as hardly to admit of having a price quoted'. The Babuckur were considered difficult: 'no amount of good living or kind treatment can overcome their love of freedom'.

Slaves kept for private use by the Nubian invaders were divided into four groups, according to Schweinfurth:

1 Boys from seven to ten years of age who served as gun and ammunition carriers for their masters. When they grow up they join the second class.
2 Native fighting soldiers who served alongside their Arab masters. 'In every action the hardest work is put upon their shoulders.' These slaves have wives and children and, the richer ones, even slave boys of their own to carry their weapons. After a raid on the Niam Niam their ranks were always increased as, delighted with getting a cotton shirt and a gun of their own, young Niam Niam would gladly sell themselves into service 'attracted by the hope of finding better food in the Seribas than their own native wilderness can produce'.
3 Women slaves who were kept in the houses. 'These women are passed like dollars from hand to hand, a proceeding which is a prolific source of the rapid spread of those loathsome disorders by which the lands within the jurisdiction of the Seribas have been infested ever since their subjugation by the Khartoumers.' However, the child of any slave, according to Muslim law, is raised as a legitimate offspring and the mother receives the title of wife. To a force of 200 Nubian soldiers were attached as many as 300 women and boys, 'a party which, as well as immoderately increasing the length of the procession, by the clatter of their cooking utensils and their everlasting wrangling, kept up a perpetual turmoil which at times threatened a hopeless confusion'.
4 Slaves of any sex who were employed exclusively in husbandry.

Only superior slaves – the clerks and dragomen – actually tilled the soil and owned cattle. Soldier slaves might be drafted in at harvest time to help, and old women, who were too weak for anything else, were employed to weed the fields.

Schweinfurth reported the price of slaves in the *seribas* in 1871: eighteen pounds of copper would obtain a *sittahsi* – literally a child six spans high, that is eight to ten years old. Women slaves called *nadeef*, meaning 'pure', were in great demand among the settlers and fetched thirty pounds of copper or fifteen Marie-Thérèse dollars. Strong adult women who were ugly were cheaper, and old women 'can be bought for a mere bagatelle'. Women or children were preferred, male slaves were considered too troublesome for trading (as opposed to keeping for oneself).

Burton wrote, 'Justice requires the confession that the horrors of slave-driving rarely meet the eye in East Africa ... in fact the essence of slavery, compulsory unpaid labour, is perhaps more prevalent in independent India than in east Africa ... to this general rule there are terrible exceptions ... the guide, attached to the expedition on return from Ujiji, had loitered behind for some days because his slave girl was too footsore to walk. When tired of waiting he cut off her head, for fear lest she should become gratis another man's property.'

18 · Varieties of affliction

A thorn is removed with a thorn. Sudanese proverb

The Nile appears as a river of life, wending its way through the dead zone of the Sahara Desert, bringing life-giving moisture to humans, plants and animals. Yet, in the nineteenth century, the Nile was synonymous with disease – the cankers of Flaubert's STDs, the agues and fevers of the explorer, malaria, plague, death. Then there were the bugs and biting insects. Speke went deaf when a beetle crawled into his ear, gnawed at his eardrum, curled up and died.

Sir Richard Francis Burton was critically ill at the moment that Speke first set eyes on Lake Victoria and pronounced it the source of the Nile. Burton probably already had syphilis, contracted in Somalia, and was always mindful of his health. For long periods in his expedition to the Nile's source he was carried on a stretcher suspended from a pole. Burton certainly knew about illness.

He is the explorer's explorer, in as much as he returned with more news of strange places than any other man, and visited more strange places than any other – from Arabia to east and west Africa, South America and India. Arguably very few men of the nineteenth century had as much experience backed by as much learning, both of language and literature, as Richard Burton. His faults included an overweening zeal and a desire to shock, which to the modern sensibility is even more offensive than it was to the more hardened Victorian. To read Burton out of context is to feel oneself on occasion among the worst kind of ranting Boer farmer, yet a paragraph later all will be reversed: 'the social position of the women is the unerring test of progress towards civilisation' is not a sentence uttered by an unthinking reactionary. Neither was he a cruel man. Despite the rumours (put about by himself), there is no evidence that Burton ever killed anyone. The poet Algernon Swinburne wrote of him, 'You cannot think how kind and careful of me he was ... I know for the first time what it was to have an elder brother. He is the most cordial, sympathetic friend to me ... and it is a treat at last to have him to myself ... I rather grudge Mrs Burton's arrival here on Monday ... in our ascent of Puy de Dôme [a volcano in the Massif Central in France] he began at once gathering flowers to press for her.'

Burton was complicated. Much of his writing was intended to jolt people out of their complacency. When he was required to be accurate, he was; and the omnivorous curiosity he displayed in *The Lake Regions of Central Africa* provided every subsequent explorer with a veritable textbook for Nile exploration. Stanley was one of the few to admit his debt to Burton's book; Speke, of course, could rarely admit he had learnt anything from Burton.

Visiting the source regions of the Nile was, *a priori*, an unhealthy business, partly because of the novelty of the possible illnesses on offer. At one point in *Lake Regions* Burton observed: 'the vast variety of diseases which afflict more civilised races, who are collected in narrow spaces, are unknown in East Africa even by name'. But there were plenty of others. He remarked that fever was the main disease, and that smallpox was the most feared and the most dangerous. He told of seeing caravans of porters with over twenty sufferers of smallpox stumbling along 'blinded and almost insensible', and 'mothers carrying babes, both parent and progeny in the virulent stage of the fell disease'.

He added that both the Arabs and the Turks practised smallpox inoc-
ulation, which was also anciently known in South Africa: 'the pus is
introduced into an incision in the forehead between the eyebrows'.
(The breakthrough of Sir Edward Jenner, the eighteenth-century scientist, was to use cowpox rather than smallpox itself as the vaccine.)
There was also a milder form, more like chickenpox, which was cured
by bathing in cold water and smearing the body with red earth.

Burton recorded the prevalence of dysentery among visitors to the
lake regions of central Africa and noted that 'as in Egypt, few are free
from haemorrhoids'. He reported that scurvy was encountered in the
upper Nile despite there being fresh meat and vegetables available,
and that the Portuguese suffered tortures from the complaint. Though
Burton knew that poor diet was the primary cause he also wrongly
imagined that damp and cold played some part in the disease. Almost
certainly explorers heading into the interior neglected to eat enough
local food, possibly from fear of being poisoned.

Epilepsy is said to be cured by the marrow of a rhinoceros' leg bone,
and an umbilical hernia by an application of powdered marijuana and
melted butter. In many cases the cure is the same for driving out the
evil spirits that possess and cause disease, the usual cathartic being the
bark of the kalákalá tree, often boiled in porridge. For other diseases
the local people resort to cautery; 'they bleed each other frequently
... a favourite place is the crown of the head'. Burton notes that 'they
cannot reduce dislocations, and they never attempt to set or splint a
broken bone'.

Diseases were divided into those of unknown cause and those caused
by *uchawi*, black magic. Detecting *uchawi* was the job of the *mganga* or
witchdoctor, his or her waist all hung around with shrivelled gourds
containing potions and cures. The people of Usumbara thrust a red-hot
hatchet into the mouth of the accused; depending on the nature and
extent of the burns, your innocence or guilt was decided. Among tribes
from near Lake Tanganyika a heated iron spike was driven into some
tender part of the body and twice struck with a log of wood; others
dipped a hand in boiling water or seething oil; the Wazegura, in times
past, pricked the ear with the stiffest bristles of a gnu's tail. An allied
tribe had an ordeal by meat that choked the *innocen*t. Others infused
water with a poisonous bark and used a fat hen as a proxy. If it survived, an appeal could be made and a stronger decoction forced down

the throat of the accused. In these trials of black-magicking, to survive the test could (though not always) mean you were guilty; and to 'fail' the test, though it meant innocence, incurred along the way death or great injury. It seems, once suspected, you couldn't win.

The *mganga* was also the chief prophet of rain. As Burton laconically remarks, 'he is a weatherwise man, and rains in tropical lands are easily foreseen. Not infrequently, however, he proves himself a false prophet; and when all resources of cunning fail he must fly for dear life from the victims of the delusion.'

19 · At Burton's grave

Because they feared the donkey they beat the load. Arab proverb

The more you read, the more ways you discover that Burton is connected with the Nile. He is Speke's, the source discoverer's, handmaiden, and his book opened up the Nile to English-speaking explorers. *Lake Regions* was the key text for African explorers. Without Burton, Livingstone would have stayed south and Stanley would have stayed home.

Burton was friends with that other Nile traveller Monckton Milnes, who shared his taste in dubious literature. We have met Milnes before when he was turned down by Florence Nightingale. Milnes must have influenced Burton's decision to set up a publishing business based in Benares (actually it was in Stoke Newington, but promoted as Benares to avoid prosecution) in order to print obscene books, most notably a no-holds-barred version of *The Thousand and One Nights*. For people brought up on Sinbad and Aladdin it comes as quite a shock that 10 per cent of the stories in the *Nights* are very unsuitable bedtime reading even a thousand years after they were first collected on the banks of the Nile in Cairo. Cairo is a city of stories and courtesans – as it always was – and the Nile seems to reflect this. A river, red with the blood of the flood, must be a source of passion, or succour – stories and sex offer both. It is no accident that the beautiful and no doubt sexy storyteller Scheherazade trades stories for her life. It is this Nile that gives life to Cairo. *The Thousand and One Nights* becomes the informal bible of the Nile, providing a narrative map of desire and inner seeking, just as the real Bible provides the framework for believers along the river bank.

These books, Bible and *Nights*, by a not uneasy happenstance accompany many Nilotic travellers – such as Florence Nightingale, who read both, equally avidly, as they travelled upriver.

But Burton's affair with the East and Eastern stories went deeper. He had immersed himself in Sufi poetry and all evidence suggests he was initiated into Sufi circles. The conclusive evidence is missed by his best biographers when they dismiss his best work – the long poem entitled *The Kasidah* – as an attempt to cash in on the success of Edward Fitzgerald's version of Omar Khayyam. *The Kasidah* features such lines as:

> Be stout in woe, be stark in weal,
> Do good for Good is good to do,
> Spurn bribe of Heav'n and threat of Hell

and:

> From none but self expect applause,
> He noblest lives and noblest dies,
> Who makes and keeps his self-made laws

and:

> And this is all, for this we're born to weep a little and to die!
> So sings the shallow bard whose life still labours at the letter 'I'.

The Kasidah, with its Sufi psychology, goes a very long way to explaining the contradictions in Richard Burton's public behaviour – not the least of which was that he followed 'the path of blame', a well-known Sufi practice where opprobrium is courted in order to discern real friends and avoid the growth of debilitating self-importance.

Knowing the central importance of *The Kasidah* to Burton, I – along with Johnny West (a fellow Nile swimmer who appears later in this book) and travel writers Christopher Ross and Matthew Leeming – decided to hold a midnight vigil in Mortlake Cemetery where the explorer's Arab-tent tomb is to be found, complete with rusty solenoid-operated camel bells (paid for by his wife using the proceeds of her biography of her husband). This was in 1990 – exactly a hundred years since the death of Sir Richard Francis in Trieste.

Mortlake is a long way from the Nile, but it's quite close to the

Thames. We climbed over the church wall and headed for the tomb (which has a glass panel in the roof so you can view Richard and his wife Isabel lying like a couple of crusader knights). We set out four candles and began reading through *The Kasidah*. It's a long poem. By two o'clock we agreed that we had read enough. The candles doused, the book quietly closed, we returned over the river to our lives, having gleaned something from the key text, the main clue to the extraordinary life of Nile pioneer Sir Richard Burton, the main tenet of which is, in short, *be extraordinary*; at least don't be afraid to try.

Cease, Man, to mourn, to weep, to wail; enjoy the shining hour of sun;
We dance along Death's icy brink, but is the dance less full of fun?

20 · At the court of the cannibal King

Although the stomach is sick, one eats. Although the eye is sick, one weeps.
Ugandan proverb

We've mentioned it before, but where exactly is Bongoland? Look at a map of central Africa from the last quarter of the nineteenth century. You'll find it in that intense spot where the Congo, the Sudan and Uganda rub shoulders and share the upper reaches of the Nile. Bongoland and its cannibals have entered the joke mythology of the twenty-first century, but they arrived in the West through the discoveries of men like Petherick and, later, Schweinfurth, both of whom, it must be said, were reluctant to attribute cannibalism to African tribes unless the evidence was incontrovertible. The theory that cannibalism among some members of the Azande – whom earlier explorers called by their Dinka name the Niam Niam – was the result of disruption by slave and ivory traders is unlikely. Petherick was there well in advance of the Arab slavers and ivory merchants; indeed, as we have seen, he arrived when the concept of trade was unknown in this region. The key point is that not every tribe in this area ate people: the Shooli, later the Acholi – the tribe of Lord's Resistance Army leader Joseph Kony – were not historically cannibals (though some claim they are now).

Schweinfurth comes across a scene in Azande country very similar to that witnessed by Cape-to-Cairo traveller Ewart Grogan, thirty years

later. He describes each residence as having a post designed for display-
ing the owner's skill at hunting and war: 'skulls of little monkeys and of
great baboons, skulls of wild boars and of chimpanzees, and I must not
hesitate to add, skulls of men! They were fastened to the erections like
the presents on a Christmas tree, but instead of being gifts for children,
they were treasures for the comparative anatomist.' Close to the huts
he discovers piles of human bones which bore the marks of hatchet
and knife, 'and all around upon the branches of the neighbouring trees
were hanging human feet and hands more than half shrivelled into a
skeleton condition ... they polluted the atmosphere with a revolting
and intolerable stench'.

But it was to the south of the Niam Niam, among the Monbuttoo, or
Mengbutu, that the greatest cannibals were to be found. The Monbuttoo were a highly advanced tribe, master metalworkers, expert at music
and making musical instruments, the women highly independent –
typically, when asked how much a curio might be a Monbuttoo man
would reply, 'Ask my wife – it is hers.' They were expert cooks, fond of
using palm oil when they couldn't find their preferred source: human
fat. Despite their advanced culture, and according to Schweinfurth, 'the
cannibalism of the Monbuttoo is the most pronounced in all Africa'.

The carcasses of those who fell in battle were divided among the
greedy victors, the bodies dried first before transport. The King at the
court of Munza preferred to eat a child every day. Schweinfurth regularly came across people engaged in preparing human meat for consumption. In one case several young women were interrupted in the
task of scalding the hair off the lower half of a human body. 'The operation, as far as it was effected, had changed the black skin into a fawny
grey, and the disgusting sight could not fail to make me think of the
soddening and scouring of our fatted swine.' In another hut he sees a
human arm dangling over a fire – 'obviously with the design of being
at once dried and smoked'. When, during a meal, Schweinfurth asked
the King why at that precise time they weren't eating human flesh,
the King replied that it was out of respect for his guests because he was
aware of their aversion to the practice. But it was being carried on in
secret, he assured them. You can tell Schweinfurth has conflicting feelings about what he's seeing:

It is needless for me to ... describe how these people obtain their
human fat, or again, to detail the processes of cutting the flesh into

long strips and drying it over a fire in its preparation for consumption. The numerous skulls now in the Anatomical Museum in Berlin are simply the remains of their repasts which I purchased one after another for bits of copper, and go far to prove that the cannibalism of the Monbuttoo is unsurpassed by any nation in the world. But with it all, the Monbuttoo are a noble race of men ...

21 · Murder *caused by* the source of the Nile

When one looks at a fool with hatred the fool thinks it is love.
Arab proverb

All the good and the great were there. The instigator, Sir Roderick Murchison, Secretary of the Royal Geographical Society; the legendary Dr David Livingstone; Sir Henry Rawlinson, Sir Charles Lyell and Lord Milton; Francis Galton, who had penned a handbook for explorers; and Clements Markham, who years later would send Robert Falcon Scott to the Pole.

We are very far from the Nile, yet we are at its source. We are in Bath, a source in its own right – of mineral waters, oddly appropriate for Burton, the great explorer who abhorred his parents' habit of flitting from fashionable spa to fashionable spa across Europe when he was young, and yet when older he was to do just the same thing. When older and still tarnished by what had been said and not said at Bath. For here he was to debate, under the auspices of the RGS, with his old friend and now enemy Lieutenant Speke. The subject: where exactly the Nile did rise.

It was this question, the supreme question of exploration, that had dogged or worried every ruler who had dealings with the Nile since the beginning of time. That is an exaggeration perhaps, but not much. We are far from the Nile, but it is fitting we are in Britain, because this was the moment when Britain began to tighten its inexorable grip on the river, a grip that would lead to war at Omdurman, the colonisation of Uganda and giant dams at the Owen Falls and at Aswan. By debating the source of a river in another country you are announcing, and advancing, one form of ownership.

Speke confided to a friend that if he had to share a debating platform

with Burton he would kick him. 'By God he *shall* kick me!' insisted
Burton on hearing this. Neither talked to the other, nor had done for
some years. Yet Burton did not look away when Speke entered the
debating hall at the old Mineral Water Hospital; instead he directed
his famously intense stare at the apparently shaken Speke. The following day Speke seemed even more agitated. He left (it was assumed for
a short break) saying, 'Oh I cannot stand this any longer.' 'Shall you
want your chair again?' a man asked Speke. 'I hope not,' he said, an
odd reply for a man who was due to return later in the day to debate
with Burton.

In the meantime worthy men spoke lengthily on exploration. The
hour was nearing for the duel. Then the report came in. Ashen faced,
the Secretary read out the news: Speke was dead, killed while out shooting during the break in proceedings. Burton crumpled. The whole
façade of his antagonism was revealed. It had been a game to him. He
wished no real ill will on Speke. The reverse may also have been true,
but now Speke was dead.

The cause of death: shotgun wound to the chest. In the nineteenth
century, deaths from gunshot wounds that were accidental – about a
hundred a year – were less likely than a suicide. In fact, a self-inflicted
gunshot wound was twice as likely to be an attempt to end one's own
life as a mere accident.

As William Guy wrote in his 1844 book *The Principles of Forensic Medicine*: 'Suicidal wounds have a character which accidental wounds often,
and homicidal wounds sometimes, lack of being inflicted in front on
the head or region of the heart.' Speke's wound was in the upper left
side of his chest. Burton had noted, years earlier, on a hippopotamus
hunt in east Africa that even when the boat was charged and almost
sunk, '[Speke] never allowed his gun to look at himself or at others.'

Had the Nile, the Red Nile, extracted this death as some sort of levy?
Or a warning: this river is not to be trifled with? It seems perfectly in
keeping with the Red Nile that settling its discovery should end in a
horrific death. The world has long argued about whether it was accidental or suicidal. It is my contention that it was neither. I think Speke
was murdered.

It started with an insult. What was it exactly, this insult? There were
so many, Speke felt, so much he had endured, as the hangdog number
two to the mighty Richard Burton. But usually one insult opens the
carapace, creates that hairline crack, through which the infection will

pass and poison the man against his former friend. Some line has to be crossed. What was the insult that started it all? Was it the insinuation of cowardice when he took a step back during the attack by spear-throwing Somalis and Burton ordered him forward? Was it the appropriation and yet at the same time dismissal of his Somali expedition diary? Or was it being told that without languages he was useless as an explorer and had only been taken along because Burton felt sorry for him?

Interest in Nile exploration reached its climax during the RGS-sponsored debate between Richard Francis Burton and John 'Jack' Hanning Speke. There was a running sore, a deep dispute between the two men that had started as early as 1855 when they explored Somalia together. It was on this trip that Speke had lost a considerable quantity of personal effects, was out of pocket for the whole expedition. And, apart from Burton successfully entering the forbidden city of Harar, the whole trip was a fiasco, both men being wounded during a night attack on their tent by Somalis. Burton received a spear through the face, and as he ran to escape he held the spear in both hands to stop it from dragging along the ground. Speke was wounded in the thigh. But they both evaded capture. It was during this desperate fight that one source of their rift can be detected. Jack Speke was plainly in awe of his friend, though, like all quiet egotists, there were some areas he considered his own turf. One suspects that bravery was one of them – but during the attack he started to fall back and Burton rapped out, 'Stand your ground, man!' Speke, in overreaction, rushed forward, thus precipitating the attack they wished to avoid, every inch the man worried that he had been accused of cowardice. He was not scared of death, even if he had been rattled by the attacking tribesmen. Speke once let slip that he had come to Africa to be killed, civilised life holding no interest for him.

This then was their great journey: to travel inland from the port of Zanzibar to investigate the great Lake Tanganyika. Which they did. While Burton was ill, however, Speke made an agreed side-journey to check another lake – which he named Victoria. After merely glimpsing this lake, Speke pronounced it the source of the Nile. It was one of the best guesses in the history of exploration.

It cannot have been easy for anyone travelling with Burton unless they were an acolyte or had a great sense of humour. From all published accounts we see that Burton was a joker, a humorist of the first rank. Speke, however, was neither funny nor inclined to japery. He didn't get Burton's jokes, though he was successful at simulating the appearance of discipleship. He adopted a very meek attitude to Burton that masked his true feelings. In letters home he castigated his leader, but Burton had no knowledge of this.

What Burton didn't bank on was the way fever and solitude played with Speke's mind. Not just weeks or months but two *years* of being sidelined in every conversation with the Arabs they dealt with must have been extremely galling. We have a modern equivalent in Gavin Maxwell's *A Reed Shaken by the Wind*, arguably a better book than Wilfred Thesiger's *The Marsh Arabs*. We sense Maxwell's frustration and impotence at having to sit through hours of conversation with Arab elders, with Thesiger in full flow and Maxwell himself, ignorant of Arabic, doodling in his sketchbook. And Burton would have made little effort, one suspects, to include the other man, who in his own proud way refused to study the language yet spent, as Burton observed, stubborn hours perfecting the use of the sextant and surveying instruments. So we have an obstinate man pretending to be an acolyte who, when presented with an opportunity, runs with it. With Burton ill, Speke leapt at the chance to explore the 'other great lake' that others had talked about.

As soon as Speke landed in England (Burton was delayed for two weeks), he sent a letter to Murchison at the RGS. Within days he was the talk of the town. He had found the lake that was the source of the Nile! When Burton landed it seemed no one cared much about Lake Tanganyika. He also found that a new expedition would be leaving soon if Lieutenant Speke's ideas about the Nile were correct. No, he would not be leading it – Speke would, and Speke had requested that he choose his own second in command. It was, from Burton's perspective, a complete betrayal.

Speke was careful to choose someone who knew no languages and had no experience of exploration – James Grant, whom we'll meet later on when he accompanies the British army against the Mad Emperor Theodore of Ethiopia (and incidentally becomes the first man to reach both sources of the Nile). Burton, pioneer of the route into the region of the Great Lakes, had been used and usurped.

We know that Speke placed an abnormally low value on his own life. And this could certainly pass for courage. He had, then, a predisposition to self-harm. The question is, was he also suggestible?

When Burton was in Buenos Aires in 1868 he met Wilfrid Scawen Blunt, then a young Foreign Office attaché. Blunt and Burton spent a lot of time together and one day Burton offered to hypnotise the younger man. Blunt wrote, 'His expression as he gazed into my eyes was nothing less than atrocious. If I had submitted to his gaze for any length of time – and he held me by my thumbs – I have no doubt he would have succeeded in dominating me. But my will is also strong, and once I had met the eyes of a wild beast ... I broke away, and would have no more.'

Speke, however, was already close to breaking point. We know that he stormed out of the RGS meeting in the morning saying, 'I cannot stand this', meaning that the anticipation and tension had certainly not been helped by Burton glaring at him. Isabel Burton reported that Speke's face, as he looked at Burton, was 'full of sorrow, of yearning, of perplexity. Then it turned to stone.' As if imploring him by body language, if not in words, to drop his war against this deeply rattled Nile discoverer. Burton did not, of course, look away. Instead, his 'basilisk stare' drilled into the weaker man's countenance. Did Burton hypnotise him? Did he somehow implant a suggestion that exploded later while Speke was carrying the means of self-destruction, a shotgun primed and loaded?

Firemen in New York City are four times less likely to commit suicide than policemen in the same urban area. One suggestion, brutally simple, is they are denied the means. Cops have guns with them all the time, firemen don't. The means are right there at your side – and in the small hours, in times of depression, a single flip decision could result in suicide. Speke had the means. He was certainly depressed. A poor public speaker with much ridiculed geographical skills, he wasn't looking forward to a drubbing by one of the finest minds in Britain. And add to that the certain knowledge that he had betrayed Burton, gone back on his word. This would, in public, be bound to come out. Speke was a prig, anxious that his honour be respected.

Burton often hypnotised his wife Isabel – it was something of a party piece. Had he hypnotised Speke during their long travels together? Almost certainly, though the key to hypnotism is that the hypnotised must want to be dominated – and this was not the case with Speke, until, perhaps, the very end. Was that look of submission enough for Burton to send the man into a self-destructive trance state? Was the sudden transformation to a stone-like expression the sign that the suggestion had taken hold? Speke said very little after seeing Burton on his last fateful encounter; oddly enough, Burton's first long poem was entitled *Stone Talk*, but this one did not.

This may sound overblown, but the later behaviour of Burton is rather curious. When he heard the news of Speke's death he was visibly shaken. He gave an alternative speech on Dahomey and then asked to be excused. Isabel reported that he was grievously upset and kept repeating Speke's name. This all suggests an element of guilt. Did he send, not just the hypnotic message that he wanted the other man to fail, to buckle, to give up, but rather, a highly specific psychic command to die? Was it a momentary lapse on Burton's part, a death sentence sent, and, once sent, impossible to retract, however much Burton may have wanted to?

One can be absolutely sure that Burton had mastered the hypnotic death stare of the Yezidis, a sect of Kurdish origin whose religion is considered to be a mix of Zoroastrianism and Sufism, learnt while he was a subaltern in the Sindh. The death stare is designed to send a psychic shock deep into the unprotected psyche of the one stared at. Reputedly it can cause madness, delusions, paralysis, death. Only by imagining oneself imprisoned within an imaginary transparent pyramid can the death stare be repudiated. It is said to be the real origin of the evil eye, and there is certainly a connection between Egypt, gypsies and the Yezidi Peacock Angel Cult, as Burton outlined in his posthumous *The Jew, the Gypsy and El Islam*.

After Speke had rushed from the assembly rooms in Bath where the great debate was going to take place, he travelled ten miles to a cousin's farm where he intended to do some shooting to calm his nerves – perhaps not such a strange thing for a man who loved hunting and killing. Certainly target shooting can calm the nerves by its requirement for stillness. But this was to be a rough shoot.

His cousin was a hundred yards away when he heard the report of a gun and saw Speke fall as he climbed over a wall. Rushing to Speke, it was found that he had a large hole in his chest somewhere towards his armpit, not the obvious place for a suicide to aim at. Because a shotgun has such a long barrel you can't in fact reach the trigger if the gun is pointing directly at your heart, but Speke was close. Most shotgun suicides are decidedly messier, with the suicide sticking both barrels in his or her mouth. To effect a heart shot one would need a string on the trigger or perhaps a hooked twig. Or perhaps the trigger could be banged against a protruding rock in a wall one was climbing over.

Whatever the case, the Speke family would be unlikely to admit it was suicide. Even today families like to conceal suicide attempts, and it was far more frowned upon a century and a half ago. There is therefore the distinct possibility that Speke really did pull the trigger with a stick or bang the gun against a stone to set it off.

Yet Speke was not the killer. Certainly he was depressed. When in a depressed state, one does not take the usual precautions. Depressed drivers tend to 'dare' others on the road, drive without seat belts and overtake without sufficient caution. Speke was an expert shot. Burton remarked that Speke would never have pointed his gun at himself or others; shooting etiquette would have been drummed into him as a farmer's son and an army officer. Anyone who is professionally around guns is very cautious – I have known ex-soldiers get very annoyed when a kid's BB gun is pointed at them (by an adult), on the grounds that any association with 'playing with guns' is plain wrong. I think it highly unlikely that Speke, in his normal frame of mind, would ever have allowed himself to be shot. And even if depressed, I think his instincts about shooting would have overridden carelessness. However, I think his will had been broken by the death stare. Combined with his depressed state, had Speke become like the driver who overtakes on a blind corner because he really doesn't care whether he lives or dies? Did Speke deliberately bang and drag his gun over the wall in a sloppy manner because he no longer cared and because he wanted to test his destiny?

The truth is harsher than this, I fear. The stare robbed Speke of his survival instinct, the thousand small decisions that keep us alive each day. He tripped the trigger on the wall and felt the impact of the left barrel full force in his chest, the shot 'led in a direction upwards and towards the spine, passing through the lungs and dividing all the large vessels near the heart'.

When Sir Richard Burton, in rare moments of conversational honesty, admitted he had never killed a man, he was wrong. Speke was killed by a single glance.

22 · It isn't over until the fat ladies are measured

Out of pure love a crow brings his friend a rotting carcass.
Egyptian proverb

Speke's second trip with Grant had been like some kind of soap opera of exploration. Petherick, Samuel Baker and Baker's wife Florence had walk-on parts, Burton was offstage just waiting for his call, and the journey, though epic and extraordinarily demanding, did not after all settle the question of the Nile's source. This would only really occur piecemeal – as Stanley and the Bakers and others gradually filled in all the gaps, ultimately proving Speke right. But on his return with Grant Speke did not have the evidence he needed to convince everyone. What he did have were some salacious tales of measuring the women of the court of Rumanika, in the environs of Lake Victoria, who were, it must be said, *extremely* fat. So fat that they would crawl rather than walk.

The irony of hatred is the inevitable imitation that develops between the hated and the hater. The hated, like the loved, begin to imitate their former oppressor. Both hate and love bestow an excessive attention, and what we look at enough we are doomed to copy. It's a kind of law of nature. Israelis ghettoise Palestinians just as they were ghettoised in Europe, suburban America adopts the dress code of the criminal classes it fears so much: sagging jeans without a belt (in case the perp hangs himself) and tattoos. So, too, did Speke ape the style of Burton, going so far as to measure the fat women of King Rumanika's court. Somehow, though Burton could get away with similar stuff, with asides in Latin and plenty of footnotes, in Speke's hands it looked like plain sensationalism. Burton would have measured everyone, or made it a footnote. Speke makes of the measuring something of a party piece, revealing his smutty-postcard sensibilities – and it was this that started the tide against him, set the scene for the great debate. The grandees of the RGS were fickle: Burton had needed to be taught a lesson, and they had done so by initially favouring Speke and sending him on this expedition. But now Speke had returned from his two-year trip with the measurements of some fat ladies but no measurements of the Nile. One geographer showed that Speke's readings suggested that for ninety miles the Nile ran uphill. Another, that he had seen the lake but at a distance, and had relied mainly on native information for his conclusions. The explorer's description of the Ripon Falls as being like a Highland stream met with incredulity that this could be the source of the mighty Nile. He was, of course, right. But, as one of Burton's beloved Arabs would have it, 'The master being wrong is more right than the student being right.'

23 · The Dinka are getting shorter

For the cow its horns are not too heavy. Sudanese proverb

Speke, for all his faults, was no racist. He enjoyed the company of diverse cannibals and headhunters and, though he might deplore their diet and table manners, he did not stoop to the usual crude epithets of the race hater. In some quarters of the Royal Geographical Society it was openly said that Speke was too friendly with the natives, that he had let the side down, but it seems to me, when you get clear of his weaknesses and foolish hatred of Burton, that he really loved the people of the upper Nile.

For the overland part of his journey, when he had to circumvent the great swamp of the Sudd, Speke travelled in the company of the Dinka, known to be the tallest people in Africa.

In the 1950s, the first time a sufficient number of Dinka were measured, they were, on average, 5 foot 11.9 inches. Many were of course much taller, with several Dinka playing for the American National Basketball Association. But in 1995 the average height had dropped to 5 foot 9.4 inches. Cause: twenty or more years of civil war and strife and habitat destruction.

In 1983 the northern Sudanese Arabs armed with Kalashnikovs the Baggara tribe of the upper Nile. The Baggara still carried their long swords, and used them when they attacked Dinka villages and wanted to save ammunition. The Baggara had enslaved the Dinka in the time of Petherick and Baker. Now they were armed with enough firepower to do it again. They rode into villages and killed the men and carried off the women and children on their horses.

The Dinka culture, like the Nuer, like the Acholi, began the process of migrating from a cattle culture to a gun culture. But you cannot eat guns, so cattle remain, albeit of less significance than before the arrival of the Kalashnikov rifle. Before the second civil war in the 1980s, the Dinka of the upper Nile were already giving up their old ways, moving to towns, converting to Christianity. The war stopped this and a great number fled to refugee camps in Kenya and Ethiopia. Many left to go down the Nile to Egypt. Some made it to America. Now, with the independence of South Sudan in 2011, some of the Dinka have returned, but the old ways are not on the surface any more. They cannot be made into picturesque images any more. People must carry them in their hearts as stories.

The Dinka were a cattle people. The cattle were hardly ever killed. They took part in religious ceremonies. Strangely, many of the Dinka who left for the United States ended up working in great slaughter-houses butchering cattle. They were happy working with what they knew, even if it was dead.

The old ways might be strange, or even wrong. In the distant past a Dinka boy might sexually stimulate a cow by licking its vulva, this being a tried and tested way to increase milk production. People doubted such stories, but in the 1980s Kazuyoshi Nomachi photographed a boy with his face in a cow's vulva and it was published in a collaboration with Geoffrey Moorhouse.

The Dinka smoke pipes bound with brass and copper wire. The tobacco is *Nicotiana rustica*, the wild tobacco also found in South America and thought to have been introduced from there. But when Petherick arrived each tribal group already had its own word for tobacco, a sure sign that they had been using it for far longer than the few hundred years the theory demanded.

The Dinka extract the four lower front teeth for aesthetic purposes. They tend to be stark naked, their bodies ghostly with ash, the facial lines looking like black cracks in the grey mask. They will sleep in ash and wear ash to keep away mosquitoes, and they burn cattle-dung fires all night for the same reason. In the morning, after the cattle have been released, fresh cattle dung will be scooped up to dry in the sun, shaped into pats the better to burn. The cattle are staked all night, each cow tethered to its own stake – you cannot stampede such an arrangement. The stakes are all in among the huts, which makes it hard to carry out a raid.

A Dinka village at dawn looks a little like a blown-up wood in the First World War, ghostly shades of destruction on the dry plains bordering the Sudd swamp with dry tree limbs poking from the ground, the remnants of old hut circles. They look random, but they work. When the huts are completed they have a grass igloo-type covering over the rough wooden structure. The top tapers to a point like the top tassel on a Nepalese woollen cap.

Dinka men are uncircumcised mainly, and they wear a circular necklace, ivory elbow bracelets, a single decorative wire around the waist, brass wire anklets. They sleep either naked or with a cloth the size of a small towel over their lower body. Sometimes a bead corset is worn around the waist, nothing above or below. Sometimes a woolly hat may be worn. The Dinka mark their faces with cicatrices like most of the southern Sudanese tribes. Unlike the Shilluk, who incise their eyebrow line with bead-like cicatrices, the Dinka have three or four V-shaped scars high on the forehead.

Devotion to their cattle is shown by polishing the horns. These cattle have horns of great size, like the cattle depicted on ancient Egyptian friezes, horns up to three feet in length. When they are not tending to their cattle the young may relax by dancing. Or they may smoke, or weave cattle ropes from elephant grass. An old man might while away time having his hair groomed with an acacia thorn. The dedicated busy themselves filling a goat's scrotum with ash, to be later used as part of a religious offering.

Because of the scarcity of water a Dinka boy will wash his hair clean of ash and earth in the early-morning stream of urine from a convenient cow. Cattle are rarely eaten. They are bled and the blood cooked or drunk fresh; they are milked and the milk drunk or turned into yoghurt and cheese. Again, in a culture with a minimum of division between man and beast, a boy will suckle direct from the cow's teat, and this might be his only source of food for the morning. If the milk is to be stored, a hollow calabash serves as a pail.

The river Dinka live in the myriad waterways of the Sudd Nile on floating islands; from above, the cloth sun-protecting tents look like something by Christo, the avant-garde sculptor. The river-dwelling Dinka are fishermen, their musculature more developed than the elongated limbs of the plains Dinka. Some of the islands are made by constructing huge piles of papyrus; others are natural formations of foliage and reeds.

The Dinka way of life survived the ravages of slavery and colonialism, but will it survive the modern world – with its automatic weapons and global culture?

24 · Ṭravel tips for the Nile explorer

For a poor person snot is salt. Ethiopian proverb

Sir Francis Galton, cousin of Darwin and inventor of both the finger-print system and the IQ test, was a great eugenics enthusiast. Unlike Speke he saw in such tribes as the Dinka supporting evidence for his own sinister racism, his belief that the African had, through gener-ations, arrived at physical excellence but not intellectual supremacy. Galton himself was not a very attractive man, though he was bright – it was he who coined the weather term 'anti-cyclone' and invented, iron-ically for an ugly man, the 'statistical beauty map of Britain' (the most beautiful lived in London, the least beautiful in Aberdeen).

He was also an early African explorer. His expedition to Lake Ngami was the start of a lifelong interest in African, and especially Nile, exploration. He chaired the controversial meeting in Brighton where Stanley tried to defend Livingstone's belief that the Lualaba was the Nile. Galton asked Stanley if the waters of Lake Tanganyika were sweet or brackish. 'There is no sweeter water for making a cup of tea,' replied Stanley, thinking he had been mocked. He then went on the attack, calling Galton an 'easy-chair geographer', 'Mr Francis Galton FRGS, FRSXYZ and I do not know how many other letters'. Stanley was being a little unfair. Galton may have been an unvarnished bigot, but he was also a genuine explorer and his book *The Art of Travel* (1872) is the dis-tillation of much real experience. It belongs, along with Burton's *The Lake Regions of Central Africa*, on the bookshelf of any self-respecting Red Nile explorer.

On the subject of donkeys – Petherick and Stanley always rode the beasts if they could – Galton wrote that asses can be taught not to kick. 'Mungo Park says that negroes, where he travelled, taught their asses as follows: they cut a forked stick, and put the forked part into the ass's mouth, like the bit of a bridle.' The forked ends were tied together behind the donkey's head while the longer piece protruded forward and struck the ground if the donkey put his head down. 'It always proved effectual.'

To stop a donkey braying, a heavy stone should be lashed to its tail. When a donkey brays it habitually raises its tail; with it weighted down 'he has not the heart to bray. In hostile neighbourhoods, where silence and concealment are sought, it might be well to adopt this rather absurd treatment.'

Crossing a river may be effected using the 'African swimming ferry'. Two large calabashes are used as a float by cutting off their small ends and joining them to make a single lightweight container. The passenger places his luggage on top of this float and then clings to it. The ferryman then balances this unstable set-up by holding on to the other side of the float and swimming, pushing the entire load across the river.

Illness, of course, was the main threat to early Nile explorers. Galton, who was trained as a physician in the early 1840s, advises that 'powerful emetics, purgatives, and eyewashes are the most popular physickings'. He advises that explorers should keep in mind the old adage, 'Though there is a great difference between a good physician and a bad one, there is very little difference between a good one and none at all.'

For a powerful emetic he suggests, 'drink a charge of gunpowder in a tumblerful of warm water or soap-suds, and tickle the throat'. For fevers he suggests prophylactic use of quinine but points out that this did not help Dr Livingstone. In the end he concludes that the banks of a river are often less affected than the low hills that overlook them. He advises never to camp downwind of a marsh, sleep between two large fires and avoid starting too early in the morning.

For the common companion of diarrhoea he suggests nothing but broth or rice water. 'The least piece of bread or meat causes an immediate relapse.' The scourge of the Nile, especially in Egypt and Sudan, however, was always considered to be ophthalmia. He recommends sulphate of zinc as an eyewash. It should be properly astringent, which you can test by tasting it. Toothache could ruin an expedition too. Galton remarked, 'An unskilled traveller is very likely to make a bad job of a first attempt at tooth-drawing. By constantly pushing and pulling an aching tooth, it will in time loosen, and perhaps, after some weeks, come out.' For thirst he recommended: 'drink water with a tea-spoon; it will satisfy a parched palate as much as if you gulped it down in tumblerfuls, and will disorder the digestion very considerably less'. For hunger, 'Give two or three mouthfuls [of food, preferably broth] every quarter of an hour to a man reduced to the last extremity by hunger.'

As for fleas, 'Italian flea-powder ... is really efficacious.' He reports a fellow explorer's experience: 'I have often found a light cotton or linen bag a great safeguard against the attacks of fleas. I used to creep into it, draw the loop tight round my neck and was thus able to set legions of them at defiance.' For 'Vermin on the Person', or lice, 'You take half an ounce of mercury, which you mix with old tea leaves previously reduced to a paste by mastication. To render this softer you generally add saliva; water could not have the same effect ... You infuse this composition into a string of cotton, loosely twisted, which you hang around the neck; the lice are sure to bite at the bait, and they thereupon as surely swell, become red, and die forthwith ... renew this salutary necklace once a month.'

Snakebites: 'Tie a string tight above the part, suck the wound, and caustic it as soon as you can. Or, for want of caustic, explode gunpowder in the wound.' Scorpion sting: 'the oil scraped out of a tobaccopipe is a good application'.

To carry an ill man Galton advises making a litter. Two lengthy poles with cross-pieces are laid on top of the sick man, who in turn is lying on a blanket. The ends and sides of the blanket are knotted to the carrying poles, which are kept from moving in and out by the cross-pieces.

Of course all the above is not much use if you cannot manage the men under your command. For this he instructs would-be explorers in the 'Management of Savages'. First, Galton counsels that:

> A frank, joking, but determined manner, joined with an air of showing more confidence in the good faith of the natives than you really feel, is the best. It is observed that a sea-captain generally succeeds in making an excellent impression on savages: they thoroughly appreciate common sense, truth, uprightness; and are not half such fools as strangers usually account them. If a savage does mischief, look on him as you would on a kicking mule, or a wild animal, whose nature is to be unruly and vicious, and keep your temper quite unruffled.

He advises that on arrival at a native encampment the occupants often run away in fright. He suggests you 'go boldly into their huts, take just what you want, and leave fully adequate payment. It is absurd to be over-scrupulous in these cases.'

Galton recognises the importance of keeping morale high with feast days and holidays. 'Recollect that a savage cannot endure the steady labour that we Anglo-Saxons have been bred to support. His nature is adapted to alternations of laziness and severe exertion. Promote merriment, singing, fiddling and so forth, with all your power.'

On flogging he is circumspect. Most of the African explorers resorted to flogging porters who stole or tried to desert. Stanley recommended a light switch, others favoured the hippo-hide whip which would raise a cut on the first lash. Galton writes, 'Different tribes have very different customs in the matter of corporal punishment: there are some who fancy it a disgrace and serious insult. A young traveller must therefore be discriminating and cautious in the licence he allows to his stick, or he may fall into sad trouble.'

On counting: 'When you wish a savage to keep count, give him a string of beads.' As each item to be counted is passed, the man counting jerks a bead from the forepart of the cord hanging in front to the rear part over his shoulder.

Of course, when managing savages goes wrong it is time to resort to coping with hostilities. Galton makes a long list of weapons suitable for resisting a native attack: for close-quarter attacks 'Buck-shot and slugs are better than bullets', but for a really good frightening effect he recommends rockets:

> Of all the European inventions, nothing so impresses and terrifies savages as fireworks, especially rockets. I cannot account for the remarkable effect they produce, but in every land it appears to be the same. A rocket, judiciously sent up, is very likely to frighten off an intended attack and save bloodshed. If a traveller is supplied with any of these, he should never make playthings of them, but keep them for great emergencies.

For keeping watch he recommends opera glasses, and 'I should be glad to hear that a fair trial had been also given by a traveller to an ear-trumpet.'

As a clever trick when being robbed he suggests the following: when approached by an armed robber and told to lie on the floor while the robber divests you of your goods, take out your revolver and, cursing, say, 'If this were loaded you should not treat me thus!' Then throw yourself on the ground as the robber in his triumph approaches. When he is in range shoot him with the 'unloaded' gun, which of course was loaded all the time. Another ruse is to keep a small pistol cocked and loaded in your wallet pocket. When asked for money reach into the pocket and fire through the fabric at your assailant.

If one is forced to take a prisoner, perhaps to act as a guide as Nile explorers sometimes did, secure him with the least amount of string by tying his thumbs together behind his back.

25 · Buying a white slave

The man who kills a lion does not pick his nose like a child.
Nubian proverb

In the nineteenth century, as we have seen, there were two approaches to discovering the Nile's source – travelling inland through Africa or attempting to ascend the river from Cairo. No one had ever managed the full ascent, not Alexander the Great's envoy, nor Nero's legionaries, nor Napoleon, nor Capitan Selim, nor the admirable Petherick. Not until the Victorian explorer Samuel Baker *and his wife* – who travelled everywhere with him – did the ascent of the Nile occur. And Baker's wife, to whom he was devoted, was certainly unusual – he bought her at a Circassian slave auction.

The going rate for a white slave in the Balkans in 1859 was about £10 for a virgin aged between twelve and eighteen, though in a glut the price could go as low as £5, perhaps the equivalent of £300 now. There were many sources: Georgia, Circassia, the edges of Greece and the wilder parts of Albania and Serbia. Turkey's vassal states in Europe were particularly vulnerable. In some Bulgarian districts each family had to give up one child as a kind of blood tax.

It was into this world that Samuel Baker, easily the most likeable of the great African explorers, burst on to the scene with a desire to be amused by the slave market in Widdin in what is now north-west Bulgaria. Baker was thirty-eight years old, already a widower and the father of four daughters in the care of his sister (two sons and another daughter having already died).

In one version of the story, the Pasha of Widdin outbid Baker for the eighteen-year-old Hungarian Florenz Sass, originally from a German-speaking part of Transylvania. Baker was so entranced by the girl that he refused to let her become the slave of the elderly Turkish governor. The same night he managed to arrange her escape and together they fled down the Danube to freedom – an implausible story at best, as Baker was on a hunting holiday at the time with an Indian maharaja called Dulep Singh. It is almost certainly the case that Florenz caught his romantic eye at the slave auction and he simply bought her.

From these extraordinary beginnings began the greatest husband-and-wife exploring team the world has ever seen, or is likely to see. It would be two years before he could set in motion his plan to reach the source of the Nile by ascending the river, attempting what every expedition since ancient times had failed to achieve. Speke may have claimed to have found the Nile's source, but somehow cutting in from Zanzibar wasn't quite as impressive as travelling the full length of the river, especially if you do so with your woman (he had yet to marry Florenz). Baker spurned the usual source of patronage, the Royal Geographical Society. Instead he sought support from a former rear admiral, Henry Murray, a bachelor who lived in Albany off Piccadilly and kept the company of explorers and big-game hunters. No women, not even slaves, were allowed in his apartments; in his bedroom were a set of parallel bars that male guests could work out on when the conversation flagged. From Murray, Baker received all important contacts, especially in Egypt. Murray, known as 'the skipper', was an enthusiastic supporter of flogging as a way of maintaining discipline, though according to Baker he exuded 'an almost womanly gentleness and courtesy'. Another contact was a former aide to Livingstone, the admired big-game hunter William Oswell. Oswell lent Baker his most prized weapon: a massive 10-gauge double-barrelled rifle and shotgun combination. The skipper, meanwhile, presented him with a naval telescope. Baker was set.

In 1861 he sent home from Alexandria for rifles, 250 pounds of gunpowder, a large box of tools and a medical chest well stocked with quinine. Unlike most of the nineteenth-century explorers Baker was independently wealthy. He asked the family company that looked after his inheritance to make unlimited funds available for his assault on the Nile. He set out on 15 April 1861: 'Left Cairo at 6am with a spanking breeze.' His notebook was not a new one, but already contained notes made during his eight years as a planter in Ceylon and during the Danube journey during which he had bought Florence (as she was now known). His handwriting had changed since then: it was smaller, less jerky, more controlled.

At Aswan, a party of Nubians came aboard to beg for baksheesh. They were all entirely naked. Baker remarked in his diary, 'I could not help thinking how much ladies must learn by a journey up the

Nile which affords such opportunities for the study of human nature.'
They then travelled overland past the cataracts on sixteen camels until
rejoining the Nile at Berber. Florence (the second Florence of the Nile,
we might note) did not like the climate at all. 'F. very ill with fatigue
and heat,' wrote Baker. But they battled on, reaching the borders of
Abyssinia, where they then spent months becoming acclimatised to
travel in remote places.

Eventually they returned to the Nile and journeyed on to Khartoum.
Here they met Arab slavers and made plans to penetrate further up
the Nile. Reaching Gondokoro, they believed Speke, on his expedition,
to be dead. But after a short stay he arrived with his fellow explorer
James Grant. Baker had been hoping that it would be he, Sam, who
would rescue Speke from trouble near the source of the Nile. But Speke,
though tired and anxious, told him, 'The Nile is settled.' Baker asked
him if there was anything left to do on the river. The reply was 'Find
Lake Nzige.' Speke in his desire to escape the rapacious King of the
Bunyoro, who had taken virtually all his belongings, had left the Nile
shortly after seeing it exit Lake Victoria and journeyed overland to
Gondokoro. He had thus missed out a huge loop of the White Nile that
native information suggested passed through an enormous lake, the
Luta Nzige. Baker decided to find this lake.

It shows Baker's courage that, knowing he would have to deal with
the Bunyoro King, Kamrasi, he still went ahead with his plan. Speke
warned him repeatedly about the devious and repugnant nature of
Kamrasi, but Baker, trusting in his immense physical strength which he
was convinced was the key to impressing Africans, was sure he would
gain the permission he needed to get to the lake. Kamrasi had odd pro-
tuberant eyes and a fickle nature. He said that Baker could of course go
to the lake. He'd even send an armed party of warriors to protect him.
But he wanted Florence in exchange.

This demand was the last of many they had had to endure during the
weeks they had been in Kamrasi's company. So far they had given the
chief a Persian carpet fifteen feet square, a Kashmiri shawl, a double-
barrelled rifle, several pairs of wool socks, handfuls of bracelets and
necklaces, even the yellow kerchief Florence wore on her head. But no,
he wanted more. Kamrasi hadn't even allowed them to stay in his capital. Instead they lodged outside the town in huts on a muddy meadow
abutting a mosquito-infested swamp.

But Kamrasi had not reckoned on the hero that was Sam Baker. After the demand had been translated – with the addition of several African wives for Sam thrown in as a sweetener – the enraged Baker leapt forward drawing his navy revolver from his waistband. He held it as steady as his fever-ridden state would allow, a few feet from the King's chest, and in a wild rage told him that if the demand was ever repeated he would kill him then and there. Florence joined in in Arabic (a language Kamrasi was ignorant of) and then the female interpreter joined in.

Kamrasi knew he had gone too far. His gross face remained impassive as he opted for less offensive gifts. That kilt Baker had been wearing when he arrived (Baker wore full Highland dress when he wanted to impress native chiefs) – could he have that? Or the compass he'd been shown? After all, good Speke had given him a chronometer. The wheedling continued, but Baker was firm. No more gifts until they had permission to leave. Kamrasi shrugged. They could go. It would take twenty days, he said. But ominously he added, 'Don't blame me if you can't get back.'

Baker and Florence were already weakened with malaria and gastric fever. The medicine chest left by Speke which they had hoped would replenish their stocks of quinine had been emptied by Kamrasi long ago. But discovering a new lake would make their name. They left with guides and a hundred-strong warrior escort. 'I trust I have seen the last of Kamrasi – a greater brute cannot exist,' wrote Baker. But this was not to be.

This is the very nature of exploration, what makes it so different from later travellers following a well-worn path. You are under the complete control of local chiefs. You have to pass through lands relying on guides you pick up along the way. You cannot afford not to trust, yet trusting too much may also bring disaster. The explorer must be a curious mix of the obsessive, the optimistic, the psychologically resilient. For all Baker's claims about the importance of physical strength it is the mental strength, epitomised by Florence's iron will to continue, that marks out the successful explorer.

Baker rode on an ox to conserve his strength. Florence, weakened by months of fever, was conveyed in an *angarep* – a sedan chair carried by twelve men. Her condition worsened. One evening Baker ordered a new handle to be fitted to his pickaxe in preparation for digging her grave. But Florence did not die, and on they went. A range of mountains grew closer and closer. The thought of crossing them seemed too dreadful to contemplate. The guides revealed nothing to them except the route for the following day. They finally reached a village Baker understood was called Parkani – in fact it meant 'very close': the lake was in front of the mountains, a mere half-day's walk away.

They could hardly contain their excitement. But when they saw the great lake, the seventh largest in all Africa, over a hundred miles long and eight times bigger than Lake Constance, worthy indeed to be named after Victoria's consort Prince Albert, Baker was too stunned or exhausted to lead his men in a round of three cheers 'in the tradition of Old England' as he had long planned. Fever ridden, in no state either to continue or to turn back, he had achieved the dream that started when he had first heard about Livingstone and had been rejected for a place on the Scottish explorer's expedition. Now, at the age of forty-two, Baker was no longer a rich big-game hunter and adventurer – he had become, like Livingstone, one of the world's great explorers.

He knew he couldn't turn back, though, until he had verified that the Nile flowed in and out of Lake Albert. This long thin lake is the receptacle for all the rivers of the region – filling a rift valley between 1 and 2 degrees North – with mountains running along both its sides. It forms such a formidable barrier the fauna changes from one side to the other. Locusts cease to be found on the other side of the lake – hence its original name Luta Nziga, which means 'the brightness which kills locusts'.

Speke's intelligence was correct – the Nile flowed in and out of the northern end of Lake Albert, the river much swollen by the other sources flowing into the long lake. It can be said that the three main sources of the Nile are, along with the Blue Nile, Lake Victoria and Lake Albert.

More waiting followed for Sam and Florence. More fever as the natives of the lake, who lived by extracting salt from the lakeside (Albert is a very salty lake, unlike the sweet water of Victoria), kept them waiting and extracted as many beads and baubles as they could. It was not the men who worked the salt 'mines' but the women who, completely naked, waded through the bubbling sulphurous gullies that fed into the top part of the lake. The women dam the hot salty ooze in little channels and the mixture of mud and salt is packed into banana leaves and laid in long pieces of bamboo which can be carried easily along narrow jungle paths.

If Baker had known it, he might have crossed the lake to continue to the Mountains of the Moon, which were only fifty miles away but shrouded in almost perpetual mist. The world would have to wait twenty years before Stanley would discover the Ruwenzoris. Here too lived the Twa tribe of pygmy people. It was Aristotle, acting on the information of Greek and Egyptian travellers, who stated that tiny people lived in caves in the Mountains of the Moon. But Baker had other things on his mind. When two dugout canoes thirty-two feet long were finally procured (the other craft mere flimsy rafts of papyrus so unstable he feared for their lives), it turned out that his men could not paddle them in a straight line. It is somewhat comic to think of Baker, having come all this way, spending the day going round in circles on the water, but that is what happened. That night Sam used his knife and axe to fashion rudders for the canoes from two paddles. He also used one of the plaid blankets that had survived Kamrasi's acquisitiveness to make into a sail. The local people were amazed: it was the first sailing boat to be seen on Lake Albert. (Years later the European tradition of cruising the lake would result in the SS *Robert Coryndon*, 'the best floating library in the world' according to Hemingway. This ship plied Lake Albert for years until it sank in 1964. For forty years its rusted wreck was still visible at the north end of the lake looking like a small *Titanic* run aground, but it had been removed by 2012.)

Sam and Florence sailed up the lake. They saw that a reedy estuary marked the outflow. The ingress was near by and they started up it to verify that it was indeed the Victoria Nile. One thing that puzzled Baker was the relative heights of Lake Victoria and Lake Albert. Though only 168 miles apart, his altitude tests – done by measuring carefully the boiling point of water – suggested that Albert was much lower than Victoria. His thermometer read 207.8 degrees, which meant the height they were at was 2,388 feet compared to the 3,700 feet of Victoria. Unless there was a large waterfall, this was not the same Nile. Florence was utterly weak but told him to continue with their search upriver. 'Seeing is believing,' she said.

Banks of weed gave way to rising cliffs. The river narrowed after ten miles to a few hundred yards. They heard a roaring noise, and turning the corner of the bending and ever narrowing river came upon the largest waterfall on the Nile cascading through a slot a bare twenty-three feet wide. Smoky mist rose high above the waterfall and the slot itself was a pounding comb of white water. At 141 feet high the falls, which

Baker named after Murchison of the Royal Geographical Society – a
canny move for an explorer to make – were high enough to explain the
anomaly in the heights of the two lakes. They had truly secured the
Nile for European posterity.

All that remained was the trip home – through Kamrasi's land.
The King had earlier sent an urgent message to Baker asking him to
return and help him in a war he was fighting with a neighbouring
tribe. Unknown to Baker, this was the start of the disintegration of the
upper Nile kingdoms, as slave-trader armies, run by such men as the
Maltese adventurer De Bono, were following the explorers deeper and
deeper into Equatorial Africa. The slavers set one tribe against another
in order to extract ivory out of the locality. It was against such a slaver-
backed tribe that Kamrasi begged for help. Baker refused. Kamrasi,
true to form, decided to starve him out, cutting off supplies and sending word that they were to be denied food along the lake. In the end
they were reduced to eating a kind of wild spinach and drinking tea
made from thyme growing on the river banks. Finally after some two
months Baker sent word that if Kamrasi despatched fifty men and food
he would at least enter into negotiations about helping the King with
his own men and guns. The food and men arrived, and Baker and
Florence began to recover on a new diet of meat and milk. They
made their way back to the capital Kisoona and began negotiations.
Baker agreed to help in defence but not in any attack. The old bully Kamrasi wanted to flee into the bush in the face of De Bono's private army
of slavers. Baker ordered that his Highland costume be unpacked, and
kilt-clad he persuaded Kamrasi that they would stay and fight. He
raised a Union Jack above the town which greeted De Bono's craven
emissaries spying out the capital for an attack. These men were told
by Baker that if they did not withdraw from Bunyoro he would inform
Khartoum that De Bono had invaded a country under British protection. If he did that their leader would certainly be hanged. The bluff
succeeded and Baker earned considerable new respect from Kamrasi.
The slavers retreated but left behind some mail for the Bakers that had
come from England via Khartoum (no doubt the slavers had posed as
friends of the Bakers while in Khartoum). These letters had taken two
years to find them – the very first postal service running the length
of the Nile river. Florence received some copies of the *London Illus-
trated News* that contained illustrations of the latest female fashions.
As Kamrasi had been unable to get his own white bride, Florence

thoughtfully cut out pictures of the women and sent them to the King.

Finally the season for Nile travel arrived and they set off for Gondokoro and Khartoum. The journey was far from quick. To hasten things they travelled across the desert to the Red Sea and then to Suez by steamer. Baker had still not married Florence, his faithful companion of six exciting years. As they neared England he became fearful of the reception his 'lady companion' would receive. He telegraphed James, a younger brother, to meet him in Paris. Here they hatched a plan to win the family – and, by extension, England – over to Florence. When they finally arrived it was to no fanfare or ticker-tape parade. Baker told no one and lived quietly for three weeks in London to satisfy the banns requirements for a marriage by special licence. Only two people attended the wedding – in St James's Piccadilly – a church large enough to hold a congregation of 2,000. The two were James Baker and his wife Louise, and both were to become staunch friends of the twenty-four-year-old Florence. At long last, one of the most eventful courtships in history had ended, as it should, at the altar.

26 · Buried alive

The person who is comfortable thinks everyone is comfortable.
Ethiopian proverb

Baker was the greatest of the Red Nile explorers. He travelled extensively on the Nile – not just a quick trip (all right, a two-year quick trip) to the source. Like all good Red Nilists he had a nose for the extraordinary and the macabre.

The death of a great king among the people dwelling in the upper Nile region of Bunyoro, now in western Uganda, was an extraordinary event. The Bunyoro controlled almost the whole area between Lake Albert and Lake Victoria and their kings – Kamrasi and later Kabarega – were a thorn in the side of Baker's sweeping ambitions. When Baker returned in 1871 he was not unhappy to hear of Kamrasi's death. He gave an account of the great funeral:

> When a king of Bunyoro dies, the body is exposed upon a framework
> of green wood, like a gigantic gridiron, over a slow fire. It is thus

gradually dried, until it resembles an oven-roasted hare.

Thus mummified, it is wrapped in new bark-cloths, and lies in state within a large house built specially for its reception. The sons fight for the throne (an exceedingly small and ancient piece of furniture). The civil war may last for years, but during this period of anarchy, the late king's body lies still unburied.

At length, when victory has decided in favour of one of his sons ... the funeral of his father must be his first duty.

An immense pit or trench is dug, capable of containing several hundred people. This pit is lined with new bark-cloths. Several wives of the late king are seated together at the bottom, to bear upon their knees the body of their departed lord.

The night previous to the funeral, the king's own regiment or body-guard surround many dwelling and villages, and seize the people indiscriminately as they issue from their doors in the early morning. These captives are brought to the pit's mouth. Their legs and arms are now broken with clubs and they are pushed into the pit on top of the king's body and his wives.

An immense din of drums, horns, flageolets, whistles, mingled with the yells of a frantic crowd, drown the shrieks of the sufferers, upon whom the earth is shovelled and stamped down by thousands of cruel fanatics, who dance and jump upon the loose mound so as to form it into a compact mass; through which the victims of this horrid sacrifice cannot grope their way, the precaution having been taken to break the bones of their arms and legs. At length the mangled mass is buried and trodden down beneath a tumulus of earth, and all is still. The funeral is over.

Among the Dinka, the rainmaker was considered the highest-status personage in the tribe. His privilege, when he became infirm with old age, was also to be buried alive.

Burial alive of the king's wives and vassals occurs all over the world throughout history. In Ethiopia it was said that the sons of Prester John were buried alive alongside their father. On his return to Cairo, Baker's attention was drawn to Ibn Battuta, who relates the death of the great Khan of Peking, who is buried with four female slaves and six male slaves and the slain bodies of his family and close friends. In this version the slaves are given a poison to drink while they are being incarcerated alive. But Ibn Battuta then relates a story he has heard from the south of Sudan 'from persons upon whose word full reliance may be placed, that among certain infidels of these countries, on the death of the king, a vault is constructed in which the corpse is laid and along with it a certain number of his courtiers and servants ... the forearms of these persons are first broken, as also their legs, below the knees ...'

Ibn Battuta was writing in 1346. Five hundred years later the same funeral rites were still being practised in the same region. But within fifty years all that would end.

27 · The madness of King Theodore and the elephants of war.

Big talk: its head is fire, its behind water. Ethiopian proverb

Things were changing too at the other end of the Nile, the Blue end in Ethiopia. An extraordinary new Christian king named Theodore had begun conquering and subduing all the warring factions around Lake Tana, the source of the Blue Nile. In 1855 he proclaimed himself Emperor of Ethiopia, father of the Blue Nile, and attempted to abolish slavery. That he ended up as an enslaver of others suggests that his efforts at abolition were at best a partial success.

Born in 1818, Theodore claimed descent from Solomon and Alexander the Great; in reality he was the son of a small local chieftain with no royal claim at all. A self-made monarch, he would make those who would mock his rightful claims tremble indeed. Having conquered all the warring Muslim tribes and unified his Christian subjects, he proclaimed himself Emperor Theodore III. The world took notice. England even sent a consul, Walter Plowden, to make a treaty with him. By then, in the late 1840s, England had realised that the Red Sea coast was worth controlling. It made sense to be friends with Theodore.

And Theodore came to love Walter Plowden like a brother. When Walter was killed by tribesmen near Gondar in 1860, Theodore avenged him by killing and mutilating *2,000* members of the offending tribe. That was a lot, even by Ethiopian standards.

The English sent another consul, Charles Cameron (of the same clan but not a direct relative of the future Prime Minister of Britain). While not a fool exactly, Cameron lacked Plowden's charm, Plowden's pull.

He lacked something, that was certain. Foresight? Nous? Whatever he lacked, his inadvertent attempt to curry favour with Ethiopia plunged that country, and Britain, into a costly war at the source of the Blue Nile, a war that produced the first and last amphibious elephant attack in history. It is quite the most extraordinary story in a river of extraordinary stories.

Cameron presented Theodore with a brace of pistols – a welcome, though possibly risky choice of gift for a man with a volatile temper and a line in mutilation. He then committed his major blunder by suggesting that Theodore write to the British authorities in order to conclude treaties beneficial to both (that is, beneficial to the Brits). Theodore took to this task with great seriousness. He knew that the British had an empress called Victoria – would she not be thrilled to hear from a fellow emperor?

The letter was about a page and a half long, full of talk of exterminating the Turks, who had pressed up from Sudan and Egypt. Also it contained a fair bit of general politesse and an attempt at brotherhood against the assumed joint enemy of Islam. The letter was sent and an answer eagerly awaited.

None came. The British had other concerns. It was the time of the American Civil War and cotton prices had quadrupled. Instead of receiving an answer by return of diplomatic bag (a process that could admittedly take months), Cameron was asked to head into Sudan to find out if it were suitable for cotton farming.

Sudan was the sworn enemy of Ethiopia. Over a year had passed and still no reply came. Not only had no reply come, but now HM Consul was slipping off to the enemy. Theodore fell into one of his increasingly common rages (his first wife, a steadying influence, had died – now he drank heavily and was more prone to anger). He turned his attention to the fifty or so Europeans, mainly missionaries and their children, who were living at that time in Ethiopia – all in Gondar. He clapped the lot in prison, and when Cameron returned all unsuspecting from his cotton excursion, he too was chained up and tortured with the skill and malice only someone as well practised in that dark art as Mad King Theodore could properly muster.

Injured but still alive, poor old Cameron managed to smuggle a message out of gaol. It was necessarily short. Probably there was little paper and less space to hide it: 'There is no hope of my release unless a letter is sent in answer to His Majesty.' This crumpled, prison-stained message found its way to Britain, to the highest ranks this time (it is thought the first missive got lost somewhere in the Foreign Office). A suitably friendly and fawning note was got up and signed by Victoria R. in Balmoral on 26 May 1864.

But who should deliver it? Given how he had behaved, it would be a brave man who ventured into the court of angry King T. Masters of delegation, the British sent Hormuzd Rassam, an Iraqi Christian who had been educated at Oxford and had assumed British nationality. It looked like a good plan and Rassam seemed keen to show he was made of stern stuff.

He travelled to the Red Sea coast of Ethiopia where he was warned he could not move inland without the Emperor's permission. So he waited. For six months. Then he decided he needed more, and more enticing, booty to win over Theodore. No pistols this time. Rassam took ship to Cairo and bought fancy glass chandeliers (Theodore lived in a tent), mirrors, the finest crystal glassware, a mass of general stores and, mindful of Theodore's thirst, two cases of Curaçao. All this was taken by ship and then packed on protesting camels as Rassam wasted no time waiting for permission and headed for Theodore's base at the source of the Nile – on the western shores of Lake Tana.

Finally in 1866 they reached it – the Little Abay or Little Blue Nile – dominated by Theodore's huge white tent surrounded by thousands of smaller ones. The question now was: would the cracked mirrors and chipped chandeliers cut it? Sadly Rassam did not know at this stage that Theodore valued only weapons as gifts.

The Emperor sent message that he was happy to receive Rassam and his party. The gifts were presented, as was the letter from Queen Victoria. Theodore waved the letter aside – of course he would – and ranted for a while about his problems with turbulent tribes and the insults he had received from missionaries. But he accepted the gifts and sent for the hostages to be released. He displayed the double-barrelled pistols that his friend Plowden had given him and said with pride that they were a gift of the English Empress herself. Rassam's hopes rose. It was to become a familiar feeling.

Just when it seemed things might be solved Theodore announced that his capital needed to be moved. Twenty thousand tents set out across the country, sometimes covering an incredible thirty miles a day. Each day supplies for the vast royal entourage were pillaged from unlucky villages along the way.

The small British party were given pride of place in the van of the expedition and Theodore was vastly attentive, sending gifts every day: plucked partridges, an antelope, firearms, plus reassuring messages that even their expenses would be reimbursed by the Ethiopian treasury. Finally a letter came stating that a relieving escort had been sent to Magdala, where the captives were being held. The letter came with a new gift – two male lion cubs.

The captives were a ragtag group of about thirty European adults and twenty-three children – British, French, Swiss and German, some of them with Ethiopian wives. Not all were missionaries; seven of the Germans were skilled artisans who had enlisted in Theodore's service to build him clever mechanical things. One is reminded somehow of the imprisoned inventors in *Chitty Chitty Bang Bang*. But even these artisans, though they had more freedom in their prison camp than the missionaries, were not destined to be set free. Yet.

Theodore had changed his mind. He had decided that Rassam should hold a trial examining the misdeeds of Cameron, who, despite having already been punished, looked set to be punished some more. Rassam visited the King at his new royal enclosure on Lake Tana at Zage, a place still famous for its coffee and its pythons. Indeed Rassam was presented with two pythons as he landed. (It's hard to work out what he was doing with all these gifts. Did the lion cubs attack the pythons while he was out negotiating?) In any case he had bigger problems to worry about: another meddling Brit called Beke.

Charles Beke was a self-proclaimed expert on Ethiopia who had claimed to the captives' relatives that he was a far better bet as hostage negotiator than the seemingly slow Rassam. He gathered letters from the relatives and landed in Ethiopia on the Red Sea coast. He sent a message to Theodore demanding an audience to obtain the release of the prisoners.

So just as Rassam had inched his way to a probable conclusion Beke had arrived to cock it all up. To a paranoid like Theodore it looked like bait and switch. Perhaps Beke was the forefront of a planned invasion and Rassam a Trojan horse? It was all a bit much, so Theodore did his usual thing and went on a three-day bender while ordering Rassam and the others to be arrested and chained up. Days later, the king, red eyed and drunk, began to read out a list of incredible charges against Rassam, but then, halfway through, apologised, gave up his tirade and allowed the prisoners to be led away to sleep in a tent.

The captives were taken to a fortress where Theodore himself laid out the carpets, an act of obeisance typical of the man. A day later he had all the hostages thrown into the dungeons. He went down and apologised to them, saying that he hadn't believed before that he was mad but the evidence before his eyes told him otherwise. He still didn't unlock them.

Bound in fetters and sometimes chained, Rassam and the others were sent back to the mountain-top eyrie of Magdala, 8,000 feet up and 1,000 feet above the surrounding plain. It was considered impregnable – accessible only by a narrow winding path. Rassam's hopes of escape were nil.

Meanwhile, the German technocrats were charged with making a super-weapon – a vast mortar made out of a solid block of metal weighing seventy tons. It was Theodore's idea. 'You Europeans are very clever,' he said. 'Make me a gun that can fire a 1,000-pound weight.' The country was scoured for metal. Fifty large copper vessels were melted down. It was not enough. Pots, pans, old spears and copper nails were added. Finally, to make up the shortfall Theodore melted down 490 silver thalers he had found while sacking the town of Gondar. All this scrap was heated up and poured into a giant mould – the barrel of the super-mortar nearly two feet across. Three days of nervous waiting followed and the mould was cracked open. The gun looked perfect. Somewhat like Saddam and his super-gun, Theodore put all his faith in this weapon.

The British tried one last time, sending an envoy of gifts and skilled workmen (to rival the German experts) to the Red Sea coast. The deal on offer was simple: you release the hostages, and you get the workmen and the gifts and no more will be said of the matter. But Theodore wanted both. And just who were these willing skilled artisans? What words of honey were used to get them willingly to swap places with people who had been held hostage for years? Luckily they were not to be tested. In the ensuing stalemate the workmen were sent home, the gifts returned to England.

In Magdala a year and a half went by. Seeds of English vegetables smuggled from the coast brought joy to Rassam. Truly he had embraced the English way of life. He planted and tended them with great care. 'Life wasn't too bad,' he wrote, 'apart from the fetters.' In the high damp altitude, near to the Equator, the vegetables grew to huge proportions. Pea plants were five feet high, potatoes monstrously large, the size of footballs, tomatoes flowered year round. One is reminded of that other source of the Nile, the Ruwenzori Mountains, where giant plants also flourish – two Gardens of Eden, of a sort. The hostages ate well; dinner might consist of soup, fish, several entrées, a joint of lamb or antelope, pudding, ending with anchovy toast or cream cheese. Arak, mead and coffee were freely available. They played whist, endlessly, and Rassam enticed hundreds of Ethiopian songbirds to a bird table in his garden.

Finally the British prepared for war. It was 1867 and the Blue Nile, thanks to the work of James Bruce and the Bakers, was confirmed as the source of the flood. It was down to control again. As early as 1093, when there had been a particularly low flood, a deputation of Egyptians had been sent to the Emperor of Ethiopia asking him to release more water (strangely, a thousand years later, when the new Tana dam is completed on the Blue Nile, Egyptians will again seek for more water to be released). In 1093 they knew that Ethiopia controlled the Nile's bounty. In 1867 they knew it too. The British needed to assert their prestige in Africa and the Red Sea. What better way than to control the whole Nile? There was also the small matter of racial pride. Were they going to let a daft foreigner like Theodore mock them from his mountain fastness? So the British assembled an army of 32,000 men, with forty-four war elephants and 55,000 pack and other animals. They wanted to make their mark, rather like the Americans and their allies when they invaded Iraq nearly 140 years later.

The explorer Baker was consulted on the currency matter. Just how would the army buy food in Ethiopia when it landed? With Marie-Thérèse dollars, but only the 1780 minting, Baker explained: 'the effigy of the Empress, with a very low dress and a profusion of bust, is, I believe, the charm that suits the Arab taste'. And, presumably, the Ethiopian. The counting houses of Europe had not enough, so by special dispensation the Imperial Mint in Vienna turned out an edition of 500,000 to be used for the expedition expenses.

The elephants came from Bombay in two newly constructed ships, with modified holds the better to deal with the awful prospect of elephant seasickness. A secret group of engineers landed unopposed at Zula on the Red Sea coast and quickly constructed a pier. The invasion army docked and Robert Napier, the commanding general, disembarked using the strengthened gangway, riding on the first in a line of nineteen war elephants (the rest were in the other boat). His salary was

£580 a month. The mahout controlling Napier's elephant, and perched up behind the beast's ears, was paid £1 a month. It was quite probably the first time since Alexander the Great that Indian elephants had been seen in Africa.

Their role was partly to inspire fear, but also to carry the heavy artillery over the rugged and roadless terrain of Ethiopia. Accompanying the army came an intelligence corps containing Major Grant, Speke's amiable companion a few years earlier in the discovery of the White Nile's source. Indeed Grant was the first man to visit both sources – the second being Stanley, who before his incarnation as an explorer was foreign correspondent for the *New York Herald*. He was here to cover the war with Theodore and had taken the trouble to bribe the telegraph operator at Aden to hold up all the newspaper correspondents' messages (such as those of the boys' writer G. A. Henty, who was there with the London *Standard*), except of course his own. The resulting coup so raised Stanley's stock with his newspaper bosses that they agreed to sponsor his search for Livingstone. So, in a way, Stanley's career was launched by the madness of Theodore.

Meanwhile the Emperor was getting nervous. It took 500 men to haul the giant German mortar up the mountain of Magdala. It was the cornerstone of his defences, a kind of V-2 rocket for the beleaguered Ethiopians.

As Napier's army plodded across Ethiopia, side-detachments were sent, with an elephant to inspire awe, into the villages along the way. Tribes united quickly under the invaders against their mad oppressor. At long last the British drew themselves up at the foot of the Magdala escarpment. Ranged in front of them were a wildly dressed army of 5,000 or more Ethiopian warriors backed by the awesome presence of the giant Teutonic mortar.

Napier loosed off some rockets. The mortar was lit – and exploded into pieces. So much for German workmanship. With skilled musketry from the British soldiers (who were armed with the .577 Snider-Enfield, which had a 600-yard effective range, four times that of the Ethiopian muzzle-loaders) it was a rout. One thousand Ethiopians were killed and only twenty-seven British wounded. It was all over for the mad King.

Theodore argued long into the night with his captains, swigging at a bottle of arak. Some counselled that the hostages should all be killed, but Theodore would have none of it. They must be released. Otherwise, he said, we will all be killed. In the midst of this swaying, hot-headed debate Theodore snatched up his precious double-barrelled revolver, gift of Victoria R., cocked the hammer and, ramming the barrel end into his mouth, fired.

Nothing happened. He'd cocked the wrong hammer, or pulled the wrong trigger. Immediately his captains were upon him, wrestling the firearm from their King. The pistol went off and the bullet scorched past Theodore's ear. The shock seemed to calm him. In the morning he sent for Rassam and asked his advice.

Theodore said, 'I thought your people were women but I find too late they are men. Men who fought bravely. I cannot withstand them so I must ask you to reconcile me to them.'

Rassam knew that, if he played this deadly endgame wrongly, four years of effort would be wasted, not to mention the time in fetters and leaky dungeons. He told the Emperor to send an envoy to Napier's army. He was sorely tempted to suggest himself, but he knew that wouldn't wash. Two other captives were despatched.

Napier sent a message back asking for Theodore's surrender and promising safe passage.

Rassam was told to gather the hostages. He went to bid Theodore goodbye. 'It is so late,' said Theodore. 'Let them go on but stay a last night with me.'

'Whatever your majesty desires,' said Rassam.

He had passed the test. Theodore acknowledged this by seeming to change his mind.

'Very well, go on, but always remain my friend or I will become a monk or kill myself,' said Theodore with a twisted-up smile on his face.

Rassam faced a supreme dilemma. Every nerve in his body was taut, his mind urging him to get the hell out of there. And hadn't Theodore himself told him to go? But, if he moved off now, then there was every chance that the rest of the captives, who were standing some way behind him (including the despised Cameron), would be held back by the capricious Emperor. Rassam spoke in a quiet voice:

'I thank your majesty but my companions are behind.' And waited.

But Theodore waved him on. Rassam hesitated. It was another fiendish test. If Rassam continued to wait it showed he didn't trust Theodore any more. He had to trust. Theodore would react badly if he wasn't trusted at this late stage.

Rassam walked on and miraculously the captives walked free some way behind him.

Theodore sent a thousand cows and 500 sheep as another peace-offering reply, though Napier turned them away and sent them back, since he had been informed that acceptance meant he had forgiven Theodore and would leave his fort alone.

The British hadn't landed forty-four war elephants to walk away now. Napier heard that Theodore might try to escape down a secret goat path at the back of Magdala. The fifty-seven-year-old general had given him enough chances to surrender. It was time to bring in the elephant-borne big guns.

Theodore, in an admirable last-ditch act of bravado, rode out in front of the massed British troops and challenged Napier to a one-on-one combat. Britain had long ago given up this chivalric ideal (though it was certainly a lot less wasteful than modern warfare – imagine if we'd sent George W. to bash up Saddam with only Tony Blair holding his jacket?). Not surprisingly Napier turned the duel down. Begged by his captains to return, Theodore wheeled his horse and disappeared up the mountain.

The end, when it came, was all too sudden. After a pounding bombardment and a half-hearted defence, the British rushed the gates of Magdala. The fortress was taken with only fifteen British wounded, two dying of wounds later.

Unnoticed at first, a bedraggled corpse missing half his head lay where he had fallen, defending the gate to the last. In his hand was a double-barrelled pistol that he had fired correctly this time, ending his own life before he could be captured. Rassam identified him as the Emperor Theodore. Souvenir hunters fell upon his corpse, but Rassam beat them back. The next day he supervised Theodore's burial in Magdala church.

Stanley wrote that the looting was frenzied and terrible. The worst offenders were the former hostages, not excluding the missionaries among them, making off with jewelled golden goblets and plate, mitres and crowns, Sèvres china, cases of Moët champagne (now why hadn't the hostages been offered that instead of mead?), ermine and bear furs, leopard- and lionskin capes, ornate saddles and highly decorated state umbrellas, tents, carpets and chests full of emeralds, sapphires and silver-set diamonds – all the treasure of Prester John.

28 · Battling slavery on the White Nile

When the river flows the wrong way make sure you are standing where you think you are before you hail a miracle. Sudanese proverb

The transformation of the upper Nile regions started with the very best of intentions: end the diabolical practice of slavery. In 1869 Samuel Baker and Florence returned to the Nile to try and improve the conditions they had found on their first journey. Appointed a major general by the Khedive (the ruler under the aegis of the Ottoman Sultan, an upgrade from the earlier title of Wali) of Egypt's army on £10,000 a year, Baker marched with 1,700 troops, a number that dwindled greatly as he proceeded past Khartoum and into the interior of Africa. He took not only his wife, the redoubtable Florence, but his nephew, Lieutenant Baker. They found the advancing front of the slave trade in the land just below the Murchison Falls on the upper White Nile. The very waterfall he had discovered five years earlier had now been subjected to the attentions of the Khartoum slavers.

> New and important countries had been investigated not by explorers but by the brigands of Abou Saood, whose first introduction was to carry off slaves and cattle. Such conduct could only terminate in an extension of the ruin which a similar course had determined in every country that had been occupied by the traders of the White Nile. I trusted that my arrival would create a great reform, and restore confidence throughout the country ... Abou Saood had sworn fidelity. Of course I did not believe him ...

Baker was also looking at ways of exploiting the resources of the country that did not involve slavery. 'It appears that at Langgo the demand for beads is very great as the natives work them into patterns upon their matted hair. Ivory has little or no value, and exists in large quantities. The natives refuse to carry loads and transport an elephant's tusk by boring a hole in the hollow end, through which they attach a rope; it is then dragged along the ground by a donkey. The ivory is thus seriously damaged ...'

At one point Baker had an opportunity to arrest the notorious slaver Abou Saoud, who was recruiting local chiefs to fight and enslave their neighbours in the southern parts of the country. 'It may seem to the public that having "absolute and supreme power" I was absurdly lenient towards Abou Saood who I knew to be so great a villain ... but had I adopted severe or extreme measures against Abou Saood, I might have ruined the expedition at the commencement.'

Baker had only 212 men and was trying to get to the Equator. He was now about 165 miles away. He contemplated releasing slaves at Abou Saoud's slaving stations but realised the problems. 'Abou Saood's Fatiko station was crowded with slaves. His people were all paid in slaves. The stations of Fabbo, Faloro and Farragenia were a mass of slaves ... Had I attempted to release some thousand slaves from the different stations, I should have required a large military force to have occupied those stations, and to have driven the whole of the slave hunters bodily.' He realised that the slaves could not have been returned home easily as they were collected from a huge area. Nor could he feed them from his own rations. He had no choice but to ignore the ravaging slave trade and move on, for the time being.

A party of native hunters was surprised by Baker's small army and fled, leaving behind its elephant spears. Baker's men returned the dropped spears to the frightened natives when they encountered them later. This caused much astonishment as the people were used to invaders taking everything from them.

In order to placate Kabba Rega, a local chief, and win him over from supporting the Arab slave traders from the north, Baker reports giving him as a present:

> One piece entire of Turkey red cloth, one piece grey calico, twelve pounds of beads of the finest varieties, three zinc mirrors, two razors, one long butcher's knife, two pair scissors, one brass bugle, one German horn, two pieces of red and yellow handkerchiefs, one piece of yellow ditto, one peacock Indian scarf, one blue blanket, six German silver spoons, sixteen pairs of various ear-rings, twelve finger rings, two dozen mule harness bells, six elastic heavy brass spring wires, one pound long white horsehair, three combs, one papier-mâché tray, one boxwood fife, one kaleidoscope.

After handing these over, Baker 'proclaimed upon all sides that the reign of terror was ended'.

But it was not.

There was a brief interlude when envoys from the Ugandan King M'tese, who had known Speke, came to visit. As credentials they brought with them gifts they had been given by Speke and Grant many years earlier: a printed book, several watercolour drawings including one of a guineafowl, and a little folding book with sketches of British soldiers of various regiments. Baker impressed the native mission with the great luxury of his travelling tent, large mirrors and other curios: 'a good shock with the magnetic battery wound up the entertainment, and provided them with much material for a report to their royal master upon their return to Uganda'. Before they left, Baker told them of Speke's death back in England. 'They had appeared much concerned at hearing of poor Speke's death; and continued to exclaim for some minutes, "Wah! Wah! Speekee! Speekee! Wah! Speekee!"'

But Baker had more important concerns. Kabba Rega had proved deeply unreliable, favouring the Arab slavers even though they were ravaging his country. Baker and his retinue drew up their battle lines at Masindi and waited.

Kabba Rega sent over food and drink to try and appease Baker. Seven jars of plantain cider were accepted and distributed to Baker's men. Shortly after dinner Baker was told by an overwrought aide, 'many of the troops appeared to be dying, and they had evidently been *poisoned* by the plantain cider!'

Never one to panic, Baker recounted:

I at once flew to my medicinal arms ... this little chest had been my companion for twenty-five years. I begged my wife to get as much mustard and strong salt ready as she could mix in a hurry ... I found the men in a terrible state. Several lay insensible, while about thirty were suffering from a violent constriction of the throat, which almost prevented them from breathing. This was accompanied by spasms and burning pain in the stomach, with delirium, a partial palsy of the lower extremities, and in the worst cases, total loss of consciousness. I opened the jaws of the insensible, and poured down a dessertspoonful of water, containing three grains of emetic tartar.

He also dosed everyone with as much mustard and salt as they could manage until 'the patients began to feel the symptoms of a rough passage across the Bristol Channel'.

By the next morning the troops, 'although weakly, were quite out of danger'. At that point Kabba Rega's men attacked. 'Suddenly we were startled by the savage yells of some thousand voices, which burst unexpectedly upon us!' Baker, who was wearing white cotton clothes, was an easy target. As he walked towards his divan or hut the sergeant walking beside him was shot dead. 'Thousands of armed natives now rushed from all directions upon the station.'

With his 'beautifully made' Holland breech-loading double rifle, Baker started firing into the attacking horde. He ordered his men to set fire to Kabba Rega's 'enormous straw buildings' which were near by. His men began to gain the upper hand using their Snider rifles against the inferior lances and rifles of Kabba Rega's band. Kabba Rega, 'the young coward, had fled with all his women before the action commenced, together with his magic bamba or throne and sacred drum'.

The battle of Masindi had been won, but Baker's ever faithful officer Mansoor was killed, receiving thirty-two lance wounds – 'treacherously murdered instead of dying on a fair battlefield', as Baker put it.

Interestingly, Idi Amin sought to return Kabarega, as he became known, to more honourable and, he felt, deserving status. Amin insisted that Kabarega was really a hero, an anti-colonial fighter. With his own unpredictable sense of humour he ordered the Murchison Falls, named after Baker's great friend and ally at the RGS, to be renamed after Baker's great enemy in Bunyoro – Kabarega.

29 · Gordon goes because Florence says so

Though the mosquito sleeps inside the house, the bee sleeps outside.
Ethiopian proverb

The Bakers retired to Devon, where Sam became an eccentric local worthy. Blacksmiths, tinkers, road menders and gypsies encountered while he was out striding the lanes would be asked back for tea in the billiard room at his estate in Sandford Orleigh. He was elected president of the Devonshire Association, and town councillor for Newton Abbot. But the old Baker, who could bring down a stag with his bare hands and a hunting knife, was never far from the surface. When a travelling strongman invited the audience to imitate his feat of snapping a chain wound around his bicep, Sam Baker, seated in the front row with

Florence, took on the challenge. Still with the massive arms that had cowed the natives of the upper Nile, Baker, with a blood-vessel-bursting grimace, huffed and puffed and broke the chain in two.

Florence kept an orderly house just as she had kept an orderly camp in the Sudan. Here there was far more luxury apparent. She liked to wear diamond tiaras. They had an Abyssinian servant, and when a footman spilled some soup on a guest she remarked in a thoughtful way, 'You should be whipped.' Perhaps in Gondokoro, but not in Devon; the remark was an observation but not an order. In fact the Bakers were very even handed. When a small boy, the son of a visitor, kicked the butler, he was imprisoned in his room on bread and water for a day. The former slave declared, 'Servants are our friends. We do not kick our friends.' Sam was equally tough on spoiled guests. When two young urchins – the future King George V and his brother – arrived for a weekend Sam Baker thrashed them for breaking the branches of a tropical tree he had earlier forbidden them to climb. Their father, the Prince of Wales, must have agreed, as he maintained his fond regard for the Bakers despite his mother's opposition to Florence on account of her journeys, while unmarried, with Sam.

Sam Baker's replacement as head of Equatoria was General Gordon (as well as exploring the region Baker had been appointed, by the Egyptian government, Equatoria's first ruler). He had pursued Baker's aim at stamping out slavery with great vigour and made enemies in the process. Now it was mooted that Gordon should take over and rule the whole of the Sudan. In an article for *The Times* Baker had written, 'Why should not General Gordon Pasha be invited to assist the government? There is no man living who would be more capable or so well fitted to represent the justice which Great Britain should establish in the Soudan.' Gordon knew better. He did not want the job, but he knew he had to find a replacement. If he managed to avoid the Khartoum assignment he had an offer to go with Stanley into the Congo, which was more attractive than being stuck in the dusty capital of the Sudan. So Gordon suggested to Baker that he and his brother Valentine, a high-ranking army officer, should take over in Khartoum as administrative head and commander in chief respectively. Gordon – who really did not want the job – travelled down to Devon and drove through the lanes with Baker, to try and persuade the older man to take this job. When they arrived for tea at Baker's estate it was all settled. Gordon was off the hook and the Baker brothers would go to Khartoum. The sixty-two-year-old former explorer was very excited – though he had reckoned without Florence. She put down her bone-china cup carefully with both hands and said with that trace of a German accent, 'You promised me that you would never go back to the Sudan without me. I do not go. So you do not go.'

One gets a rare glimpse of the contribution Florence made to Baker's success. She provided, one suspects, the judgement that he lacked. If Baker had gone he might well have ended the way Gordon did. And Gordon, incidentally, was not at all pleased that anyone, and a man's wife no less, should block him. Baker led him from the drawing room with a doleful air. 'My dear Gordon,' he said, 'you see how I am placed – how can I leave all this?' Florence later remarked that Gordon had hypnotically powerful blue eyes that were very hard to resist – she did not condemn her husband for falling prey to them, though she never forgave Gordon for trying to pass on a deadly mission to a man past retirement age.

Gordon was duly sent to the Sudan with the object of staging a withdrawal there in the face of the Mahdi's forces. And he was really the wrong man, given all the years he had spent building up the British presence there and subduing the Arab slave trade. He had too much invested and this led to the dithering that brought about his downfall. But it seems that, had a certain telegraph not been sent, the whole Gordon fiasco might have been avoided. Lord Cromer related in his memoirs that when he discovered Gordon was proceeding to Khartoum via the Red Sea port of Suakin he immediately telegraphed that this was inadvisable, the reason being the open rebellion of the tribes that lay between Suakin and Khartoum. If Gordon had continued via Suakin he would have been held up and eventually turned back – by which time the need for him in Khartoum would have evaporated. But Gordon changed his route and went to his eventual doom via Cairo instead. Cromer wrote, 'If I had not interfered as regards General Gordon's route, a point which seemed at the time to be one of detail, the course of history in the Soudan would have been changed and many valuable lives, including probably that of General Gordon himself, would have been saved.' And there might, ten years later, have been no battle of Omdurman in which so many died and a certain English subaltern called Winston Churchill rose to prominence.

In 1893 the Bakers, Florence and Sam, planned to spend the following year in Somaliland, hunting lions. Sam was now immensely fat

and suffering from intermittent gout. He died of a heart attack before
he could leave. Somewhat ahead of his time, he had asked to be cre-
mated in the newly built crematorium in Woking, the first to be built
in Britain.

Florence lived on in Devon for another twenty-three years. Whenever guests arrived she wore her finery, everything she had been denied
during her travels in Africa. And all visitors were forced to eat the
immense cream teas her husband had so loved.

30 · A strange occurrence

The Nile is great, greater still is a man who sincerely notes his own faults.
Egyptian proverb

The story, however, does not stop there. Often, when writing a book
such as this, which requires the sourcing of hundreds of volumes of old
and often hard-to-find books, one is struck, forcibly, how much coincidence, or serendipity, plays a part in the finished work. I started writing
this book in Egypt, within sight of the Nile. The Arab Spring revolution of 2011 made me reconsider what was the best place to carry on
the uninterrupted work necessary for such a large project. I ended up
living in Dorset, not so far from a friend who lived in Dowlish Wake in
Somerset, which turned out to be the ancestral home of the Speke family.
I then travelled up north and gave a talk at a school in Dumfriesshire.
It was here, in Thornhill, that I discovered that Joseph Thomson had
been born (well, two miles from Thornhill), the African explorer who
first named the Thomson's gazelle (and about whom I had been reading
in my research on Nile exploration). I started to obtain books – some
second-hand, some new, many through the marvellous interlibrary
loan service. In a bookshop about a mile and a half from my house
I found a reprinted edition of *Ismailia*, Samuel Baker's account of his
attempt to subdue the slave trade in southern Sudan. The book was
missing a map and was only £10 – a bargain. When I got it home I
found inside it a letter typed on thin blue paper dated 20 July 1963 –
in good condition and almost the same age as myself. The letter was
from the great-grandson of Sam Baker, Valentine E. Baker, presumably
named after Sam's brother, though an internet search found nothing

beyond references to Chet Baker singing 'My Funny Valentine'. The letter itself concerned a visit the great-grandson Valentine had made to Gulu in Uganda, home to the Samuel Baker School. He had visited in the 1960s to donate some books by Baker as well as a handwritten letter from Baker to Abou Saoud, (or Aboo Sood as he sometimes spelled it), the double-dealing Arab slaver whom he defeated in his attempt to stamp out slavery.

But this upper Nile story twists and turns like the Nile itself because the Samuel Baker School is only about an hour from where Joseph Kony, founder of the Lord's Resistance Army, was born. Kony staged raids on its dormitories and kidnapped children for his army. One of the ex-Sam Baker schoolboys, Moses, who would rise to become a trusted lieutenant before defecting back to normal life to resume his studies, was interviewed by Matthew Green, author of a book about Kony called *The Wizard of the Nile*. I got in touch with Matthew. In a further twist I found we had been to the same college and had even shared the same teachers.

The letter to the slaver appears on page 138 of *Ismailia*. So the great-grandson of the writer had copied the original letter and then sent it to someone ('Mr Hudson' is all it is addressed to) who had put it in a book containing the same letter, which some fifty years later I bought in a second-hand bookshop in Dorset which I visited only because it was within walking distance of my house. Here's the letter:

Aboo Sood, Sir,

You arrived here on the 10th inst with a large quantity of cattle stolen by you and your people.

You, knowing that the Bari natives were at war with the government, have nevertheless been in daily and friendly communication with them.

The Baris of this country are rendered hostile to all honest Government by the conduct of your people, who, by stealing cattle and slaves from the exterior and delivering them here, have utterly destroyed all hope of improvement in a people naturally savage but now rendered by your acts thieves of the worst description.

It is thus impossible that I can permit the continuance of such acts. I therefore give you due notice that at the expiration of your contract [he nominally worked for Baker] you will withdraw all your people from the district under my command.

At the same time I declare the forfeiture to the Government of the cattle you have forcibly captured under the eyes of my authority.

Signed

    Sam W. Baker

      Governor General

The original letter, still at the Samuel Baker School, was handwritten. I fold up my version, from Baker's great-grandson, and return it to the safety of his great-grandfather's book. I am sure Kony's lieutenant Moses must have seen the letter, the original, while he was at school. I'll surely tell Matthew Green, maybe at my next college reunion. I am beginning to realise why the Nile has such a hold on people. It connects up all stories.

31 · Mountains of the Moon no. 2

The word of God is like a grinding stone. Sudanese proverb

The Red Nile connects up all stories – maybe – but it certainly keeps returning us to the old stories. Millennia after Aristotle wrote of the strange Mountains of the Moon, they appeared again in all their ghostly significance in the accounts of the new European explorers.

Burton and Speke naturally had different theories about where exactly the mountains were. It took the superhuman efforts of Stanley, however, finally to identify their true position.

Burton rightly pointed out the many holes in Speke's argument for Lake Victoria being the source of the Nile, or even being one lake and not many, but he did not, after the RGS had backed Speke's expedition, seek to prove his own theories on the ground. This was left to Stanley, who in his incredible 1874–6 expedition circumnavigated Lake Victoria and Lake Tanganyika, thus proving that Speke's inspired guess about the source was correct. The geography hinted at by Ptolemy's map of the Nile's source was proved to be substantially right. Only one thing remained – where and what were the Mountains of the Moon? In 1876 Stanley's able assistant Frank Pocock claimed that he saw white-topped mountains through the mist as they camped near Lake Edward, which connected with Lake Albert to form a major reservoir of mountain water that entered the White Nile. But it would take until the end of the disastrous 1887–9 Emin Pasha expedition for the Mountains of the Moon to be properly discovered.

Emin Pasha was a German who pretended to be a Turk. Stanley was a Welshman who pretended to be an American. Emin Pasha was appointed to run the Equatorial area of Sudan, a replacement for General Gordon. Though he had left behind a wife and children in Germany, Emin Pasha had reinvented himself as a man of science and learning. When Gordon – who was now in charge of the whole of Sudan – refused to evacuate Khartoum he was overrun by the dervish army of the Mahdi. A dervish is, ordinarily, a Muslim seeker after truth, a kind of would-be mystic. Dervishes who have found what they seek become Sufis, and the whole of North Africa and Arabia is host to many different groupings of Sufis and dervishes. In the 2011 Egyptian revolution, Sufi orders provided moderate Islamic resistance to the extreme Saudi-influenced and -funded Islamists known as Selafis. So in general they are a force for good. However, in nineteenth-century Sudan the word 'dervish' became misapplied to Islamic fanatics – who we might call jihadists today. They allowed themselves to be whipped into a frenzy of anti-European sentiment by their leader, the 'mad Mahdi'. These 'dervishes' became the core of the army which then persuaded local tribes to instigate a national rebellion.

Emin Pasha was sufficiently far south to be out of reach of the Mahdi's supporters. Moving his Egyptian and European staff and army further south, Emin Pasha took to patrolling Lake Tanganyika in a steam boat. He also sent mixed messages of despair to the British government. In fact Emin Pasha was a great fool, something Stanley discovered only when he had spent a year trying to rescue him.

The British, anxious that they should not have another Gordon-type disaster on their hands, were only too pleased when Stanley was recommended to stage a relief expedition. Perhaps it was the semi-official nature of the expedition, or the fact that it would be transporting a large quantity of arms and ammunition to the embattled Emin Pasha – whatever the reason, Stanley departed from his usual practice of employing men of a lower social status than himself, people he could dominate totally. Instead he engaged several British army officers and sons of the moneyed classes. The decision was to prove a terrible mistake. When the expedition was forced to divide in two, the so-called rear column commanded by a Major Edmund Barttelot spiralled into a jungle-induced anomie and despair. The young aristocrats and soldiers beat their native servants mercilessly. All of them had native mistresses, a practice Stanley disagreed with.

Then things took an even more macabre turn when James S. Jameson, an heir to the Jameson whiskey family in Ireland, paid for a young female slave who was then given to cannibals to be cooked and eaten as he sketched the whole proceedings. Stanley could not believe this had taken place, but when he finally relieved the rear column he was able to open the now dead Jameson's personal box, to find the drawings he had made. This, and the charges of murder and brutality brought against the other officers under his command, were to ruin Stanley's reputation for ever. He was known as Mata Bulai, 'the breaker of rocks', because of his selfless work alongside native road-builders during his work establishing trading posts in the Congo, and this epithet took on a more sinister meaning when the ghastly events of the Emin Pasha expedition were revealed. Stanley, for all his obvious gifts, was fatally poor at judging the characters of those above him on the social scale. He was repeatedly duped by the psychopathic King Leopold of Belgium, he was tricked by the cunning adventurer Pierre de Brazza, and when presented with feeble specimens of the ruling classes assumed they would live up to their public school rhetoric of honour and duty.

Once Emin Pasha was contacted, it transpired that he wasn't quite sure if he wanted to be rescued or not. Certainly, the amount of supplies and ammo brought by Stanley was pitifully low after all the depredations the expedition had suffered. Indeed it was Emin Pasha who had to feed Stanley's men after they had been living for months by foraging in the Ituri Forest. But Emin Pasha's hold on his men was more fragile than his sensitive ego cared to admit. When stragglers failed to keep up with the expedition he would not order them to do so. When his men openly revolted he did nothing to quell the rebellion. In the end, though, he did leave, along with the remaining members of his embryonic 'government' of Equatorial Sudan.

From Sam Baker to Gordon to Emin Pasha – an explorer, a soldier and a scientist, all defeated in the end by the country and its conditions. By the time they reached the Mountains of the Moon, Stanley could barely walk a hundred yards. The thousand-person-strong expedition crossed the Semliki river in three canoes – it took a day and a half, which was fast going, despite an attack by fifty members of the War-asura who killed two of Stanley's men. The constant attritional warfare Stanley had suffered since leaving the lower reaches of the Congo now ceased. The people around Lake Edward were routinely oppressed by the Warasura and they welcomed Stanley's column with ample gifts of food: 'Not a bead or yard of cloth was demanded from us.' The explorer established the Semliki's source in Lake Edward, and since the Semliki fed Lake Albert it meant that the Ruwenzoris were one of the ultimate sources of the Nile – just as Ptolemy's map had predicted. If Burton had not been so keen to shoehorn Lake Tanganyika into the role that Lake Albert played, he might not have exposed himself to being so wrong about the Nile's source. In any case, Stanley had sewn it all up: the Nile really was solved – as far as the geographers were concerned.

The Ruwenzoris are formed by crystalline rocks uplifting some three million years ago. The same tectonic movement formed the rift valley of Lake Albert and Lake Edward – and shut off Lake Tanganyika from the Nile basin (Burton would have been right if he had speculated about the Nile of several million years ago). The range is some seventy-five miles long by forty miles wide and is most famously home, as we have seen, to an 'Eden-like' habitat unique in Equatorial Africa. William Stairs, one of Stanley's officers, made one ascent to over 10,000 feet in the Ruwenzoris, but it was not until 1906 that most of the peaks were climbed by the Duke of Abruzzi's expedition.

Stanley's later life was curiously misshapen. Away from Africa he seemed to lose direction. He married Dorothy Tennant – a woman of superior social caste, as he saw it – who dominated 'the breaker of rocks' mercilessly. Stanley was offered the chance to be *de facto* ruler of an embryonic Kenya and Uganda, but his wife (echoing Florence Baker) forbade him, or at least put such emotional pressure on him that he turned the offer down. She was fascinated by politics and practically forced him to stand for parliament in Lambeth. He got in, and found politicians just as he had suspected – conniving and unreliable, all talk and no action. His greatest pleasures came in solitary walks and caring for his adopted son – also illegitimate but, unlike Stanley as a child, loved.

32 · The Mahdi's sword

Men may say otherwise but the rains always come. Ethiopian proverb

So Stanley leaves our story, for the time being. Meanwhile, back in darkest Africa, Sam Baker's successor as ruler of Equatorial Egypt was, as already noted, none other than General Gordon. His success at sub-duing the slave trade was considerable; but it did nothing to inhibit a messianic vision of his own role in subduing the whole of Sudan for his masters in Cairo. Nominally this was the Turkish Egyptian khedive; in fact it was also the British government. Their enemy was the Mahdi, who had raised an army in Sudan against the Egyptian Turkish pashas who ruled his country. Eventually the Mahdi's dervish troops would kill the British representative, General Gordon.

Like some mythological warrior, the Mahdi was empowered by carrying a special 'lucky' sword. It was a gift of the Sultan of Darfur, who did not read and therefore did not know that it was a Frankish sword, carried by a latterday crusader intent on liberating Tunis from the rule of the Ottomans. The sword weighed two pounds ten ounces. It had a hammered steel blade and a brass hilt and was inscribed 'Charles V Holy Roman Emperor'. Its blade was 31.75 inches long and the handle 6.25 inches. That such a blade could be in an infidel's hand was truly a mystery.

Charles V, Holy Roman Emperor, had ruled Spain, Austria and the Netherlands in the sixteenth century, and paid for his reconquest of Tunis from the Ottomans with the gold that Francisco Pizarro had extracted from the Incas. This sword, then, was paid for by one con-quest and used in another. When Tunis fell in 1574 the new rulers were the Beyliks, Turks who ruled on behalf of the Ottoman Empire. They were merchant adventurers, equipped with the best weaponry of Damascene steel, and had no use for the booty left behind by the fleeing Franks. The sword, though beautiful, was traded with a local Tuareg chief who carried it for sixty years and his son carried it for forty. The sword crisscrossed the Sahara, drawing blood in the raids of the Tebu of Tibesti. Once a *haddad*, one of the feared and despised yet most necessary iron workers of Africa, hammered and filed down a deep nick in its blade. He told the owner, a Garam tribesman, that it was a holy sword from the Franks, but this was soon forgotten. The sword was cleaned in the sands, scoured of blood and sharpened with the circular grit stones left behind by prehistoric man, grinding stones for when the Sahara was a place well watered, overrun with game, with gazelle, giraffe and baboon. The climate grew worse in the eighteenth century, hotter and drier, and the tribes that lived around Uweinat, at the border of modern Sudan, Libya and Egypt, began to weaken. The Garam dispersed and some were conquered by the Darfuri tribes. The sword, in its elaborately sewn leather scabbard, was captured and given as tribute to the Sultan's great-grandfather. That it was a sword of Frankish origin was now widely known, though no one could read the inscription, and it was thought that one day it would have a special significance. It was said to be the sword of Richard the Lionheart, who had proposed that his sister marry Saladin. In a sense it was a crusader's sword, and using it against the English, who backed the Turkish Egyptian ruler, was seen by the Mahdi as right and fitting.

Gordon was killed on the steps of his palace, fighting bravely to the last. He may have lacked foresight but he was no coward. The Mahdi had intended that this sword be the end of Gordon. He wanted to sever Gordon's head with it. In the end the head of the blue-eyed, fair-haired Scot was brought to him poked on to the end of a dervish lance. This was set outside Gordon's palace to be pelted with stones by all passers-by.

When the Khalifa, the Mahdi's successor, was eventually hunted down, a year after the battle of Omdurman and the reconquest of Khartoum, there was no sign of the sword. The Khalifa was shot while he sat with his men. There was only one survivor of his inner circle – Osman Digna, who escaped while wounded early in the battle. Digna had earlier inflicted the humiliation on the British of being the first foreign commander to break their famous infantry square. At the battle of Tebai, Digna's men surprised the British into allowing an opening in the square, the military formation that had remained unbroken since before the defeat of Napoleon. The confused soldiers then retreated in disarray, though they did ultimately win the battle. When asked how they had managed this great feat one of Digna's lowliest soldiers replied, 'Because we did not know the square was invincible. No one had told us.'

Digna was captured a year later and spent eight years in prison at the place where the Nile flows into the sea, Rosetta – the same prison from whose walls the Rosetta Stone had been plucked a half-century earlier.

He always maintained he had returned the sword to the desert, leaving it in the safekeeping of another tribal sheikh, waiting for the right time for it to be used again.

33 · Wild swim

God does not hurry. But what he sends to the earth, always arrives.
Sudanese proverb

This is a long book so I decided to have a rest, let someone else take over for a while. My good friend Johnny West is a far better swimmer than I. In fact I had discovered that I was not only a poor swimmer, I was a cowardly one. But instead of lashing myself I decided to draft in the talent to complete my self-set mission: swim the Red Nile. Years ago I had shared a flat in London with Johnny West. He joined Reuters and I went to Japan to teach English and study aikido. His first posting was Cairo and, on his invitation, I visited him there. It was the start of an excitement and interest aroused by the city that led to me moving and living there. Since this book is partly a result of my life in Egypt, Johnny West could be called its instigator.

By chance he was visiting Khartoum and agreed to a bout of wild swimming far beyond my meagre capabilities. What follows is all-round clean-cut war correspondent, and now oil consultant, Johnny 'Two Niles' West's version of his Red Nile swim – his attempt to swim the junction of the Blue and White Niles. Sensibly he had chosen a time before the main flood (when White is more powerful than Blue) in early May. Later on the vast flow of the Blue Nile would have made the attempt even more foolhardy than it already was.

'I took the hotel driver Mahmoud the day before to do a recce. I'd already decided to start on the Blue Nile, flowing sharp west in its final stages, and swing round where the two Niles met to end up in Omdurman on the other side. So first we looked for the entry point, just by a large public garden with several tea houses. Mud banks fell away precipitously from where we were standing, covered in modern consumer crap – squeezy juice bottles with straws, plastic bags, biscuit packets forming a wave of human flotsam you had to wade through on dry land to drop three yards down to water level.

'"The currents are treacherous," Mahmoud said as we looked down. I smiled politely. The seatbelts in his taxi didn't work and it was clear from the way he had woven through the traffic that he only had loose control over the steering of his old battered mongrel taxi. He wasn't exactly Mr Safety.

'"Did I tell you about the electric fish?" he asked, as we sped over the bridge to Omdurman to find the destination port. "If there are enough of them, they can paralyse you. Oh, and the fishermen's nets. Bound to drag you down," he said, avoiding a stout woman and her many shopping bags by inches as he sped up to overtake an even crappier taxi.

'Mahmoud was having fun. Why not? When you do this kind of thing regularly, you recognise that you are fodder for other people's paranoias, and even their schadenfreude. Once I was recceing swimming the River Derwent which flows through Hobart, Tasmania, and struck up conversation with an angler on the banks. "Aw, the sharks'll get you, mate," he said. "River's full of 'em." Research later showed that the last time anyone was known to have been attacked by a shark in the estuary was 1878. OMG, I thought as I looked at him. This bored old man is sledging me, recreationally. Since then, I'd learned to factor in schadenfreude as a motivation when you ask advice about swimming any body of open water.

'And that was what Mahmoud, and several others, had been doing. Currents, electrocution, fishermen's nets. Eventually we found the spot I thought I could hit, amid the remains of the fort which had hosted the Mahdi's last stand in 1898. We drove back and agreed I would find Mahmoud outside the hotel at six the next morning.

'Khartoum was already busy by then, or at least the thoroughfares across the bridges that connect the three dislocated limbs of the city. I climbed out of the cab and waded through the plastic tide down to water level. Gave my glasses and clothes to Mahmoud at the top. And struck out into the Blue Nile.

'My original plan, informed by anxiety over how wise it was even to be attempting this in the first place, was to swim straight across the hundred-yard stretch to Tuti Island, then walk round, or over, the rich alluvial farmland, find the right spot the other side, and strike out across the White Nile to the agreed landing spot in Omdurman. Once I could actually feel the Blue Nile, though, its current brisk and no-nonsense but lacking in any malicious intent, I devised a new plan.

'I would just stay midstream and be carried down to the meeting point of the two Niles, round Tuti Island, then just swim fast and obliquely across the White Nile. If I struck out about a quarter of a mile downstream of the intended landing point, I should be able to make it.

'So I floated along gently, the warm muddy waters peacefully enveloping me. As always, the city just fell away once I was in the river. I'd had the same sensation swimming across the Thames at Tower Bridge. It doesn't happen at water level. It's only once you are *in* the water. The river becomes the filter through which to see the city, not the other way round. The muted hubbub of Khartoum's seven million denizens on their way to scrabble their livings for another day became the backdrop to the curious birds – some kind of pigeon? – flying overhead and following me down the river. A couple of fishermen's boats bobbed past and then – moment of panic – my foot hit one of the nets. It's always a shock to strike something in the water when you think you should be free, and I wished sorely that 9/11 hadn't happened and I still carried my Swiss army knife everywhere. But I shook loose and came down to the junction of the two Niles. By this time I'd been in the water perhaps fifteen minutes, travelling the best part of a mile but scarcely swimming more than a couple of hundred yards.

'At the junction, the current really picked up. The White Nile comes crashing in against Tuti – you can see from old maps that the shape of the alluvial island has changed quite considerably even from colonial times – and the two rivers funnel past the western edge of the island north towards Egypt and the Mediterranean. By now the current was perhaps at the speed of a gentle jog – which feels fast when you judge your movement against the land.

'But it's a river! The current runs parallel to, not against, dry land. If you don't mind where you land, the fastest river current in the world in a straight-banked river is actually irrelevant. Just be ready to walk a couple of miles in your trunks. I listened to the ever more insistent traffic. I could see waves of it passing over the six-lane bridge to Omdurman to the south.

'The current was so fast it seemed best not to plop along. Conserve energy midstream, then, when the time is right, plough quickly to the shore, fast and furious. When I could see the Mahdi's fort ahead of me, I whirled my arms and gave the two Niles my best front crawl. In the middle of large bodies of water you lose real perspective so I just couldn't tell how far across I was. I saw Mahmoud and his battered yellow taxi waiting ... then I backstroked a little, looked up again, and he was gone. I was already overshooting.

'I no longer had any fear the river would drown me. But I had a keen interest in limiting how far north I landed and in how much of the city's effluents I'd be exposed to. I buried my face in the water again and whirled into my best front crawl. I looked up and looked up and I was still offshore hundreds of yards down from where I'd intended to land. A bridge was coming up and beyond it some kind of industrial complex which wouldn't be a whole lot of fun, but I still seemed quite far out to midstream.

'Until I put my legs down.

'And discovered that, even though I was fifty yards off the shore, the water was only thigh deep. A meander had cut out a huge swathe of shallow bank on the western side. So I waded ashore to wait for Mahmoud, who had driven round; he was performing his prayers. He was all smiles and appreciation in time-honoured sledging tradition – respect to the event. Ten minutes later we were back at the Acropole Hotel in time for breakfast, nursing our secret, debriefing George Pagoulatos, the nervous proprietor, a little pleased with ourselves.'

34 · Fuzzy-wuzzy

The Nile said to the crocodile, 'I can live without you but you cannot live without me.' Nubian proverb

This was the river they were fighting over. On the one hand the British, on the other the men with *hairstyles*. Who were these demon soldiers of the desert, the so-called fuzzy-wuzzies, one of the tribes who supported the mad Mahdi, and considered by the British to be a great menace?

There were clues in the caves at Beni Hassan on the banks of the Nile about 125 miles south of Cairo. The wall paintings are extraordinary. One long sequence of two men wrestling allows you to reimagine, exactly, the martial arts of 4,000 years ago. It was at Beni Hassan that Bruce Chatwin saw paintings depicting a people making obeisance to the Pharaoh, wearing their hair in the style of the 'fuzzy-wuzzies', the Beja nomads of Egypt and Sudan (called fuzzy-wuzzies by the British, the Beja were notoriously fierce warriors). The pictures were 5,000 years old; the Pharaohs were long gone but the Beja are still here.

I went down to the Nile at Minya, after seeing the caves at Beni Hassan. Unlike the grotty grey of Cairo, Minya is sparkling clean, an efficient urban centre. I hired a felucca to see what the Nile would feel like. It was perhaps a little wider than at Cairo – the Nile again reverses expectation by widening as you go up towards the source, at least as far as the Sudan. The river was windy, but despite Herodotus claiming there was no breeze caused by the Nile, it is always windy and almost always blowing from north to south, against the current and helping any boat to go upstream. The boat I hired was piloted by a solemn old sailor who smoked in the high breeze, cupping his fag end expertly when we went about.

It was in Minya in the early nineteenth century that Ibrahim Pasha, the son of Muhammad Ali, returning from his expedition to subdue Senaar in Sudan, heard about the prevalence of robbery along this stretch of the Nile. Several villages were known to participate in a kind of piracy here. He commanded that the *kiasheff*, leader of one of these supposedly criminal villages, supply him with the robbers who had disturbed this part of the river. The chief would not talk, so to compel him he was given 500 lashes of the *kourbash*, a terrible punishment indeed. The *kourbash* is a braided strap, about a yard long, of hippo hide; its hard edge and narrow whip-lashing tip were notorious for cutting the victim. It was a much hated tool of Ottoman suppression along the Nile; as Churchill would write, 'Patriotism does not grow under the Kourbash.' (Strangely, the *chicote* used by Congo slave traders and the *sjambok* of the apartheid regime in South Africa were both whips made of hippo hide.)

But even after 500 lashes this man did not confess or reveal a single name. Ibrahim then ordered him to be stripped and beaten with red-hot rods of iron. Incapable of resisting such torture, the man gave up 200 names, 150 of whom were executed. In view of the way the information was obtained, it is quite probable they were all innocent.

Before visiting Beni Hassan I'd been to a cultural festival on the Red Sea coast at Marsa Alam. The Brits and the Turks are long gone, but here were Beja dancers, fuzzy-wuzzies, not fighting now but laughing and performing music with a one-stringed violin and drums – still here and still with the same hairstyles.

35 · Iroquois Indians on the River Nile

'Oh tongue, I am slapped for you,' cried the ear. Sudanese proverb

The Beja did for poor old Gordon in the end, but not before the Gordon relief expedition under General Lord Wolseley tried their best to save him, in 1884–5. There was a considerable delay in setting out up the Nile to Khartoum (the overland route was blocked by desert and hostile tribes). The problem was the cataracts, the rapids that turn the White Nile intermittently into a whitewater torrent between Aswan and Khartoum. No ordinary boatmen were deemed able to battle such rapids. Experts were needed – and were fetched, from Canada. Which is how Indians of the Caughnawaga branch of the Iroquois tribe ended up fighting the Red Nile.

'My name is Louis Jackson and I am one-half Caughnawaga Indian; having lived all my life with them I know their language. When General Lord Wolseley expressed a desire for the best Canadian boatmen to take the Gordon relief expedition up the Nile he asked for Caughnawaga Indians. I had no intention of going as I had heard discouraging talk about the Egyptian River Nile, moreover I was engaged in securing my crops. But it was explained that I, owing to my command of English, was best suited to go and look after our Caughnawaga boys, so, in the end I agreed.

'The Caughnawagas are strictly speaking an offshoot of the Mohawks, one of the divisions of the Six Nations, formerly in occupation of the area now called New York, and known to the French by the general name of Iroquois. Long ago they were resettled at the head of the rapids of the St Lawrence river opposite Lachine, on a tract of land ten miles square or 64,000 acres. Unlike many of our aboriginal brothers their spirit did not fade on this small area of land, for they quickly became the true masters of the river, and the rivers of the Canadian Provinces are without end. With some small mixture of white blood the Caughnawagas maintained always their Indian customs, manners and language; also the alertness and powers of endurance of their forebears. They know water well; they know how to take a birch canoe over rocks and cataracts as well as any man alive. Without them the relief army of the Nile would have been lost. Lost once perhaps going upstream, lost for certain coming back down again. Of course it did no good, Gordon was dead from the start, but that didn't matter. The Caughnawaga Indians did their part, eighty-five of them and five lost, all told.

'Colonel [James] Alleyne told us an army is only as good as its rations. We had good rations and so did those who came after us, because we ferried their rations up stream, over rock and backwater, past the worst of the falls and rapids of the Nile. We had Armour's beef, bacon, preserved meat, mutton – salted and tallow sealed – vegetables, Ebswurt's crushed peas which boiled long made a tasty soup, pickles, pepper, salt, vinegar, hard biscuit, flour, oatmeal, rice, sugar, tea and coffee, tinned cheese, jam, lime juice, tobacco. Each boat was of the York type, not exactly, but similar, keeled whalers for sailing; and fitted out to carry ten days' rations, good rations as I have listed above, for a hundred men. And the boat could carry ten men with all kit and military accoutrements and about ten hundredweight of ammunition. Peter Canoe, who had no English, spoke better with the Arab swimmers we had than those who knew that language. The Caughnawagas are proud of never swimming, they are practically born in a canoe and when they leave it they are prepared to die rather than swim. James Deer, when he saw the rapids, said we had been better in our birch canoes, and he was right, but they couldn't have been handled by the soldiers who knew oars but not paddles. (And we had brought paddles all the way from the St Lawrence, expecting canoes.)

'Our ship took us to Alexandria and then by steamer we went through Egypt. We saw cattle lying perfectly still in the water with just their heads out. The sight scared my boys as to what the heat would be like further south. And it was terrible heat, but there was always a wind. We called the Nile the windy river because it is windier than any river we know in Canada – almost always a north wind which is the most useful against the current.

'The river itself in many places was about the same width as the St Lawrence opposite Caughnawaga, which the boys remarked on often. In one settlement of the Egyptian people we saw people in small mud huts and more rats at a glance than I had ever before seen in all my life. Their own boats were made of wood, about twenty feet long, with gunwales three feet high, made of mud, hard baked mud that kept out the water very well; the sails were peculiar, overhanging the mast at the foot. The sheep in this place looked like dogs dragging long tails on the ground and the dogs looked like the Esquimaux dogs I have seen in Manitoba.

'At one place we stopped before reaching Assouan, the only place we stopped by day, a young Christian Egyptian took me to a sacred tree of great healing power. If you wished a person to be cured you drove a nail into that tree, and I must remark that nails are scarcer than money in this country. The tree is nothing much to look at, studded with nails of all patterns it goes up about four feet then lies along the ground for about thirty feet.

'At Abu Simbel I heard there were great statues sixty feet high with toes three feet long but I regret I did not see them as I was fully engaged in collecting the cholera belts for my men. Everyone, soldiers and voyageurs, was required to wear these belts made of strips of flannel twelve to fifteen inches wide. I was told by soldiers who had long served in Egypt and the Soudan that they were very useful against the cold and damp that helped spread cholera and dysentery.

'The British soldiers were all fit and young; I saw none over the age of thirty. Nevertheless, before leaving the Nile I had the pleasure of seeing two of my Iroquois carry off the first prizes for running at the United Services Sports day held under the patronage of the Wady Halfa station commandant.

'We moved further and further up river, lining the boats past the long lines of cataracts. Going up some minor rapid with eight Dongolese on the line, having just passed the worst place a couple of the men ashore fell to fighting and the rest let go the line to join in or part them and I was left at the mercy of the river. That was something of variety! These Dongolese were entirely unused to boats and did just the opposite of anything you would expect. They are all excellent swimmers and able to cross the river at almost any place. When making long distances they make use of the goatskin bottles they use for carrying water, but full of air; scolding was no use as they neither understood nor cared. I may mention another peculiarity of theirs. Each had many scars all over his body. When one fell sick I saw the reason: he was cut by another and the cut was filled with sand.

'As the river fell with the season we saw more crocodiles. Peter Canoe said he had the moccasin on his foot eaten by one and we were polite enough not to disagree. Colonel Alleyne and Abbé Bouchard, with the help of a powerful glass, pronounced one brute sunning himself on the exposed rocks far off, to be twenty-five feet long. When I signalled for dinner all headed for the shore and it was here Louis Capitaine was so unaccountably lost, within sixty feet of the shore. Louis had the bow oar in Peter January's boat and rose when nearing the shore. He was as sure-footed a Caughnawaga Indian as any but he lost his footing and fell into the foul stream. One hundred feet passed before he was seen to rise. Lieutenant Peter, a good man, and always quick to the rescuing, threw a life preserver, though it was far from Louis who was certainly having his trouble staying afloat. Lieutenant Peter ordered in our best Arab swimmer, Suleiman, and without these swimmers we would have been a spent force long ago. Suleiman dived like an arrow, slicing into the water, and in a few strokes was at the spot where Louis had been. But in our watching of the swimmer, in that brief moment, Louis Capitaine was lost from sight. I was sixty yards behind Peter's boat and I swung wildly at the water, stirring it up with my twelve-foot beech oar, plunging those horrible depths as best I could, which was no good at all. But my grief was nothing to that of Colonel Alleyne, who took the whole blame for it on his shoulders. I believed he would cry but he did not, but he did not eat a thing that we offered that evening when we came in to make our fires and cook up the Armour's beef rations they gave us each day. Suleiman kept swimming the waters until nightfall and found Louis's helmet which he held to his chest; he was shivering. Colonel Alleyne held an inquest that night and despatched me to the telegraph station at Semnah to send the sad news of Louis's death. He hired native swimmers to keep searching and left money for a decent burial if they found the body; but as we moved on I do not know if they ever did. There is an epitaph to this story: a few weeks later Colonel Kennedy showed me a copy of the *Ottawa Free Press*. In it there was a long and colourful account of the death of a man called Captain Louis Jackson. We all thought it bad but Peter said in his high laughing voice that now Louis Capitaine had got his promotion my widow ought to get his pension.

'I must mention a curious sight I saw at the funeral of an Egyptian. Before lowering the body into the grave they put a small coin into his mouth. It is their belief that the dead must cross the river to reach their "happy hunting grounds" and the penny is to pay the ferryman.'

(Based on *Our Caughnawaga Indians on the Mighty River Nile* as told by Louis Jackson.)

36 · The Maxim and the Nile – a short history of a machine gun

After you throw the spear you cannot catch the end of it, nor the words you have spoken in haste. Ethiopian proverb

The Gordon relief expedition failed. Even if the army had set out earlier they might still have been beaten by the huge forces of the Mahdi, lacking as they were that crucial piece of equipment, the single most useful tool in subjugating Africa to colonial rule: the Maxim machine gun. When General Kitchener returned (he had been on the staff of the relief expedition), this time as leader of the forces set to avenge the humiliation of Gordon's murder, he would have with him his Maxims. There had been mechanised guns before, but none this light, so efficient and so fast firing. The basic design remains in vestigial form in all machine guns to this day, proving the Mephistophelian genius of Hiram Maxim.

Hiram Maxim was probably someone you would not want to know. As well as inventing the world's most efficient killing machine circa 1880 he was a multiple bigamist who upped and left his family in America and never returned. He had lawsuits pending with almost everyone he dealt with. He never forgot a slight. He was also a mechanical genius. His other credits include the first tethered flight (with an aircraft powered by two steam engines), a bronchial inhaler called 'the pipe of peace', an incandescent lightbulb (it is still debated today whether he or Edison or Swan got there first), various radio appliances and an early helicopter.

The Maxim was the world's first fully automated machine gun. It was a breakthrough because it was genuinely automatic – the recoil of each shot advancing the next bullet into the chamber. Though not light at sixty pounds, it was much lighter than the six-barrelled Gatling gun. Since the barrel is a large part of any gun's weight – and cost of manufacture – having only one was far preferable to having six or more. Also the Gatling required hand cranking, whereas the Maxim conformed to the magical idea of automaticity, with one touch of the trigger enough to set it chattering death across the battlefield. This meant that only one person was needed to operate it – another important advantage over the two-man Gatling gun. The final feature of the Maxim that made it so effective was its comparatively long range – over 2,000 yards – compared to the Gatling gun's 400 yards.

In his expedition to relieve Emin Pasha in 1887 Stanley took with him: two tons of gunpowder, 350,000 percussion caps, 100,000 rounds of Remington ammunition, 50,000 rounds of Winchester ammunition, and a prototype Maxim machine gun with its portable stand. Stanley was outraged that people should think he needed this to fight his way across Africa – why, he explained, he had already done that armed only with Snider rifles. This great load of ammo and the Maxim were intended for the use of Emin Pasha when they reached him. Yet, in the end, Stanley had to use the Maxim against the Wasukuma tribe during the last, supposedly easy stage, of his expedition to relieve Emin Pasha in 1887–9. In the thirty-two years since Burton and Speke's first crossing in 1857, an increasing number of explorers and then missionaries had crossed the plains between the Indian Ocean and Lake Victoria. Stanley noticed how high the transit fee known as the *hongo* had become – some missionaries being charged £270 to cross three days' distance of land. Guns, too, were not so unusual. When the Wasukuma began massing, Stanley attempted to make peace, but to no avail. Wasukuma entered his camp and killed a man; seventeen were shot by Stanley's Wangwana porters in retaliation. The Wasukuma were bunched around the camp in their hundreds, waving spears and rattling long knives against shields. Stanley had earlier, during peace negotiations, been struck at by a spear and had not retaliated. Now he did. The Maxim was set down from the bier on which it was being carried. The barrel was carefully attached, the cartridge belt unwound. This would be the first time in history that an automatic machine gun would be fired in anger. It was probably Lieutenant Stairs, the rearguard commander, who fired. The results were electrifying. Only one man was killed, since everyone else fled. The noise alone, 600 rounds a minute, suddenly shattering the silence of the savannah, sent the attackers running for their lives.

Stanley had used the gun reluctantly, because to have relied on such a fearsome weapon contradicted his great plans for Africa: after all, how can you say you are helping these people if all you do is kill them? But the next generation were less circumspect. The Maxim took no part in the exploration of the Nile – it came too late for that – but it definitely played a key part in its subjugation. Frederick Lugard, who was sent to Uganda by the British East Africa Company, took the same prototype Maxim to back up his authority, and killed far more people than Stanley ever did. Its first test in prolonged conflict came with the Rhodesian Matabele War of 1893. In the battle of the Shangani, fifty men armed with four Maxims overcame a force of 5,000 attacking Ndebele warriors. But even bigger victories would come. It has been stated by believers in British superiority that the Sudan was administered by eighty-three political officers in the early twentieth century. In reality it was run by the reputation of the Maxim at Omdurman.

As Hilaire Belloc put it:

Whatever happens we have got
The Maxim gun and they have not.

37 · The slaughter

While crossing one river ask about the others you still have to cross.
Sudanese proverb

The Mahdi's forces, now under his deputy the Khalifa, could not be allowed to run the Sudan. He began threatening Egypt, even launching small war expeditions across the border. If he wasn't stopped, it was reasoned in Cairo and London, the whole Middle East could be set ablaze. The British had bided their time, but now, in 1898, they had a plan.

By an odd irony Kitchener had been present at the bombardment of Alexandria, which in 1882 was the event that triggered English involvement in Egypt. In 1884, as an aide de camp he tried everything to get an expedition going to relieve Gordon before it was too late. The government had dithered, chose Wolseley instead and the time lost resulted in Gordon's downfall. Ten years after the death of Gordon, and now a general, Kitchener sought revenge in the form of retaking Khartoum. (As an interesting aside, the only love of Kitchener's life was his fiancée Hermione, who was the daughter of Valentine Baker – Sam's brother. Sadly she died in Cairo of typhoid fever.) Kitchener believed it essential to either secure Khartoum or get out of Africa altogether. And now, with cotton growing on the Nile that needed water, control of the river was essential. It was possibly the first river war in history.

Kitchener was, like Gordon, an engineer. He had been educated at

home in Ireland, commissioned in the army, and early on drew admira-
tion for his mapping of the Levant. The border of Israel and Lebanon
stands where it does today because that was where Kitchener stopped
his survey. He was a man quite at home with his own company, spoke
good Arabic and took no notice of unasked-for help or unfriendly criti-
cism. If he had not proven it to his own satisfaction he took no one's
word on it. When asked how he would reconquer the Sudan his answer
was: build a railway. It was the engineer's answer. The desert was too
short of water to allow a massed army to travel. The river had defeated
them before despite the Iroquois boatmen. The only sensible method
was a railway.

So Kitchener built a railway, and he built a bridge. The 1,000-foot
bridge over the Atbara, the other main tributary of the lower Nile after
the Blue Nile, was built in forty-two days by an American firm with
mechanics imported for the task, a sign of the shifting world order.

The railway finished, Kitchener, like a man on rails, slid his vast
army into position against the dervish hordes. He had 8,000 English
soldiers and 17,000 Egyptians. The dervish army numbered 50,000.

Winston Churchill wrote about his own experience of what followed, the bloodiest battle fought on the Red Nile, in *The River War*,
an extraordinarily accomplished book for a twenty-three-year-old. It
explains with lucidity how the British came to be opposing the vast
dervish army and is informed, partly, by Churchill's own role in the
battle as a cavalry subaltern. At the battle of Omdurman three things
made a vast difference, in fact created the template for the tactics
employed to such disastrous effect in the First World War: accurate
artillery, accurate, rapid and long-range rifle fire and Maxim machine
guns. With these three elements the dervishes did not really have a
chance once they had opted for a setpiece battle on an open plain –
with minor relief features easily scoured by accurate artillery.

First, let us examine the artillery. It was no accident that Napoleon
was an artilleryman. The nineteenth century saw the rise of big guns
as the defining force of battle. The invention, in 1803, by Henry Shrapnel, of the shrapnel shell gave momentum to the whole development
of exploding munitions delivered through guns. In the 1860s the
gas-sealant band on a shell was perfected, allowing shells to be fired
through a rifled barrel – with a consequent great increase in accuracy.
Even without the machine gun, long-range accurate artillery with
exploding shells was a devastating force to be reckoned with.

Next came accurate long-range rifle fire. The rifle used at Omdurman by the British was primarily the Lee-Metford, a .303 rifle that evolved into the highly successful weapon of the First and Second World Wars – the Lee-Enfield. It was a rifle capable of firing eight shots (or ten, on some models) very rapidly by use of a bolt mechanism. The first British breech-loading rifle that used a cartridge – the Snider-Enfield – which was employed by Samuel Baker in his anti-slavery forays, was already a vast improvement on anything the Arab or native chiefs were armed with. The Snider, as already noted, was accurate to 600 yards and a trained man could send ten rounds a minute against three rounds a minute for a muzzle loader in expert hands. It used a metal-cased car- tridge that could travel well and suffer rough handling. In short, the Snider returned the advantage of firearms to the imperial colonisers of the world. The Martini-Henry consolidated it, but the repeating Lee- Metford raised it by the power of two.

And finally the Maxim gun. It could fire up to 600 rounds a minute – equivalent to 200 muzzle-loading riflemen. But a Maxim could be fired by one man (though it was easier with two). As we have seen, it was first used by Stanley in his rescue of Emin Pasha and became syn- onymous with African colonisation. Its effect was not just mechanical, it was also psychologically devastating to come under such sustained fire – probably, in the case of many African troops, for the first time in their lives.

In addition to field batteries there were gunboats on the Nile, placed at either end of the British and Egyptian army, safeguarding the flanks and the river. The gunboats were equipped with 12- and 12.5-pounder guns, 4-inch howitzers, Maxim machine guns and powerful search- lights. The guns on board were manned by Royal Marines, though the crews were a mix of Sudanese, Egyptian and British sailors. The gun- boats had been shipped in sections by sea and rail and then assem- bled on the Nile. There were ten and, whatever happened on land at Omdurman, these boats effectively sealed the fate of the river.

Omdurman, then, was a stage set for a slaughter. As the vast der- vish army charged across the open ground the British guns remained eerily silent. Then the artillery opened up. Churchill described what happened:

In another minute they would become visible to the batteries. Did they realise what would come to meet them? They were in a dense

mass, 2800 yards from the 32nd field battery and the gunboats. The
ranges were known. It was a matter of machinery ... They topped the
crest and drew out into full view of the whole army. Their white banners made them conspicuous above all ... Forthwith the gunboats,
the 32nd British field battery, and other guns from the *zeriba* [a fortified camp] opened on them. About twenty shells struck them in the
first minute. Some burst high in the air, others exactly in their faces.
Others, again, plunged into the sand, and, exploding, dashed clouds
of red dust, splinters, and bullets amid their ranks. The white banners
toppled over in all directions ... It was a terrible sight, for as yet they
had not hurt us at all, and it seemed an unfair advantage to strike
thus cruelly when they could not reply.

Thus did the dervish army come to be beaten before it had even engaged
with the British. However, there was still some more equitable fighting
to be had – the last charge made by lance carriers of the British cavalry.
It was this charge that Churchill had the good fortune to be a part of.
He was attached to the 21st Lancers who made the charge, though he
was actually an officer of the 4th Hussars.

It was all an accident of course. The 21st Lancers were sent in to
clear up some pockets of dervish resistance. The group they charged
seemed 'scarcely a hundred strong'. But these men did not flee, they
knelt down and started shooting. 'On the instant all the sixteen
troops [about 350 men] swung round and locked up into a long gallop-
ing line, and the 21st Lancers were committed to their first charge in
war ... bullets struck the hard gravel into the air, and the troopers, to
shield their faces from the stinging dust, bowed their helmets forward
like the Cuirassiers at Waterloo. The pace was fast and the distance
short.'

Then, as the Lancers galloped forward, a crease in the ground, a dry
watercourse in fact, revealed a horrible secret: 'from it there sprang,
with the suddenness of a pantomime effect and a high-pitched yell, a
dense white mass of men nearly as long as our front and about twelve
deep'. All of a sudden it became imperative to maintain the velocity of
the charge and break through their line. 'The British squadrons struck
the fierce brigade with one loud furious shout. The collision was pro-
digious. Nearly thirty Lancers, men and horses, and at least two hundred Arabs were overthrown. The shock was stunning to both sides and
for perhaps ten glorious seconds no man heeded his enemy ... several

fallen Lancers had even time to remount. Meanwhile the impetus of the cavalry carried them on.'

The fight was on. The dervishes gave no quarter, hamstringing horses, pressing their rifles into horse flesh and firing at point-blank range, throwing spears with great dexterity and wielding their heavy swords. The Lancers fought for their lives with lance and pistol. In two minutes, though, it was all over, and the cavalry had broken through and were clear of the dervishes. 'The men were anxious to cut their way back through their enemies ... [the main battle] might have been a massacre; but here the fight was fair, for we too fought with sword and spear. Indeed the advantage of ground and numbers lay with them.'

But reality sank in fast. In 120 seconds of contact five officers, sixty-five men and 120 horses had been killed or wounded. The Lancers dismounted and using their accurate Lee-Metford carbines, which easily outranged the dervish muskets, drove their enemy back. In the end modern armaments had won the day again. The rest of the battle was a mopping-up operation.

38 · Kitchener makes his bones

A son goes out to war in the morning; he comes home when God wills.
Ethiopian proverb

The Khalifa's forces were defeated at Omdurman – the world's most extraordinarily unbalanced battle, with 10,500 Arabs slaughtered and only forty-seven British killed (and 382 injured). These are the figures of a massacre, not a battle. Yet European weapons and tactics, communications and logistics created this imbalance. The sheer scale of the victory no doubt contributed to the heady confidence of the Europeans when they started their own little war in 1914; yet the real model of future warfare was the mass carnage on both sides of the American Civil War.

Kitchener then had a problem: what to do about the Mahdi's bones. A European with little experience of the Middle East might have let them lie in their tomb in Khartoum. Kitchener knew better. The tomb was destroyed utterly. The naturally mummified corpse was taken. The head was dumped in kerosene – 'for future disposal', said the gruesome Kitchener. He had to be dissuaded from turning the skull into an ink-well. The rest of the bodily remains were cast into the Nile.

There is a strange symmetry to this act, as if Kitchener, despite his long association with the region, only half understood the mythic qualities of the river. We have seen that in ancient times, drowning in the Nile was thought to confer immortality. Casting the Mahdi's bones into the river perhaps symbolized his rebirth, not his ultimate destruc-tion. In 1947 his tomb was rebuilt by one of the Mahdi's youngest sons; the dream of a purified Islamic state is still very much with us, long after Lord Kitchener remains best known for his impressive moustache and his demand that 'Your country needs YOU'.

A good place to remember him is on his Nilotic island near Aswan, a gift to him from the Egyptian (read 'British-backed') government. The island is a menagerie, as Kitchener loved animals. It is located at the most symbolically important spot on the Nile, its navel in the ancient Egyptian world.

39 · Two gentlemen of Fashoda

'Oh river what makes you cry out loud?'
'The stones blocking my way!'
'Oh stones what makes you rattle with anger?'
'The running water pounding on us.'
    Sudanese proverb

It was 1898 and Kitchener was busy trying to reconquer the Sudan. Meanwhile, Britain's eternal enemies of the last millennium, the French, were busy with their own plans for world domination. They had somehow lost the Suez Canal, through the ineptitude of the Egyp-tian Khedive who had bankrupted the country, allowing the British to buy it up. They did not want to lose the Nile too. The French, in unconsidered moments, revealed their deeply held belief that, since Napoleon had been the first European to conquer the Nile, the Nile was *de jure* if not *de facto* French. Jan Potocki, the Polish Nile traveller who wrote in French and authored the *Thousand and One Nights*-like novel *The Saragossa Manuscript* (turned into a great 1960s movie – a favourite of Jerry Garcia and Martin Scorsese), mentions in his narrative *Voyage in Turkey and Egypt* that the French are a people of intellect, the Spanish a people of passion and the English a people of action. He implies that when these peoples attempt something outside their realm of expertise they become either inspired or ridiculous – an English passion, a Spanish theory, a French adventure. And the Fashoda Incident, as it came to be known, was a truly French adventure.

Yet they were also somewhat careful. They did not wish to offend the paper rulers of Egypt, the Turks, even as they wished to oust the force behind them, the English. The French, with their interests in west and central Africa, knew that control of the whole continent was about controlling the Nile. Churchill, in *The River War*, states wrongly that the Nile drains a quarter of Africa. The real figure is a tenth. But the exaggeration has a truth – the Nile *controls* a quarter of Africa, perhaps more. A look at the map will explain why: with the north blocked off by the Sahara, the control points on the Mediterranean are Gibraltar, already British, and Cairo. We have seen that controlling the Nile controls Cairo, and by extension the eastern Mediterranean and its most important exit to India and the East. But that is the Med; what about Africa? The centre of Africa has two exits, the Congo and the Nile – control both of these, and you control the centre. The French already had the Congo, but without the Nile they were limited to the western side of the continent. If you take in the Blue Nile and the White, truly the whole eastern half of Africa down to the Equator is within your purview – you have the water source and you have the means of transport.

Naturally the British hold on Egypt looked impregnable, but the Nile did not rise in Egypt. If the French could cut it off somewhere higher up they would achieve their objective like a prankster standing on a garden hose yards away from the bemused gardener holding the nozzle.

The British did not take any of this very seriously until Victor Prompt, a French hydrologist and friend of the French President, delivered a paper before the Institut Égyptien in Paris explaining how the Nile could be controlled by a dam at Fashoda, at the southernmost end of Sudan. 'Egypt could be ruined,' he said, by vengeful operation of this dam. And with the ruin of Egypt, or its threat, would return some measure of control over the Suez Canal.

The French, in a way that was truly romantic (and an intellectual, when he turns to adventure, is always a romantic), decided to send an expedition to cut off the Nile and claim it for France. The expedition would leave French territory in Gabon, traverse the most inhospitable parts of central Africa to arrive at the Nile at Fashoda. The man they sent was Jean-Baptiste Marchand, who would make a river journey across Africa the equal of Stanley's and yet would leave the continent a failure, a blackguard, a mountebank and a usurper.

Jean-Baptiste Marchand was born in 1863, the eldest of five children. His father was a cabinet maker, not a rich man, and Jean-Baptiste left school at thirteen to become a junior copying clerk to a local lawyer, employed chiefly because of his round, clear handwriting. Jean-Baptiste had a broad forehead, wide but deep-set eyes and a small, undistinguished-shaped head, but his gaze, reportedly, was intense; his nickname in the army was, not surprisingly, 'John the Baptist'. For six years he laboured as a copyist, all the time subject to intense 'visions' of a future exploring Africa. He idolised the great explorers – Baker, Burton, Speke, Stanley, especially Stanley, all of them British. He was religious, yet sought inspiration in all religions. At one point he was so taken with Islam that he dressed and lived as a pious Muslim.

With the help of his lawyer boss he gained admission to the Marine Infantry, which offered the best chance of being sent to Africa. After three years in the ranks, in France, his burning ambition and great competence were recognised: he received a commission. Finally he was sent to Africa, landing at Dakar in February 1888. He was twenty-five years old – not bad going. For all those who insist that access is denied to those that seek entrance to the hallowed halls of professions usually monopolised by the rich and entitled, there are all these counter-examples littering the annals of exploration: Stanley, Petherick, Marchand, Livingstone (Livingstone had worked at thirteen in a weaving mill, yet by taking night classes he gained enough of an education to become a doctor). What characterised them all was an intense desire to go to Africa.

For seven years Marchand suffered fevers and illness, yet he weathered the climate better than most. He *enjoyed* it. He had also formulated, or refined, the plan he had dreamed of as a boy back in Thoissey, a small town near Lyons. The dream: to out-Stanley Stanley. He did not see Thoissey again until September 1895. On that first holiday home in France he put up a formal scheme to the Ministry of Colonies: he would be the first to carry the tricolore across Africa. His route would be new, untrodden by a European before. He would go further and faster than Stanley. He would at last be on an equal footing with the gods of his youth, his heroes, and would live his visionary dreams.

His seven years in Africa had made him no less prone to visions, but, like many, he needed to kill the source of his childish inspiration in order to achieve it: he began to hate the people he had once idolised – the British. Along with his fellow *soudanis* – the name was given to officers of the French Sudan, the easternmost part of French West Africa – he saw that the British were behind everything that spelt trouble in Africa. They were behind slavers though they professed to be against slavery, they pushed forward native kings hostile to French rule, they sought, successfully, to block French ambition in Africa at every turn. In other words they were the controlling power. The Germans, in contrast, were well thought of. It is easy to be popular when you have no power.

Marchand's plan, the one accepted, was his most simple: to beat the British to the upper Nile. Kitchener's railway had yet to be started. Omdurman was only a name in the gazetteer. It looked good.

But when Marchand landed in Libreville, the capital of the French Congo, in July 1896, the country was in uproar. One hundred and fifty Senegalese had been sent to accompany the expedition, but they had been held up by de Brazza, the Governor, who claimed that troops not under his direct control would upset the delicate balance of the Congo. The balance looked already to be upset, yet Marchand soldiered on; finally he confronted de Brazza about the lack of armed support and the condition of the country. De Brazza would be reported to the highest authority, if he did not co-operate. De Brazza gave way and Marchand set out to pacify the country between Luongo and Brazzaville (laughably beyond its namesake's control). Six months after their arrival in the Congo the expedition arrived at their real starting point. As Burton said, there are many 'starts' to an expedition. They carted with them 13,000 pieces of luggage intended for the expedition, for resupply of French outposts along the way, and for establishment of the fort intended at Fashoda.

How big was a piece of luggage? Certainly a porter could carry no more than three or four pieces. One piece of luggage was a box of seeds, including *haricots verts* which one of Marchand's lieutenants, Émile Landeroin, would later grow in the swamps of the Nile. En route he provided, even in dire conditions of swamp and fever, haute cuisine with heroic roux and sauces made out of native butter and mealie flour, poured over whatever fell to hand: Nile perch, tilapia, reed buck, buffalo, crocodile. They travelled upriver in a steamship, the *Faidherbe*, which would be their sturdy companion until the last.

Marchand led by example. The expedition doctor wrote, 'Our chief is so enthusiastic, so persuasive, that he manages everything by his own example ... he never seemed to rest. Everyone was caught up in his urgency and wished to follow him, to feel himself one of us.'

Over a year later the expedition had steamed up one of the narrowest of the Congo's tributaries, the M'bomu, managing to reach a point 130 miles from what was hoped would be a navigable tributary of the upper Nile. Between the headwaters of the Congo and the Nile lay a 2,000-foot-high forest plateau. On one side the water drained into the Congo, on the other it went into the Nile, but in the middle there was nothing for the *Faidherbe* to float in. In a move reminiscent of Werner Herzog's 1982 movie *Fitzcarraldo*, their small steamer was sawn into sections to be carried by porters across this divide. More pieces of luggage. It took weeks to do this in a systematic enough way so that the ship stood a chance of being reassembled once they reached the other side. Marchand himself took a demonic interest in the dismantling of the ship, in the exact record of each nut, bolt and rivet – lose a bolt in the Ituri Forest and the ship might never steam again. They had many porters, sturdy Yakoma tribesmen, to carry the bits, but one vital part of the boat could not be subdivided: the boiler. It took several days to work out what to do. Marchand encouraged the whole team to brainstorm the problem. You can imagine what a Gallic fervour of ingenious thinking this would bring on. They thought of a sedan-chair-type arrangement with extended poles for the porters to carry – but it was impossible, too heavy. They thought of transporting the boiler in a kind of rope hammock – too unwieldy. Finally, with a kind of naive brilliance, Marchand cut to the heart of the problem: they would reinvent the wheel; it was decided to roll it the entire 130 miles to the Nile.

But to roll a wheel you need a road. So they built one.

It took a thousand porters to make a suitably wide and level track. A path was surveyed and cut, then widened and flattened. Logs were laid to make a rough road. The chief engineer, Jean Souyri, almost became demented watching his precious boiler being jolted over roughly hewn tree trunks laid over crags, dry watercourses, ridges and pits, swaying as it was jerked from rock to rock, closer and closer to the now sacred destination of the Nile. The boiler was fourteen feet long and about four feet in diameter. Since it had to be rolled along its long axis, the road had to be fourteen feet wide. Wide enough for a humvee in fact; a vehicle which, unfortunately, they did not possess.

Having been travelling for over a year, the expedition was now spread out over about a thousand miles of country. Lines of communication were stretched almost to breaking point, but still Marchand pushed on like a crazed prophet determined to reach the upper Nile before the British could claim it. And the *Faidherbe* was not the only boat they carried: in the rear there were two metal whaling boats, also in parts, carried head high by the chanting Yakoma.

Imagine rolling a boiler from London to Birmingham, and then some. Around Coventry the jungle would give way to the dusty, rocky plains of the watershed. It was still hard going, and now they had to search out waterholes and straggly trees; finally they arrived at the upper Sueh, which flowed into the top of the Sudd swamp and eventually into the White Nile.

In a mad exercise of Imperial Meccano, it was time to reassemble the *Faidherbe* and continue the journey. Despite Marchand's explicit records it was not a quick job. As they laboured to fit the jigsaw puzzle of the steamboat together, they saw that time yet again was against them. The rainy season was passing, and the river was getting lower by the day, ominous rocky pools forming as they watched. It looked as if the porters would need to shoulder their burden again – along with 90,000 rounds of ammunition, many hundred kegs of bordeaux and champagne, vin de Banyuls and 'le corned beef', much scorned though the latter was. As the water lowered, the *Faidherbe*, *sans* boiler (it would have weighed the ship down too much going over rocks), was put into accelerated reassembly and dragged over rapids a further one hundred miles. They hoped they would meet a great river that would bear them north without need of an engine. But here, by the side of a muddy tributary, at last beaten, they had to wait until the rains came. Four more months ... and now they were separated from the very heart of the ship itself – the boiler.

Sans boiler the noble *Faidherbe* would be useless against the current. She had no sails and was too heavy to row. So another wooden road, a neat parody, we can now see with the comfort of hindsight, of

Kitchener's railway. Along this road, which ran alongside the dry river, the boiler would be rolled to the new resting position of the *Faidherbe*.

So in the south we have the French, quixotically making a wooden railway along which to roll a ship's boiler. Up north you have the passionless, idealess *rosbifs* building a real railway – rails and sleepers and all – and they were winning. Kitchener's army was already at the junction of the Atbara river and the White Nile, getting closer by the day. The British had steam trains while the French didn't even have a boiler.

Engineer Souyri gave up in disgust and retreated back to the Congo. Days after he had left, the boiler arrived. Marchand's men then rebuilt the engine slowly, painstakingly, relying on diagrams in their now rotting notebooks.

In the kitchen garden the expedition's doctor grew lettuces, radishes, spinaches, aubergines, cucumbers. When a Dinka chief walked thirty miles with a brother who had, he said, been constipated for seven weeks, a terrible ailment it has to be admitted, the doctor mixed up a remedy involving spinach, cod-liver oil, senna pods and pepper. The results were said to have been explosively satisfactory. But still the rains did not come.

Unbeknown to Marchand, the British had meanwhile won yet another war – slaughtering the Mahdi's men and taking Omdurman, all according to plan. The Prime Minister Lord Salisbury would probably have offered a face-saving formula to the French. The territory that Marchand had traversed along the Bahr el-Ghazal could have been given to the French, and, if the French government had not at that moment just imploded over the Dreyfus Affair, a more conciliatory attitude might have been taken. But Salisbury's Cabinet were not so diplomatically minded. They had won a war that had cost few lives but a lot of effort; they would not be denied their absolute rights over the Nile.

Britain had a big army very close to Fashoda. The French, though on a war footing, with the navy in the process of mobilising, were very far from being able to fight a war in Africa over a few acres of swamp. Britain was willing, had an army *in situ* and a navy vastly more powerful than that of France. That didn't stop the French drawing up an invasion plan – of Britain! The tentacles of the Nile reach everywhere. Control of a river in Africa was leading towards a great war in Europe.

The *Faidherbe* was moored on the Nile at Fashoda, where Marchand

and his men had built a camp. A few miles downstream were the British, who had travelled upriver as soon as Omdurman had been fought and won. The British were demanding that the French leave. The French wouldn't. It was all very polite on the surface. There was no attempt to tear down the tricolore. Kitchener knew enough not to be heavy handed. The stand-off continued for months. The invasion plan was seen to be impractical and was withdrawn.

Meanwhile there was one last chance for the French to assert themselves, a 10,000-strong Ethiopian force with several Cossack mercenaries and a French citizen named Faivre and a Swiss citizen improbably called Potter.

The then Ethiopian emperor Menelik II (before being emperor he had been imprisoned by mad Theodore, though he ended up marrying Theodore's daughter) had started sending Ethiopian troops south and west from the Ethiopian highlands to claim more of Africa. They had with them European advisers who naturally sought also to advance European interests. These men could lend their force to a joint French–Ethiopian claim to the upper waters of the Nile. The only problem was that the Ethiopian soldiers couldn't see the point of marshy, disease-ridden Equatorial Africa. They found the conditions of travel so appalling that, though they reached the Nile, it was with a reduced force of only 800, the rest having deserted or died, lost to dysentery and malaria. When it came to asserting France's claims alongside Ethiopia's, they planted two fluttering flags side by side on the bank. Two Ethiopians swam out to an island to push their claims a few yards further, but of the French/Swiss force only Potter (or was he perhaps a cunningly placed British interloper?) could swim, and he was now delirious with fever.

Even with this failure, the French government clung to the hope of a solution that would be to their advantage. In the end they ordered Marchand, somewhat humiliatingly via a letter sent through Kitchener, that one officer should be sent to Cairo and then to Paris to further the decision-making process. Time passed, and conditions for the British were markedly worse than for the French. The French knew how to live. They sent daily baskets of produce from their gardens sown with European vegetables to Kitchener and his men, who were living on army biscuit, roasted hippo and a sort of Nile weed thought to be nutritious. There were a dozen deaths a week in the British camp, which was situated on the toad-infested mudflats downriver from Fashoda.

The temperature was often over 40 degrees and not even Kitchener's officers had mosquito nets, whereas Marchand and every one of his Senegalese and Yakoma men had been using them since their departure from the west coast of Africa.

In the end the five months of waiting became too much for Marchand. He went to Cairo himself to plead with the French Ambassador to support his tenuous hold on Fashoda. The answer was not only no, it was a no that transformed Marchand at a stroke from being a man who had led an heroic force to being an isolated adventurer, an obsessional nut, an embarrassment. He was warned not to wear his uniform in Cairo for fear of giving offence. Unable to save face, the government in Paris sought to use Marchand as a scapegoat, claiming that his well-stocked fort in Fashoda was 'on the verge of starvation'.

Marchand was so disgusted that he never again spoke of Fashoda. Like his government, he desired to wash that memory of the Nile for ever from his life. He wept openly at the handing-over ceremony to the British.

To justify his journey, perhaps only to himself, Marchand decided to continue with the gallant ship *Faidherbe* up the Sobat river into Ethiopia. It is the Sobat that pours 'white' silt into the Nile and gives the lower river its name. It was slow and tortuous going as they were now running against the current. The river grew rockier and drier, the *Faidherbe* ground against stones and finally bottomed out on a ledge of limestone and began to take on water. She would go no further. Rather than simply leave her, the expedition unanimously agreed that she deserved a more dignified resting place. Two days of hard slog saw the completion of a little dry dock. With huge effort the *Faidherbe* was dragged into it and saluted, then toasted in one of the last bottles of champagne they had left: 'Our brave little ship! May she rest in peace.'

They trekked on for six weeks to Addis Ababa, Harar and finally the French port at Djibouti. The going was rough and stony but it was a blessed relief after the swamps and jungles. At the edge of the Indian Ocean they hoisted the tattered tricolore they had raised with such high hopes and lowered in shame at Fashoda. Marchand perhaps wept again. It is not recorded. Back in France the expedition was sidelined by the establishment, but over the years the reputation of Marchand's incredible journey grew – though only within the French-speaking world. In Britain his exploits are all but unknown.

Rusted remains of the steamer *Faidherbe* lie to this day on the banks of the upper Sobat, tribute to the determination of Capitaine Jean-Baptiste Marchand. Sadly, though, the boiler was taken out to be hammered into tribal weaponry many years ago.

40 · The first trans-African traveller, circa 1898

'Don't come to me, I will come to you,' said the malaria.
Upper Nile saying

The days of the old Nile explorers were merging into a new age of colonial expansion: explorer + Maxim = colony being the general equation. The extent of European penetration into the Nile region around the turn of the twentieth century made for safer travel – if you were on the right side. This meant that much longer journeys through Africa were now possible.

Possibly one of the most unPC travellers was the empire builder Ewart Grogan, who in 1898–1900 became the first man to travel from the Cape in South Africa to Cairo, via the headwaters of the Nile. Grogan had failed at school and university in England, and had gone to South Africa to make his fortune. When he asked a young woman to marry him, she said she would not unless he proved he could succeed at something. So he rashly decided on his plan to become the first man to traverse Africa from south to north.

Mentored by Cecil Rhodes, Grogan saw Africa as one big opportunity for the British to extend the reach of their empire – through hard work, not mere appropriation, it must be said. Grogan was immensely tough and brave, a Cambridge dropout and a first-rate shot. His comments on people with a darker-hued skin are probably what has kept his otherwise fascinating account of walking from Cape to Cairo out of print, other than the poor print-on-demand copies which render some pages unreadable.

Grogan enters our story when he hits the Nile basin in eastern Rwanda. His Watusi guide had introduced him to some 'ape-like creatures leering at me from behind some banana-palms'. One of these creatures is described as 'a tall man with long arms, pendant paunch, and the short legs of the ape, pronouncedly microcephalous and prognathous'. These creatures were easily alarmed, but once they realised that Grogan was friendly they explained by sign language exactly how to capture elephants – which was one of Grogan's interests (he treated the whole trip partly as an extended hunting holiday). Grogan writes:

> I failed to exactly define their status, but from the contempt in which they are held by the Waruanda, their local caste must be very low. The stamp of the brute was so strong on them that I should place them lower in the human scale than any other natives I have seen in Africa. Their type is quite distinct ... and, judging from the twenty or thirty specimens that I saw, very consistent. Their face, body and limbs are covered with wiry hair, and the hang of their long, powerful arms, the slight stoop of the trunk, and the haunted, vacant expression of the face, made up a tout ensemble that was terrible pictorial proof of Darwinism. Two of them accompanied me to Mushari ... they showed me the ease with which they can make fire with their fire-sticks.

These primitive people were not pygmies – their height ruled that out – so who were they? Grogan could, of course, be telling a whopper. Yet earlier, when shown the carcass of what is obviously a giant mountain gorilla, he doesn't embellish it by saying he has seen a living one. Grogan does, however, report the local rumour that these gorillas carry off local maidens from time to time. King Kong must be a hard-wired myth.

Of course people lie all the time just to tell a good story – and what could be a better yarn than a personal meeting with the missing link? And by showing the modern African's dominance over the primitive hominid – from which he evolved – the account supports similar European notions of superiority over the African, notions which Grogan definitely subscribed to.

Yet it is important to note that Grogan came from a different age and, it is obvious from his writing, was far from enlightened about the abilities of people very different to himself. I don't think he ever questioned for one moment his assumed superiority over the native African. Nor do I think that the character he displays, which is bluff and rather open, is congruent with the sly insertion of a bit of racial propaganda. He's a racist, but an unthinking and undogmatic one, the kind who 'loves' (and patronises) Africans rather than hates and despises them, and he sees as a 'threat' not the Africans themselves but other Europeans who would colonise the continent if the British weren't smart about it.

Liars aren't parsimonious with lies. They tell them in bunches. If you read an account by a liar such as Colonel Fawcett (who disappeared in the Brazilian jungle in the 1920s), you find every page has vagaries and amazements such as sixty-foot anacondas (there has never been a captured and recorded anaconda exceeding twenty-two feet in length), lost jungle cities and a paste used by Indians to dissolve stone. Liars don't hold back and tell just one pointless fib in a book of 378 pages.

If Grogan is to be believed, and the matter-of-fact way he presents his story, with no hint of drama, suggests he should, then it is quite possible that he encountered a last surviving group of a hominid such as *Homo ergaster/erectus* (*ergaster* is usually considered to have preceded *erectus*, but sometimes the names are used interchangeably). We know from hearth evidence that *Homo ergaster* could use fire and we know he was a tool user. The fact that Grogan's creatures have wiry body hair is also suggestive of what we know of *Homo ergaster* and earlier pre-*Homo sapiens* hominids. That such a group could have survived so long in isolation is remarkable, but far from impossible. *Homo erectus*, we know for sure, survived in Asia until less than 10,000 years ago. In the rest of the world he died out 200,000 years ago – or so we believe. Recently it has come to be accepted that Neanderthals and modern *Homo sapiens* may well have interbred. Some even consider that later *Homo ergaster/erectus* may also have interbred with *Homo sapiens*. Could Grogan's 'missing link' have been a group of such hominids? We know from fossil evidence that *Homo habilis* and *Homo erectus* lived alongside each other for thousands of years. Perhaps, too, this happened for far longer than imagined between *Homo erectus* and *Homo sapiens sapiens*.

But it was not this information that interested the British authorities in Cairo, to whom Grogan reported (breathlessly perhaps?) at the completion of his stupendous hike. Ernst the Norwegian runner would have been proud of him. No, the information the British coveted was about the Atem river. Grogan suggested that this river could be used as an alternative channel to the Nile, which was so thoroughly blocked by the papyrus and elephant grass of the Sudd. It was the Atem which would later feature in the plans for the Jonglei Canal. The Nile was slowly succumbing to man's control, or so it seemed.

41 · Connection and control

The water that was helpful in the dry season they curse in the rainy season.
Central African proverb

Is this the right moment to bring it up? I'm not sure. But it has to
be said, at some point in our lengthy Nile journey, that the river was
losing its mystique, its magic; it was being sized up. Mapped, measured,
dredged, dammed. In 1904 the first current meters were installed. From
now on the speed of the Nile could be known with accuracy throughout the year. Previously spot-checks on its speed had been made by
measuring the time a dropped float sped along a measured section of
the river. Kitchener had reinstalled the Nilometer at Khartoum; indeed
one of the first acts of the British as they entered the Sudan was to
establish measuring gauges in Dongola. The Egyptian High Commis-
sioner Lord Cromer told the British government that the importance of
such measures to Egypt could not be 'overrated'.

Measurement. The nineteenth century saw the standardisation of
measures and the triumph of measurement ... and of standardisation.
If it moved, it was measured. If it didn't, it was also measured. If it
had to be stopped from moving to be measured, then so be it. After
measurement came standardisation. It was easier that way. It's a childish thing, this desire to measure. Children love measuring, counting
paving stones, listing numbers. But its results are very useful, to those
who seek control.

Another sort of measurement had been initiated by General Gordon
during his years as Governor of Equatorial Egypt – now South Sudan.
He had been the first to organise scientific map-making of the upper
Nile and its tributaries through the Sudd. Eventually the whole Nile
would be mapped – more thoroughly than many rivers in Europe. Certainly far far better than the Amazon, the Mekong or the mighty Oxus.

The Nile attracted stories. It was the river of stories in the age of
stories and mythology. Then as man moved into the scientific age it
became the river to be measured and mapped. But whereas stories lead
men to the source, maps and measurement make him bolder. They
tempt him with the promise of control. Stories connect, that's what
they do. Stories demand only to be told and retold. Measurement
is only useful (except to the Aspergerish part of us) in as much as it

promises control over something valuable. Control is very tempting, since it confers power.

Seeking the source of the Nile was a search for information that led to maps that led to control that led to dams that led to the river being broken up. Strangely, the Nile started life as many small rivers all connecting up. Then it became, through the abstraction of the hydrographers, a single entity – the Nile basin, draining a tenth of all Africa. Now, as dams proceed in Ethiopia and Uganda, one can see it becoming broken up again, into local streams, no longer a unified whole.

If the effect of the Nile on human history can be unearthed, or unsubmerged, then it must be a form of psychohistoriography – the play of place and time on the way men think. The object of war, the world's first tank general J. F. C. Fuller wrote, 'is to change the enemy's mind'. The Nile changed men's minds. It still does. But, whereas before it changed minds through stories, it now changed them through the promise, the lure, of control.

Of course, even in the past the Nile had been controlled. Didn't Menes change its course? Wasn't Lake Moeris an early version of Lake Nasser? Kind of – but this control, limited by limited technology, did not replace the power of Nile stories. Stories lead to greater understanding. Measurement aims too at greater understanding, but that measurement must also become part of a story, albeit a scientific one, if we are to consider things 'understood'. Control cuts off understanding prematurely because it is action before we have full understanding.

The more we understand, the greater our paralysis. And this is a good thing. Willcocks, the designer of the Aswan dam, learnt late in life that perennial irrigation, which replaced the old flood-based basin irrigation, had allowed the bilharzia worm to multiply and virtually destroy the strength of the Egyptian fellahin. Even today it is said that the Upper Egyptians are fatally weakened by the effects of bilharzia and the smoking of bango (cannabis) to relieve its symptoms. For what? For more cotton exports? That was always the justification for the earlier dams on the Nile.

Understanding leads to paralysis – of that which is destructive. The Nuer people who would lose their livelihood if the Jonglei Canal were completed call the Sudd 'Toich', which means 'Gift from the Mother'. They live in alignment with the Sudd and use its suction-pump swamp-like attributes as a benefit – a store for water in the dry season. To the Arab slavers and the explorers who followed, the Sudd was simply a barrier, something to be burned and hacked away – so that we could better control the river. Ignorance of the Nuer might lead us to do this. But the more we understand them the less likely we are to interfere.

Stories connect. Stories lead to understanding. Measurement can lead to better stories of a scientific kind, but usually it tends to fuel fantasies of control. Control is acting before you have full understanding. Surfing is not about control of waves, it is about riding them, it is about alignment with the giant forces of nature, not attempting to deadlock them and wrestle them to the ground. Control leads to a backlash, unforeseen circumstances, unsustainability. Can you surf the Nile? In a few places – just below the Owen Falls, maybe a few stretches of the Blue Nile. But not many. Perhaps that gives an indication of why attempts to control the Nile are always a step forward and a step back. It's not easy to be in alignment with nature. But we need to be. When our control fantasies have all faded, become stories of disaster instead of inspiration, our children will turn to other stories that promise a more positive return. The only 'everyone wins' stories out there will be those where surfing will be the paradigm, not a fistfight with mother nature.

And yet for all the common-sense appeal of a sustainability imperative – that every development be subjected to the simple test: is it globally sustainable? – there remains a sneaking suspicion that we are looking at the wrong thing. To clarify: the population of Egypt since the first barrage was built has increased tenfold. The population since the second dam, the high dam, was constructed in 1970 has increased from thirty-four million to eighty-two million in 2012. That huge increase is, in biological terms, a great success. Since Malthus made his gloomy predictions between 1798 and 1826, a sudden increase in population has always been seen as presaging a collapse. My wife's uncle told me he remembered seeing rabbits colonise an island in the River Nile (I did not even know there were rabbits in Egypt, but there are) when he was a boy; they ate everything and then he watched them starve, get thinner and thinner and die off since none could escape (now they would probably be eaten first, owing to the increase in human competition for land in Egypt). Yet humans at every turn manage to defeat this depressing prophecy. In fact the human race just keeps getting bigger and bigger. What we can be sure of is that it is at the expense of other creatures – maybe even rabbits. Wild animals, great herds of buffalo and elephant moving between the bends of the upper Nile – these have all disappeared, or are fast disappearing. Poaching for ivory and bush-meat intensifies, especially with the very real Chinese demand for ivory increasing with that country's prosperity.

Or take the 100,000 Nubians who were instantly deprived of an ancestral homeland as Lake Nasser flooded. Can their loss be balanced against electric power for poor farmers? Increased irrigation, leading to increased food production leading to increased population? That increased population starts building on the farmland – shades of the rabbit population – but in this case they are saved by cheap wheat imports from Russia and the US.

Attempts to control the Nile either to increase the economic wealth of Egypt or to benefit from its strategic guardianship of the Red Sea/Mediterranean corridor usually result, as we have seen, in the Nile turning red with blood. No gain, no pain, it seems. Increasingly, almost no change is painless.

Technological improvements that lead to population growth lead to war, wars that are often fought using the fruits of the same technological improvements. When all-out war is too costly, as it is now, proxy wars, internal wars, crime wars, ideological wars become the new form that conflict takes. Terrorism – though ghastly and disruptive – kills far fewer people than traffic accidents. In a global sense it is a non-event, yet we shower it with attention because our need for conflict, driven by population pressure, requires some kind of outlet. Sport appears to serve a similar purpose, a release from the cabin-fever of modern existence, but with beneficial rather than harmful results.

The secret of storytelling is not control. You cannot 'plan' a good story. Instead you have to set off, as if on a wide river, and see where you end up. The best advice is to reincorporate what has already happened but in a new way. Joke tellers do this all the time, using something that was mentioned ten minutes ago in a new and witty context. As Hitchcock said, 'If you show a gun in the first few minutes then you have to show it being used, the audience demand it.' So, though stories move forward in time, they actually look backwards, weaving what has happened, what was implied, into a more interesting pattern. Compare this to a desire to control the future. Here you are looking ahead, hoping that you have taken every contingency into account. There is no room for improvisation. Everything must be strictly thought out in advance. You can't improvise a giant dam.

The problem with big things like dams is that people get very attached to the idea of them. They then refuse to look at all the evidence dispassionately. They have too much emotional capital invested in their pet project. Then there is the money aspect – the contracts, the employment. Those that make the future are almost uniquely unsuited to predict it, which is a pity. This is left to storytellers, who by delineating our very human follies give us insight, great insight if we care to look carefully, into what is likely to happen in the future.

We have strayed a long way in our look at control and understanding. If we are truly interested in looking ahead I have only one question relevant here: what will happen to the Aswan dam when it starts to crumble? Will it be rebuilt every few decades, like those Japanese temples – different wood but identical design for 750 years? In Japan they still train craftsmen to work as they did 750 years ago. Maybe we don't need to do that with the Aswan dam; it was pretty rough and ready in its time. But are we really looking at a river dammed for as long as humans run this planet? Something in me rebels at this idea. I am not sure why, but one day I suspect the River Nile will run unhindered all the way to the sea from its source. (In this fantasy I see people waving the river on its way rather as they wave the Olympic torch through distant villages.) Maybe we just need to learn to let go. The desire to control is human, the ability to forgo it truly superhuman.

42 · More cannibals at the source of the Nile

After the war has passed: 'I will buy a spear,' says the fool.
Sudanese proverb

But back in 1898 fantasies of control were at their height. It was easier, too, to fantasise about controlling the Nile when its people were seen as either missing links or bloodthirsty cannibals. If they should suffer when we dam rivers and build canals, who cares? They aren't even properly human, are they?

Cannibals. You can't have the Nile without cannibals. Grogan, when he wasn't meeting the missing link, spent some of his time hunting big game and some of it wading through swamps and hacking through the jungles of central Africa. He also encountered cannibals in the Kagera river region.

We have already made the acquaintance of the Kagera river: it flows into Lake Victoria and constitutes the Nile's furthest source. For a river and not a lake to be considered a source the river should have sufficient current for its contents provably to cross the lake and arrive at the outflow. In 1994 this was attested to in horrific fashion when the bodies of butchered Tutsi floated out and across the lake propelled towards the Ripon Falls exit. A hundred years earlier similar remains had been discovered by Ewart Grogan.

Grogan embarked on his journey because, he said, Rhodes had inspired him with the idea of a railway running from Cairo to South Africa. In the late 1890s the route had not even been walked, let alone surveyed. Twenty years earlier, Stanley had fought countless battles with angry natives in his river journey across central Africa, and this put off all but the most courageous or foolhardy. Grogan was of a different generation when he set off in 1898. He was imbued with the South African familiarity with the continent. He did not fear Africans, and he saw Africa as a potential home, not a version of hell there to be conquered and then left alone. He also had the immeasurable advantage of starting from a familiar base with people he knew and trusted; whatever horrors emerged, he would have that connection to draw on. And finally, though the territory might be difficult, the people intractable, the provisioning inadequate, he had the supreme psychological benefit of knowing that explorers, men like him, had already been there. Though no one had made the journey he planned, every section of it had been completed by an illustrious forebear in the previous twenty or thirty years. Grogan would simply be joining up the dots. *Simply.* The journey would take two years and make Grogan a famous man. He would go on to be one of the founding forces in Kenya, building the first sawmill, brickworks, and Nairobi's biggest and most expensively appointed hotel.

Simply. Not really. The journey was still tough and dangerous. In Rwanda, in the forests where the Nile rises, he came across scenes reminiscent of the later massacre of Tutsis. He wrote of seeing 'dried pools of blood, gaunt skeletons, grinning skulls, and trampled grass [that] told a truly African tale ... the diabolical noise made by the onrushing natives decided me that the matter was serious. I questioned my guide as to their intentions, and was scarcely reassured by his naive remark: "They are coming to eat us."' Grogan fired his rifle at the attackers and they disappeared. Exploring the cannibals' huts so recently vacated, he continued:

Loathsome, revolting, a hideous nightmare of horrors; and yet I must tell briefly what I saw.

Item. – A bunch of human entrails drying on a stick.

Item. – A pot of soup with bright *yellow* fat.

Item. – A skeleton with the skin on, lying in the middle of the huts; apparently been dead about three months.

Item. – A gnawed forearm, raw.

Item. – Three packets of small joints, evidently prepared for flight, but forgotten at the last moment.

Item. – A head, with a spoon left sticking in the brains.

Item. – A head, one cheek eaten, the other charred; hair burnt, and scalp cut off at top of forehead like the peel of an orange; one eye removed, presumably eaten, the other glaring at you.

Item. – Offal, sewage.

Item. – A stench that passeth all understanding, and, as a fitting accompaniment, a hovering cloud of crows and loathly, scraggy-necked vultures.

Every village they passed 'had been burnt to the ground, and as I fled from the country I saw skeletons, skeletons everywhere; and such postures, what tales of horror they told! … A beautiful yellow covers this spot on the map, with a fringe of red spots with flags attached, denoting stations of the Congo free state … the whole system is bunkum … the stations marked do not exist; and read, mark and inwardly digest: I have to pay a licence *to carry a gun* in the country.'

A year before Joseph Conrad's *Heart of Darkness* was published in serial form Grogan witnessed scenes that could have been lifted out of the novel. The culprits were raiders from the Congo, encouraged by the amoral Belgian experiment in using murder and slavery to extract rubber and ivory from the forest. Askaris, or Force Publique soldiers, armed by the Belgians, led a riot of theft and murder into the surrounding territories. Behind them came the Congo cannibal tribes such as the Baleka, or Bareka. According to Grogan's researches they were 'well made and pleasant featured, averaging not more than 5ft tall. Their possessions – baskets, shields, knives etc. – are very crude, and their dress consists of air and an occasional scrap of hide, human or otherwise. Whether they have a definite country or not, I cannot say; some natives told me that they have, many days' journey west of Kivu, while the majority say that they lead a nomadic existence like a flight of locusts, eating up just as effectually whatever they come across.'

43 · An Army of the Lord ...

'Look at what I do,' said the river, and flowed. 'Listen to my ways,' said the river, and roared. 'And you say it is my fault that I have eaten this person?' said the river when a man drowned. Ethiopian proverb

Fast-forward a century. The upper Nile regions have seen colonisation and then the retreat of Europeans following independence in Uganda, the Congo and Sudan. In the school in Uganda (the school my bookbound letter referred to) named after the explorer Samuel Baker, students have achieved fame of a different kind, notoriety even, as abductees into Africa's largest child army. Just as the rootless Bareka recruited young warriors in the time of Ewart Grogan, so Joseph Kony of the Acholi tribe – who have never been cannibals, unlike the Azande (formerly known as the Niam Niam) – has specialised in kidnapping young people, some barely in their teens, in order to fight for a state independent of the Bugandan authorities in Uganda.

Since Joseph Kony and his Lord's Resistance Army have been leading a nomadic existence in the same corner of Uganda/Sudan and the Congo for over twenty years, their success at achieving statehood is limited. During that time, on their path crisscrossing the White Nile, back and forth, this army of children, now grown older, has been accused of every kind of atrocity. Mainly they stand accused of abducting children to become wives and soldiers, beating peasants to death with millet pestles, cutting off the lips of those who betray them and the legs of those who ride bicycles, since the bicycle is the fastest way to relay a message of an attack happening and therefore sabotaging it. Joseph Kony has a thing about bicycles, no doubt the result of numerous cases of their deployment as vectors of early warning. When the journalist Matthew Green sought to interview him, a tube Green had with him containing sting-relief ointment was nearly the cause of trouble because of its resemblance to bicycle inner-tube repair solution. Kony has, not surprisingly, been routinely portrayed as a nut. Green, in his book *The Wizard of the Nile* (never mentioning but nodding at

The Wizard of Oz), is shocked when he finally meets the man by how ordinary he is. Adolf Eichmann and Heinrich Himmler provoked similar reactions. Reports that Kony was a monster were circulated by the government of President Museveni in their quest for money from the coffers of the West. It is always implied that Kony's barbarism is somehow linked to the colonial experience of the early twentieth century. And yet it seems naive to assume that a mere sixty years of colonial domination could really have much impact on a landscape and people thousands of years in the making. Kony remains an enigma. In fact in the only interview he has ever given he was interrupted when he tried to explain his mindset: that in the bush they have no medicines but plenty of spirits, and it is the spirits which tell them what to do and what to eat in order to get better. Strip away the cultural trappings and he is talking about intuition, how, when we are emotionally detached from the outcome, we can tune in and obtain insights that benefit us. Most mathematicians and physicists report such 'magic' in the way they arrive at their theories.

One is on tricky ground pointing out the good points of a mass killer and child abductor, yet the point is, as Hassan al-Turabi (the intellectual behind Sudan's Islamisation in the late twentieth century) is quick to point out: Africans did not drop an atomic bomb, ignite Dresden or build concentration camps. We conveniently forget our own near history when we rush to condemn another nation. We, in Europe, simply have better machines for killing. Not that one wants to condone evildoing; more to the point, one doesn't want to inhabit that murky ledge where evil-doing captures our imagination. For my own purposes it is germane to point out that Kony is merely the most prominent, or most visible, of a tradition of witchdoctor leaders that characterises the preferred African political set-up. In France one could say they have witchdoctor intellectuals; in America the self-help gurus and entrepreneurs are the witchdoctors – by that I mean people who hand down a complete recipe to every one of their followers, content to interfere at a micro-level in the lives of those followers and mostly lacking in any sense of self-doubt or any desire to rid themselves of said followers. Instead of witchdoctor you could read guru.

Joseph Kony is still in the bush, leading his child army in ever decreasing circles from Uganda to the Congo and probably back to South Sudan now that it is in a state of war against North Sudan. Kony has received money from the North to help destabilise the South before, and no doubt he will again. It is quite conceivable that he will live out his entire life as a vagrant warlord – perhaps the last of the great warrior chiefs of the upper Nile.

44 · First football match in the upper Nile

He who does not recognise a hint will not understand even if told plainly.
But do try! Ethiopian saying

Kony's most trusted men all come from his own tribe, the Acholi. But what kind of people are they? Perhaps there is something to be said for the football theory of national identity – or perhaps not ... Some believe that the way a nation plays football reveals the inner qualities of the country, though it is of course an untestable hypothesis. But here goes.

The tribe of Joseph Kony, the Acholi, were largely unknown to the outside world until the arrival of missionaries in 1902. The Reverend Albert B. Lloyd wrote that this proud and warlike tribe were adorned with iron and ivory rings, the lower lip pierced with a rod of glass, bottle glass polished smooth, about four inches long. 'This gives a most curious effect, especially when the wearer is angry, for he will draw it up, and thrust it outwards, like the sting of a hornet.' He described at length the hairdos of the 'young bucks', featuring a cone of matted hair with an empty cartridge case stuck in at the top. On the crown of the head, just behind the cone, was fastened a curved spike of ivory, the point bent towards the front. The spikes varied in length from two to six inches. On their wrists many young men wore circular blades made from steel and padded against the wrist with leather. This kind of weapon was well known further north and east but never further south of Acholi country. Kony's army still wore such wrist knives in the twenty-first century.

The Acholi carried a 'peculiar knob-kerry' – a long stick with a thick ring of iron shrunken on to one end. It weighed two pounds 'and the indentations made on the craniums of the people with this weapon are quite common in every village'. Again the knob-kerry's use has been supplanted in the present era by the similarly effective millet pestle.

Lloyd and his fellow missionary, 'both being fond of football, conceived of the idea of introducing the game to the Acholi'. Neither missionary knew much of the Acholi language, so it was impossible to explain what the rules were. They hoped that by example the young Acholi warriors would pick it up as they went along. At first the Acholi men looked at each other as if to say, 'Is it a fight or fun that we are after?' As soon as someone could do so, the ball was grabbed. Then that man was seized, carried off and shaken until he released it. The goalposts were forgotten, the sides all mixed up and 'bumps and bruises rained upon us ... in the first half-hour we spent much more time on our backs than on our legs'.

If a player received a cut that was too big to be ignored, the traditional remedy was to stitch it up with a long thorn pressed through the flesh and bound at each end with a fibrous thread. As soon as the wound healed, this was removed. An even more ingenious form of stitching was to use the so-called bulldog ant, whose large mandibles do not release their grip even if the ant is killed. Drawing the flesh together the ant is held firmly and allowed to bite, puncturing the two sides of the wound and drawing it together. The ant's body is then twisted off. A line of such ant heads holds a wound together until it has healed – about the time the ants' heads begin to disintegrate. Almost certainly one can see Kony's men, without modern sutures, resorting to such methods today.

It gradually dawned on the Acholi, gashed and wounded from their efforts at football, that the object was not to fight but to enjoy a game, and that to kick the ball through the goalposts was the main point of the thing. 'Some of the men were beautiful runners and with their long legs could accomplish much more than we civilised folk, with all our clothing and heavy boots, could hope to do.' Football became an established event at 4.30 p.m. every day, except when the drums of the village announced a drinking bout. Lloyd would then declare football 'off', as 'the young bucks would come out to play full of drink and in no fit state to take their exercise quietly'. He was able to conclude, 'I shall long look back with pleasure upon the really splendid games we had, after Acholi boys had learned that no bloodshed was necessary.'

45 · Short cut: the Jonglei Canal

The small path may be small but it can bring a person to the big path.
Sudanese proverb

Though the Acholi now occupy the northern part of Uganda, the tribe originated in Bahr el-Ghazal, in the region of the great swamp of the Sudd. Like the Mountains of the Moon, the Sudd is one of the places on the Nile one keeps circling and returning to, crucial to the Nile narrative.

To recap, the Sudd acts like a regulatory cistern at the heart of the Nile. Man sees it, like anything natural, as poorly designed, over-engineered and full of redundancies. Yet the Sudd has a function beyond wasting the river's water; it smooths out the White Nile's flow and serves as a meteorological magnet for central Africa, yoking in weather and wildlife, preserving the region from the irreversible trends of desertification. But the Sudd, from the point of view of Victorian mechanical man, was simply a big marsh. It ought to go. God's work needed some trimming. Especially now that the river had finally been dammed.

After the explorers and slavers and the wars came this final solution. It was seen as a British–Egyptian project as the whole of the Nile was now under British jurisdiction. If a series of dams could be erected from the source to the sea, then the old problem of flood and famine would be abolished. Sir William Garstin, a tough engineer who made the first real river survey of the upper Nile (the early explorers always cut off the corners of the river, going overland when the going got too tough in the canyons and gorges), discovered that the real source, in a hydrological sense, was, as we have already mentioned, not Lake Victoria but Lake Albert. This was because the swampy lakes between Victoria and Albert did not actually increase the flow – the same amount entered Albert as left Victoria. So the first dam could be built at Lake Albert and this could become a giant reservoir with ease, as Lake Albert had very steep sides. But the big problem was that all this stored water would then have to pass through the Sudd – the world's biggest swamp. This meant that a great deal of it would be lost.

Garstin had already traversed the swamp, leading men in an incredible effort to clear the first waterway through it. This involved attaching cables around huge acreages of papyrus and literally tearing it out.

In many places the fabled Nile was only three feet deep. But once a way had been forced through the Sudd it became increasingly clear what the real problem of the Nile was: the sheer size of the Sudd.

The Sudd swamp is bigger than England, and it's all marsh, a giant sump for the White Nile pouring out of Uganda. Its name comes from the Arabic *sadd*, meaning 'block' or 'barrier', and for centuries the Sudd was precisely that.

Wetlands are like fallow fields, floods, deserts, all the things we can't quite see the point of except that they look nice. The Sudd, too, it is now conceded, might have a point beyond being a giant bog that wastes the valuable water of the Nile. But its ecological virtues were less appreciated a hundred years ago when the idea of the Jonglei Canal was first mooted. This straight canal, 225 miles in length, would provide a short cut from the top to the bottom of the swamp, cutting the wetlands out in a giant loop. Now, with the disasters of Lake Chad and the Aral Sea – both dried to a tenth of their former size – it can be seen that draining a marsh is not an isolated move. And all the consequences of such a move cannot be known since every wetland is different, has different dependent ecologies – human and otherwise. One navigates the Sudd through a series of cuts made in the vegetation. Sometimes, in the past, more often than not there were moments when the Nile was completely blocked. When Samuel Baker penetrated south down the Nile in 1864 he cut through such a wall of vegetation that he accidentally drained that section of marsh, leaving his boats high and dry. He escaped from this predicament by building a dam of clay and timber behind his boats, enabling them to float clear again. Baker's channel was cleared again by dredgers in 1911 but closed anew during the First World War. Only after the Second World War was a permanent series of cuts through the swamplands finally made. After these blockages one reaches the 300-mile stretch known as the Bahr el-Jebel. The view from the rusty motorboat deck hardly changes the whole way as vegetation twelve feet high blocks the view on either side, apart from the odd tantalising entrance to lagoons. Jonglei, a village originally of only a few huts, was chosen by the British hydrologists of the Egyptian Irrigation Department to be the site of the great canal which would bypass all the above by slicing through the drier land on the right-hand side.

After sixty years of thinking about it, the digging started in 1979. All great dams seem to acquire iconic machinery. Almost like mechanical gods these machines promise great things but are ultimately defeated. In Canada, the Bennet dam on the Peace River, which created the largest open water in the Rocky Mountains, required that the area to be flooded should be logged first. Two super giant log crushers/manglers/pushers were employed to clear the area. One got stuck and lost beneath the floodwaters. The other remains outside the town of Mackenzie – a giant yellow behemoth, part rotovator, part Transformer, part gigantic mechanical folly. Neither did the work they were designed for, since the ground proved too bumpy for the giant machines to traverse. Like some doomed First World War tank they got stuck in every ditch and ravine they encountered.

The Jonglei scheme had a truly monumental digger – it looked like a Meccano monster fashioned from breaking up a Mississippi paddle steamer and mating it with an agricultural feed plant. The huge scooping wheel at the front, however, seemed to work. Called Sarah, the giant cutter ploughed through the soft laterite soils and lower clays at a goodly rate. By 1984 seventy-five of the 225 miles were all that remained. But though Sarah worked, the world around her collapsed into war.

Thirty years on, Sarah is still there, rusty, but not as rusty as you would think considering she was also hit by a stray missile during the long-running civil war between the south and the north of Sudan. You can peruse her bulk on Google Earth at the point she reached furthest south. Now peace has been signed, there is revived talk of completing the Jonglei. Let us hope not. Let Sarah rust in peace.

46 · Love on the Nile

When they like the mother, they kiss the daughter. Nubian proverb

The Jonglei Canal may never happen, especially as the new country of South Sudan has the more pressing concern of war with the North on its hands. This element in the chain of river control is missing, but slowly, throughout the twentieth century, the other elements fell into place.

Sir William Willcocks, the great engineer responsible for the first Aswan dam, the dam that really changed the way the Nile was perceived, was not sure, at the end of his life, whether damming rivers was quite the complete good he had thought it to be. In his retirement he tried to stop yet another dam happening in the Sudan. And failed.

We may have had enough of the well-documented ecological impact of dams, the spoiling of the fishing and the spread of bilharzia, but there is an often overlooked benefit: their impact on romance. The dam's effect on passion.

The first dam at Aswan was built in 1902, as mentioned earlier. It heralded a new era of steamboat travel previously made difficult by the cataracts between Aswan and Wadi Halfa. The era of the affordable Nile cruise, the ultimate romantic getaway, was made possible by the dam. With a railway link from Cairo one could avoid the longueurs of Middle Egypt, which hard-core travellers such as Flaubert took in their stride, take ship at Luxor and steam upriver to Aswan and Wadi Halfa, now submerged by Lake Nasser but in those days a thriving Nile port. The first dam raised the river and half submerged some of the temples, allowing tourists a unique amphibious experience, seemingly doomed like any good romance.

The second dam, opened in 1970, but effectively filling up for the previous six years, completely submerged a country: Nubia. This was the romantic country that interwar tourists such as Agatha Christie were the last to travel through.

Christie visited Egypt many times. The first time she fell in love with her first husband Archie Christie. But she had, for some reason, an aversion to sailing the Nile until her marriage to her second husband, Max Mallowan, an archaeologist fourteen years her junior. In 1933, when she was forty-three, they took a romantic cruise up the Nile, which naturally became one source of inspiration for the archetypal Agatha Christie mystery *Death on the Nile*.

Agatha Christie made her Nile journey a decade after the discovery of Tutankhamen. The excitement of that find provided a new impetus to Nile tourism. Christie visited almost all Nileside sites, including that of Akhnaten's palace at Amarna. She was so taken with Akhnaten she wrote a play about him. It has been performed only rarely – by amateur and repertory theatre groups. It has never opened in the West End, which may have something to do with its having eleven scene changes and over twenty speaking parts. I think, though, there is an excellent case to be made for turning *Akhnaten* (or maybe it should be *Akhnaten!*)

into a musical; with Nefertiti, Akhnaten and Tutankhamen all involved it would make a spectacular production.

Christie's love affair with the Nile not only resulted in the Poirot novel *Death on the Nile*, she also collaborated with the Egyptologist Stephen Glanville on a whodunnit set in ancient Egypt called *Death Comes as the End*.

With Glanville she had an intimate correspondence, reflecting a relationship that remained platonic but emotionally was every bit a love affair. Ten years younger than Agatha, Glanville had, she always said, 'a talent for living'. Glanville would confess to friends that he was in love with the homely detective writer; and she kept his letters bundled with those from her husband. When Agatha wrote of Stephen to Max Mallowan she always sandwiched any praise of the Egyptologist with extravagant praise of her husband. Stephen would jokingly refer to his attraction to Agatha with his friend Max, who perhaps chose not to be too aware of what was really going on.

Mallowan himself was an Assyriologist not an Egyptologist, and there is no doubt that Agatha loved him. Perhaps *agape* and sex went well together for him, whereas *eros* and a shared dream of love on the Nile were reserved for Stephen.

Christie's Egyptian novel *Death Comes as the End* ('a novel of jealousy, betrayal and murder in 2000 BC,' my 2001 reprint warns me) contains some of the clunkiest dialogue she ever wrote. Usually her characters speak entirely convincingly in their narrowly defined but acutely observed surroundings. In ancient Egypt Imhotep, the world's first architect, paces up and down saying, 'Can I not do as I please in my own house? Do I not support my sons and their wives? Do they not owe the very bread they eat to me? Do I not tell them so without ceasing?' Imhotep as Victorian Dad, perhaps, but not a patch on her usually precise capture of contemporary mores, speech and character. Agatha should have stuck to the present, and she knew it: only her love of the Nile allowed her to stray.

47 · Agatha's trunk

When the bull is in a strange country it does not bellow.
Sudanese proverb

It felt almost as if I had cruised the great river, after watching again, following a long gap, the 1978 film of *Death on the Nile*. The novel and the film are quintessential Christie material, as if the mystery of the past, the archaeological subtext so to speak, parallels in some necessary way the forensic exertions of the rotund but astute Poirot. A Frenchman called Auguste Mariette was the founder of Egypt's first archaeological museum, the French having always had, since the debut of the *savants* under Napoleon, a proprietorial attitude to ancient Egypt. It was another Frenchman, François Champollion, after all, who worked out the key to reading hieroglyphics. And, strangely, it was in Champollion Street, just behind the great museum in Cairo, that some of the bitterest fighting of the 2011 revolution took place, as if control of the country should be decided under long-departed French eyes. So French, or even Belgian, intellectual superiority in mystery solving is a key part of the Poirot/Nile scenario, one ramping the other up to a sort of critical mass – for just as *The Hound of the Baskervilles* defines Sherlock Holmes, so *Death on the Nile* seems to define not just Agatha Christie but some essential element of Nile romance.

There may be a simpler explanation. The Nile is *the* river of death. As we have seen, crossing to the western side, where all the tombs are, was the fate of all who had died, the Nile becoming a veritable Styx. One might even say that Christie had stumbled upon the red nature of the Nile – because *Death on the Nile* is, of course, a story of thwarted passion as well as murder.

I had always assumed that Christie made only one visit to Egypt, but actually she made several. I became intent on tracking down some of the details of her own Nile experience, not so much as a further insight into her work but rather because of a fellow feeling for another confirmed Nilist.

Agatha Christie's favourite Cairo hotel was not the Mena House, which is out by the Pyramids and always touted as 'her hotel' (in fact she only ever stayed there briefly and didn't enjoy her stay); she much preferred what is now the Marriott on Zamalek, a place previously known as the Gezira Palace Hotel. Agatha had first stayed there in 1910 with her mother. They remained for three months for 'the season'. It was Agatha's coming-out season – far cheaper than a similar affair in London and considered almost as good. On the same island was the celebrated docking facility for Thomas Cook. From here one could travel to Luxor or Aswan aboard the SS *Setti*, the PS *Tewfik* or as Agatha did, the PS *Karnak*, which became the model for the paddle steamer in *Death on the Nile*. It was at this wharf that the celebrated archaeological booty from Tutankhamen's tomb was unloaded in 1923, en route from Luxor to the Egyptian Museum in Cairo.

Agatha's hotel, the Gezira Palace, stood, in her day, in sixty acres of beautiful gardens. It borders the Nile, and was formerly the palace built for Empress Eugénie, wife of Napoleon III, when she arrived for the opening of the Suez Canal and, reputedly, had an affair, consummated in one of the gazebos in the gardens, with Khedive Ismail. The Gezira Palace is today, in its nucleus, very similar to what it must have been like in Agatha's time. The ceilings are high and the fans turn the air lazily, high above you. But when Agatha returned in 1933 with Max Mallowan she would have been disappointed not to stay at the Gezira; in the early 1920s it became the private residence of Habib Lotfallah Pasha, returning to its hotel role only in 1961. But the island of Zamalek, also known as Gezira (which means 'island' in Arabic), was always the start of any journey up the Nile. From here she would have proceeded up to Luxor and another favourite hotel, the Cataract at Aswan. On all these journeys she was never one to travel light, and it is interesting to glean from her own accounts what she actually packed.

In her memoir about helping her archaeological husband Max, *Come, Tell Me How You Live*, she recounts the humiliation of having to buy 'O.S.' clothes – 'outsize' – for her journey. She resorted to the 'tropical department', first for a sola topee ('brown, white and patent'), though she is tempted by a double terai hat, which was available in pink. The double terai was a much esteemed traveller's hat as it had a double skin, thus protecting your head from the sun. Being too large for sailing trousers or jodhpurs, Agatha plumped for plain coats and skirts made of shantung. This was a woven raw silk cloth, with a rough texture, hard wearing and favoured by the wives of empire builders. 'I am transformed into a memsahib!'

Other specialised clothes would include a Burberry coat and skirt – most useful for the cold winter nights one can experience on the Nile.

This set of garments 'unites the freedom of the upper part of a Norfolk jacket with expanding pleats, and the smartness below the waist of a skirted coat'. It was recommended for shooting, walking and golf – and Agatha was a keen golfer, especially in her youth. She had even tried surfing when, on a world tour with her first husband, she stopped in Hawaii. Strangely, she is probably the first Englishwoman ever to have stood up on a surfboard.

But there will be none of that on the sedate Nile cruise. She might include, again for the surprising cold of the Egyptian night, a pair of ladies' fleeced knickers bought from Dickins and Jones. Agatha was a keen motorist and for wet weather included her motoring rainproof made of gabardine with a camel fleece lining.

She would have quite a few evening dresses for special occasions, and these would require the dress shield, or dress preserver – essential when few dresses were washable and dry cleaners might be few and far between. The dress shield went under the armpits and stopped the dress becoming drenched in smelly perspiration. It was especially useful for ballgowns. In this era before the widespread use of deodorants the smell of ladies' perspiration was not considered offensive. Indeed in Agatha's ball-going youth 'gentlemen used to like what we called a "bouquet de corsage"'.

Then there were the accessories: hat guards, motor scarves, puggarees (hatbands for further sun-protection), night socks and night caps, garters and eyeglass cords, bootlaces and dressing-gown girdles; cork soles, belts, several fans from Liberty, two 'housewives' (handy collections of needles, thread and tiny scissors), hairbands, Indian gauze combinations, Milanese silk knickers, cream Japanese silk petticoats, linen knickers and a tea gown. Then there were a dozen fancy cambric handkerchiefs and a dozen bordered handkerchiefs with the monogram 'A.M.' and not 'A.C.'.

Agatha hated zips but bought a zipped travelling bag: 'life today is dominated and complicated by the remorseless zip'. In the trunk would also be several 'fountain and stylographic pens'. Agatha always believed that a pen could work for years without giving trouble in England, but the moment you went abroad it would go on strike, 'either spouting ink indiscriminately over me, my clothes, my notebook and anything else handy, or else coyly refusing to do anything but scratch invisibly across the surface of the paper'. She took just two pencils, as pencils are 'fortunately not temperamental'.

Next would be not one but four wristwatches. One to wear, three to pack. The sandy winds that blow around ruins were deadly for an ordinary wristwatch of the 1920s and 1930s. She would reckon on a watch lasting a week at best.

Books of course. Often she had to relinquish space to make room for those of her husband. A plaid rug for picnics. She was ready for anything, it seems, even love on the Nile.

48 · King Tut's swift

The birds of different rivers speak different languages. Ethiopian proverb

Agatha, married to an archaeologist, met Howard Carter several times. In the early years after his great discovery of Tutankhamen's tomb in 1922, he was to be found ensconced each winter in his desert dwelling where he worked on cataloguing all the remains he had found. The building was a cube of mud with a tiny garden lying in the shadow of the house. His laboratory, where he unwrapped mummies, was in the Valley of the Kings. Melting off the resin that sealed the mummies' shrouds with a soldering iron, he found within the wrapping jewelled objects more wonderful even than those that had been stacked in Tutankhamen's tomb. One intrigued Agatha Christie when she later saw it: a ring of blood-red carnelian carved in the shape of a migrating swift – along with swallows, swifts are constant winter migrants to the Nile valley. The red sun's shape is attached to the swift, the setting sun which must die each night, the soul which must fly like the swift to another place unknown.

I had seen a swift land awkwardly on a clifftop out in the Eastern Desert. There was some danger in this. If the swift could not flap its way to the edge to drop off into a thermal, it would die, as its legs are far too weak to carry it anywhere and it can neither perch nor walk. To make a nest the swift must catch its materials on the wing – floating pieces of hay, feathers, seed pods falling – and take them to whatever eave or overhanging rock it favours. The construction is plastered together with saliva, a less attractive nest than that of the house martin, whose masterful lodgings are made from wet mud pellets and grass plastered to the side of a wall.

Coming from England as I do and growing up with house martins nesting under the eaves of our house and swallows and swifts feeding at sunset on the insects above the cornfields, I had the sense growing ever stronger that the world as I saw it was, without intention from me to force it that way, circumscribed by familiar faces that all along my Nile journey – through reading and travelling – kept appearing, as if to remind me that life itself is as connected as a river system, that the tendency towards unity outweighs the forces of entropy. In short I saw swifts following the course of the Nile south. They are the original explorers of the Nile, from sea to source and beyond.

It isn't difficult to confuse house martins, swallows and swifts from a distance. Closer up, swifts are the larger, sleeker and more aerodynamic, house martins the smallest and chubbiest, with white underparts to identify them. They all fly south in winter. I have been in the desert and seen one exhausted, a house martin, perched on the wing mirror of a Land Cruiser, panting for breath it seemed. The Bedouin driver fed it water in a saucer and it revived, flying onwards towards Lake Nasser.

Though Aristotle mentions the migration of swallows down the Nile, this knowledge was not widespread. As late as the time of Gilbert White, the eighteenth-century clergyman naturalist of Selborne, it was thought that some birds hibernated during the winter. Swallows rarely migrate in very large groups unless held up in fog or other difficult weather; then, groups can accumulate rather like the bunching of walkers at a single stile. They depart at different times and make their way over Europe in the autumn and across the Mediterranean and down the Nile to east and southern Africa.

The first men migrating north had only to follow the birds flying overhead. They must have followed them down the Nile to the sea and beyond. And, millennia later, come the new migrants, people like Agatha Christie and Howard Carter, returning each year to the East, like swallows and swifts in their own right.

Part Six

BLOOD ON THE NILE

From assassination to revolution

1 · To the end of the Nile

A sharp thorn, moving with the river's flow, stabs without being seen.
Rwandan saying

The Nile fascinates. It mesmerises tourists such as Agatha Christie, but it also captures the minds of men set on wielding power and influence. Influence bears the same relationship to power as a stag's antlers do to his status: there is an assumed and useful correlation between size and fighting ability, but it is not set in stone. A weak deer with fine antlers may be able to bluff his way for a very long time. It is fascinating to see those Mesopotamian statues and friezes of symbolically full-antlered stags as if they were saying *this is a man*. So, with the Nile, controlling it has an influence beyond any physical power it can exert.

But influence it has. And the way that influence was focused and amplified in the twentieth century was through the construction of dams.

Three of the world's greatest engineering feats are still to be found in Egypt: the Pyramids, of course, but also the Suez Canal and the Aswan high dam. And the last two (and probably the first) are not the result of a professional engineer, a committee of responsible technocrats or a government ministry. Both the Suez Canal and the Aswan high dam are the result of two amateurs who just wouldn't give up. In the case of the Suez Canal it was the failed French diplomat Ferdinand de Lesseps. De Lesseps capitalised on having been the tutor of the then ruler of Egypt, Khedive Ismail. This immensely fat royal was starved by his father but secretly fed spaghetti by de Lesseps. The Khedive never forgot, and forced de Lesseps' plan through against, at first, stubborn French and British government disapproval.

One suspects, reviewing the history of the Red Nile, that history is not made by parliaments, committees, companies – it is made, rightly or wrongly, by determined individuals or small groups of determined individuals. Just as Lenin toppled Tsarist Russia with nineteen fellow revolutionaries, so too are many of the events we have examined the result of determined, if not obsessive, individual action by people who might have no official backing. Outsiders in many cases, who find themselves through sheer persistence in the right place at the right time for their one-shot message to ring home.

In the case of the Aswan high dam, the British had for years considered Egypt's section of the Nile to be just one piece of the whole river. They contemplated controlling the river nearer the source – using the Owen Falls dam to turn Lake Victoria into a reservoir, cutting a canal through the Jonglei, draining the Sudd and using dams on the Blue Nile, all to take complete control of the river from source to sea. But politics was never going to let this happen. Upstream countries such as Sudan, Ethiopia and Uganda could be coerced into grudging co-operation but never really trusted with controlling Egypt's water supply. The dam of 1902, its height raised in 1912 and 1933, was considered a brilliant work of engineering. But it had simply never occurred to anyone to build a second dam there so big that it would turn the whole of fertile Nubia into a giant lake. To the British, such an act of violence against the homeland of an indigenous people would have been unthinkable. Whatever else may be said about the British Empire, its track record of defending minority and tribal cultures within the countries it ruled is impeccable compared to the treatment many received after independence. The British treatment of the Nagas in India, the Penan in Borneo and the Nubians in Egypt was far better than what was meted out after the countries' majority groups took power. That Egypt gained a hydropower system and a source of reliable water benefited the farmers downstream. It had no benefit at all for the 100,000 Nubians who lost a homeland that had been theirs since pharaonic times.

No, it was far too audacious an idea for a government-paid British engineer to come up with: to plug the Nile permanently and flood Nubia. Crazy. But one Egyptian, of Greek origin, Adrian Daninos, had precisely this idea. Rather like the great engineer Isambard Kingdom Brunel, who claimed that his life's work was just the physical completion of ideas he had had before he was eighteen years old, Daninos, an agronomist by training, came up with the first part of his plan in 1912 when he was just twenty-five. His father had been an archaeologist, and the son was trained first in Cairo in agronomy and then in Paris as a lawyer. He married a Welshwoman and lived his whole life in Cairo.

In 1912 he came up with the idea of adding a hydroelectric station to the 1902 dam at Aswan. Included in the scheme was a plan for a nitrogen-fertiliser plant. This scheme was presented to the Egyptian government time and again, with improvements and changes, through the First World War and the Second, until in 1948 it had mutated into a scheme, the first ever mooted, to try and hold back the entire Nile flood behind a single dam. There was something preposterous and momentous about this challenge to nature. Daninos had made many journeys to Nubia and had calculated that above Aswan a single dam could stop up the whole Nile valley for hundreds of miles. A gigantic lake could be created. All earlier plans were designed to slow the river but at least deliver some of its annual floodwaters. The new plan insisted that everything could be stored and released when needed and not wasted during the high waters of the summer months. From previous schemes which planned to hold back 13 billion cubic yards of water he leapfrogged to one that proposed stopping in its tracks 186 billion cubic yards. The thought of the world's greatest river penned up behind one wall of concrete was just too big a leap of faith – the leading government engineer Dr Harold Hurst wrote of the Daninos proposal, 'the claims are somewhat exaggerated and the difficulties passed over. It is a very long way from this stage to the presentation of the final project ...' – and again the high dam looked likely to disappear. By this time Daninos had added to the plan a steelworks using the hydropower electricity generated and a lock to allow ships to pass through the dam.

If Nasser had not come to power in 1952, it is likely the high dam would never have been built. There would have been no destruction of Nubia, no problem with a lack of silt in the delta, no collapse of the sardine fisheries that thrived in the Nile flood as it entered the Mediterranean, no spread of bilharzia through the stagnant canals that could be used year round, and of course, no hydropower, no steelworks, no increase in agricultural yield, no freedom from African control of the river, no reduced harvests during the drought years of the 1970s and 1980s.

Those who say the dam was essential to the welfare of Egypt are talking nonsense; not one of the highly experienced British engineers with over a century of meddling with the Nile thought the dam was possible, let alone necessary. Only Nasser's revolutionary zeal made such an audacious thing happen at all. Arguments about its overall utility miss the point: it is here to stay. The silt that used to cover and nourish the delta now spreads itself along the floor of Lake Nasser, which at 350 miles long is one of the world's largest man-made lakes. In 500 years, it was originally estimated, the lake would have silted up and no dam would be possible. But recent studies show siltation is far less than was previously imagined.

Strangely, once Daninos' plan was taken up he was shouldered aside by the Russian and British and Egyptian contractors who finally built the dam. He ended his days in 1976 living in a small flat in central Cairo trying to interest the world in a new plan to crisscross the planet with canals that would end food shortages for ever.

2 · Inside the *dahabiya* with Sadat

On the day birds learn to speak they will say: 'Disappear! Disappear!'
Egyptian proverb

But we're ahead of ourselves again, carried along by the dreams of the likes of Daninos, Nile dreams which would be used by Nasser, and his successor Anwar Sadat, to make Egypt not only independent in terms of power and food, but independent too from the grand strategic aims of the great powers of the twentieth century.

Let's take up from where we left off with Agatha and turn to a less romantic fellow denizen of the *dahabiya*: Anwar Sadat. Perhaps there is another way of looking at his life, a Nile perspective, that starts with his birth in the Nile delta village of Mit Abu el-Kom, travels upstream via a humble houseboat and ends with his traumatic assassination in 1981.

Sadat's original name was el-Sadaty, which means 'followers of the masters'. This refers to one of the many Sufi groups found throughout Egypt, and indeed throughout the whole of north Africa and the Middle East. Their proliferation and influence were noted by Richard Burton (himself a Sufi), and, years later, as we have already noted, it was during the 2011 revolution that Sufi groups resisted the fundamentalist Salafis, intent on destruction in the name of an Islam alien to most people of the region.

But Anwar el-Sadaty was no Sufi, which is probably why he changed his name after the first revolution in 1952. His father, though born into a very poor peasant family, was reasonably well educated thanks to the unceasing efforts of his mother, who sold butter door to door to the wealthier peasants. He came to the attention of a section of the British Medical Corps who were studying the alarming rise in bilharzia noted in the delta since the introduction of perennial irrigation. They needed an interpreter and someone to liaise with local villagers. So a river disease was Sadat's father's, and Sadat's, ticket out.

Sadat's father was transferred with the Medical Corps to the Sudan. His mother found him an ex-slave to marry, Sitt el-Barrein, 'woman of the two banks' – a true Nile name. It is not recorded from which part of the upper Nile she had been snatched. Despite the best efforts of Baker and Gordon the slave trade continued well into the twentieth century. I was introduced to a smiling African in Siwa whom everyone called 'the slave'. He was about fifty and his father had been a slave brought via the desert route from Chad or the Sudan.

That Sadat's mother was a Nilotic African would connect him to the source of the Nile; it would supply him with truly African credentials in a world where such credentials had begun to mean something; it would also be a source of humiliation and shame in the formative years of his life when his family moved to Cairo. Sadat's father took another wife, and then another, who bore him nine children. Sitt el-Barrein was at the bottom of the pecking order, beaten in front of her powerless son when she failed to clean the house correctly. Naguib Mahfouz's novels abound with the kind of domestic tyrant that Sadat's father became. It is a tyranny encouraged by the tyrannised in the fond belief that the tyrant will protect them from other petty tyrants. In Sadat's case it made him outwardly servile and submissive, but within, all the evidence suggests, he was burning with an ambitious rage – one that would spur him on to joining a secret pro-Nazi group and aiding the German war effort under the nose of the British invaders who had provided his father with the wealth to become the tyrant he was.

While Sadat's mother and father lived in Sudan, they would travel back and forth from the delta on a post boat, an overcrowded steamer or sailboat plying the waters up to the first cataract at Aswan. His mother, when pregnant, which she was four times, would make that long journey back to the delta so that the children would not be born in Sudan. As an unborn child Sadat would have felt the slow rhythms of the river as he travelled south inside his mother; as a boy he grew up playing in the waters of the Nile. He would have known the flood and all the work it entailed. His happiest memories were all of this Nile village, an existence which abruptly ended when, aged six, he went with his family to live in Cairo. His father was stationed at Abbasiya barracks – hardly any distance from the place where Sadat would ultimately be murdered.

As a young man growing up in Cairo, Sadat would have known that the *dahabiya* houseboats were the kind of place where actors and actresses might relax after a show. Sadat had dreamt of being an actor – he once answered a magazine ad asking for new talent with a letter in which he declared, 'I am a young man with a slender figure, well built thighs and good features. Yes – I am not white, but not exactly black either. My blackness is tending to reddish.'

The *dahabiya* was the main mode of transport in the golden age of Nile tourism, from the late nineteenth to the mid-twentieth century. It was something of a barge, not so dissimilar to the Oxford University Boat Club barges moored on the Thames, with a flat bottom and a shallow draught. It could be seen as a direct descendant of the kind of barge used by Cleopatra and all subsequent Nile travellers of the Islamic epoch; it could be rowed or sailed using two masts – a large foremast and a smaller mizzen – both rigged with the lateen sail seen on dhows throughout the region. The cabins were on deck, which was cleaner, lighter and more convenient than having them below deck. The upper deck is the province of the passengers; the lower deck houses the crew.

The kitchen, which was a small shed containing a charcoal stove, was near the bow between the foremast and the prow. The cook was protected from the wind by both the shed and a moveable awning. A *dahabiya* could be as little as sixty and as much as a hundred feet long. Some were luxuriously fitted out with grand pianos, gilt-framed mirrors, bookcases and divans. The crew had no quarters to speak of – simply a box with their few possessions and a brown blanket to roll up in on the foredeck. Though the Nile is favoured by southerly winds that counteract the current, when the wind was down the crew could be expected to tow the boat along the bank from dawn until dusk. This they reportedly did cheerfully, singing songs, smoking and chewing on sugarcane grabbed from the bank. When there was no towpath they could punt all day and move the barge that way.

During the summer months the *dahabiyas* would be moored in Boulaq in Cairo where the captain, or *reis*, would supervise their over-haul. Over time some of these moored *dahabiyas* became houseboats used for nefarious pleasure-seeking purposes, but they could also be simply rented out as places to live. In time they became a fixed part of Cairo life, so much so that Naguib Mahfouz wrote a novel about life on a houseboat for a group of hedonistic artists. When two German spies hid in Cairo during the Second World War they did so on a houseboat, one with a large antenna disguised as a washing line. The antenna-maker, one Anwar Sadat, was a signals officer in the Egyptian army. He had become a kind of actor, first idolising the Prussian style, even going so far as to wear a monocle, then playing the more demanding role of a spy and resistance fighter.

That he was able to escape the usual fate of a spy in wartime was a tribute to his charm and luck. He would go on from being an underground radio operator to becoming one of Nasser's co-conspirators against the British.

3 · The adventure of the Hungarian Boy Scout leader

The hyena that is going to eat you does not cry out first.
Ethiopian proverb

By the time of the Second World War the Nile was all about Egypt. The Red Nile was all about Egypt: this was where the huge showdown between the new Black and the new Red would occur – the Black of the Axis countries and the Red of those allied to the Soviet Union, which from 1941 onwards bore the heaviest burden of the European war. The Red and the Black were duking it out in the north African desert while the diplomats of Cairo grew exceedingly nervous and burned their papers. (Sadat would have seen them in action, and indeed paper burning, when he became president, was a yearly ritual for him – he would start a personal bonfire in the grounds of his Nileside house (which is still in the Sadat family – in 2009 Jehan Sadat greeted tourists there for an exclusive cocktail party, a former first lady reduced to being a gimmick for an expensive Nile tour), or the annual fire would be held at his ancestral village of Mit Abu el-Kom, incinerating all offending and incriminating documents that had accrued in the previous twelve months.)

Back in 1940s the Nile waited for its new masters. Though the British controlled the headwaters of the White Nile in the Sudan and Uganda, they knew that mere riverine control was not enough in these times. To control the Nile in military terms meant, very largely, retaining control of Cairo.

With the Axis advance on Cairo came a need for intelligence from that city. The Germans, for a while, benefited from an American leak in security engineered by the Italians. This was hardly enough. Rommel decided to place some spies right in the heart of Cairo, oddly enough on a boat on the Nile.

In 2006, driving through the Western Desert of Egypt, close to the Libyan border and the huge wilderness plateau of the Gilf Kebir, Richard Netherwood and his team of amateur desert explorers and historians discovered the original spy camp of Count László Almásy, the Hungarian adventurer, explorer, soldier and espionage agent upon whose life Michael Ondaatje's novel *The English Patient* (and Anthony Minghella's 1996 movie) is based. I met Netherwood in Cairo and was impressed by his can-do approach to modern desert archaeology. In the camp they had discovered German-made batteries, German newspapers and German tyres – all mummified in the desert air (tyres last particularly well – from a distance, their sand-polished exterior makes them look very black and new). Netherwood's method was based on being a well-travelled desert driver himself. When he saw a place that looked like a good campsite he was certain it would also have appealed to the 'English Patient' some sixty years earlier.

Working from Almásy's books and correlating possible campsites with his descriptions and Google Earth pictures, they decided a number of locations could be where the German team had rested up while infiltrating two spies into Cairo in 1942. This was Operation Salaam, which has gone on to inspire novels such as Ken Follett's *The Key to Rebecca*, *The English Patient* and the much underrated *Cairo Foxhole*, a 1960s epic with Michael Caine in an intriguing bit part. None of these productions, however, has given enough prominence to the part played by the future President and leader of the Egyptian people Anwar Sadat.

Sadat had managed to get an education, just as his father had. As a man of ambition he resented the presence of the British occupiers. Unlike wealthy Egyptians, who were insulated in their palaces and motorcars from British army arrogance, the poorer folk felt the injustice of a foreign ruler keenly. Sadat wrote of his hating the sight of a British NCO in the military police riding his motorbike at full pelt through the streets of Cairo, forcing people to leap out of the way. And the two-tier justice system whereby British subjects were not tried in Egyptian courts for crimes committed in Egypt rankled with all Egyptian patriots.

The Second World War naturally brought such antipathy to a head, with the hundreds of thousands of British and allied troops moving through Cairo. While watching a Second World War movie with my mother-in-law, who was about ten at the outbreak of the war and living in Cairo, she remarked on a bar-fight scene with drunken Scottish soldiers fighting English squaddies – 'Like in Cairo,' she said. My father-in-law told me, shortly after I married his daughter, how he had been on protest marches as a young student during the war. Anti-British sentiment, as in India, was rife. Hitler became a popular name. Indeed it has seldom been remarked upon that the full name of the general who headed the governing military council after Mubarak was deposed in 2011 was Mohamed Hitler Tantawi, the 'Hitler' being quietly dropped in the 1970s. Sadat, like many Egyptians, sought to aid Nazi Germany not out of direct affection, but to destroy the common enemy of Imperial Britain.

In a strange reversal, the original English Patient initially preferred to help the British, not the Germans. Count Almásy had been schooled for a while in Eastbourne and had many friends among the group of explorers known as the Zerzura Club, so named because membership required one to have spent time searching for the lost oasis of Zerzura. Almásy was complicated; as well as exploring he was the founder of the Hungarian Boy Scout movement, a glider champion, a chainsmoker and a homosexual. In the First World War he had flown in the Austro-Hungarian air force; this together with his unusual background led the British to decline his offer of help, despite the obvious desert expertise. Rommel was less circumspect and Almásy was employed to smuggle two Germans, Johannes Eppler and Hans Sandstede, into Cairo right under the noses of the occupying British.

By driving hundreds of miles through the desert – and stopping at the camp that Netherwood found – Almásy was able to reach the Nile 600 miles south of Cairo. From there, the two spies proceeded, dressed as British soldiers, by train to Cairo. There they rented a houseboat which they shared, improbably, with a bellydancer. You can see how their minds were working: instead of skulking around like spies, let's be right out in the open. Officers enjoying time off at the Kit Kat Club were encouraged to continue the party on the houseboat. Eppler, who had been brought up in Egypt, was able to pass as a wealthy Egyptian, while Sandstede posed as an American. Though the British at Bletchley Park were on to Almásy's journey through radio transmissions made by Rommel, they did not know he was transporting spies. It is possible, had Eppler been less flamboyant, that the duo might not have been discovered.

Sadat was appointed as the radio expert for this comedy act. He wrote, 'I had an appointment to see the transmitter. The first thing that surprised me was that they were living on the Nile houseboat belonging to the famous dancer, Hikmet Fahmy (who had danced for Mussolini before the war). The surprise must have shown on my face, because Eppler laughingly asked, "Where do you expect us to stay? In a British army camp?"'

Eppler told Sadat with pride that a Jewish intermediary had changed money for them. He also boasted of having Jewish Egyptian girls enact sex fantasies for him by pretending to be virgins. He said he was 'deflowering' one every night. Sadat was not alone in thinking that this was a doubtful strategy for keeping a low profile. Hikmet Fahmy grew jealous and started complaining about 'the Germans'. Soon the British started to investigate. It wasn't hard to work out that there was a radio on board as it was the only boat with a washing line made of cable, not rope. Sadat could not fix the transmitter brought through the desert, but he did carry out some repairs on an American transmitter the pair of comedy spies used, a radio obtained through the Swiss Legation. When Eppler and Sandstede were arrested, Sadat was given away. The military police searched his house, but the radio was in the women's section and the police were too mindful of Eastern tradition to insist on searching the harem. Without that evidence against him, Sadat was able to avoid a death sentence. He spent the rest of the war in prisons of varying degrees of laxness – in one, the Zeitoun, he was able to take a taxi into town at night, spend an evening at a pension run by a Frenchwoman and visit the Abdin Palace on his way home, where he was to make a complaint about prison conditions to the royal entourage of King Farouk, who were powerless and yet indignant about British interference in Egypt.

Sadat, despite his later involvement with the revolution that deposed King Farouk in 1952, was useful to the palace. He became the contact point for the hitman Hussein Tewfiq, who had graduated from killing drunken British soldiers to assassinating highly placed pro-British politicians in the Egyptian parliament. That Sadat should end his days with an assassin's bullet, or bullets, in his body seems karmic retribution for having been an assassin's pimp in former times. The British were not despotic: during one attempt Sadat was smuggled out of his poorly-guarded prison to help during the hit, then returned to his cell.

Sadat never made a secret of his assassin's past. In his autobiography he relates how he handed over two grenades to Tewfik as back-up for the murder of the politician Amin Osman; he mentions boastfully how Tewfik could easily have got away after the killing (he was caught instead). When it was Sadat's turn four grenades would be used in addition to the bullets; one of the assassins could, too, have escaped being caught ...

4 · Lawrence on the Blue Nile

Drinking coffee requires a snack, talking with a King requires a gift.
Ethiopian proverb

Let's go back a bit. It's 1941 again. Imagine the credits rolling on one of those Pathé newsreels – all churning tank tracks and saluting soldiers. 'Hitler's steel battalions sweep into Mother Russia while in Africa hope is all but extinguished ...' For months it looked very much as if the British would be driven from Egypt by the might of the Axis armies. If Rommel could keep up his momentum the Germans and Italians would reach the Nile and seal the fate of the Suez Canal. As we have already mentioned, the British had so little faith in their own defences that the Embassy began burning its documents. The smoke pouring from the grounds of the British residence was so great it was believed, at first, an incendiary bomb had been dropped.

Further south not a dog barked against the British in the Sudan; the Sudanese preferred British masters to Italian ones. The British could send a force down the Blue Nile and into Khartoum, squeezing Egypt from both sides. No wonder they were burning documents in Cairo.

In Europe things did not look any more hopeful. The British had been driven from Dunkirk. There had been failed campaigns in Norway and Crete. The allies needed a victory, anywhere.

Enter Orde Wingate, one of the strangest generals of the Second World War, a man who gave his briefings in the nude while combing his pubic hair for lice with his toothbrush. Wingate, who had coincidentally spent time in the Egyptian desert looking for the same lost oasis of Zerzura as the Hungarian Almásy (though one imagines he would have sneered at being called a member of something as insignificant as an explorers' club), was given the job of securing the other end of the

Nile – the source of the flood, Lake Tana. By securing Ethiopia the Nile would be secured. The back door into the Sudan and Egypt would be closed. Even if Egypt fell, at least the British could perhaps effect what the Italian rulers of Ethiopia had been promising for six years but had so far failed to do: turn the Nile off and bring Egypt to its knees.

The Italian plan had the diverted water, instead of flowing out of Lake Tana at the Tis Abay or Tissisat Falls, travelling down a giant thirty-mile-long tunnel (aptly enough a scheme rather like this, bar the bringing of Egypt to its knees, is at last being built by an Italian contractor). The planned pipe would deliver water to the arid plains which could be sown with all manner of crops – perhaps with something of the success shown by Rassam with his giant vegetables.

Grabbing Abyssinia was a very long shot. The basis of Wingate's army was tiny, barely a hundred men, divided into action groups of a single officer, five NCOs and a nucleus of Sudanese Defence Force soldiers. The plan would work only if these men would be able to recruit and lead the thousands of Ethiopians who had a grudge against their Italian masters. In short, it was Lawrence of Arabia on the Blue Nile.

In Egypt the British were suffering in the oppressor's role; further upstream on the Nile they gambled on playing the opposite role, as liberators. Wingate had been successful in Palestine raising a Jewish defence force against Arab incursions. He became a staunch Zionist, if not a bigot, urging Israelis to bayonet the 'dirty Arab'. Wingate was a great believer in the fear-inducing effect of eight inches of cold steel in your stomach.

He looked, and behaved, like something out of the Old Testament. He used the Bible as a tactical manual, preferring, like Gideon, to attack at night using lights and noise, as Gideon used pot smashing and torches, to give the impression of a much larger force. He called his Ethiopian army 'Gideon Force'. A fellow officer, W. E. D. Allen, wrote, 'His equals were inclined to bait him, and the more easy-going went in fear. But the same fervour that made him goad men to almost super-human effort insisted later that their courage be recognized.'

To reach Ethiopia Wingate followed in reverse the route of Bruce, pushing upwards through the Sudan and along the Blue Nile. Then, for some reason, possibly to avoid their route being anticipated, he insisted on marching to strict compass bearings rather than following existing tracks. Instead of managing the thirty miles a day of King Theodore, the army beat its way through thornbush and thistle patch. And to repeat a story told earlier – repeated because it is so damn bizarre – whenever a well or waterhole was happened upon, the eccentric Wingate would rush to the head of the column, drop his trousers and pants and bathe his nude backside in the water supply. Strangely, his men followed him ardently. Allen wrote, 'His narrow blue eyes, narrow set, burned with an insatiable glare. His spare bony figure with its crouching gait had the hang of an animal run by hunting, yet hungry for the next night's prey. Some demon chased Wingate over the [Ethiopian] highlands ... perhaps to what is called greatness, perhaps to that failure to integrate [the various selves of the personality] which is called unhappiness.' Not that Wingate was well liked, he wasn't. But being well liked and getting men to follow you are different in war and peace. One senses that men knew Wingate would win.

It was not completely straightforward. Local chiefs were canny, wanting arms without having to fight with them. Wingate split his Gideon Force into parts under different European officers, each sent to recruit the nation to his cause. He had a trump card which he played to the full. At the head of his army rode, on a mule, Emperor Haile Selassie, deposed after fighting against the Italian invaders in 1936.

Selassie, christened Tafari, which becomes Ras Tafari (ras meaning 'head' or 'chief'), was simultaneously becoming a messiah to the people of Jamaica. Leonard Howell, a globe-trotting Jamaican of a religious turn of mind, found himself at the coronation of Haile Selassie (also in attendance would be Wilfred Thesiger, one of Wingate's Gideon Force commanders – perhaps they even stood next to each other at some point). Howell was greatly impressed by this African Emperor and on his return to Jamaica started preaching the good news that would become Rastafarianism. Though his and Bob Marley's lives overlapped (both died in 1981), Howell never adopted dreadlocks.

Selassie, then, was also a man with charisma. Together with the prophet Wingate they began to persuade the tribal factions of Abyssinia that the Italians would be beaten. Picking their way over the thorn-studded hill country with camels and mules, Wingate's tiny force gradually accumulated local support. In the end he marched into Addis Ababa with Haile Selassie. The remnant of the Italian army in Ethiopia were harried and tailed by four or five Europeans, 140 Sudanese and a few hundred Ethiopians. The Italians abandoned a ravine of the Blue Nile that they had been trying to hold and scrambled towards the mountains in the north. One of the few Europeans with this part of

Gideon Force was Thesiger, later to achieve fame as a desert explorer. He was given orders by Wingate to hold a narrow panhandle of land between two plateaux. Meanwhile Wingate attacked from the rear. In total over 8,000 Italian troops surrendered. In the end, more than 20,000 members of the Italian colonial army would be imprisoned. The Blue Nile was again in British hands. Wingate had given people at home something to cheer about, stiffening the resolve of the rest of the allied troops engaged in the north African campaign.

We know so much about the mad Wingate not just because of the fame of his bum-cooling eccentricities, but because in his tiny army (when you exclude the Ethiopians and Sudanese) there were some exceptional men who accompanied him: as well as Thesiger – Laurens van der Post and Hugh Boustead. Thesiger would go on to become the iconic explorer of the 1950s. Van der Post would write exceptional books about his time in Japan later on during the war – which were turned into the David Bowie film *Merry Christmas Mr Lawrence*; he would also become a confidant of Prince Charles (who, in true six-degrees fashion, would later meet the former terrorist Sadat while on his honeymoon with Princess Diana). Boustead had been, with Almásy and Wingate, a member of the Zerzura Club; he had also been on two Everest expeditions.

Thesiger was described by a fellow officer as 'donnish and shy, though with a taste for hard living that surpassed even Wingate'. Van der Post amazed everyone by his constant activity and his abilities as both vet and medic. He was the only one who did not lose camels in the stony passes above the mile-deep canyon of the Blue Nile. He was also an overt Christian, though this translated into action – helping others – rather than preaching, and was naturally welcomed.

These interesting and unusual men were attracted to, and driven by, the ultimate oddball, Orde Wingate. Wingate brought a religious perspective to war. For him every war was a holy war. If he couldn't make it into one he wasn't interested. In Palestine, David Ben-Gurion said that Wingate, as a passionate Zionist, taught the Jewish settlers everything they needed to seize control of the land that would become Israel. In a highly dramatic few years Wingate would go on to attempt suicide, found the Chindit army in Burma, catch typhoid from impulsively drinking water from a flower vase in Iran (this was part of the Gideon mentality he favoured – Gideon picked only men who lapped up water like animals rather than decorously using their hands to scoop it up) and ultimately die in a plane crash before the war ended.

It doesn't always do to find out too much about your heroes. When I met Thesiger in his London flat about ten years before he died he told me that 'Van der Post "went off", started believing his own propaganda. Though he was a very nice man when I knew him earlier.' Thesiger himself was the model of self-deprecation. He cooked me boil-in-the-bag curried rice and showed me the giraffe thighbone he had used to beat off a mugger in Kenya.

On another occasion I met the last-surviving member of the Zerzura Club – the ninety-five-year-old Rupert Harding Newman. When I mentioned Hugh Boustead's name to Harding Newman (who also knew Almásy), he said, 'Awful man. Horrible little man.' What could one say? Explorers, war heroes, 'great' men, all drawn by the river for one last Nile adventure ... oddballs, freaks, misfits who had found at last their place in the scheme of things.

5 · The high dam changes the score

The river that flows into a lake only reaches the sea by changing its nature to become clouds and rain. Sudanese proverb

And, with a little help from such men, the British won the war. Roll credits. Oh, second feature: how they lost their empire.

Had those wonderful British hydro-engineers become too bogged down in the Sudd? Lost their political nous? Or transferred their will to rule people to simply ruling water? Whatever the complex reasons, by the late 1940s the empire was being dismantled and the dwellers on the banks of the Nile were seizing control of their inheritance. And one way to do this was to build a great big dam.

I started researching this book with an undisguised hatred of the Aswan high dam. Now I am not so sure. It is almost too easy to see in the high dam evidence of hubris, of man yet again overstepping the mark. The more one studies the effort expended by the Greek Egyptian Daninos to get the thing even on to the agenda – petitioning constantly from 1912 to 1956 through three wars and a revolution – the more one begins to admire the sheer breathtaking scale of the project.

In order to be built on a gravel and sand floor the dam could not be a straight barricade of concrete, as the lower Aswan dam is. Instead it took advantage of the burgeoning discipline of soil mechanics effectively to become a false hill, a new part of the landscape. Just as the Suez Canal was an attempt to rework nature and physically change the world, so too was the Aswan dam.

Seen from the side, the Aswan dam looks like a very shallow-angled pile of gravel. It extends upstream for over half a mile, which gives the highest point a gradient of less than 1 in 5, which is very shallow indeed for a dam. By spreading itself so far back upstream the dam provides a gradient for silt to be deposited and a substantial guarantee against any kind of collapse. It had always been a concern that the dam might be blown up by Israelis during one of the several conflicts in the later part of the twentieth century (the latest coming in 1998 with a threat by Avigdor Lieberman, who later became Israeli Foreign Minister, that Israel might nuke the Aswan dam; he was later sacked for fraud). But, short of a direct hit by an atomic weapon, the sheer size of the dam beneath what is visible on the surface militates against its easy destruction by force.

As mentioned earlier, recent studies on silt deposition have also proved surprising: far less silt has been deposited than was previously estimated. Almost certainly the slowing of the Nile before it reaches Lake Nasser causes silt to be deposited further up the river, effectively reducing the river's gradient and speed before it enters the lake. Though it is estimated that the lake will be silted up in 500 years, the truth is that no one knows how long such a thing will take. And now, with work proceeding on an enlarged dam on the Blue Nile, and the Atbara already dammed, silt production will be reduced still further.

The engineering problems of the high dam were not just about logistics and shovelling vast amounts of crushed rock into place. A suitable curtaining method was needed to extend far below the dam to stop water seeping through the river bed and appearing on the other side – as constantly happened with the barrage, which was also built on sand (the rock bed of the Nile being miles deep in the delta, as we discovered earlier). The curtain devised at Aswan was an Egyptian engineer's invention – a series of 'pipes' of grouting – cement and sand – were injected 135 feet down to the granite bed beneath the dam (a granite bed which German engineers set at eighty-five feet until their work was checked and they were fired for a sloppiness which could have resulted in a disastrous flood under the dam). The curtain of closely set vertical pipes extends down to the granite base. This forest of underground pipes spreads fully the width of the river and sixty-five-feet upstream from the dam base. Water may seep under the heaped-up sand, rockfill and gravel of the dam but it cannot penetrate through the curtain.

The Nubian people in Sudan lost half their town of Wadi Halfa. Many were relocated to a new town, New Halfa, very close to the Atbara river dam. Were they happy? Is anyone happy at losing their ancestral land? Though they had suffered before when the first dam was built, and suffered again when the dam was then raised, it appears that resignation rather than anger was their response at being moved.

The Egyptian contractors building the dam – who worked with the Russians after a purely Russian attempt with Egyptian labour had failed – claimed that fifty men a year were killed in the building of the structure. One of the most high profile who died was the obsessively driven chief engineer Amin el-Sherif. He moved permanently from Cairo and spent fifteen or more hours a day in his office at the new dam. He started a system of night shifts in the summer to overcome the heat. Powered by generators attached to the old dam, electric floodlights lit a hellish scene of excavators and dumper trucks working through the night to build the vast earthwork. El-Sherif had to report every day how much rock had been shifted, and he managed to bring the project, which had been a year behind, up to speed by the end of 1962. His job done, he took a drive to survey his work from the comfort of his black VW Beetle. When the car didn't move, workers went to investigate and found the fifty-year-old el-Sherif dead at the wheel.

Though Germans, Britons and Russians all like to claim the credit for the Aswan high dam, it was made possible by Egyptian labour and, though this is often overlooked, by a very high level of Egyptian engineering skill.

6 · Cold War blows on the Nile

A man struggling with a brave man cannot afford to be shy.
Ethiopian proverb

The dam captured the public imagination. Students volunteered in their hundreds in 1963 to help keep the dam on target. Here was Nasser not only reclaiming the Suez Canal but giving his country a giant project in which everyone could join in and celebrate. But though it was later represented to the world as a Russian-financed Egyptian triumph, in fact this most recent attempt to control Egypt's Nile had its roots in the broken dreams of Britain and its new competitor on the world stage – America.

The standard story is that Nasser got British, American and World Bank backing for the dam, then, when he bought arms from the Czechs, the deal was off. But this Cold War cover actually obscures the truth. For a start, the deal with the Americans and the British was made *after* the deal for Soviet-controlled arms. The British could live with Nasser buying weapons from the Eastern bloc as long as they still controlled the Nile.

This was the plan: by agreeing to finance the dam the British hoped to retain control of the Nile basin for years to come. They had been virtually bankrupted by the Second World War but insisted on punching above their weight by relying on their special relationship with an increasingly irritated United States. The World Bank and the US would provide most of the cash for the new dam, but the British expected to benefit the most by dominating the agenda about Nile control for the next two decades – which is how long they thought the dam would take to build.

The Americans, meanwhile, were busy with their own covert plan – still ongoing – which was to reduce British influence in the Middle East and replace it with their own. By capitalising on the need of the British to appear as important as they had been before the Second World War, the US leviathan used British nous and intelligence to kick-start America's own infiltration of the Middle East – partly to secure oil reserves and partly to find a market for arms sales. Rivalry between the US and the British would outstrip concerns over Soviet influence and find its arena in the lengthy distractions of the Nile basin.

The Americans, with a wealth unimaginable to cash-strapped 1950s Britain, were pushing ahead with several hydrological aid projects along the length of the Nile. Called Force 4, the project had an energetic manager operating in Ethiopia, much to the appreciation of Haile Selassie and the disquiet of the British. Restored to his throne by the eccentric Wingate, Selassie, with the help of Force 4, was reviving that long-held plan to divert the wealth of the Blue Nile away from the apparent wastage of Egypt. The British were concerned but could do nothing about it.

They relied on American cash elswhere and had to agree with American plans or prepare to be ignored.

Nasser had come to power by ousting the General who had been the face of the coup against King Farouk. He had capitalised on American dislike of British power in the Middle East to build strong links with the CIA. These links would help in the financing of Daninos' project, which had come to his attention almost as soon as he and the other so-called Free Officers (including Sadat) who led the coup had come to power.

First, to the applause of the Americans he had to rid himself of troublesome leftists who wanted to claim the revolution for themselves. Then it was the turn of members of the Muslim Brotherhood to be purged. There was nothing in this behaviour to suggest someone singing from the same songsheet as Moscow, and the Americans were pleased (the CIA were represented in Cairo by Miles Copeland, father of the former Police pop star Stewart Copeland). It did not seem unreasonable to offer Nasser the money for the dam, even if he had just bought some cheap weapons from the Czechs. Better them than the British, who were getting very annoying about their right to determine Nile policy for the world.

The British incentive to go along with the high dam was simply the offer of a seat at the table. There had been initial consternation that the old 'century storage' plan (creating a storage lake big enough to withstand a century's worth of variable rains), involving the great central African lakes, the Jonglei Canal and the Blue Nile, was to be ditched or side-channelled perhaps. In an abrupt about-face the British under Prime Minister Churchill, sixty years almost since he fought in the River War, still believed they could turn that seat on the dam committee into more influence than their financial contribution suggested. And the dam would take years to build, especially with all the conditions that were attached to the loan.

Naturally Nasser refused to abide by many of the conditions and the British were content to let the project 'languish', since they knew that an even bigger stumbling block would be the loss of Sudanese Nubia when Lake Nasser began to flood. It seemed inconceivable that Egypt would ever reach an agreement with the Sudan, and it was part of the work the British had assigned themselves to broker such a deal, naturally extending their control in the region at the same time. Churchill had seen Britain go from being the masters of the Nile to waiting for scraps to be thrown their way. All the folly of Suez and its aftermath can be traced to the forgivable inflexibility of men quite suddenly down on their uppers.

Nasser, following in the footsteps of Muhammad Ali (who claimed that Machiavelli had nothing to teach him about cunning), outfoxed the British by establishing contact with the Sudanese military. These men, some of whom had trained in Egypt with Nasser in earlier times, felt a strong kinship with the Egyptian revolution. In 1958, the Sudanese army staged a coup. When Sudan's Prime Minister stepped down they took over, and with great goodwill came to a quick agreement with Nasser: Egypt would pay £15 million compensation for the flooded land of Nubia (later Sudan would receive another £30 million to redress all the destruction caused by the dam).

There was now no negotiating role for the British. It also looked as if Nasser would get this thing done far more quickly than anyone had anticipated. Without the British there to be humiliated and bullied there wasn't much point in the Americans financing the dam – and they already had control of the Blue Nile through their Lake Tana project. Nasser suspected they would cancel – and as a test he suddenly agreed to every one of their stringent conditions for the loan. Getting wind of this the Americans promptly cancelled their offer, leaking the information that it was because of Nasser's turn towards the Eastern bloc. Which was a prophecy easy to fulfil. The Russians, however, found Nasser no pushover.

That it was British–American rivalry that sank the loan to build the Aswan dam is supported by the disastrous reaction to Nasser's emboldened occupation of the Suez Canal zone in December 1956. The Americans continued to back Nasser against the humiliated British. Now control of both the lower Nile and the canal had slipped from the seventy-year-long grasp of the dying British Empire. The British Cabinet discreetly discussed the suggestion that the Nile could be turned off at the Owen Falls dam, which had been opened only a few years previously. But beyond petty revenge there seemed little point in punishing the wily Nasser this way. He had won.

In Cairo, on Zamalek Island, incidentally reclaimed from the Nile by the work of William Willcocks, there stands the famous Cairo Tower, with its revolving coffee shop at the top. It wasn't revolving when I went up, but the view was certainly worth the slightly scary lift ride. Although the Americans withdrew their finance from the Aswan dam, they did pay some development money at the beginning. It was with this money that Nasser built the Cairo Tower. (There is now a better, and higher, revolving restaurant, good at night, on top of the Grand Hyatt on the tip of the old island of the River Mamluks, Roda. Ride up to the fortieth floor and you'll be able to see almost the whole of Cairo).

7 · Countdown to an assassination

Unless the vein is cut, blood will not flow. Egyptian proverb

The Nile flows on. Even after being dammed at Aswan, it flowed on. The Israelis have used the dam's vulnerability to their advantage; at regular intervals, as we have noted, a hardline Knesset member will mutter about the possibility of bombing the high dam. But they never will. Even supposing that it could be blown up, if the dam broke millions would lose their lives: in a country of over eighty million people, at least sixty million live within the floodplain of the tsunami that would be released by a destroyed Aswan dam.

Sadat understood the possibilities of coming to terms with Israel. In his historic manoeuvring to regain control of the Sinai he saw that the humiliating defeat of the 1967 Six Day War, when Jordan, Egypt and Syria all lost territory, though tragic for the Palestinian people, was only a problem to the Egyptian people if they could not regain their own lost territory. Sadat managed that with the Egyptian–Israeli Peace Treaty of 1979 and gained the Nobel Peace Prize into the bargain. From being described by Henry Kissinger as a 'donkey' he went to being hailed, also by Kissinger, as a statesman 'as great as Bismarck'. But it would not save him from being killed.

Sadat was truly a Red Nile president. Being half black African, previously a source of some shame, he could now exult in his Africanness. He saw the Nile as one way of linking all the African nations behind a world player: Egypt. He chose Aswan as his favourite winter quarters, symbolic centre of the Nile and the gateway to Africa; he would be Africa's voice. Indeed Sadat became so enamoured of foreign affairs that he neglected what was happening alongside the banks of his own river in Upper Egypt – in Sohag and Asyut and a hundred other Nileside

towns which resented modernisation when it resulted in higher prices
and wealth for a tiny minority. In 1977, as Sadat met with the Yugoslav
leader Marshal Tito in Aswan, guests asked why there were burning
buildings in the town. Anwar Sadat had to telephone his own office
in Cairo to discover that his people were rioting over the rise in bread
prices.

The building of the dam dragged Egypt into the industrial age,
through increased power supply and a revolutionised irrigation system.
What this meant were huge changes – increases in crop yields, but also
changes in the pattern of work. Men from Upper Egypt could earn far
more working in factories in Helwan (no longer an idyllic spa town, but
now, in what some thought an assertive act of irony, transformed by
Sadat's predecessor into the steel and concrete town of Egypt, a place
later to be synonymous with causing respiratory ailments rather than
curing them). These Upper Egyptians and displaced Nubians found
work as *bawabs*, or doormen, stonemasons and drivers in the rapidly
expanding cities of Cairo and Alexandria. Here their natural conserva-
tism was seen as potential fuel for the long-running power plans of the
Muslim Brotherhood, a banned Islamic organisation that would later
achieve Egyptian office in the 2012 election.

Modernity along the Nile had meant prosperity to some; to others,
as we have seen, it had brought bilharzia, disrupted age-old agricultural
practices and replaced a culture of punishingly hard work followed by
complete rest with one that demanded constant slogging away. It was
a brusque welcome to the modern world. Though Muhammad Ali had
instigated this turn to modernity, and the British had accelerated it, it
was Nasser who made it ugly yet took the credit; and it would be Sadat
who would take the blame. He was a thwarted actor who had posed
on the world stage as a ruler of the Red Nile; he would die as one, shot
down by his own men who believed he had led them too far away from
the traditional virtues of an imaginarily idyllic Nile existence ...

It was a few days before the 6 October Parade in 1981. The parade
was held every year to celebrate the Egyptian victory in the 1973 Yom
Kippur War with Israel (a victory in as much as it kick-started the return
of the Sinai, Sadat's aim, but tactically only successful in that the Egyptians crossed the Suez Canal). The day actually commemorated the successful storming of the Canal, further memorialised in the name of a
bridge across the Nile and a new suburb of Cairo, 6 October City. The
parade always lasted several hours as trucks of soldiers, tanks and gun

carriages drove past Sadat and his generals and other prominent folk seated in a raked concrete stand.

That day an irresistible package had arrived for the President of Egypt, from London. Sadat was excited to discover that his Savile Row tailors had completed the new uniform ahead of time. In his Nileside residence in Giza, which had been sequestered from a former army officer of the old regime, Sadat took his time trying on the new uniform. It was exquisitely tailored, a slim fit that in comparison made his Vice-President (and successor) Hosni Mubarak look positively stodgy, despite being ten years younger. Sadat found that the attractive lines of the slim-fit uniform would be spoiled by wearing a bullet-proof vest, so three days later, when dressing for the 6 October Parade, he left the vest at home.

Sadat, like many world leaders, had a soft spot for theatrical uniforms and decorations – he had uniforms designed by Pierre Cardin as well as by Savile Row tailors. In his youth he favoured cropped hair, a monocle and a swagger cane. Once he was president he carried his field marshal's baton like a pharaoh's *ankh* and crowded his chest with medals. Only recently he had awarded himself the green silk 'sash of justice'. His sense of being an actor was enhanced by all the hours of TV footage in which he starred. He increasingly liked to spend hours alone watching the old video tapes, the filmic record of past triumphs: the address to parliament after the 1973 war, his journey to Jerusalem, his several TV appearances in America. Most of his day would be spent in interviews, almost all filmed. At night he would eat a light dinner, meet more people, then from 10 o'clock onwards watch imported and recently released films (even before they reached the censor) in his private cinema. He usually watched two a night, though he would be snoring before the end of the second. By the time of his assassination this latterday Pharaoh was living largely in a bubble of his own design.

On 6 October, Sadat's last day had begun like most in the latter years of his presidency. He had gone to bed fairly late after watching a film. He had risen around 9.30 a.m. and eaten his preferred mix of honey and royal jelly followed by a cup of tea. Later he would munch on low-fat cheese and a low-calorie wafer. Sadat ate little as he was careful about his weight. He had then taken some light exercise and received his daily massage.

Sadat had announced a few days earlier that he would ride to the parade in his open-top Cadillac. He had taken to making trips in this car (which was reminiscent of the vehicle that saw the end of JFK), yet it seems the assassins never contemplated an assault on the car, possibly because the route would never be disclosed beforehand. Certainly Sadat, like most world leaders, was safest when there was no prior warning of his movements. With no warning he could wander through a crowd without protection – assassins need days and days to prepare. Somehow the profession does not attract the spontaneous type . . .

Striding out of his palace in Giza, he left behind on the side-table his field-marshal's baton. Later, Jehan Sadat, the President's wife, would say she had seen this as a bad omen, though quite how bad she had had no idea.

Not that there weren't security measures in place. The Americans had contributed over the years, it was rumoured, $20 million to keep Sadat from being killed. This included signals intelligence and an elite unit trained by the US to deal with any attempt on his life. But in keeping with Sadat's desire to appear at his most uncluttered before the TV cameras of the world, the elite unit were banished to a position behind the reviewing stand where they would not get in the way of the cameras. The President was like a Hollywood superstar – if it wasn't filmed it didn't exist. When Prince Charles and his new bride Diana were passing through Egypt on their honeymoon in August that same year and asked that a picnic with Sadat not be filmed, he was annoyed and puzzled. His love of appearing on television certainly did not make him popular, as he imagined it did.

The head of the Presidential Guard, a brigadier general, explained later that his main task had been making sure that only those invited took a seat on the stand and that the food and drink consumed by Sadat were checked personally by him. The old habits of Nile rulers die hard. It was as if they were protecting against medieval assassins armed with poison when they should have been aware of twentieth-century ones armed with rifles and grenades.

It took some hours for the truck carrying the killers actually to pass the stand where Sadat was sitting. This reviewing stand, which looks like a small section of a football stadium, is situated on the main road to the airport. It is still there, though the chipped concrete at the front has long been repaired. You can see that the front edge of concrete is very thick, and if one lay down on the inside up against the wall (which is what Hosny Mubarak did) you'd be perfectly safe from gunfire. Sadat, however, did not consider such a manoeuvre until it was too late.

At the parade stand Sadat asked Bishop Samuel of the Coptic Church and the Sheikh of Al-Azhar to sit next to him. It was for the cameras, of course – the man of power living in peace with the two religions – but it was the right message to be sending to an Egypt intent on division; it was, however, too late to heal the rifts already about to engulf President Sadat. The religions did not fare equally in the face of fate: Bishop Samuel was killed but the Sheikh of Al-Azhar survived.

The gun lorries, roofed over with metal hoops designed to hold canvas, came to a halt. It's easy to see why no one suspected anything. On the footage shot by a news team covering the event it looks like a breakdown. The plan had been to recruit the driver as part of the team, but this had proved impossible. It was Khaled, the leader of the assassins, who came up with the simple expedient of ordering the driver at pistol point to stop the lorry. It hardly swerved out of line. Here is yet another instance of the colossal luck that attached to this attempt. Everything was lining up against Sadat, as if destiny had determined that his time, indeed, was now up. If, as had been planned, the lorry had been under the care of a sympathetic driver it would have driven closer to the stand than it did. From where it stopped to the stand looks a good seventy yards. By driving this distance adequate warning would have been signalled to Sadat that something was wrong, and he would have been able to duck down behind the concrete barrier of the stand. (One wonders how simple it would have been to install a long window of bullet-proof glass running the length of the concrete lip – indeed Jehan Sadat was behind such a windowed balcony at the side of the main stand.) Sadat, of course, would never have agreed to this, as it would have looked too much like hiding. There was also the precedent of Nasser, who, after an assassination attempt, had not flinched, had in fact issued an on-the-spot invitation to any future killers, announcing his fearlessness of death.

Khaled, the lead assassin, came from the small Nileside town of Mallawi. Mallawi not only had a sizeable Coptic Christian community, it was a bishopric of the Coptic Church. It was also famous as a place that the Holy Family visited on their journey into Egypt. Kum Maria, not far from Mallawi, is revered to this day as the spot where the Virgin Mary stepped ashore during the journey of the Holy Family up the Nile. Yet it is precisely in these towns with a significant Coptic presence that the terrorists of the Egyptian Islamic Jihad proliferated. With the uncertainty that comes with modernisation, age-old disputes were again visited as the 'real cause' of current problems.

Khaled was a successful student. Though not clever enough to enter the elite arm of the air force, he still qualified for officer training with the artillery. Ironically, one indeed of many ironies, had he been an air force pilot he would not have been in a position to take Sadat's life.

For a year, ever since the big crackdown by Sadat on everyone who had opposed him in word and deed, but especially word, there had been open talk – if such a thing is possible – among clandestine groups that the President should be assassinated. Killing a ruler is prohibited by most interpretations of the sayings of the Prophet, but the new younger firebrands of the Islamic jihadist movements took their inspiration from the hypocritical Mongol Muslim rulers of the twelfth century who would drink alcohol and eat pork while professing to be followers of Islam. Baiburs had defeated such Mongols, so it was seen as legitimate to take arms against a leader who was not a 'real' Muslim. A book written and privately printed by an imam called Farag Atiya extolled this viewpoint.

That Khaled would ever read such a book or even meet its author was again an unlikely coincidence. Khaled wanted to get married (history would have been very different if he had done so) and in order to do so needed a flat of his own. While wandering around the neighbourhood of Boulaq he noticed someone addressing the faithful with vigour and enthusiasm at a nearby mosque. This was in 1980, a year before the assassination. Khaled approached the preacher, Farag Atiya, hoping that the man might help him find a flat. Farag realised that this young army officer was just what he needed. He befriended him and gave him a copy of his book, *The Absent Prayer*. Khaled was one of the very few actually to get a chance to read this book, because when it came to the notice of Colonel Zumr, the originator of Islamic Jihad in Egypt (and the world), the precursor of Al-Qaeda, Zumr declared (in the days before the internet and the anonymity which that provides) that the book was inflammatory and would serve only to arouse suspicions and get people arrested. So 450 or more of the original 500 copies were burned.

It wasn't the sole reason for Khaled's conversion, but, rather like that select few who read the first Harry Potter novel when it came out in a tiny print-run and then felt superior, Khaled, having read one of the rare fifty originals, felt honoured. He now knew he wanted to serve the cause.

On 23 September his chance came, though again he sought to avoid the final act. He was summoned by his commanding officer and told to lead the 333 Artillery Battalion's eleven gun carriages during the 6 October Parade. Khaled asked to be excused. He had already told his family that he would be returning to Mallawi for 8 October, which was the religious ceremony of Eid el-Adha. His commanding officer was adamant – he would have to lead the gun section of the parade. This would place him at the front of eleven lorries towing 131mm guns. At that moment Khaled knew his hand had been forced by fate. Given his commitment to ridding the world of Sadat, and given that he had tried to avoid this fate, this was an unambiguous message that the assassination was ordained.

Other methods of killing their leader had been proposed and rejected: an attack on Sadat's helicopter was deemed impossible as he always took three of the five that the Egyptian army owned (as long as he wasn't loaning them out to visiting movie stars – when Elizabeth Taylor arrived he addressed her as 'Queen', after her role as Cleo, and let her take one of his helicopters). Usually you never knew which one he was in.

An air attack on his rest-house next to the barrage (the very house, much adapted, that years before Mougel Bey and later Scott Moncrieff had directed operations from) was turned down by none other than Colonel Zumr on the grounds that death could not be guaranteed. Zumr, who hailed from the Nileside village next to the barrage, probably wished to spare his neighbourhood from being the centre of such an operation and the retaliation that followed. He would be arrested after the assassination and his life spared owing to his opposition to the attack. Zumr, who led an abortive uprising in the upper Nile town of Asyut, always believed that the shooting of Sadat was premature.

In another curious irony he would spend the duration of Mubarak's regime in prison. When the Arab Spring revolution took place in 2011 he was released. He then, after thirty years in gaol, announced, 'The coming period does not at all require armed struggle with the ruler.' That the man who imprisoned him, Mubarak, is now himself in prison is rather bizarre.

Khaled went to his mentor Farag Atiya (the hunt for the flat apparently long ago given up) and told him of the role he had been given during the parade and his conviction that this was destined to be the moment to take Sadat's life. Perhaps a factor that hardened Khaled's

resolve was that his elder brother in Mallawi was a member of one of
the fundamentalist groups picked up by security forces on 3 September
– twenty days before he received his orders to lead his section of the
parade.

Khaled asked Farag to find two accomplices. In two days Farag
rounded up three men including Muhammad Farag (no relation of the
other whose first name was Farag), 'the marksman', who had been the
army target-shooting champion seven years running. They all understood that 'an element of martyrdom' was involved. An element! This
was wishful thinking, or perhaps an acute perception to keep feelings
corralled, not let fear get in the way. All three must have known they
would die, but all three agreed that it was worth it. All of them were
either reserve or former soldiers doing civilian-type jobs and all had the
trademark thick beards of religionists. These were dutifully shaved off
before the mission. It was a curious enactment, *sans* irony, of the Arab
cautionary saying to the over-religious, 'I fear, my friend, that your
beard is so long it is now mounting a challenge to the hair on your
head.' So, beardless, but still bearded in mind, they moved ever closer
to their nightmare destination.

The one problem Khaled had was that the driver of the truck was
the only driver in the unit, so there was no alternative to him, and certainly he was no sympathiser to their cause. He was scheduled for the
parade and was indeed looking forward to it. Khaled's proposed solution was to give him a sleeping pill before the event and then take over
himself at the last minute. But when the conspirators tested a sleeping
pill on Muhammad the marksman it had no effect, so the plan was
abandoned. It was at this point that Khaled decided simply to force the
driver to pull over at pistol point.

The next obstacle was an order, indicative of Sadat's lack of trust
in his own army, that all ammunition and all firing pins be removed
before the parade. This caused Khaled some consternation, and with
some difficulty Farag obtained four pistols, several grenades and some
firing pins for automatic rifles. But it turned out that the collection of
each section's ammunition and firing pins would be conducted by the
section leader – Lieutenant Khaled. It was doubly fortuitous since the
illicitly obtained firing pins were obsolete and didn't fit.

Getting his three accomplices into the truck had also been very easy.
Despite the driver's interest in taking part (maybe because he got to
drive), the parade was not popular with soldiers. It meant hours of

sitting in the sun without food and water. So finding places in the truck was easy. One soldier who should have attended was ill, and two more had requested leave – and were rather pleased that they both received it. The necessary identification and paperwork were all drawn up by Khaled, as this was his usual job anyway with regard to his section.

Having replaced three members of his team with the assassins, Khaled hinted that these new men were from 'intelligence', possibly there to keep an eye on everyone else. When officer Khaled shared his food with the new privates under his command, his batman was so surprised that he assumed that Khaled was trying to curry favour with the intelligence men.

The day before the parade all units were camping in tents. Khaled arrived with a battered Samsonite briefcase containing the ammunition and the firing pins. A brigadier drove through the camp with a loudspeaker and announced that all arms were to be concentrated in special storage tents. Khaled detailed two of his new men from 'intelligence' to be in charge of section security. One collected the firing pins while the other guarded the tent where all the arms were stored.

On the day of the parade, 6 October, Khaled and his men rose at 3 a.m., ready to move out at 6. Khaled took four Egyptian AKM assault rifles – semi-automatic machine guns with a collapsible stock – from the arms store in the tent and loaded them in the truck, placing four hand grenades in a helmet covered by a scarf. To identify the loaded weapons when stacked with the others of his section he placed a piece of cloth in the barrel of each 'live' gun.

The order was given to move off. Here, again, Khaled was lucky as his truck was on the right-hand side of a column of three, nearest to the reviewing stand.

At the parade six Mirage jets roared overhead spewing coloured smoke from their tailpipes. Everyone who was there remembered this and somehow linked it with the assassination. (During the 2011 revolution the appearance of jets over the Nile at Tahrir Square also signalled the end of Mubarak's regime rather than, as he intended, its rejuvenescence.) It was at this very moment, which couldn't have been planned better since it was so perfect a cover, that Khaled's truck came alongside the parade stand. Sadat was at this point sitting down. Khaled pulled his Makerov pistol out and told the driver to pull over. The frightened man simply jammed on the brakes. Khaled did not try to argue, he just reached under the seat for the grenades and jumped out of the cab. He ran forward and at this juncture Sadat stood up, because he believed that this was part of the parade and the man approaching was there for a reason – to be greeted by his leader.

Khaled threw a grenade which landed in the stand at Sadat's feet but did not explode. At this point Sadat should have dived for cover. Khaled threw another. By this time Muhammad the marksman had stood up in the back of the truck and taken careful aim, resting the rifle on the metal sidepiece of the open truck. He started to fire.

Some survivors later said that the irregular rifle shots sounded like a backfire. And, from the evidence of the 2011 revolution, they do sound similar, the only difference being the slightly more contained sound of the AKM. But it is an easy mistake to make, especially when you are not expecting rifle fire.

The nearest member of the Presidential Guard was Brigadier Sarhan. He ducked like everyone else and spent some time telling Sadat to duck too. But Sadat remained standing even when it became apparent that he was under attack – one interpretation is that his outsize ego just couldn't comprehend his impotence. He reportedly shouted, 'Mishma'oul! Mishma'oul!' (Outrageous! Outrageous!) at Khaled before finally falling over. It was as if he believed so much in his own power that mere words of disapproval would stop the assassin's bullet

A wave of panic swept over the 2,000 people in and around the main stand. Many later said they had believed that the jets were also attacking, that they were part of a co-ordinated assault. In the stand everyone shrank lower as Khaled approached, firing continuously. A third grenade exploded, and Muhammad and his fellow assassins jumped down from the truck (quite a height) and ran forward, firing from the shoulder. Khaled stood right in front of Sadat pumping round after round into him, though later reports suggested it was a ricochet and not a direct hit that killed him. He was hit thirty-seven times. Khaled reputedly shouted to Mubarak and others near to Sadat to get clear, that he only wanted to kill the President. For a good minute there was no opposition to the attackers. In fact Muhammad the marksman was not only uninjured, he managed in all the confusion to get clean away. Of the other attackers, Khaled Islambouli and Essam el-Qamari were wounded and taken prisoner – and beaten very badly. Both received cracked skulls and had their knees broken during interrogation. The fourth member of the team, who had elected to come on his own initiative, was killed in the attack. (It was at his house that the assassination team met and, though Khaled had asked for only two others, he was allowed to join.)

Sadat and seven others were killed and there were twenty-eight wounded.

In the footage of the assassination, as the firing continues you can see chairs being thrown towards Sadat in a vain attempt by the former Prime Minister Mamdouh Salem to protect him. Very soon after the firing had finished, Mubarak can be seen being hustled away to safety. Already people knew that Sadat was dead and were recognising Mubarak as the new leader.

Muhammad, the marksman who got away (on the film footage you can see the assassins scarpering like schoolboys out of an orchard where they have been caught pilfering), made his way to the house of his relatives. Perhaps he believed that the puny uprising co-ordinated by Colonel Zumr in Asyut would spread through the nation. Instead the security forces did what they always did and worked their way through his relatives until they found him. It is interesting to speculate that had Muhammad had an exit strategy in place – say a Bedouin smuggler willing to drive him across the Libyan border – he might well have escaped for good. Instead, he waited for a revolution that didn't happen and found his martyr's end along with Khaled Islambouli.

8 · Murder bros

All rivers want to join each other. Men say they do but live their lives differently. Sudanese proverb

Even assassinating world leaders can be a family business. Khaled's brother attempted to assassinate Hosny Mubarak in Ethiopia in 1995.

Mubarak only narrowly avoided being killed by Muhammad Islambouli and other fellow terrorists. Outside Addis Ababa his quick-thinking driver, faced with gunmen, did a perfect reverse-skid turn and hightailed it back to the airport where the presidential jet was waiting with its engines running.

Incidentally, it was the security chief Omar Suleiman (who briefly took over after Mubarak was deposed) who saved Mubarak from a further attack by ordering the return to the plane. A little down the road was a second wave of assassins planning to finish the job. By the irony that invades the whole warp and weft of political intrigue along the Nile since the beginning of time, Khaled's brother Muhammad had been one of the causes of Khaled's involvement in the attack on Sadat in the first place. Khaled, it may be remembered, had taken up arms partly because of the incarceration of Muhammad. Now Muhammad had adopted the family trade against Mubarak. In all, Mubarak would survive six assassination attempts.

As for the assassins, their eighty five-year-old mother Umm Khaled Islambouli unrepentantly told an interviewer in 2012 that she was 'very proud' of Khaled and Muhammad. Muhammad lived for years in Tehran, 'where they named a street after him'. In an even less repentant move, his daughter married Osama bin Laden, and she and her child now live in Qatar. Muhammad eventually tired of Iran and flew back to Egypt. For a few years he was in prison, but he is now free and living in Egypt along with his mother.

One woman: two world-class assassins and a great-grandchild to the world's most wanted terrorist. Children of the Red Nile.

9 · Do not forget this is a red river

A visitor is like a passing flood. Ethiopian proverb

Egypt is the gift of the Nile, wrote Herodotus (though my pal, the satirist Mahmoud Zeydan, calls Egypt 'the git of the Nile'). Egyptians consider the Nile synonymous with Egypt. It is of course bigger than that. Our story has moved up and down the Nile as the Red Tale has taken us. Sometimes Egypt has been the focus, at other times Sudan or the very source regions in Uganda and Ethiopia. In the nineteenth and early twentieth centuries, the importance of control began to fragment as dams were proposed, breaking the river into sections. With the completion of the high dam Egypt entered a new phase of autonomy. For the first time in history, it was no longer dependent on the rains in central Africa and Ethiopia. But these places, the headwaters, are just as much the Nile. Indubitably they are part of the Red Nile, as the following horrific tale will show.

When a dead body falls in water the rate of putrefaction is altered, the 'extinction of animal heat' is accelerated, cadaveric rigidity sets in faster. And in creatures, including man, which are hunted to death, the onset of rigor mortis is especially quick. And these people were hunted to death.

But is this the right way to begin this story? Surely the fact that the place has been doomed before may be by happenstance, but happenstance is still reportable, still lives on in our minds. This place, a river medium sized, brown with earth-carrying water, is how it looks; a brown washing machine is its only significant waterfall, the Rusomo Falls, a short, compact waterfall, brown water narrowed down. This is where the only bridge over the Kagera was built, the bridge that carried so many to safety as they fled in April 1994. What went under the bridge, what went down the river, cannot be forgotten.

Especially by the people of the lake. The people of the river killed their friends, enemies, neighbours, pupils, masters, but the people of the lake only endured. They had endured already one disaster, they would endure another. The lake people who lived by the mouth of the Kagera inhabited a place known as the landing, Kasensero landing place. A beach on the edge of Lake Victoria, a mile or so from the exit of the brown river, the Kagera, which snaked back into the diseased heart of Africa.

Kasensero was where the first case of 'slim' was diagnosed in the lake regions of central Africa in 1982. The first case of AIDS in Uganda, Kenya and Tanzania. Though the disease had been fomenting in the Congo since the 1930s, it is believed, and had transferred to Haiti (many Haitians worked in the Congo in the 1960s and 1970s), it was from the doomed lakeside village of Kasensero that AIDS spread like the plague it was into Africa.

It was never a pleasant place. The landing attracted displaced people, drifters, people unwelcome in their own villages. The fishermen were often drunk, it was said. They made full use of the large number of prostitutes in town. From these people, from this town, the disease spread across the lake into Kenya and Tanzania and down the highways of Africa to Zambia and Zimbabwe. It spread north to Kinshasa and Entebbe.

Though it was known as 'the AIDS village' for many years, it is known for other reasons. You would think that AIDS would be enough suffering to pile on to one settlement of tin-roofed housing, dirt roads, a poorly stocked clinic. Even now with the penetration of AIDS so complete in Africa, Kasensero has only three nurses working full time at its AIDS clinic. There are families of twenty-four children looked after by a single grandparent.

But God, when he sought to punish Job, did not stop after round one. He kept going, piling it on. When God sought to punish the Pharaoh he sent plague after plague, and he turned the river red with blood. This is what happened to Kasensero. This is what happened to the Kagera river after the events of 6 April 1994.

People resort to biblical terms because they seek a story to explain what has happened. The Tutsi were the children of Ham; they were, supposedly, of Hamitic origin, cattle people who had drifted southwest over centuries from their homelands in Ethiopia. They had found the ripe jungle gardens of Rwanda and Burundi to their liking. Bringing their cattle they had displaced easily the original pygmoid people, the Twa. As for the other immigrants, the Hutu people of Bantu origin, they formed a society of a kind with the minority Tutsi. There was some intermarriage and a blurring of differences, but the conventional wisdom was that the Tutsi were blessed with straight noses and paler skin and cattle-owning tendencies while the peasant farming Hutu generally put up with things.

The reaction of the Twa is not recorded. There are no books written in Twa, a secret, almost lost language, since the Twa in modern times mainly use dialects of Bantu languages such as Rundi and Kiga. Down to only 1 per cent of the population by 1994, they are losers in history that we never hear about.

The bridge was the crossing place. Across the bridge came the Belgians in 1916, taking over from the Germans before them – short-lived masters – and adding their own twist to the Hutu and Tutsi saga. They encouraged the rift between the two people, had the tribal group noted and stamped onto identity cards. After independence in the 1960s these cards would remain.

The river would get clogged. It is not unusual in the case of a violent death for a 'cadaveric spasm' to occur, when the victim has been subject to terrible excitement and nervous exhaustion. It is not uncommon upon the field of battle to see the death expression, the expression at death retained rigidly in the face, the weapon still grasped tightly in the hand. Some of the bodies were like that: still clutching the hand of a child, also dead, both floating down the brown river, now red. Many were without heads, many of the men without genitals. The people of

Kasensero saw all this, for they were the ones called by God to bury the murdered ones, mainly Tutsis, and Hutu who were friendly to Tutsis.

The numbers will always be debated. The African scholar Alex de Waal puts the figure at over 750,000 murdered. Not that the Tutsi were without their own history of violence. In one of the least reported mass killings of recent times, 100,000 Hutu in Burundi were killed by Tutsi and Tutsi supporters in 1971. Was it something about this place, the very geography of it? Both of these peoples had come from other areas in Africa. Only the Twa were true natives. There is no record of the Twa being anything other than peaceable jungle dwellers. Maybe they should have been left alone. A fond hope; we would all be best off left alone, but we are not, nor ever will be.

Just below the bridge at the Rusomo Falls the river looks like the River Wye in Wales after a heavy rain. Day after day a body a minute went under that bridge – sixty an hour, 1,440 a day, 10,080 a week. Week after week. Many smaller tributaries of the Nile run into the Kagera, including the most distant source. It is hard not to see this act as some kind of symbolic desecration of the Nile itself. It is said that the Hutu were sick of the Tutsi claim to be from Ethiopia. They wanted to send them back to the place where the Blue Nile meets the White.

Rigor mortis sets in particularly early in the feebly developed muscles of the newborn. When a body has been decapitated rigor sets in slowly, perhaps after ten or twelve hours – but then it persists for more than a week, even when the weather is warm. Some of the bodies washed up on the beach at Kasensero could be carried to their graves with ease, still stiff as boards.

But many more did not wash up, they washed *into*. The Kagera is the true source of the Nile and its current is such that there is a perceptible movement from its mouth to the outflow at the Ripon Falls, now of course submerged. This slow current propelled bodies far into the lake. They began to raft together, rotting in the Equatorial sun.

But before putrefaction comes lividity. The skin loses its elasticity and the flesh its firmness, and the blood, once evenly distributed, gravitates towards the lowest-lying parts. Hence the deep violet tint of the occiput and the back, the places where the lungs and brain rest and slowly fill with blood. Sudden death is characterised by extensive lividity – when there is not substantial blood loss during the killing. When the arms and head have been removed, there is less blood to discolour the corpse, however violent the death.

The bodies begin to rot. One to three days after death a greenish discoloration of the abdomen. The eyeball becomes soft and yields to pressure. Out on the lake you see the inflated balloon of a belly, and then another, and another in the far distance. On one knee perches an interested crow.

Three to five days will see the genitals, if they are still present, a dirty brown-green. The whole of the abdomen a deeper shade of green now. Patches of green appear on the back and lower extremities. Gas, as we have seen, bloats the abdomen and now forces bloody froth from the mouth and nose, on those bodies still possessing these features.

After a week the odour of putrefaction is well developed. It is an odour none can ignore, nor forget. It lay in miasmic waves over the lakeshore. Even the fish, depleted in recent years, were driven away. That is why the people of Kasensero started to fetch the bodies in from their rafts of rotting flesh and bury them. As one resident put it, 'Fish was losing market so we took it upon ourselves to bury them at different points.'

This is still a contested matter. It is thought that over 6,000 bodies were washed ashore or removed from the lake, and buried at Kasensero. The monument erected there to the slain of the Kagera is for only 3,000. Out in the lake, the ones that did not get driven back by wind and waves and were taken by the current, who knows how many disappeared into the depths, the relatively shallow depths, of Lake Victoria? (Not to mention those who crossed the lake and went over the Bujagali Falls.)

The people went over the bridge escaping to Tanzania. Underneath, the bodies were thrown into the river. Genocide and rivers have an ancient history. During the Spanish Inquisition, Protestants in the Netherlands had their backs broken with iron rods and then were thrown into the river. It was found, in the era before crematoria, to be the fastest way to get rid of people who disagreed with you.

The inner organs have their own rate of decay. The brains of infants rot quickest, followed by the stomach, spleen and liver. The adult brain is next. Slower to rot are kidneys, bladder and pancreas. Last to putrefy is the uterus. After ten days the cornea has collapsed, the veins have become red cords visible beneath the surface, the anal sphincter has relaxed. Soon the skin will begin to peel off.

Machetes and AKM and AK47 rifles kill more people in Africa than any advanced form of despatch. In the lake the bodies have been killed by even simpler means: hoes, adzes, heavy wooden poles tipped with iron.

10 · Rehab's story

Seven times one may fall and seven times rise again. Nubian proverb

The bodies, some Rwandans said, would be flushed down to the sea. The several dams and the slow-moving Sudd would make this unlikely, though particles of the dead would, over time, pass through Egypt to the sea. The Nile had been desecrated before, and will be again, though naturally one rebels against such a thought.

The particles of the slain pass by and the Egyptian fellahin do what they have always done, they dig. They dig canals, they dig levees, they dig crops. And they measure out their water with the pipette mentality of a scientist – when they aren't sloshing it all over the place, perhaps in the remembered excess of the highest flood.

After Sadat's assassination Egypt was ruled, as we have seen, by his lucky Vice-President, Hosny Mubarak. Lucky – he took a shot but survived, which of course guaranteed that no one could seriously blame him (though conspiracy theorists have tried very hard). But despite greater and greater wealth being generated through construction projects, mainly in Egypt and the Sinai, things did not become easier for the poorer people of the delta and the banks of the Nile. Discontent rumbled on. Was the Nile itself guilty?

The impact of the dam was being felt in a way no one had predicted. Perennial irrigation had brought an increase in food. But, as already noted, the lack of flood silt meant far more fertiliser was needed. Food production rose but so did its cost. The dam electricity allowed for greater modernisation. More food and better healthcare saw the population soar, a population increasingly kept from the available wealth of Egypt. Sadat's 'open door' policy was continued and brought more and more imported goods into Egypt as well as tourists to the new boom town of Sharm el-Sheikh (which Mubarak loved so much he lived there most of the year). The country also saw a slide into greater corruption and the rise of a class of ruthless businessmen capitalising on their connections with the Mubarak clan.

Many who chose not to participate left Egypt to earn money to send home, one of the few ways they could improve their standard of living in a country where the *wasta*, or influential connection, was necessary to get a job. Indeed, after the Suez Canal, gas production and tourism, remittances from workers abroad are Egypt's largest foreign-currency earner.

Before I came to Egypt I was living in Oxford. We had two very small children, and my wife arranged for a girl to come out from Egypt for a year to live with us and help out. This girl was Rehab. She spoke no English. She was twenty-two, a bit spotty, and wore platform shoes that my mother-in-law threw away because they were so smelly. Truth be told, Rehab didn't like washing that much. Her room, my old study, had a stuffy, fetid but not entirely unpleasant smell. She had a small TV, supplied by us, but she never watched it. Around 8.30 p.m. or 9 she would go to bed and sleep and that was that. Not that she got up early – she didn't, unless I knocked on her door, which I did every day.

Rehab, when she smiled, had a lovely face. If you caught her unawares, her face in repose was distorted into a grimace, grim indeed. She looked after my newly born daughter with infinite patience, walking her around and around the garden to keep her sleeping. Because she knew no English my two-year-old son was soon speaking Arabic. Then Rehab herself picked up odd words of English and used them with great inventiveness. She would sit on the doorstep, the *mastaba*, as they say in Egypt, and engage passers-by in conversation. In one year she got to know more people in our street than we had in the preceding three. With less English than I have Italian, which is practically none. Always cheery and smiling, always keen to make contact, say hello. She used to go to the supermarket and target people who looked as though they might speak Arabic. She actually did find a woman who lived two streets down – an Egyptian who had married an English Muslim convert. Rehab got to know her daughters – slightly bewildered English girls in headscarves who spoke no Arabic. Rehab met a Mexican girl and asked us if she could invite her round, as a treat. The street was her preferred meeting place, though the Pakistani lad got a bit too interested and had to be dissuaded. Rehab was supposed to be engaged to a young man back home. This year away was to earn enough to buy a washing machine, a great ambition. She also loved charity shops, of which there are a goodly spread in quantity and quality in affluent Oxford. She bought vast quantities of children's clothes for her nieces and nephews and a great trunk which, when we took her back to Egypt after her year with us, took up two and half baggage allowances.

Rehab had had jobs far worse than ours. In fact our job, though limited in terms of Arabic-speaking opportunities, was heaven compared to the job she had done for two years in Lebanon where she had been locked indoors when the owners went out. She had worked since she was twelve, though she had been to school, off and on, too. She could read and write. I always wondered, though, about her set scowl – until she told me of her first job.

'I was twelve and so they sent me to the fields. There I was given the worst job because of the noise: watching the pump. Every hour or so I had to fill the pump with fuel oil. If you let the pump run dry they beat you hard because it breaks the pump. You sit for twelve hours watching the pump, you can't do anything, not even play because of the noise, but you do. But you have to be careful not to let the pump run dry, though I did once.'

The Nile has always had its *sakieyehs*, waterwheels driven by buffaloes treading a circuit, and *shadoufs*, to raise water into a canal or, often, to rid a place of too much water. But since the building of the British dam in 1902 the activity has become year round instead of being concentrated around the three months of the flood. And the flood raised water levels, so, without it, the height the water has to be moved through increased. This problem was exacerbated by the building of the high dam, but was then 'solved' by the introduction of the ubiquitous diesel pump, which is the sound you hear as you walk through the delta, over the perfect manicured fields without a scrap of space wasted.

We had an allotment in Oxford by the river and when we arrived Rehab borrowed, with smiles and gestures, a spade from our eighty-year-old neighbour (we'd never dream of borrowing tools) and set to making a raised bed to grow carrots. Egyptian towns and villages might look a mess, but, as I often repeat, Egyptian gardens are beautiful. They lay out the vegetables with just enough aesthetic awareness to make looking at the fields a pleasure. In Holland you see the same careful use of each square yard as you do in Egypt, but not with the same flair, the mixing of a few flowers with a crop – to combat pests, they will tell you, but also adding to the look of the fields. The habit is carried with them. Police recruits will water and care for a raised bed next to their shack of corrugated iron, where they are supposed to watch the road; farmers' boys, they stoop down to water plants and make tea on a three-stone fire when their superiors are absent. If you walk by the Nile in central Cairo, in Maadi, or Zamalek or Imbaba, you'll see market gardens of elegance and beauty that seem to contradict the searing ugliness of the concrete and cars around you. Why should that be? Another Nile mystery. Anyway Rehab was a natural gardener, fast and efficient and looking for things to keep her busy.

You read about agricultural yields, which have undoubtedly gone up since the creation of both dams. But without the Nile silt the Egyptian farmer had to manure his fields for the first time ever, now he uses chemicals, and the dependence on fertilisers is complete. Then there are the problems of declining fish yields, growth of algae, canals blocked with vegetation, bilharzia – all this, and yet for me it is the image of that smiling girl, her face, when in repose, turned into a set scowl by the requirements of the machine.

11 · A load of Toshka

Touching the teat will lead to milk stealing. Ethiopian proverb

Sadat's legacy lived on, appropriately, in a canal that bore his name. The Sadat Canal, like the Joseph Canal of yore, was designed to carry away Nile water in excess of what could be stored. Satellite pictures from on high initially showed a string of three lakes growing, through run-off from the main lake, on the western side of Lake Nasser. But funny things happen to lakes out in the desert. The third one has dried up, it seems; the others are clogging up with reeds and swampland. The problem, as Willcocks would have seen immediately, is not irrigation, but drainage. The lakes have no exit except the sky. Like Lake Qarun in the Fayoum they are just getting siltier and saltier, slowly dying.

But Toshka in Egypt means more than these run-off lakes. Toshka, also known as 'Mubarak's Pyramid', was the last desperate attempt by a Nile leader to alter destiny. His, his country's and the Nile's.

Toshka was the most grandiose scheme ever conceived by an Egyptian government (if you discount a British plan in the 1930s to flood the Qattara Depression west of the Nile delta with seawater to drive a waterwheel perched on its edge, around the place where the battle of Alamein was fought). Toshka was nothing less than an attempt to create a new Nile, a second valley running parallel to the old Nile. By diverting water along canals from Lake Nasser, the oases of the Western Desert, it was planned, could be linked up to become vast new hubs of industry and agriculture. Some 20 per cent of Egypt's population would move there. In one swift (well, rather slow) move, but only one, all of Egypt's problems could be solved. Population growth, lack of land, increasing food demands, job requirements.

Just as the Aswan high dam was designed to solve all Egypt's problems in the 1950s, and, of course, didn't. The idea was a fantasy projection by a president who knew he had done little but maintain the status quo since the death of Sadat. A president streetwise enough to know that the ever younger population were not going to put up with jobless overcrowding for ever. But Toshka was not the right answer. Those children who watched, as I did, in 1997–8 the endless propaganda films on the TV about the dream of Toshka, who read the children's books by Egypt's leading writers commissioned to encourage belief in the fantasy (one book had a resident of the 'new' valley writing to her cousins in the 'old' valley saying how large her house was, what a nice garden she had). Those children were in their twenties in 2011. Instead of living the Toshka dream they stoned the police and started a revolution.

By 2005 Toshka was beginning to falter. The 'Toshka' brand of cigarette (yep, they even produced one) became unavailable. The road to 'Toshka City' remained a road to nowhere. Water was pumped into the Sheikh Zayed Canal, but it went nowhere too; even now the canal is still 40 miles short of the first oasis, Baris. I once made a camel trip with a Bedouin from Baris (which, with added irony, is the way most Egyptians say 'Paris'). He told me that in the summer the temperature is often over 45 degrees, too hot for a slow-moving, fast-evaporating canal. The desert, too, complicates things. Its own aquifers mess with the irrigation run-off, causing a general rise in salinity. My Bedouin friend told me, 'There is a good reason we mainly grow dates and olives on irrigated land in the desert. Everything else turns the land to salt.'

Toshka vegetables reach rich folk's supermarkets such as Metro and Carrefour. Some are even exported abroad. Only private agricultural companies can make the land pay. The smart money is not made by feeding the Egyptian poor but by lining the pockets of the already rich. Which would be OK-ish, if the money trickled back into Toshka – but it doesn't. No sane Egyptian would want to live there if they had the choice. In 1997 we heard all about the schools and hospitals that would be built – but so far, none have been.

The 'second phase' of the plan was quietly dropped seven years ago – in this phase two million acres were supposed to have been snatched back from the desert as prime agricultural land. The quantity of reclaimed desert is controversial. Some claim 16,000 acres have been cultivated. Others declare it is as shockingly low as 1,000 acres.

In short, it's a mega-project disaster. According to the US State Department, which has, through various forms of aid, funded some of Toshka, the budget for the whole fiasco is an incredible $87 billion. But the publicly available figures for the Egyptian budget don't even mention the Toshka project.

The Nile deceives. The Nile gives dictators grand ideas and then refuses to let them come true. The bankruptcy of Mubarak's vision for Egypt becomes the literal bankruptcy of the grand plan. The new President, the Muslim Brotherhood candidate Muhammad Morsi, brought to power by the revolution, soon turned his back on Toshka, partly because of its association with Mubarak, but partly because it's the sane thing to do. The Brotherhood have said, 'The answer to our problems is not in big projects. It's about simple things ... affordable housing and investment that leads to jobs.'

The year 2005 was when the Toshka dream died. It was about this time that Mubarak handed over a lot of the decision making in Egypt to his son Gamel. From 2005 onwards I noticed Egyptians getting gloomier and gloomier. The rich got richer through corrupt construction deals (Gamel's version of a big plan) and the poor scurried around in a world that was speeding up and getting poorer at the same time.

12 · Revolution on the Nile

The blade of the axe does not cut stone. Egyptian proverb

This is how it happens: a country comes into existence because of the bounty, the sheer good luck, of a flood, a summer flood that makes it easy to grow a surplus of grain. The country becomes rich, waxes and wanes, is invaded and repulses invaders. Then important people decide, like the proverbial farmer and his golden goose, to kill the goose that lays the golden eggs. They dam the river. This means, at first, that more food is grown, more people can be supported, and, very easily, the population increases. So the river is dammed again and even more people can be fed. But the cycle cannot go on for ever. What has happened is that the dynamic of the river has been replaced by a static model of economic growth – a model that is clearly unsustainable in such a country as Egypt. More and more people have nowhere to live; they migrate to cities and attend school and have no jobs. These are the people of the revolution. They will bring down the leader of the country, the spiritual successor of the man who dammed the Nile. It is a poetic revenge by history, perhaps.

It starts with something you don't believe. All wars and revolutions and disasters have this moment of disbelief. It can be monstrous – when I saw the Twin Towers collapse I thought at first I was seeing a movie, having accidentally been switching across channels. Or it can be a minor disbelief, nothing out of the ordinary. I was round at my pal Roland's house. He's an artist and so is his wife Lucy, who teaches at a big international school with many rich Egyptian kids in attendance. She came home from school that Monday and said, 'All the kids are saying tomorrow's protest will be a big one.'

I hadn't given it any thought and my wife Samia – she's a journalist and should know, it's her job after all – turning to speak from her glowing laptop that night said, 'It'll be nothing. It's all talk.'

It was the biggest demonstration in Egyptian history.

It was then I knew that things were not going to go away. If a Tuesday could bring out that many people, a Friday would be, had to be, enormous.

Again, you don't believe it even as you are watching it. But you believe the sounds of your neighbourhood, you believe the sight of young lads running past your house holding iron bars and sticks and bottles half full of petrol.

Egyptians had never risen against their own leader before. Nasser had ridden an anti-British wave, not an anti-royalist one. Before that it had been, since Cleopatra's time, just a succession of invasions, one taking over the country from the last, while the fellahin kept managing the canals and irrigation ponds and *shadoufs* and worrying about the flood. Clever Egyptians had always managed to rise to the top, and Egypt has a way of making anyone who stays there into an Egyptian.

As for the Egyptian people themselves: 'You can't keep them out,' mused Professor George Scanlon to me one evening at the Italian Club shortly before the revolution happened. He meant it in the broadest possible sense: not just the pressure of an increasing population demanding its share, but a kind of Egyptian safety valve. Egypt has a way of bending the rules so that a kind of institutional inclusivity always develops. When too many poor relations have wangled their way into somewhere exclusive, rich people move on and start another club, school, beach resort. But it's temporary; the process is inexorable and works to level the country and iron out what might be constricting and damaging differences in another less flexible culture. Scanlon, Professor of Islamic Art, had excavated the ruins of Fustat, the first site of an Islamic Cairo, and had lived in Cairo since the late 1940s. Now he had just retired after the American University moved their campus from Midan Tahrir to way out past the ring road in a reclaimed bit of desert. Ironically a bigger, uglier campus, for more students, further reducing its exclusivity.

It seems that Egyptians have managed to find some sort of accommodation with their rulers since the beginning of time. Now it looked as if they were changing their tune and going for a knock-out blow.

Before the revolution we'd moved away from our Nileside apartment, though I was still writing there. Our new place was in New Maadi, a good half-hour's walk from the river. Quite close to where our apartment block was built were found remains of 'Maadi man', a prehistoric ancestor of the ancient Egyptians who built the Pyramids. Maadi man had lived off the bounty of a stream that fed into the Nile, now called Wadi Digla. Symbolically, perhaps, the dry streambed is being laid with giant pipes to function as a sewer for the new towns being built in the desert. Walking to work I can follow the sewer to the river, which sounds worse than it is.

When the revolution happened, you could hear from our apartment (which is on the third floor) the guns firing on the Corniche. My wife had wanted to join the protests as she's Egyptian, and sympathised with the idea of removing Mubarak. That he was gangster, a reasonably benign one, but still a gangster, I knew. It was obvious. In a gangster state the poor and the weak are victimised by the police. In a healthy police state like Morocco it is the rich who are targeted for tips and small traffic bribes. In all my time in Egypt, driving a high-status 4x4 I had been stopped only once by a policeman – and then it was to ask for a lift. In Egypt, if you had a big 4x4 or a Merc and possibly a BMW, then life on the road was one long green wave ... but not for much longer.

I was in two minds. I knew Mubarak and his rich cronies were corrupt, but I had benefited, a bit, from their corruption. I had written travel brochures for the Egyptian Tourist Board, which derived its money from revenues in Sharm el-Sheikh – which was built up with Mubarak money and favours. I used the fast internet in Cairo that was a direct result of decisions taken by the Prime Minister – a creature of Mubarak. As had many of the rich kids currently protesting against him. It was all confused in my mind. I saw then that it is always young people and angry or retarded older people who make revolutions. A normal person, as they get older, sees how incredibly complex the ecosystems of politics and reform are. Everything depends on everything else. Mubarak may have ripped off the Egyptian people in one sense, but he had kept them out of war for thirty-eight years. In the Middle East that was quite an achievement. I had benefited from the high-speed internet this Prime Minister, a tech head, had brought in. It was faster to log on in Cairo than in Oxford, I found. I had benefited from the ATMs and the ludicrously cheap gas – 10p a litre, less for diesel. That gas had fuelled cheap desert holidays when we burned over the dunes with ten jerry cans in the back to be refilled without even thinking. Ten jerries in the UK would cost about £300 to fill. I had benefited, but I had also lost out. The new rules allowing lax lending had driven up the new-car population and the overall car population by about 300 per cent in many areas. The road along the Nile was heaving night and day with cars. The accidents were horrendous. In rich areas like ours everyone's kids had cars too. An empty street I used to walk along was now impossible to park in. To walk along it was like striding against the madness of crowds, mechanical crowds. I'm whining about the traffic and there's a revolution happening outside my window.

The word itself vouchsafes the experience. What exactly is a revolution? Do the means of production have to change hands? Must the leaders of the *ancien régime* be executed? I think about this, I honestly do, as I lie awake hearing the noises of the revolution outside and the telephone ringing as friends and family call in to report what is happening outside their apartments. Not that it seems quite like a revolution on that first Friday. Some kind of crackdown is feared, must be forthcoming. The hysteria mounts and we watch amazed to see police cars and trucks burning, on TV, all over Cairo.

I wake to hear the doorbell ringing: it is Umm Sabrine, who comes every Saturday to clean our flat – come rain or ... revolution. Umm Sabrine, the mother of Sabrine, has crossed the city from her neighbourhood in Sayeda Zeinab, a poor area where, she tells us, the locals have torched the notorious police station, one famous for torturing and abusing suspects. Many of the attackers came from the slaughterhouses in that area and the police ran away, she said, after a short battle. I don't even know Umm Sabrine's name, no one seems to, though I've met Sabrine her daughter who isn't half as nice. Umm Sabrine must be about seventy; she complains of her health but she keeps working every day of the week. She's always early and has no fear of heights – often you'll see her leaning right out of window like a rock climber, keen to get it clean on both sides. She is illiterate, and has the gift of the gab and good timing. She is humble but assertive – a good combination. She tells me in all seriousness that her daughter has seen the Suzanne Mubarak Library on fire and the shops of Nasre Street looted and destroyed. The coward in me vied with the curious soul. I set out to investigate.

Everywhere was quiet, though in the distance there was the occasional sound of gunfire, which you get to be an expert on very quickly because, when people are free to fire guns, they do so much of it that the nuances of the noises made by each weapon become burned into your consciousness. I used to be a little disbelieving of war-movie lines in which 'incoming' was dissected with skill, both type and direction. I now saw it was a lot easier than bird watching, there being far fewer species of gun and their reports all so distinctive. The workaday metallic flatness of Kalashnikov fire. The resonant firework boom of a howitzer. The backfire sound of a shotgun. I'm not sure if I heard any pistol fire. I congratulated myself on these observations, this coming up to speed with weaponry and war.

I encountered very few people at first but passed more and more as I approached the roundabout in Nasre Street – where a day later a policeman would be murdered, a policeman who had long been reviled for taking money from people, it was said, a man whom I had driven past many times without wearing my seatbelt (an offence in Cairo only since the rise of Mubarak's son Gamel). Certainly a revolution is a time for settling scores. But right now there were no police about. None. In a police state that's a strange experience. It felt unexpected and full of possibilities; it reminded me of waking up as a child in England and finding it had snowed in the night. The police had left their vehicles, abandoned them. Many were burned. They had given up the little pit-stops they favoured, with the spiky anti-drive barricades and a tin roof to provide shade. All these huts had been destroyed, often down to the foundations. One place I had always rather resented having to step off the pavement to go round, resented the cocksure officer who sat in his black Toyota pickup with a raised covering for troops in the back – his little place was completely destroyed. It felt mighty good to see that, and, I noted, without police everyone was much more polite. Much more.

In the only supermarket I could find open there was a great queue for food. A woman, well dressed, well made up, the type who would have pushed in or been haughty and rude, was self-effacing and polite – normal actually, fear had made her normal. I thought now why revolutions are so intoxicating. The social order is reversed. The last shall be first and the first shall be last.

13 · Roland and the jets

Wood that is wet from the river must be forced to burn.
Ethiopian proverb

I am at Roland's enjoying the view from his balcony. I am not sure why he is living in Cairo, maybe to get better views than you would living in England. Like me, he's after the material. He mainly paints landscapes of the desert and sometimes cityscapes, which he makes look like views of desert cliffs and escarpments because often they include such features, the Moqattam Hills blending into the Citadel and north Cairo quite effortlessly. Roland is a big beefy bloke, painter as welder would be the type, not uncommon. In fact he told me he used to earn money as a welder before his art began to sell.

Like many artists Roland has an interest in the military, in planes especially, but tanks will do. He tells me about a battle between loot-ers and the army he watched yesterday from his balcony. The wall of the satellite area opposite (one of Egypt's major telecom centres with giant satellite dishes angled up to the universe), which the looters tried to breach (usually defended by policemen dozing in prison-style watchtowers, now by the army, but for three days by no one), is pockmarked with AK74 rounds and quite a few holes from the heavy machine gun on the tank – maybe 12.7mm, Roland speculates. The holes are big, but even the 5.54mm rounds can make a hole in concrete if they hit at the right angle. So the message is: don't expect to be safe behind a solid concrete wall unless it's more than three inches thick, maybe a lot more. The looters, or 'thugs' as everyone calls them (from the direct translation of the Arabic word *baltagi*), were armed with AK74s too. The army killed two of them and hauled one other away. The rest escaped.

'Killed them?' I ask.

'Yep, they certainly looked pretty dead from up here.'

This is both good and bad news. Good, primarily. When the main source of trouble is the thugs, which it is, then any deaths are a relief. If you have a family at home behind a barricaded door armed only with a headhunting *dao* I picked up in Nagaland and a couple of kitchen knives and a wooden sword, then any deaths among the bad guys are welcomed. We know they are the bad guys because they are attacking protesters whose only crime is to sit down in Tahrir Square. A bunch of kids mainly, some of whom I know quite well like Amr, who was there the night they were charged by horses and camels and said it was a lot more frightening than it looked. He said the government would have won if only they hadn't been so stupid as to close off all the exits. Intent on a total slaughter, they missed victory and ended up defeated.

The army are considered the good guys because, though they aren't arresting Mubarak, they are stopping the thugs from attacking ordinary people away from Tahrir. In the square they just watch and wait.

The thugs are armed gangs recruited by businessmen over the previous decade to protect their interests. When a shop has a dispute in Cairo with another shop, they send round a few blokes with iron bars to break up the shop front and dish out a few beatings. They also throw stones and even plant pots. *Our* plant pots on one occasion when the internet café below us was targeted by the furniture store above it for hanging a sign too low and thus blocking the internet café sign. The fight was thick and furious, but no real bloodshed despite the mean and deadly-looking iron bars everyone was wielding. That's the thing about fights, wars, struggles – the number of injuries seems disproportionately lower than the armaments would suggest. Except the First World War, the Hutu–Tutsi massacre and a few other counter-examples. I suppose I am talking about war as a means and not war as extermination.

The thugs have been swelled by prisoners let out of Tora Prison, which is just over the autostrade from where we live. Over the concrete flyover and down about half a mile of leafy suburban streets and you're at our house. Gangs of thugs were repulsed by homeowners on Saturday night, the biggest night of battles for our neighbourhood. On Sunday morning the army put a tank on the crossroads a hundred yards from our street. A big khaki tank. The people carried sticks and knives to defend their shops and homes and set up roadblocks. This is a posh neighbourhood. I always spoke English at the roadblocks and usually someone smiled. Egyptians have a great sense of humour, possibly the world's best, when they are not scared. When they get scared they lose their sense of humour totally. I once drove through a checkpoint without permission in the Sinai and dared crack a joke to the fuming officer who stopped me. Normally he would have laughed, but in the Sinai they are scared and it was only because I had my son with me that I wasn't arrested and given a hard time. As it was, he shouted a great deal at me. Nervous. Scared. No sense of humour. I tell Roland as we look out and we agree that the English sense of humour, though vastly overrated, is not allowed to disappear when the shit hits the fan. It's supposed to flourish. You put a brave face on it. Actually I can think of several Egyptians who were cracking jokes the whole time, so maybe I am completely wrong.

But Roland and I are feeling like we have been in a war and it's a good feeling until we hear shots. 'Over there,' says Roland – we are both getting better at this game. Roland has his binoculars but we've both seen the movie. The glasses may catch the light, give our position away. 'Shall we go in?' I say. We go in and watch from inside through the open balcony doors. Why risk it? That's a revolution for you: you're always asking yourself, 'Why risk it?' So you end up holed up at home and not going out. Except it's perfectly safe outside, maybe even safer than before because there are far fewer cars.

In a car you feel safer until you see a hold-up, then you feel scared, trapped; you work out how to open the car door, roll out into the dust and leg it. You understand pretty early on why war correspondents keep doing what, on the surface, looks like a shit job. They do it for the *incredible* sense of newness you get when a country suddenly goes from normal to unfuckingpredictable. I walked out of my house, down towards the Mubarak Library. The street was empty except for a few burned-out cars, a police truck still smouldering and a few young men taking pictures of said truck on their phones. They all looked nice enough guys. The only scare was about five motorbikes each with two up roaring by. *Baltagis* ride bikes usually followed by a couple of Peugeots crammed with blokes. But they are gone. The Mubarak Library is fine. No looting, no fire, even the flag is still flying, and the two caretakers are wearing their blue and yellow uniforms looking wary but reasonably cheerful.

This incredible sense of newness, this feeling that you are an explorer in a new land, doesn't go away because every day there are new developments, new outrages and new signs. One day the US Embassy bus is attacked by a mob – stoned, the news report says. This sounds … terrible, until I talk to someone who was actually on the bus: one stone went through a back window and everyone is fine. But it's enough to convince even the diehard Americans to leave. I start to formulate a rule: if there is no local evidence of something reported then it's an exaggeration or an outright lie. Foreigners are being attacked, comes the report. I see no evidence of it in my neighbourhood, but then all the foreigners are leaving. Every day, in forlorn little convoys of microbuses and their favoured giant 4x4s. I can't help thinking, 'Fucking cowards, fuck you you arsehole businessman, you oil worker, you bank scumbag. You lord it over everyone but when the going gets tough you leg it! Fuck you!'

A day later I am enquiring about 'the last flight out' offered by the British Embassy, who, after they have ascertained that we are truly British, are very helpful in that understated, competent way the British excel at. If 9/11 had happened in Britain the emergency services would have got everyone out alive, one thinks on such occasions, though of course plenty would disagree and probably volubly too. The American in the airport I see blubbing is quite a sight. He is about fifty-five, as fat as a cream cake, cone-shaped in his Hawaiian shirt. 'I been here twenty-five years. Twenty-five good years,' he keeps blubbing. Come on, chum, put a sock in it. Obviously he loves the expat lifestyle and has made it permanent. The barbies, the big cars, the trips to the beach, horseriding round the Pyramids at dawn, getting to shout at people lower down the food chain than you. Put a sock in it, fatso, you'll live to play another day. But that is all in the future after my capitulation, my caving in, my fleeing from the revolution.

After leaving Roland's I increase my range to visit my pal Matthew, a librarian at the American University. On the way I hear lots of shots quite close. When I arrive at Matthew's he is packing up, ready to leave. I tell him things aren't too bad, but I am interrupted by the longest burst of gunfire I have yet heard. Really loud. It's hard to argue against in any sense. Matthew says the other American teachers agreed to defend the block by staying up all night in shifts. But they started drinking about nine and by eleven-thirty they were too pissed to do much, so they all went to bed leaving Matthew to guard the block (with the Egyptian doorman and his assistant) all night long. In a way it didn't matter since they weren't attacked, but understandably Matthew is pissed off, and tired. On my own building, because it is right next door to a mosque, there is no shortage of defenders. The mosque PA, which is bolted to a pole about a foot from our balcony, is now a source of comfort and support rather than loud call-to-prayer broadcasts at 5 a.m. The mosque relays information throughout the night, 'The thugs are in the next street. The army is at the crossroads. More thugs in Gazeir Street.' It is very comforting. Private enterprise is represented in our street by two internet cafés, frequented by small boys who lean on our cars and break off the wing-mirrors. The cafés have provided nothing for the community since I have been there bar a place for small kids to play shoot-'em-up games that they also play at home. In this time of trouble the cafés are locked down with iron gratings over the windows. The mosque never closes and is a real force for unity and help in the community when it is under attack. And I don't even like the caretaker at the mosque, a grumpy old devil with a huge praying mark on his forehead.

So Matthew gone, Roland phones and says he is going too. My wife Samia says she will stay and I should go. I say I'll stay, but the next day there are reports that more foreigners are being targeted downtown. It gets harder to argue against rumours when they seem to affect you personally. I start to rationalise. My son is refusing to go outside, whereas my daughter at least walks round the neighbourhood with me when I make a sortie. My son has built a barricade of all his toys which he calls 'the nest'. It seems perverse to carry on in this sort of scenario when we could be back in England watching it all on TV at his grandma's house, playing footie in the park and listening to audiobooks of horrible histories. So quite quickly I decide to go. Buying the tickets online (they've turned the internet back on now) is done in two ticks. We are off tomorrow, it seems, just like that.

14 · The author leaves his story

The axe does not sharpen itself. Sudanese proverb

I had been here seven years; I thought I would live here seven more, like the biblical lean and fat years, seven seemed a good number. Now I was leaving, running for home, another home.

'I've never seen a real tank before,' says my son on the way to the airport, 'and now I've seen nine.' Yep, real tanks with swivelling guns that line up on you as you approach, tanks at every motorway sliproad, on-ramp, watch out the army is out in force. The country is locked down tight, no one could move around the ring road – which we are using to get to the airport – if these tanks decided to trundle into the centre lane.

I made my plan, which was basically to go early but not too early. The curfew was until 7 a.m., or was it 8? No one seemed to know. I knew that first thing the local barricades were still up and people were tired and jumpy from a night of watching. By about 9 a.m. things were more normal, everyday life had started again. By 11 a.m. they were starting to get a bit nervous, which worsened until the curfew again at 3 p.m., or was it 4? So, tactically, the best time to be on the ring road was 9–9.30 a.m., even though our flight wasn't until 2 p.m.

Yes, compared to that SAS raid on Benghazi I'd been reading about only the other day it was tame stuff: being driven in a taxi by our trusted taxi driver Gamel, we were stopped only once by a fairly bored bunch of soldiers who wanted to look in the boot as we approached the airport. Everyone was alert in the car, waiting for something to go wrong. It felt exciting but also boring. The boring part of war is you can't get on with your own life. At first that's a giant relief, and I'm sure a lot of heroes are people whose own lives were tedious and irritating and war offered a welcome release. But my life, though moderately dull by any standards, still held a few attractions, and once all the fun of sneaking around and going through roadblocks and checkpoints and seeing what places had been looted and what hadn't, once that became, not routine, but somehow less interesting, then I wanted to get on with what I wanted to do, such as make a trip up the Nile to Luxor to investigate something I needed for this book, so though it was an interesting experience it wasn't a life-changing one. I wasn't about to drop everything and become a war correspondent.

Partly it was the fact that I didn't have the same instincts as war-correspondent types. For my friend Steve, who's been shot at by Israelis, carried wounded Palestinian children and made a film about the aftermath of the Jenin massacre, the revolution meant finding out what was really going on. The night snipers were defending the Interior Ministry; he kept going closer and closer until he passed a group bringing back a dead body. They begged him to go back but he went on. Then he met some more with another dead body who begged him even more strongly to turn back. 'That begging wasn't the normal kind of alarmist begging you get in Egypt, it was quiet, it had the ring of truth all right.' He turned back. But not before he had shot film of the hospitals and prowled around all over the place. And, unlike me, who look Egyptian enough until I open my mouth, Steve looks foreign, foreign and tall, and carrying a couple of cameras. But still without fear of going anywhere. My own inclination was to avoid all the places that others were going to. Why go to Tahrir Square? Why snoop around with a camera? It wasn't my country. It wasn't my revolution. I felt this quite strongly. I guess it meant I wasn't a revolutionary at heart, whatever my former protestations had been. I liked sneaking around my neighbourhood, seeing how *that* had changed, seeing what I knew and what was familiar, but I hardly ever went downtown these days, and anyway, what would I do? Chant?

I'm not a team player and revolutions need team players. I wasn't Egyptian and going to ogle seemed brainless. My wife went downtown to join the crowd for a day – this was the day, the turning point it now seems, when the *baltagi* rode into the square on horses and camels. She'd left before that happened, and it was lucky she did, because they locked the square down until 12 p.m. As I said, my pal Amr said he would have fled, everyone would have fled, if it hadn't been locked down. In a way, the army had saved the revolution by forcing the protesters to unwillingly face the *baltagi* ... and win.

After my wife had been downtown once, I said why go again? She wanted to go but I thought she'd shown enough solidarity. We need you here, safe and sound, I said. Several times. But still she was staying, to look after her mother and our apartment, or that was thrown in as an extra, a spin-off from looking after relatives. The apartment might be tempting. I had already lost my car – stolen one night from a supposedly safe place quite near to where the Carrefour hypermarket was looted.

Later, watching looters at work in Britain I realised what an amazingly well-orchestrated job had been done on Carrefour. Not only was the entire hypermarket relieved of all its goods but so were the surrounding shops. One cousin of my wife's who lived near by (it was his driveway from which the car was nicked) reported that the looting was 'steady like a breeze' all night long, trucks and vans and cars, no arguments, no frenzy, just slow and steady and methodical looting, leaving the hypermarket quite bare by morning. Later it emerged that the government had probably encouraged this highly public act in order to show that the country was under attack. Bad, greedy men are often assumed to be stupid, but they avoid being over-clever, over-sophisticated. Badness and greediness don't go with creativity and imagination, not long term; crooks tend to stick to what works and then repeat it. The bad, greedy men who ruled Egypt had worked out how the carrot and stick worked long ago. Letting a bit of looting happen would reward their thugs and let the world know Egypt was under attack. Why Carrefour and not, say, my street? Because Carrefour would be in the news. It was, in my experience, the only serious bit of looting that happened. In our own street I found a broken drinks machine. That was it. Then my mother-in-law was mugged – the day we left for the airport. It gave a new impetus to leaving, though surely it should have been her instead of me? Two guys, they looked normal, not angry, quite well dressed, zoomed up on a motorbike as we faffed around by our taxi making an obvious show of bags and suitcases. The bike was on us in seconds. I remember thinking What's that bike doing so close? – and then seeing my mother-in-law, who is seventy-six, fighting to hold on to the bag, but she's canny and let go without being pulled over. I ran after the bike for three steps, she ran for more. Impossible. I shall never forget the face of the bag snatcher. There was no hint of malice or even victory – simply the look of a job done, perhaps the job was a little harder than expected, almost a quizzical look; you'd never clock this guy as a robber in a hundred years. Looked like a shop assistant or a government clerk.

Gamel, our trusted taxi driver, started to make excuses about his heart, how he couldn't run after them because of his heart. I said no problem, I didn't run either. It was impossible, they were too far ahead, though every bike I saw from then on with two riding I scrutinised. I would not forget that face.

And then my trousers were stolen. First the car – my favourite ever vehicle, a short-wheelbase Toyota Land Cruiser specially adapted for desert travel with one-ton rear springs and no back seats etc etc. Every time I got into that vehicle it brought a smile of fun and satisfaction and growling macho potential to the accelerator foot – a rumbling menacing truck of a car on massive tyres ... nicked. Probably now it was in Libya or the Sinai with a rocket launcher bolted to the back. It did, however, have a few technical issues that needed fixing, and strangely I felt, after waves of nausea, a pinprick sensation of relief – I wouldn't have to get it fixed after all.

Not so my trousers. These were again my favourites. A pair of zip-off North Face trousers I had used for several desert rambles and had found excellent in every way. They had been entrusted to the boy who carried our wet laundry on his bike – in a plastic crate tied to the back – to the place where it was ironed for a small fee. He left his bike outside our building and asked the *bawab*, a man of immense laziness, to watch it for him. While he went into the shop, probably for cigs as he had, aged 13, just taken up heavy smoking. In England, agreeing to watch some-one's belongings for them is a risky thing. It carries responsibilities that can be a bit nerve-racking. Not so in Egypt. People agree to do things that would normally incur huge responsibility (like watching my car, for instance) with scarcely a second thought. If you want to understand Egypt, think of a nation of students: enthusiastic, humorous, up for a party, unreliable, gregarious, fun, not to be trusted with a car if it doesn't belong to them, nor trousers it seems ...

So during the revolution crime increased exponentially. In fact it must have gone through the roof if I experienced three crimes against me and my family in such a short time – a few weeks. In a way they were all crimes of opportunity – and Egypt had been such a safe place that one had become more lax than one would be in London. I'd say Cairo is probably like anywhere else in the world – London, Paris, New York. It's still way safer than Nairobi or Jo'burg.

Anyway the boy's bike was stolen and so were the trousers. The man who employed the boy and owned the ironing business agreed to pay me £50 for them. I knew he wouldn't. He did give me £20 though. Which was something.

Then we received a call (this was after I had returned to Egypt – we fled, stayed abroad for six weeks, realised things were fine, bar the thieving, and returned), a call from the police. They said they had caught my mother-in-law's mugger. This call came at 8 p.m. and was answered by my wife. She and my mother-in-law were instructed to go down to Bassateen police station to identify the bag-snatching criminal. 'Isn't it a bit late to be visiting Bassateen?' I said, but they brushed me aside in their eager desire for justice. When they arrived by taxi at the police station, however, they found it besieged by protesters of various kinds, all chanting, some armed. Inside, the supposed thief was a young lad of fifteen who, my wife said, looked incapable of any crime. But the tough detective said he came from the area's most notorious crime family and was guilty of many such motorscooter muggings. But he was not the man. Then, in a moment of supreme uproar, that very boy's family advanced on the station to break him out. The detective ran, unholstering his gun as he went, leaving my wife and her mother with the chained and grinning criminals. All the policemen were needed, letting off rounds above the protesters' heads, who were all now ducking, and fire was exchanged with the crime family before they scarpered in a fleet of broken-down Peugeot 504s. Before that happened, my wife and my mother-in-law, alone with the tethered crooks, looked in vain for a back entrance to the police station. Eventually one of the handcuffed prisoners pointed out a side-door. They left and were picked up by the same quick-minded taxi driver who had been circling the area waiting for them to leave. It was quite a night, all told.

15 · Baboon wars

The love of the baboon: in times of dew she carries her young under her, in times of rain she carries her young on her back. Sudanese proverb

In my journeys along the Nile I had seen hippos and crocs and learnt to be cautious of both. But I was most careful with baboons. A big alpha baboon, whatever the primatologists will tell you, can be real trouble. As we heard earlier, he can tear your head off he's so strong. I think the baboon gods of the ancient Egyptians or the earlier baboon cave paintings I had seen in the desert, were a warning. In a simple and direct way, now backed up by extensive zoological studies, they suggested what becomes of some men in power. Those cave paintings had baboon bodies and human heads, and some were headless baboons, the most dangerous kind perhaps.

They say an alpha-male baboon, head of the troop, top of the pile, has about three years of easy living. Then someone will try and knock him off his perch. Mostly, during his reign of power, a baboon just has to nod or grimace and a young buck goes scuttling away. His rep settles all. But baboons transfer in. New males arrive to take their rightful place and to widen the gene pool and squire the resident females. One of these dumb young bucks may have a go at the chief. He'll be beaten. That doesn't matter. People who derive their ideas about fighting from boxing don't realise that losing is the least of your worries. Losing means pretty much nothing. What counts is recovery time and the desire, or the foolhardiness, to have another go. Mubarak had no more recovery time; the Nile would soon have a new ruler.

EPILOGUE

I am finishing this book where I started, in my flat by the Nile looking out at the square of blue that is my touchstone, my connection with the river. Despite the unrest of the elections, the rumoured death of Mubarak (at the time of writing, in January 2013, in hospital rather than gaol, the same hospital in which my father-in-law had his pacemaker fitted), and the ongoing possibility of million-person demos in Tahrir Square, everything looks pretty much as I remember. There are still plenty of cars – too many, in fact – driving around. The shopping centres look full, and although tourism is about 30 per cent down foreigners still walk around in their sandals and shorts, bearing their small rucksacks. In short, the Nile keeps on flowing, however red things may become.

We have seen how this river has always attracted stories of passion and bloodshed, we have witnessed the way the Nile first burst its banks and flooded down to the sea only a few thousand years ago, we have learned that it is a relatively new river rather than something as old as the hills it flows through. Yet it is also the river of history, of human history, and the river of classical times, be they Greek, Roman or ancient Egyptian.

There is a real sense that writing the history, or biography, of a river will involve a tale both fleeting and vague. This could never be the case with the Nile. From biblical times to the battle of Omdurman the Nile has seen bloodshed and drama on a vast scale. How to render that down to a scale both readable and comprehensible has been our challenge here.

Recently I had the chance to visit the Sudan again. The plane, as luck would have it, flew into Khartoum in daylight and had to circle a while before landing. In a seemingly endless cycle we passed again and again over the place where the Blue Nile surges into the White. It was as if the Blue Nile was rolling back, something aged and inadequate, a shot in the white arm of an elderly relative, and, like the blood coursing through a junkie's syringe, the red flow was visible from thousands of feet up in the sky.

This cyclical rejuvenation of the river when the water is most needed, in summer, means that, unlike the ravaged Chinese rivers that are spent before they even reach the sea, the Nile is harder to suck dry, harder to kill. Man looks at the river, a picture of the dynamic reality of life, and tries to impose his static vision upon it. He tries to make that river into something tame and predictable, a resource to be milked. But a river, as we have seen, has a tendency to see red, to influence life in all sorts of strange and unpredictable ways.

A lot has happened in Egypt since the heady days of January 2011. After Morsi and the Muslim Brotherhood took power in a supposedly free and fair election, things began to change with increasing and depressing rapidity. It became clear – in Egypt – that the Brotherhood had one agenda for home consumption and another message they would broadcast in English via their effective PR machine. Carte blanche to clerics to incite violence against the Christian community and Shiite Muslims resulted in churches being burned and Christians losing their lives. Ties with jihadist groups – overt and covert – were strengthened and the Sinai descended into a chaotic no-go area. Jihadists were allowed to return from Afghanistan. Prisoners convicted of killing police in the 1990s were released. During the tolerated attack on the US Embassy in Cairo, Al-Qaeda flags were visible, as they were in many Brotherhood demonstrations. Power outages in Alexandria and Cairo were so lengthy food was rotting in the shops. Tourism was down 50 per cent and the Egyptian people had had enough.

It was not a narrative the West could understand. Wedded to concepts of commitment and consistency, journalists who 'got' the Arab Spring because it fitted their naive notions of revolution and renewal couldn't grasp the dual fact that a people would both want to be rid of a tyrant and also want to reject the 'democratic' results of a following election. First, of course, an election in Egypt is not the same as one in West Hampstead or Woking. In villages a 'big man' will offer chickens to people who vote for him, or drive around intimidating people into giving him their approval. In all probability the narrow win of Morsi was sanctioned by the army as the most politically acceptable result at the time. The army thought it could work with the Brothers and turned a blind eye to election law. But it was not to be.

30 June 2013 saw a spontaneous uprising by the Egyptian people against the policies of the Brotherhood. Even my 80-year-old mother-in-law attended the rally in Tahrir square. As one joke went: 'Nasser couldn't get rid of the Brothers, Sadat couldn't, Mubarak couldn't. But in two years they got rid of themselves.' Despite their social work, free clinics and legal services, the Brothers showed themselves more suited to agitation than ruling a complex modern nation. Crime had exploded; people could not find work.

But Westerners still persisted in imagining the Brothers were on the side of democracy – as they busily removed the basic framework that allows democracy to work and which we take for granted: an absence of lawlessness, an independent judiciary, the ability to feed yourself, equal opportunities for people regardless of gender or religion. As my friend Amr pointed out – and he was one of the keenest supporters of the 2011 revolution: 'If you need a gun to feel safe, if your family cannot go out at night, if you have no money – what use is a "vote"?' We have taken hundreds of years to refine our legal system and sense of law and order, justice and fairness. Universal suffrage is the cream on that cake – not the substance of it. To expect a people nurtured under centuries of benign, and not so benign, autocracy – as we have seen in the stories in this book – to suddenly embrace our highly developed notions of democracy is to ask and expect too much.

An interesting example I saw recently compared the worldwide export of the British invention of the roundabout with democracy. In Britain and France roundabouts work well. In other places they don't. In Egypt you need a traffic cop on each entrance of a busy roundabout otherwise there will be gridlock. In fact a straight intersection works better because at least one line will keep moving. We don't realise it but a roundabout is built on a whole set of assumptions about etiquette and fairness. If something so simple can fail under the slightest pressure, is it any surprise that cosmetic applications of democratic politics will also fail?

Tourists are coming back. The future is a little brighter.

A VERY SELECT BIBLIOGRAPHY

Books beget books and big books require a lot of begetting. In Cairo I was kindly offered the use of the AUC library by Matthew Ismail, while in England I used the Bodleian and the unique, invaluable, though sadly no longer free, interlibrary loan service. I bought many books over the years from the famed booksellers in Ezbekiya Gardens (which I wrote about in my book *The Extinction Club*, London 2001). I also found many excellent books in English and Arabic in the superb Kotob Khan, Maadi, Cairo (a great place to have a coffee too, by the way).

Rather than list over twenty pages every tome I consulted or from which I pulled one fact or insight, I've made a list of everything I have used that I think the reader will further enjoy. Some sections have more books recommended than others, but this is the accident of research rather than an unstated preference for that era. If you have some particular interest that may be served by knowing a more recondite volume not listed below please feel free to get in touch via my website: www.roberttwigger.com

One: Natural Nile

R.E. Cheesman, *Lake Tana and the Blue Nile*, London 1936
George Cotter, *Ethiopian Wisdom*, volume 1, Ibadan, Nigeria 1996
J.S.R. Duncan, *The Sudan*, London 1952
F. Clark Howell, *African Ecology and Human Evolution*, London 1964
H.E. Hurst, *The Nile*, London 1952
Richard Leakey, *The Making of Mankind*, London 1981
Patrick Synge, *Mountains of the Moon*, London 1937
William Willcocks, *Sixty Years in the East*, Edinburgh 1935

Two: Ancient Nile

Kenneth Bailey, *Jesus through Middle Eastern Eyes*, 2008
Wallis Budge, *The Nile: Notes for Travellers*, London 1890
Richard Carrington, *Tears of Isis*, London 1959
Amelia Edwards, *1000 miles up the Nile*, Leipzig 1878
William Golding, *An Egyptian Journal*, London 1985
Adrian Goldsworthy, *Antony and Cleopatra*, London 2010
Matthew Ismail, *Wallis Budge*, Kilkerran, Scotland 2011
Barbara Mertz, *Red Land, Black Land*, New York 1978
Barbara Mertz, *Temples, Tombs and Hieroglyphs*, New York 2007
Alan Moorchead, *The Blue Nile*, New York 1962
Alan Moorehead, *The White Nile*, New York 1960
Karol Mysliwiec, *Eros on the Nile*, New York 2004
Paul Perry, *Jesus in Egypt*, New York 2003
Anthony Sattin, *The Pharaoh's Shadow*, London 2000
Stacy Schiff, *Cleopatra*, New York 2010

Three: River of the Believers

Philip K. Hitti, *History of the Arabs*, London 1967
Robert Irwin, *The Middle East in the Middle Ages*, 1986
Joel Kraemer, *Maimonides*, New York 2008
Stanley Lane-Poole, *Saladin and the Fall of Jerusalem*, London 1898
Amin Maalouf, *The Crusades through Arab Eyes*, London 1984
Fatima Mernissi, *The Forgotten Queens of Islam*, Cambridge 1994
P.H. Newby, *Saladin in his Time*, London 1983
Ahmed Al Shahi, *Wisdom from the Nile*, Oxford 1978
Bradley Steffens, *Ibn Al-Haytham*, Greensboro, North Carolina 2007

Four: The Nile Extended

James Bruce, *Travels to Discover the Source of the Nile*, 5 vols, Edinburgh
    1790
Juan Cole, *Napoleon's Egypt*, Cairo 2008
Louise Colet, *Lui*, Athens, Georgia 1986
Max Gallo, *Napoleon*, Paris 1997
Al Jabarti, *Napoleon in Egypt*, Princeton 2010
Martin Kalfatovic, *Nile Notes of a Howadji*, London 1992

Philip Marsden, *The Barefoot Emperor*, London 2007
Francine du Plessix Gray, *Rage and Fire*, New York 1994
Anthony Sattin, *A Winter on the Nile*, London 2010
Ataf al-Sayid Marsot, *Egypt in the Reign of Muhammed Ali*, Cambridge 1984
James St John, *Egypt and Mohammed Ali*, London 1834
Ferdinand Werne, *Expedition to Discover the Sources of the White Nile in the Years 1840, 1841*, 2 vols, London 1849

Five: The Nile Damned

Richard Burton, *The Kasidah*, London 1974
Richard Burton, *The Lake Regions of Central Africa*, London 1860
Agatha Christie, *An Autobiography*, London 1977
Agatha Christie, *Death Comes as the End*, London 1945
Agatha Christie, *Death on the Nile*, London 1937
Winston Churchill, *The River War*
Cromer, *Modern Egypt*, 2 vols, London 1908
Matthew Green, *The Wizard of the Nile*, London 2008
Richard Hall, *Lovers on the Nile*, London 1980
John Hanning Speke, *Discovery of the Source of the Nile*, London 1863
Arthur Hawkey, *Hiram Maxim*, Staplehurst, Kent 2001
Mary S. Lovell, *A Rage to Live*, London 1998
Dan Morrison, *Black Nile*, New York 2010
John Petherick, *Travels in Central Africa*, London 1869
Georg Schweinfurth, *The Heart of Africa*, London 1873
Laura Thompson, *Agatha Christie*, London 2007
Patricia Wright, *Conflict on the Nile*, London 1972

Six: Blood on the Nile

Paul Carell, *Foxes of the Desert*, London 1960
Mohamed Heikal, *Autumn of Fury*, London 1983
Tom Little, *High Dam in Aswan*, London 1965
Samir Raafat, *Cairo, the Glory Years*, Alexandria 2005
Anwar el-Sadat, *In Search of Identity*, London 1978
Viscount Wavell, *Allenby in Egypt*, London 1943

ACKNOWLEDGEMENTS

I owe you all: Matthew Ismail, Ian Preece, Bea Hemming, Andrew Kidd, Samia Hosny, Wak Kani, Shaun Bythell, Joyce and Ian Cochrane, George Feltham-Parish, Maria Golia, Zohra Merabet, Steve Timpe, Jon Bjornsson, Mahmoud Sabit, Haajar and Mustapha Majzub, Paul Gordon and Lynne Chandler, Jihan, Mario and Manel Trinidades, Steve Mann, Ed O'Grady, Charon Mokhzani, Chris Ross, Richard Head, Richard Netherwood, Dave Morrison, Roland Prime, Lucy Westwood, Jessica Fox, Mahmoud Mohareb, Yusuf Zeydan, Steve Carter, John, Will and Rupert Seldon, Marie Shelton, Nick Owen, Gerard and Barbara Flynn, Naomi Darlington, Denys Johnson-Davies, Dan Morrison, John Paul Flintoff, John Crockett, Matthew Green, Paola Crochian, D'Arcy Adrian-Vallance, Hugo Dixon, Mark Dixon, Adrian Turpin, Arita Baaijens, Carlo Bergmann, Ramsay Wood, Gill Whitworth, George Scanlon, Patty Schneider, Ian Sansom, Ian Belcher, Boris Johnson, Richard and Claudia Mohun, Hassan, Homda, Ian Singleton, Chris Stewart, Tahir and Rachana Shah, Leon and David Flamholc, Aaron Fuest, Hassan Webster, Mihail Ivey, Floyd Evans, Peter Davies, Ryan McCliment, Christoper Watson, Jug Rushbrooke, Sonali Wijeyrathne, Stuart Dodd, Martyn White, Johnny 'Two Niles', Doris Odden, all donors and loyal blog readers. Abu Nasr, Mohamed, Hassan Ezzat, Pius, Theodore, Father Ecklund, James Carter III, William Coles, Antony and Jean Twigger, Babu Ramlingham, Peter Davies, Aoife O'Driscoll, Frank Nasre, Ben Forster, Tarquin, Anu and Al Hall, Garry Shaw, Clara Twigger-Ross, Rachel Barker, Enrique Turbot, Nigel Hale, Stu Pask, Jeffrey Lee.

INDEX